"Ms. Cooke has written an ambulatory history of New York City admirable for its scholarship and still more admirable for the sensitivity of her intuitions about the city's past—intuitions that serve the needs of those of us who, though we have spent our lives within its borders, find its essence difficult to comprehend. How many times New York has built itself up, knocked itself down, and built itself up again! As if taking us by the hand and conducting us from street to street, Ms. Cooke evokes the sights and smells and sounds of all those earlier New Yorks. In a hundred unexpected places, she unearths clues to the transformation of a grubby fortified trading post into the greatest of cities. The many levels of ancient Troy are far easier to make out than the many levels of contemporary New York; we have reasons to be grateful to Ms. Cooke for opening our eyes to its accumulated wonders. Wherever she leads us, we are happy to follow."   —BRENDAN GILL

"*Seeing New York* is no ordinary collection of walking tours. Instead, it is an interpretive history of the city, full of insights and little-known facts, that is grounded in particular places and neighborhoods. If you love history, or love New York, you will love this book."   —KENNETH T. JACKSON
Barzun Professor of History and the
Social Sciences at Columbia University, and
editor-in-chief of *The Encyclopedia of New York City*

"Where has this book been all my life! I was born in New York City, raised in New York City, lived all my life in New York City. Hope Cooke's invaluable book of walking tours through all the boroughs answers questions I didn't even know I had about New York City. Best of all, Cooke's witty tours make the city brand new. Seeing the city through her eyes transformed this jaded bird into a wide-eyed tourist. No visitor to New York should be without *Seeing New York,* nor, for that matter, should any true New Yorker. Don't leave home without it."   —JOHN GUARE
Playwright

"Hope Cooke's remarkable and eloquent *Seeing New York* penetrates behind the streetscape and its facades, into the heart of multi-ethnic and socio-cultural changes that continue to shake New York City. They expose themselves, uniquely and in fascinating detail, to her sharp, inquiring gaze, and in her sprightly text. Once Cooke's way-of-seeing catches hold, exploring New York and other cities will never be the same."   —GRADY CLAY
Author of *Real Places: An Unconventional Guide to America's Generic Landscape*

"Hope Cooke guides us on an intriguing journey through the American metropolitan phenomenon that since the seventeenth century has been inhabited by people from every corner of the globe. Her historical and sociological accounts of Harlem demonstrate clearly the need for us to preserve this tiny cultural enclave, replete with architectural gems, so that generations to come will be able to walk the streets and admire the buildings that so many noble and notable African Americans have called home."
—THOMAS J. BESS
Executive Director, Landmarks Harlem, Inc.

"Hope Cooke's *Seeing New York* invites the walker to appreciate its points-of-view on the physical and social city with a spirited mixture of insight, affection and outrage. Ms. Cooke has come home to the myriad wonders of her metropolis. At the same time, she feels a special kinship with the New Yorkers displaced by the numerous injustices of the city's growth. To go around New York with her is to be enriched by the observations and connections crowding her itinerary but also to feel the loss that goes with history. This persistent recognition of what's at stake makes her unusual narrative specially rewarding."   —PAUL SPENCER BYARD
Partner in Platt and Byard Architects and former President of the Architectural League of New York

Seeing New York

IN THE SERIES

Critical Perspectives on the Past

Edited by

Susan Porter Benson,

Stephen Brier,

and Roy Rosenzweig

HOPE COOKE

Seeing New York

History Walks for Armchair and Footloose Travelers

 TEMPLE UNIVERSITY PRESS Philadelphia

Temple University Press, Philadelphia 19122

Published 1995

☺ The paper used in this publication meets the requirements of the American National Standard for Information Sciences—Permanence of Paper for Printed Library Materials, ANSI Z39.48–1984

Printed in the United States of America

Text design by Tracy Baldwin

Library of Congress Cataloging-in-Publication Data

Cooke, Hope, 1940–
    Seeing New York : history walks for armchair and footloose travelers / Hope Cooke.
        p. cm. — (Critical perspectives on the past)
    Includes index.
    ISBN 1–56639–288–8 (cloth). —ISBN 1–56639–289–6 (pbk.)
    1. New York (N.Y.)—Tours. 2. Historic sites—New York (N.Y.)—Guidebooks.
3. Walking—New York (N.Y.)—Guidebooks. I. Title. II. Series.
F128.18.C66 1995
917.47′10443—dc20   95–2972

Contents

Preface

When people ask what I've been doing for the past fourteen years, I usually say, "er, I've been working on a spatially pegged history of New York," not "I've been writing a guide book." Two thousand five hundred years ago I wouldn't have had to be so circumspect in certain circles. The earliest theorists were tourists. *Theoria*, "theory," originally meant "beholding," seeing the sights, gaining a worldview through looking, listening, sensory perception, memory, and imagination as well as the intellect. The aim of *periegetes*, the tour guides who led people around Greek cities, was to represent, even reconstruct, the integrity of places, the coherence between person and place.

When I started this book, my need for ground under my feet, for a sense of belonging (from the same stem as *longing*), was extreme. A few years earlier I'd returned from living in the Himalayas, where I'd spent my adult life. Before that, I'd been at high school in the Middle East. When I came back from Sikkim with my children, my sense of displacement, bewilderment (living in the wilds), was profound. Though I'd been brought up in New York as a child, my confines had been narrow, a somber sphere in the east sixties guarded by impassive doormen. Mostly, my outdoor world consisted of the school bus stop, our apartment's side street, and the south tip of nearby Central Park. School existed isolate in its own geographic bubble near the East River. My calibration to surrounding space, and to *time*, had been further weakened, or, at least, skewed by the fact that I was an orphan, raised (along with my sister) by an elderly British nanny. If Harriet and I had any exterior reality, it was the Kentish countryside of Johnny's pre–World War I England, not the bleak, if respectable, blocks below us.

When I first reentered New York, I had no immediate family and few coordinates to help me end my estrangement abruptly. Before I could start to make my own shape here as an adult, I was impelled to absorb the city. Belonging had to grow as slow as bone.

But there was no resting place, no place to begin my incorporation. Even as I sought to calibrate myself to my surroundings, the ground around me was undergoing the same tectonic shifts I was. In 1973 when my children and I moved to Yorkville, on Manhattan's Upper East Side, a cluster of plasticky outbuildings, fast-food shops, and chain stores, following the new Gimbles East, had just begun to replace many of the old German stores and services along 86th Street. For years, the living memory of the Third Avenue El, torn down only in 1956, had served as a divide beyond which most realtors did not cross. Now that the memory of the El was fading, development surged, the phenomenon sped by new landmark laws blocking high rises to the west. (The Fifth Avenue–Lexington Avenue precinct had wealthy residents, powerful enough to shape their environs.)

As Yorkville's elderly tenants departed through death, or defeat by rent hikes, owners razed their walk-ups. Tenements dating from the 1880s, when the neighborhood had expanded as a working-class suburb for Germans and Irish, made way for sliver towers. Third Avenue pubs once serving the navvies who'd built the El (1878) and the 59th Street Bridge (1909) became singles bars, refurbished in Faux Irish, for young professionals moving in.

While enough ethnic institutions remained for people still to characterize some sections of Yorkville as German, or East European, essentially the neighborhood was lava'd over. Its immigrant energies, once spilling over in scores of organizations, funeral homes, specialized travel agencies, literary clubs, gymnasiums, and music societies, now shrank to a few cake parlors and marzipan displays. Entrepreneurs tore down the Rupert Brewing Company, the last remnant of the "malt related" industry that at one time employed a fourth of the neighborhood. The new co-ops (which stole a city street) took the name Rupert Plaza. Jaeger House, the neighborhood's central *turnverein*, was ignominiously recast as a branch of the Spaghetti Factory restaurant chain. Soon afterward, a co-op complex rose in its stead.

The events in my neighborhood were nothing new. Since its foundation, the only constancy in New York has been change. In 1824 James Fenimore Cooper remarked that fewer than five hundred houses built before 1783 survived. An editorialist in an 1856 *Harper's Monthly* wrote, "A man born 40 years ago finds nothing, absolutely nothing, in New York he knew." Edith Wharton thought New York's constant rebuilding would make it "as much a vanished city as Atlantis or the lowest layer of Schliemann's Troy."

As a returnee, with a mighty need for surrounding place to relive life's broken ties, provide groundedness, I was dismayed, if occasionally exhilarated, by the ceaseless unraveling. The fact that I was a writer with no timetable to keep, my only office the city's streets, made me particularly susceptible. On the days I felt secure, Manhattan's maelstrom was pure energy. On shaky days, the boundlessness made me yearn for limits or, failing that, at least a vantage point.

Gradually, it dawned on me that while my need for correlation to place was great because I lacked tenure, most so-called native New Yorkers were equally exiled, equally alien, without an emplaced sense of self. For whatever reasons—one being that Freud abstracted psychology from grounded experience, specific place, another being the sheer difficulty of reading an occluded city—most of my friends lived as disjointedly, as marginally as I did. Though in some ways our privatized, subjective sense of the city was rich, it not only denied us a grasp of the city's development but also our own niche in its continuum. (While my friends and my disorientation took the form of alienation, in some other cities people occasionally go mad through private attachment to place. In Jerusalem, for instance, dozens of foreign tourists, overwhelmed by the religious and historic weight of the town, often break down at associative sites, "becoming" John the Baptist, King David, or Sampson—a (mis)identification psychiatrists call the "Jerusalem Syndrome.")

Not only did the people I meet not try to see the city in a holistic way, most of them didn't even articulate their lack of "grasp" as a problem. Unless you happened to be a complete castaway, it was too big a deficit to see. Too many other needs clamored for attention.

In the eyes of some of my friends, most of them divorced single mothers, New York was a citadel of broken romances, each apartment building a place where something had ended—denue, or whatever is the opposite of venue. We all had internalized responses to the city's dangers and knew how to dart up empty subway stairs in case of lurkers. We also knew its spatial etiquettes (related to danger) and could tell to an inch the proper distance to leave between ourselves and the person getting cash from an ATM. Otherwise, except for spatially embedded memories of lost loves, we had little compass. I myself, who have a somewhat dyslexic sense of direction, will never forget that downtown subways are *always* on the west side of New York avenues: the figure of a man I used to go out with keeps departing down the subway stairs again and again, his winter coat flapping as he turns to look back. (I once used this axiom after moving to Brooklyn—

to my cost. As we know, Manhattan is at the city's core, hence it *had* to be downtown from my new home borough. Down is always the heart. Manhattan could *not* be uptown flung someplace on the periphery. One day, accordingly, I took the F train from the west side of Bergen Street in Brooklyn, certain I was headed for the "capital." It was a great shock, when the train suddenly rose above ground, to find myself over the Gowanus Canal. Worse still, even today I believe it was the *subway,* not my anthropomorphic principle, that failed me.)

To remedy my rudderless state (also to return some local reality to life when household grief and tragedies unfolding in Sikkim threatened to consume me), I began to go on weekly walking tours. Not single-minded architectural circuits, which I found took away meaning still further from "built remains," but excursions designed to decode how processes of social change had reshaped the city's terrain, and how in turn, social relations had been conditioned by both built and natural environments. (Most of these walks were led by eclectic enthusiasts recruited by the YMHA, which was, more or less, unique at the time in sponsoring *social* rather than art historical tours.)

Our outings were strenuous. A ten-mile hike across the Bronx's Grand Concourse, a three-hundred-foot descent into the cathedral-size caverns of the new water main in Van Cortlandt Park, a bridge over the River Kwai march on a 100-degree summer day to explore Whitman's New York and Brooklyn, a seven-hour walk along Broadway, Manhattan's spine, from Bowling Green to Times Square. Spatial connections as well as the sheer physicality of place became vivid to me in a way we're denied when we rush purposefully from A to B.

Noise: jackhammers, police sirens, brass bands, boom boxes, rush hour traffic (it was always rush hour) permeated the air, insisting on the present. So did the weather: layers of hot sweaty skies or drilling cold.

Despite the sensory tug of the immediate, satisfying in itself, I began to make ties back over time, to sense that it was possible to reconstruct the forkings that have led us to the contemporary world. The very difficulty of exploring New York, the need to heighten spatial and historical imagination, served as goad. The places we puzzled over had been veiled with overlays of later generations, their uses transformed, their demography altered. But we found clues (same stem as *clod* or earth) in the terrain itself, in the shoreline curve of an eighteenth- or nineteenth-century street, now blocked in by rings of landfill. The remains of our history, fragmentary though they may be, are there, in our city streets, decodable. The city is informing us through its street names, its buildings, but many of us don't know how to see (and consequently come to think it's not important to do so). Our sense of place, our historical sensibility, atrophies still further. Living air-rooted in high rises enhances the disassociation.

Despite my need to end my urban atomism, for quite a few years after my "reentry" a contradictory urge in me also enjoyed my marginal poise. Some part of me *liked* the perchedness, the slightness of apartment life, the need for constant adjustment of self to place, self to symbol. If my situation was a little precarious, there was also the promise of surprises. Leaving Manhattan's flux, taking a house somewhere, moving to a more niched community seemed like going from novelist to character.

When I finally was ready and anxious to move to a more planted situation, I was lucky. I recognized it, as they say in romances, at first sight. A little brownstone in Brooklyn, a house with a yard and a wisteria arbor, in a neighborhood with a candy store where, unsolicited, they gave you change for phone calls. My children were leaving for school and college, Yorkville was being rubbed away, even the view from our window had vanished since the dome of the octagon asylum facing us on Roosevelt Island burned and collapsed in on itself. Willy nilly, I sensed my weary vertebrate bones were carrying me to Brooklyn, the home borough.

(The word *home,* the dictionary says, is more often used as a modifying adverb with *going* than as a noun. In this sense the word includes not just the fact of shelter, the Penelope of being there, but the Odyssey of return, the hint of past separation. Perhaps it is this suggestion of apartness that makes the word so fraught with meaning, refuge, compared with the merely material *house.*)

The neighborhood where I moved is a residential community and erstwhile dock area south of Brooklyn Heights. Its origins go back to 1846 when local investors started a Manhattan-Brooklyn transit link in the form of the Hamilton Avenue "funeral ferry" to speed corteges from Manhattan to Green-Wood, the great Victorian cemetery in the nearby Gowanus Hills. (The ferry also suited Brooklyn entrepreneurs building up the port to the south, but the Brooklyn negotiators hid this more self-serving purpose.)

Only a few of the streets in my neighborhood are landmarked, however, most of the architecture—Italianate and Greek Revival—is still intact. The area has never become rich enough during its several incarnations to modernize, or poor enough to ebb away. It is an "ideal" nineteenth-century urban space, its rowhouses set back in deep gardens unusual in New York. As our block is a virtual cul-de-sac, children choreograph elaborate ball games, jump rope in the street. Old people sit in serene captaincy near their front doors or on their stoops.

In contrast to Manhattan, the coherent spaces of my new community made it look possible at first to read its past without much effort. I was comforted by becoming part of a continuum simply through buying in as occupant. Streetscapes here exuded symbols that both invited and satisfied nostalgia. *Nostos:* "home," *algia:* "pain," a painful ache for home. Interestingly, the word *nostalgia* had changed meaning, from its original 1780 usage, "homesickness," to its current meaning of longing for past time, just around the date buildings here went up. Carroll Gardens, the realtor name of my new neighborhood, assuaged both.

Despite the fact that when I moved in my kids had gone and I was living alone, my new surrounds were so nurturing I felt fully centered with no need for perspective. It was only after some months I realized the chance to burrow, to borrow stature in an intact built environs such as Carroll Gardens, was not a substitute for knowing where I was. Here, no less than in Manhattan's urban overlay, it was necessary to read the landscape, to puzzle out the social and cultural constructs imposed on the space over time.

Unlike the protean development of most Manhattan neighborhoods, Carroll Gardens was intended (as far as commercially developed sites will allow overall planning) as a codified, stratified commuter suburb, its most expensive houses radiating out from a luxury park in the center. Equally costly houses and handsome Protestant churches lined the tree-planted avenue on the spine of land leading down to our elite parent community, Brooklyn Heights. The Irish immigrants who'd come to work on construction and local docks lived in the locality's lower margins, out of sight of the neighborhood core. Many settled just east of my block where the land drops down to the Gowanus Canal. Though our street exudes serenity, a *rus in urbe* remove from change and turbulence, its developers, in fact, designed it as a masonry stage-set to protect the original residents from what lay beyond.

As I walk east along the street from the bus stop to my house, the cornices of the brownstones overhang, extending the domestic shelter. Since the buildings to the west near the luxury park are a story taller, the effect, heightened by the gradient of the land sloping toward the canal, is one of induction. I'm led along the street of diminishing rooflines, drawn by its perspective like the miniature walker in Renaissance drawings.

The houses at the lower-caste end of the street, which serve to cut off the end of the block, making it into a semi-square, are not only smaller in scale but have no brownstone veneer on their brick walls. By chance, and custom, they are painted red and contrast with the rather smug brown-stones along the way. Looking slightly meager, yet stubborn and redly defiant, the little houses introduce a frisson of Hopperesque vulnerability, the hint of something disquieting just beyond the frame that makes our block's solace doubly precious. It is only afterward one notices the chimney looming over the buildings that belonged to one of the many factories opened near the Gowanus in the last century. As always when they could, the wealthy built on high ground, leaving the cholera lowlands to noxious industries and the immigrant poor. The bare brick houses at the end of our block are a baffle, a screen, to hold the two apart.

But shape shifts. Today, Carroll Gardens' residents are mainly Italian Americans descended from the Bari men (and their women) who replaced the Irish as longshore workers in the 1890s. It took half a century to gain the high ground, but the Italians have now imprinted their symbology on the neighborhood so completely it's hard to envision the years of struggle it cost them to move up from the industrial canal and riverside.

Despite New York's cold season, Bari's heirs have turned the deep front yards here into extensions of interior space, as they do in southern Italy. Back lots are left for basics—laundry, the occasional vineyard—while the street gardens are presented as virtual chapels. Old men, mixing careful blues, keep bright-robed Madonnas freshly painted. Some images of the Lady stand encased in humming neon lights, some in grotto niches, the so-called bathtub Madonnas. Several of the shrines, including one dedicated to Saint Lucy, the benefactress of the blind who stands life size, smiling wistfully, holding her martyred eyes before her on a plate, are intended to be visited by passers-by. Even some of the miniature Madonnas have life-sized flagstone paths leading to them, as if one *might* do pilgrimage.

Throughout the day, church bell chimes weave a web of sound, defining the neighborhood's time. Until a few years ago, two sacred processionals defined the neighborhood's space. On Good Friday, Christ's image is taken out of St. Stephen's Church and carried through the streets by a horse-drawn hearse, while other parishioners lead Bari's patron, the Virgin Maria Adolorata, down separate streets in search of her son. When they reunite at last near the church, the entire community enters to sing mass, the reunion more profound and moving than the death. The other festival, a summer rite when parishioners carried the Virgin through the bounds of the neighborhood blessing each important household along the way, stopped in 1991. In part it ended because of displacement.

In the late 1970s, as people from outside the community (such as myself) arrived in Carroll Gardens searching for decent, affordable housing, rents rose, and many younger Italians were forced out of the area. Though some were happy to leave for newer neighborhoods in Bensonhurst and Staten Island, many felt anger, particularly as household in-fighting grew, one family member wanting to sell, another to stay.

Paradoxically, the powerful Italian ethos of the neighborhood, the Mediterranean "songline" established over years, may have itself contributed to the plight of old-time residents here. From the late 1970s on, even after the 1987 crash stalled real estate activity in most of the city, the community's nearness to Manhattan plus its mellow "European flavor" drew newcomers. Not long after I'd moved in, local activists, recognizing the double-edged weapon of "Old World Charm," began to fight back with alternate imagery. Despite their pride in the positive ethnic profile they'd managed to assert since winning the high ground, a few even drew on negative stereotypes of Italians borrowed from old movies supposedly set in this neighborhood.

"Red Hook, our name is *not* Carroll Gardens, but Red Hook!" Juliana, a local community board member who joins our party uninvited, flings this gritty, dangerous word at the group walking (not led by me, thank heavens) through our leafy side streets. Juliana hurls this imprecation, invocation, of a nearby "bad neighborhood" to ward off further encroachment on this area's insufficient housing. (By the late 1970s tours had come to be feared by many communities as being introductory walkabouts for "gentry" house buyers.) In case people can't hear her, she is also wearing a T shirt that says "We're FAMILY" in big letters and then the statement about being Red Hook. At the time, the district's rechristening as Carroll Gardens was fairly recent. Until then we had technically been South Brooklyn, but also sometimes had been considered part of the sullen land tip farther south of here.

Juliana's use of the name was deliberate, summoning up a beautiful, if rather grim, nineteenth-century industrial landscape where Civil War–era warehouses and stubbles of worker housing stand surreally juxtaposed to Manhattan's prow across the harbor. It was here at the Atlantic Basin Docks, soon after they were opened in the 1840s, and again during the draft riots, that immigrants, Irish men in those days, tried to burn the grain elevators taking away their livelihood. It was near here in the 1960s that Italian longshoremen fought to keep their jobs, striking to stop the containerization laying off most of the workforce. They lost, and shipping moved to New Jersey ports, which had greater space and better transport for the bulky new freight.

It is not this imagery, however, that Juliana seeks to invoke, though the desolation of Red Hook today, the past loss of shore work, the future risk of losing the waterfront to developers altogether, are related issues. It is the mass media imagery of violence, the filmic memories of bloody cargo hooks slung from longshoremen's waist belts, that Juliana uses to shock. Though the derivation of the name Red Hook is of banal Dutch origin, *red* from the color of the soil, *hook* from the land spit jutting into New York harbor, the words sink like a talon into the mind, imprinted in our consciousness by sensational crime reporting of the 1930s and later movies. (Ironically, most of the gangland activity happened here, off piers in Carroll Gardens, [South Brooklyn], not in Red Hook. It was the press at the time who cavalierly borrowed the more dramatic nomenclature, which Juliana and other local activists later borrowed back when gentrification, regentrification, began.)

Guilt and fear are probably among the reasons we tend not to look at our urban environs as carefully as we might. It is painful to open our eyes to the struggle over interpretations (and habitation) that goes on in this densely ancestored, contested city. Through no fault of our own, city dwellers live in conflict with each other. But the political and psychic cost to ourselves for *not* knowing where we are is greater still, the disability made worse by generational dislocation. In my case the lack of ties I'd felt when I first returned from Sikkim to America was underscored by an exaggerated—even for this society—absence of family structure and history.

Preposterously, owing to a constellation of reasons (chiefly, that no one had told me as a child, and I was later too scared to ask), I'd never known if my mother, who'd died in a plane crash when I was an infant, was interred, and if so, where. It was not until some time after I'd moved to Brooklyn that I'd learned she was buried right here in Green-Wood, the cemetery whose opening at mid-nineteenth century had given rise to the development of Carroll Gardens. She is buried in the fringe area near the heavy iron fence bordering the daily hum of traffic on Brooklyn's Fifth Avenue. I'd driven by a hundred times.

In a newly translated seventeenth-century Dutch journal there is an account of how the Munsee Indian tribe that lived in this part of Brooklyn once passed the contents of treaties and contracts down through generations. During negotiations, a tribe member held a different shell in his hand as each article came up for discussion. When an agreement was reached, the specific meaning of each marker was recounted. "As they can neither read nor write, they are gifted with a powerful memory," the diarist wrote. "After the conclusion of the matter, all the children who have the ability to understand and remember it are called together, and then they are told by their fathers, sachems or chiefs how they entered into such a contract with these parties." The children, the journal went on, "are commanded to remember this treaty and to plant each article in particular to their memory." Later the shells were bound together on a string, put in a bag hung in the house of the chief, and the young warned they must preserve this memory "faithfully so that they may not become treaty breakers, which is an abomination."

The following study of New York City's built environs and its weave of meanings over time began as an effort to implant memory, to end displacement—at heart, to come home.

Acknowledgments

I offer deep thanks to the New York Society Library, where I did my earliest research for this work. The wood-paneled reading room of the library is a burrow of safety from life's vagaries, while its open stacks are an invitation to explore life to its outer reaches. Marc Piel presides over both domains with a generous heart. My next institutional debt is to the Brooklyn Historical Society, whose librarian, Clara Lamers, helped me ransack its archives. Wayne Furman at the New York Public Library embodied helpfulness, as did the staff of the Prints and Photographs division of the Museum of the City of New York.

My major debt by far, however, is to my friends at the New-York Historical Society. Thank you librarians, May Stone and Mariam Touba, and the series of willing apprentices whom I worked to the bone. Upstairs, in the Print and Photo Division, thank you Dale Neighbors, Wendy Shadwell, Diana Arecco, and Laird Ogden, who strove heroically (feverishly is probably a better word) to help me get the material I needed when it looked like the institution would collapse, leaving my project half done. Rarely have I seen people work with such grace under pressure. At the same time they were doing their own tasks under horrible circumstances, they fought to keep the society alive to safeguard the collections entrusted to them. Not only myself, but the society and the city are in their debt.

Joan K. Davidson, another person who did yeowoman work to save the NYHS, was also a benefactor of this book: she gave a generous grant from the J. M. Kaplan Fund for maps and illustrations.

I gratefully acknowledge Gordon Klopf, former Dean of Bank Street College, who gave me my first job as cultural geographer; and the Museum of the City of New York, who invited me to run its walking tour program for several years. Through these walks I met splendid fellow city sleuths, all of whom have informed this book.

I've been fortunate to have several individuals give me immense help on particular chapters. April Tyler, now a Democratic district leader in Harlem, gave me insight on various aspects of my Harlem chapter. Professors Madhulikha Shankar Khandelwal and Khe Young Park provided valuable background on Asian Flushing. Professor Tom Jorge was a main source of information for the Dominican chapter. (Mistakes or skewed interpretations are my own.) Franny Eberhart of the Historic Districts Council rendered gracious assistance in fact checking.

Had it not been for Temple University Press, there might not have been any book at all, and (horrible thought) the following narrative might still be just in my head. My fond gratitude to everyone at the press, David Bartlett, Janet Francendese, Charles Ault, Henna Remstein, and Ann-Marie Anderson. Barbara Reitt, my copy-editor, has been an inspiring commentator as well.

I owe appreciation to historians Roy Rozensweig and Suzanne Wasserman, who looked lovingly over the text as part of their job, and Professor Edwin Burrows, who looked painstakingly over the earlier chapters as a labor of love. Graphic artist Shan Jue did the beautiful maps. Carl Lee, friend and sometime cartographer, helped with my easts and wests. Vincent Virga, generous as always, offered wise counsel on the illustrations.

Thank you dear Palden, Kesang, and Hope Leezum, who've traveled much of this road with me and who've worked hard to make two countries home. And as for Mike: Mike Wallace, my husband, has not only given minute commentary on the many incarnations of this work, but has shared his passion for finding connections, for bringing past to present. We met just as I was embarking on this project, and he, coincidentally, was starting his own mega-treatise on the city. My being, as well as this book, would be less without him.

A Note to Readers and Walkers

The walks in this guide explore New York's development from its founding through the present. Starting in the Dutch era at Manhattan's southern tip, the walks proceed in rough chronological timeline and northern progression to the upper end of the island, also exploring parts of Brooklyn, Staten Island, and Queens at key moments in their formation. My hope is the tours will aid city dwellers and visitors in understanding how the metropolis came to be as it is, how New Yorkers evolved to be as we are. Each walk offers traditional architectural and art historical insights into the neighborhood covered. The primary focus of each tour, however, is on developing an integrated understanding of sites (and epochs) we often see in isolation. Underlying all the particular facts in the book, I have tried to suggest general strategies for decoding space and architecture, skills the reader can use in any surroundings.

Some specific points:

Time

Except for Walk 2 (South Street and Snug Harbor) and Walk 8 (Whitman's New York), which take you farther afield, each itinerary can be done in about two and a half hours. (This estimate does not include travel time to the starting points.) Alternatively, you can make a day of it, loafing and eating as you go.

Safety

The most important consideration is common sense. Like most cities, New York can be a dangerous place. Always be alert to what's around you. If possible, go with a friend, and go only in daylight hours when there are sure to be plenty of people about. If you are a bit uncertain about visiting some neighborhoods, go in a car or use that chapter for armchair traveling. You also can telephone the local police precinct or Chamber of Commerce (listed in the telephone directory) for update information.

Street Strategy

I urge walkers to read each chapter before starting out. This will provide a framework for seeing that can ease your way. Once on the route, be alert to opportunity, improvise in places where it would be safe and fun. Try to go on days you think things will be open. Churches, for example, are generally open only Sunday mornings, without a special appointment. You will find a million attractions along the route that have not been noted. Also, I fear, some of the sites charted for you might be gone by the time the book is out, victims of New York's endless overhaul. Each walk has an accompanying map with the route marked, but be ready to be flexible if you come to a vanished site. Another point is that, though precise walking routes are given, not all the locations mentioned in the text have been assigned numbers, in an effort to keep the maps as clean and legible as possible. Also note that although the dotted lines on the maps follow the route, they do not invariably follow the side of the road the text describes. Moreover, the compass directions for Manhattan are not true points but have been adjusted somewhat for the island's north-south street grid plan, which follows the island's shape rather than compass desiderata. The minatory finger is a device to alert you to visuals, as is the boldface type used for sites under review.

I apologize for the omission of chapters on places and people that should have been included but for space limitations. I am particularly sorry about leaving out the South Bronx, which, contrary to public opinion, is undergoing amazing, even visionary, reconstruction.

I wish I could go with you. I am getting separation anxiety after these many years of planning your itinerary—as Whitman said,

—loth, O so loth to de-
    part!
Garrulous to the very last.

Seeing New York

1

Manhattan and the Harbor

Subway: IRT Broadway–7th Avenue (train 1) to South Ferry.
IRT Lexington Avenue Express (trains 4, 5) to Bowling Green.

This walking tour will look at reasons past to present for the territorial huddle at Manhattan's tip. It's hard to understand New York as a port anymore, to feel Manhattan as an island. Down at the Battery you get a better sense of the city's founding as a harbor sentinel.

*S*tart at **Castle Clinton ❶**, *in the southwest corner of* **Battery Park.** *(Today, the fort built before the War of 1812 holds the ticket center for the Statue of Liberty and Ellis Island ferries.) If it's a sunny day, I suggest you sit on a bench facing the bay to read this introduction.*

Eleven thousand years ago New York's first natives, descended from Asian migrants by way of frozen Bering-land, left only light traces, spearheads—rough paleolithic flints—when they trekked New York's forests. Thousands of years later the hunters slowed their endless circling and started to camp in semi-permanent settlements, clusters of bark and sapling longhouses. (The remains of almost eighty sites fringe the city.) Though population grew after the introduction of slash-and-burn agriculture not long before the Europeans arrived, land remained plentiful and habitation seasonal.

After planting in early summer, the various kin groups that made up different tribes would strike camp—the women porting the baggage—and move to clamming sites around the harbor. For easy carrying the women baked corn, their staple crop, into cakes called *pone* (our "corn pone") and stored some kernels for next season's seed in underground stone jars. Ancient mounds of shellfish near the Harlem River show that Inwood was a favorite resort, despite clouds of annoying "muskettas." The beach running along the East River shore at Pearl Street was another.

Foot-battered trails webbed the camps together. The most important way on Manhattan was the north-south track from Westchester to the island's tip, today's Broadway. Indians from Staten Island, lower New Jersey, and Brooklyn who came to Manhattan to take the path are supposed to have landed at **Kapsee,** the rock on which Castle Clinton stands. (The name means either "sharp rock place" in the Delaware language, or is a derivation of "little cape" in Dutch.) Kapsee, now buried in Battery Park landfill, was then an island outcrop among other jagged gneiss rocks jutting off the island's southwest tip. This makes the start of the north-south trek problematic if not downright aquatic—but this is the tradition.

In contrast to today when New York and New Jersey wrangle over development, the tribes living around New York harbor worked out cooperative rights. The Reckgawawanc (a subordinate tribe of the Weckquaesgek in Westchester), who kept seasonal camps at Carnegie Hill, East Harlem, and Inwood, controlled Manhattan's north. The Canarsie from Brooklyn had usage over the greater part of the land south of 59th Street and also "held" most of the islands in the East River and the lower harbor. Staten Island "belonged" jointly to the Canarsie and the New Jersey Hackensack and Raritan communities. The Hackensack had sway in Sapokanikan, a cove in Greenwich Village.

To say the least, the European explorers who first happened by New York had different views of landholding than the Indians. When the Canarsie tribe "sold" Manhattan to the Netherlands' West India Company director, Peter Minuit, in 1626, they would have assumed the deal to be an arrangement for usage only. Furthermore, they did not even have gathering rights, let alone title to the upper part of the island, a point the northern tribes raised into the eighteenth century. But all that lay in the future.

The first explorers didn't put ashore. Nonetheless, the men—all of them hired mercenaries—claimed and named the land around the harbor for the foreign princes who were paying. The first known scout to arrive was Giovanni da Verrazano, a Florentine sailing for the King of France in 1524. Hinting at still earlier European-tribal encounters, thirty canoes of friendly Indians paddled out to meet the ship. As a storm blew up, Verrazano pulled anchor without landing but logged the "steep forested hills" and the "beautiful stream"—the latter-day Hudson. Back in France mapmakers recorded the visit. "The beautiful stream" became the "Vendome" after a French prince, the outer bay the Gulf of Santa Margherita after the king's sister, the harbor and its islands the "Angouleme,"* a title of the dauphin.

One year later Esteban Gomez, a black Portuguese of Moorish descent sailing for the Spanish king, probed local shores. Ice drifts stopped this explorer also from disembarking, but Gomez rechristened the waterway to the west of the island before leaving. This time it flowed as the "San Antonio," in honor of the saint's day on which he'd arrived.

In 1609 Henry Hudson, an Englishman working for the Dutch East India Company, dappled into New York's upper harbor (by then called Esteban Gomez Land by some in Europe). Fearing shoals, he slowed his ship and threaded his way through the lower bay taking constant soundings. Like earlier explorers, Hudson (actually his mate) remarked on the harbor's fragrance, its "sweet smells of grass and flowers and goodly trees." Unlike earlier navigators, he and his men pushed up the west river in hope of finding a shortcut to the Indies, the goal impelling his journey. Hudson's party

---

*This naming might also have honored Jean Ango, a Dieppoise merchant who bankrolled the monarch.

reached the current site of Albany before turning back. For a few years the west river became the "Mauritius" after a Dutch national hero, Prince Maurits. Eventually, the water, "Mahican," "the river that flows two ways," would take Hudson's own name.

By 1610 Dutch entrepreneurs (mostly migrants from the Caribbean) were hectically gathering furs from upriver tribes. Since the Renaissance, men of standing in the cold northern cities had been wearing broad-brimmed fur hats similar to those Brooklyn's Lubavitchers own today. Until then, the Dutch had bought pelts from Russia, but the Muscovites were hiking prices. The Hudson offered "water-proof" beaver skins for soft currency—kettles, duffel cloth, hoes, liquor. It also offered sexual perks. Soon, European diseases began to disable, then to destroy the tribes.

In 1613 a Dutchman from the Netherlands, Adriaen Block, arrived to explore the territory's potential. His ship the *Tyger* burnt. (Construction workers digging the new subway turned up the charred ribs beneath clay riverbed near the present Twin Towers in 1904.) After a dank winter in a dug-out pit on Broadway, Block carpentered a replacement with Indian help. When he sailed for home with a cargo of furs, he repaid the favor by transporting two tribesmen as exhibits. Block's show-and-tell impressed the Netherlands' governing body, the Staats General. Though undermined by almost constant warring with Spain, the council resolved to expand its overseas possessions, "passages, havens, countries and places."

Somehow the profusion of prints showing Dutch interiors, sheltered Vermeer spaces where the only exterior is sunlight slanting through casements, has come to rule our thinking about the Netherlands. Also, children's books popularized at the turn of this century in a bid to promote New York's Anglo-Knickerbocker origins give us cloistered images, snug cupboard beds in paneled rooms belying the voraciousness, viciousness, of Holland's imperial expansion at the time. Even Dutch maps of the era have become valued as lapidary fantasias, not the high-tech documents of global reach they were.

The government granted Block a three-year monopoly for trading. It also sanctioned the founding of a fort near Albany as an outpost for gathering skins. Such a deadly melee began when Block's tenure

Early maps showed the Hudson as the region's important feature. The Dutch picked Manhattan's site to guard the river's mouth.

ended that Dutch merchants appealed to the Staats General to create a single trading company along the lines of the directorship started a decade or so earlier to exploit Asia. (By the way, beavers are back in force, posing a problem to upstate ecology as they dam up scores of waterways.)

Various Dutch cities chartered the *West* India Company for two purposes—mining the new-world territory Holland already claimed, and seizing Brazil along with several West African slaving ports recently founded by other European powers. When the cities divvied up the stock in hand, Amsterdam took New Netherlands, the land between Delaware and southern Connecticut.

Thanks to the roughshod staking of claims, title wasn't clear, and overlaps proved frequent. James the First of England, for one, had, in fact, granted the same land New Netherlands encompassed to the Plymouth colony some twenty years earlier. To reinforce ownership, declare its paramountcy, the West India Company decided to show the flag, or rather the company logo, as the infant venture wasn't a national enterprise at all but a purely commercial undertaking.

The company's hapless standardbearers turned out to be thirty Walloon families shipped from the Netherlands under a company director, who scattered his clients around the territory like human shields. Amazingly, given the bleak conditions, the new arrivals, including those assigned to the little island off Manhattan's tip (later Governor's Island), managed to return a freight of furs to Amsterdam.

The following year the company sent out a hundred more Walloons, livestock, seeds, arms, and an engineer to build a fort at the Hudson's mouth. The idea was that a bastion at Manhattan's southern tip would ensure Dutch control over the waterway leading to upriver fur supplies. The engineer, trained in the grand Renaissance manner, planned a massive star-shaped redoubt. There was even talk of turning the whole southern end of Manhattan into an island fort by cutting a channel through the swamp at present-day Broad and Beaver streets.

The sorry mud castle the engineer eventually produced with the help of Angolan slaves seized from a Spanish ship bore little likeness to the drawings. Even so, because of up-state Iroquois wars, the company decided to move most of its far-flung settlers (except the Albany fur traders) down near the stockade for protection. Fort Amsterdam became such an important anchor it influenced the town's development through today.

Who were these people, who in the words of a New England contemporary "huddled rather than dwelt?" First, they were not Dutch but Walloon, French-speaking Protestant refugees who'd fled to Amsterdam from

present-day south Belgium to escape the Spanish conquest of their province. Conditions here were too raw for anyone but the stateless.

From the beginning New York was ruled by a fort, a brute fact shaping the town's spaces and mores.

The Walloons had tried their best not to come to New Amsterdam. Some had been twice dispossessed, first of their country, second of their jobs. (The list of the first Walloon passengers to New York has been lost, but we know that other Walloon ventures abroad at this time were undertaken chiefly by textile workers displaced by shifts in the flax and wool weaving trade.) Few had wanted to go to an outpost banning private trade and manufacturing. The Walloons begged the English to allow them to settle in Jamestown, the British colony in Virginia. They shipped out under the Dutch West India Company only after the English said a definitive "no."

Unlike New England ventures to the north that had a colonizing and ideological basis as well as a profit motive, New Amsterdam was begun solely as a company town, its single objective money. As the company conceived the cantonment here to be a commercial entrepôt, not a determined "peopling," the ragged band of arrivals weren't even colonists, let alone settlers. They were company *servants* under contract for six years. This distinction shaped the city's demography, social history, and spaces.

Discontent ran so deep that, despite their original hope of settling permanently in the new world, most contract holders fled back to Europe once their time was up. The company's offer of free land to anyone who would stay on swayed only a few.

Even the company directors were careerists with no inherent loyalty to nation or firm. Peter Minuit is an example. First, like others stationed here, he was not Dutch, but rootless, a French Calvinist who'd later moved to Westphalia and then to Amsterdam. Not long after his Manhattan purchase, the West India Company recalled him to Europe to answer charges, largely fornication and theft. Minuit revenged himself, or rather took a new career option, by returning here to help Swedes found a colony in Delaware that later challenged New Amsterdam.

Despite housing improvements and other company efforts to ease life (mainly bringing more African captives to serve as municipal slaves), few volunteers signed up for the hardship post. Those who did come broke the West India monopoly laws as far as they could. The fort's barracks were stuffed with beaver skins waiting to be smuggled out—and Indian girls who had been smuggled in.

The settlement was a company town founded for commerce.

In 1639 the company surrendered its exclusive control over the trade that had led it here. To no avail. Even after opening the fur trade to all, even after offering free passage to the outpost, it still couldn't entice many Dutch to come. Hollanders remained a bare majority among the adventurers from Britain and other European states who made up the shortfall. In 1643 a visiting Jesuit priest noted eighteen languages—perhaps counting the West African speech native to the town's captive work force.

The single goal New Amsterdam's voluntary residents had in common was the impulse to make money. The place to do that was down by the shore of Manhattan's southern tip. From early on, the pull to be down at the island's southern end was such that land had to be added to accommodate.

☞ Look across at Staten Island. The hills there (up to 409 feet) are the steepest on the East Coast after Maine. Originally, Manhattan looked rather like this—its name (first mapped as "Manatus" in 1639) means "hilly island" in Algonkian. Things soon changed. Today, except in the north, Manhattan is so lopped, filled, and flattened it's hard to get a sense of how it once appeared.

Landfill in the lower city began in the 1680s and continued for three centuries. From the Battery to Midtown, both shores of Manhattan have been extended into the river by roughly one to four blocks. Down near the old fort section the padding is even greater, and land south of City Hall is two-thirds wider than when Minuit bargained with the *wilden* or "wildmen," as the Dutch—conveniently for their appropriative purpose—called the Indians. (For their part, the tribesmen called the Dutch *Swanniken,* "from the salt sea"—the same derivative as *sewant,* the shells later used as currency.)

Except for the Kapsee Rock chain, Battery Park itself sits on made-land swelled out over the years. After the Revolution when the city finally tore down the ancient Dutch fort, patched and operative through British rule, it dumped the rubble here. Most of the fill, however, occurred in the 1840s, when pipe laying for the new Croton water system freed up tons of slurry.

☞ Look northwest at **Battery Park City,** the most recent addition to Manhattan's tip. (The name "Battery" incidentally, came in the 1690s from the harbor defenses around the fort.) Before leaving here, you might visit **Castle Clinton's Diorama Exhibit** showing the battery's development. It is well worth the time.

*W*alk north through Battery Park enjoying the acrobats working the ferry crowds and the vendors selling garish watches.

Since the publication of "Tricks and Traps of New York" in 1853, tourists have been warned about peddled time-pieces. Olden-day versions were often empty gilt cases holding no clock work machinery.

*C*ross over Battery Place to **Bowling Green ❷** and then sit on the steps of the Custom House (site number 3 on your map), which occupies the site of the old fort.

Landfill began from the 1680s,
as people huddled near the port
at Manhattan's southern tip.

Not only is this comfortable, but by keeping your back to the imposing Custom House you can (somewhat) keep a timeline in the densely overlaid space. Though all the city is a palimpsest—a tablet written on, erased,
and written on again until only traces of past markings are legible—this
heart of Manhattan is more inscribed than most.

☞ The "Company's Negroes," who built most of what scrappy infrastructure the town possessed, developed a short strip of the old Indian north-
south trail from the fort to the company planting fields near Fulton Street.
Gradually, the thoroughfare assumed the name Breede Wegh, or **"Broad
Way."**

The other tribal path the Africans improved was a northeastern track
serving farms the company developed for leasing out to its servants. Within
a decade, all the farms but the governor's fief had been abandoned,
mulched back into wilderness, but the Bowery road remained, and remains
through our day.

The third and last route the authorities developed in a semi-planned
manner was a path along the East River shore between the fort and today's
Broad Street. In 1633 the company paved the river road with shells from
nearby Indian middens, ancient garbage dumps. As the seawracked road
gleamed palely on starry nights, people called it Pearl Street.

Since the beginning householders had fixed their dwellings near the
east side of the fort. (For the first several years they lived in bark-lined pits
roofed with sod, seven feet under ground. Later, they built wood shelters.)
In contrast to the Hudson, the East River was protected, ice-free in winter.
Moreover, its axis was Europe. Like many of today's immigrants in Queens
who feel comfort and connection to Asia or South America living under
JFK's flight path, early company employees could watch the occasional
Dutch ships anchoring in the East River and turn their faces homeward.

Except for Pearl, other streets down here to the lee of the fort started
life as helter-skelter footpaths linking the settlements of huts the townsmen
built at will. It was only (with a few exceptions) twenty years after the outpost opened that the company got around to formally granting ground lots.

In 1647 the company ordered a new director up from the West Indies
to shape the muddle into a viable fur-trading and slaving depot. By now
the Dutch had started to lose the more lucrative parts of their empire to
their French, Spanish, and English rivals: this derelict port town was something of a last stand. The newcomer arrived "peacock-like with great state
and pomposity" to find a straggle of cabins and a few public buildings—an
ill-equipped shipyard, one or two stone warehouses holding export to-

bacco leaf, a brewery and tavern, some ruined windmills, and a crumbling fort.

Peter Stuyvesant set to. First, he appointed a board of surveyors to regularize the city and force householders to fence their land. Next he ordered a tax on imported wines (a basic source of revenue, as one-eighth the town buildings were in some way liquor related) for repairing the fort, completing the new church inside it, building a wharf at the foot of Whitehall Street, and raising a paling by the shore to stem erosion. That same year the martinet soldier ordered all adult males to donate twelve days' work on the fort per annum or pay stiff fines. Miffed townsmen compared their new governor to a Muscovy duke.

*C*ontinue to keep the Custom House to your back; don't turn around!

Although New Amsterdam was a garrison-ruled company town, and early portraits of the settlement—all from the navigator's harbor perspective—show the fort as the paramount town feature, it was always a shambles. Rooting pigs hunting food in the weedy earthworks (never faced with stone) almost pulled down the ramparts: the public made off with struts for firewood, even William Beekman, a selectman.

The fort's purpose was as shaky as its structure. Originally, the stockade holding the governor's house, a barracks, and a mill had been conceived as a defense against European enemies rather than against the Indians. From the start, however, higher-ups at the settlement had been trading with the English, their supposed foes, both here and in New England. In fact, it was English carpenters from Connecticut who had built the new Dutch Reform Church inside the plinth stockade.

☞ **Bowling Green:** In early days, company soldiers drilled on the plot facing the fort's main entrance fronting Broadway. Later, as the name tells, part of it served as a bowling green.

Stuyvesant organized periodic cattle fairs here—the only market in town. Unlike English settlements planned around commons, the town had no civic forum. The land in front of the fort had some limited public uses but never was a proto-democratic gathering place or center in the sense of the New England greens. Bowling Green (actually shaped rather like a thumb print) is genetically coded, the DNA of a town founded for trade, ruled by might.

Tradition has it that Peter Stuyvesant was bowling here when a British force sailing for the English king's younger brother, the Duke of York, arrived off Kapsee in 1664. Surrender was abject. The town's citizens had been chafing under autocratic West India Company rule, and York's governor swore to protect, even enhance, New Amsterdam's trading rights.

The conquerors renamed the settlement New York after its new owner. The outpost's condition, however, stayed much the same, a garrisoned port whose purpose was to send income to Europe—in this case to the Duke of York. Though His Grace's interest in taking New Amsterdam coincided with the larger British interest of smashing the Dutch empire, it was mainly the duke, a chronic debtor (he even owed his governors), who stood to gain.

Under the British, market days here increased to three times a week, but Bowling Green remained a military parade ground and the fort stayed the town's pivotal site.

In the 1730s when new property tax laws led to a spurt of gentrification, the city rented out the space to two well-connected men. For a token rent, they enclosed the ellipse as a paying park (". . . keeping it in turf, and making a bowling green with walks there-in for beauty and ornament of said street"). Imposing brick townhouses soon went up around the little enclave and it became known as the "Court" end of town.

Even if never planned as a community node, the green had its public moment in the period leading to the war when crowds rallied here. (The fields around latter-day City Hall were also used oppositionally by unorthodox preachers and radical artisans.) A few propertied men conspiring in city coffee houses spurred some of the move to break with Britain; the bulk of agitation, however, was outdoors by working men, often here in front of the fort.

In 1765 Sons of Liberty protesting a new colonial tax broke into the fort's stables and burned the governor's chaise, two sleighs, and the royal coach. The vandals' vehicular target wasn't as sophomorically chosen as it might look to modern eyes. Until recently, New York had been a "walking" city. With only two exceptions—Wall and lower Broadway—the streets had no sidewalks. Pedestrians made their way in the center of the roads, competing with horse and hand carts. The new coaches appearing in town were an arch symbol of crown and class. (This perception continued even after the Revolution, when a famous actor suffering from gout kept an apologetic picture of crossed crutches on his carriage with the motto "its either this or these.")

Iron fence: In 1776 crowds gathered again. This time they came to topple the gilt lead statue of the king loyalists had erected here a decade earlier to thank him for canceling the Stamp Act. Smashing through the protective railing (raised in 1771), the crowd pulled the equestrian statue off its base and shipped it to Connecticut foundries to melt into shot. For good measure, they also packed off the crowns (some say balls) on the fence stanchions.

☞ Rub your hand along the top of the fence's larger rail posts. Thrillingly, in this city where nothing lasts, you can still feel the gash of the mob's hacksaws.

During the occupation by the British the fort served as their military headquarters. At war's end in 1789, the city finally razed the old colonial tumulus, incorporating the rubble into Battery Park, distributing the wood for fuel to the poor. Since New York had already served as the nation's pro-tem capital and harbored the hope of becoming the Republic's permanent headquarters, the city built a pillared mansion on the site, thinking it would become the presidential residence and office. After New York lost its capital status, the building held the state governor and infant arts organizations but soon declined into a "genteel" boarding house.

At the close of the 1812 war the city razed the old structure and auctioned the site to developers who put up Federal houses. The area took the nickname Nob's Row. Briefly. Within decades the nabobs had moved up-town to flee the tide of immigrants landing at the Battery and the reek of shoreside industry. Steamship offices moved into the houses until they, in their turn, were torn down in the early 1900s to make way for the new U.S. Custom House.

☞ Finally, we get to look at the former **Custom House** ❸ itself—it's hard to maintain a timeline in the face of such a dazzling construction. First, note that the building turns its back on its source of revenue, the harbor. Bowing to the financial and shipping trade grown up around the port, architect Cass Gilbert axised the structure toward Broadway. Despite its land orientation, the exterior foams with nautical detail: dolphins, cockleshells, tridents, the sterns of ancient "triremes," and scallop shells. Heroic statues on the facade recall ancient and modern seafaring powers. The four statues depict America's worldview at the time. To the far right as you face the building, an exhausted Africa slumps over a vacant-eyed sphinx. To the far left an otiose Asia meditates unconcerned over prostrate slaves. (Help is at hand, a Christian missionary presence in the shape of a rising cross looms behind her over her shoulder.) Next to the door, on the right, regal Britain sits back, overly satisfied with her dignity and spoils. One knows that keen Miss America leaning forward to the left of the entry soon will take global leadership. A bonneted plains Indian crouches behind her rallying her on to success.

For the past two decades, the building has been empty, managed by the General Services Administration, a federal body. Ironically, or fittingly, it has just reopened as part of the Smithsonian's National Museum of the American Indian, so New York's first inhabitants are represented here after all (their artifacts looking puny and wilted in the grand classical interior.)

*W*alk south on Whitehall Street to State and then turn right to **New York Unearthed,** ❹ a new archaeological museum at 17 State Street. Telephone (212) 748-8600.

A creative judge sentenced the owners of this building to set up a museum in perpetuity as punishment for digging their foundation without the required site evaluation. The exhibit offers a fine neighborhood chronology.

The next stage of the walk will resume exploring the "Dutch" town and then work its way into the "English" city and beyond. (The De Lancey House, now Fraunces Tavern, will be an exception to this strategy, as, like Bowling Green, it merits its own biography.) The connective link in all the eras is the town's tie to the harbor.

*D*ouble back over Whitehall Street and walk north up Water Street to **Coenties Slip.**

☞ The clinch of town and sea, commerce and port, are inscribed in our land patterns. The neat rectangle to the east of Pearl once served ships as a small water berth. Note the street signs "Coenties Alley" and "Coenties Slip" marking the old water and land divide.

☞ The yellow boundary on the pavement at Coenties and Pearl marks the **site of the old City Hall** ❺ or Stadt Huys. The lines show us that the building stood so close to Pearl Street, then the city's shore, that waves sometimes lapped the building's walls and chipped away at its foundations.

The building opened in 1641 as a public tavern put up by a governor tired of entertaining English traders at his home inside the fort. This is remarkable if you stop and think about it—in theory, the Dutch feared the English and in large part had built the fort to defend against their incursion. So here is the governor, not just trading with the enemy, but building a guest house for them and appointing an English secretary "because of the great number of English who come daily to reside here with us."

The five-storied stone public house was the town's key building after the fort. Its steeply pitched tile roof flanked with end-chimneys and crow-stepped gables consoled homesickness, or tried to. The lightless basement held many of the town's malcontents, men and women jailed for New Amsterdam's endemic "quarreling, fighting, smiting and beating."

In 1653 when the West India Company finally granted the town a municipal charter, the local government upgraded the city tavern into the Stadt Huys or City Hall. It still kept functioning as a pub, but a new town council of citizens met here regularly—rather like Rotarians who gather today at local hotels.

The new council had been hard won. Stuyvesant had agreed to its formation only after prominent townsmen, in the face of what looked like the long-feared British invasion, had refused point-blank to defend the city. To get his palisade along present-day Wall Street, Stuyvesant not only had to consent to the council but, worse, give it jurisdiction over the town's excise tax on drink. For the next decade the two kept crankily at odds, the council stressing laws shaping the quality of life, rudimentary zoning, street improvements, the governor—with reason as it turned out—harping on military preparedness.

The gabled brick Stadt Huys, or City Hall, evoked old Amsterdam, or tried to.

Remarkably, neither body provided the town with a public drinking source. Private citizens dug the **earlier well** in front

of the Stadt Huys. (We'll come back to the later well in a moment.) In the Dutch city, unless you had money enough for a roof cistern or a private well such as this one, you were dependent on ponds for drinking water. The Dutch canon of cleanliness was difficult to uphold, and housewives sprinkled Rockaway sand on their floors to tamp down muck.

*T*urn left and walk up Coenties Alley, a route the city cut through to Stone Street to connect the Stadt Huys with the municipal distillery supplying its liquor.

Despite New Amsterdam's first ordinance banning immoderate drinking, to stop ruined tipplers from "pawning goods to tapsters," alcohol was the underpinning of the early town's finances.

*T*urn right into Stone Street, a dark curving corridor that follows the angle of the city's old shoreline at neighboring Pearl Street.

From early settlement, elite Dutch families, including brewers, lived on winding Stone Street, then segmented into "Browers" or Brewers Street to the south of Coenties Alley and "Hoogh" Street or High Street to the north. As districting laws hadn't yet come into fashion, many residents kept their distilleries near their homes.

☞ Stone Street got its name in 1656. It was something of a boast, as it was the town's first road to get paving. The cobbles you see today are from the mid-nineteenth century, not original.

People with houses fronting on the street furnished the stone and leveled the track we are walking on, but the citizen council underwrote construction. Until this time the weighty brewery carts and draft horses had struggled and sunk in sewage and mud. As the excise tax on liquor funded most municipal operations, it was quick to sanction improvements for distillers.

☞ At the bend in the road, notice the **front-end gable house** faced with yellow glazed Holland bricks.

When wealthier merchants arrived from Holland after New Amsterdam gained citizen rule, houses of locally kilned brick and ballast bricks from the Netherlands replaced slapstick frame. A few who could afford to ordered Delft tiles and oak furniture shipped from home—some households, at last, began to have the safe, snug rooms we remember from our story-book Dutch.

☞ This house is *not* a serious effort of replication, but a historical whimsy built early this century. Nonetheless, to a degree, it serves as illustration.

First its alignment. In the hectic Dutch trading cities, narrow plots forced houses to be axised gable-end toward the street. In consequence, the gable-to-street architecture came to be a sign of urbanity per se, an emblem of living in a densely settled and so, theoretically, desirable part of town.

From there, the gable-end style had come to represent prestige pure and simple, the reason why England's landed gentry adopted the mode in 1688 when it reached Britain with the Dutch monarchs, William and Mary. As most of New Amsterdam's settlers were from urban backgrounds with far more genuine links to the tradition than the English country gentlemen, they also sought the prestige the familiar shape signified. Moreover, the nostalgically gabled buildings had a practical side—the construction aided easy access (through hoists) to upper floor storage space.

As well as re-creating the architectural symbol of congestion, the settlers also willfully managed to duplicate the real thing—no mean feat in a near pristine land.

By the 1650s, when the town swelled with noncompany servants and property began to be a more important commodity, speculation drove the impulse to huddle at Manhattan's tip. (The citizen council had won the right to parcel out town lots from Stuyvesant, a key concession.) Like some landowners today, many recipients held on to ground lots, waiting for values to rise. The masses of town tulip gardens visiting diarists noted were bane to the West India Company in Amsterdam. Time and again, headquarters ordered Stuyvesant to enforce development. Like Saint Paul writing to the Corinthians, the governor issued injunction after injunction to New Amsterdammers forbidding them to hoard unimproved property. The last law, in 1663, a year before the British takeover, threatened to auction any undeveloped lots.

Turn left when you reach the small alley, **Mill Lane,** ❻ *that leads in to South William Street. The cut, dank even today, was originally called Slyck Steegh (as in slick) or Mud Alley, because of its location near the boggy creek at Broad Street. Don't bother to walk into South William Street, a much-changed thoroughfare, but simply look down to your left.*

A structure on the site of present-day 32–34 South William Street (formerly Mill Street) housed one of the few industries in the Dutch city—a mill grinding the cedar bark used for mordant by the tanneries around the Broad Street swamp. According to the 1660 Cortelyou map of New Amsterdam, some of the "Company's Negroes" were quartered in a dormitory above the mill until they got their own land plots in 1644.

A decade or so after the Africans departed, the mill's upper floor may have become the first house of worship for the twenty-three Jews just arrived in New Amsterdam as refugees from a Dutch colony in Brazil. (Their old persecutors, the Portuguese, had recently seized that territory from their Dutch rivals, bringing the threat of the Inquisition with them to the new world.) The uncertainty about the exact meeting site of the first congregation here comes from Stuyvesant's early strictures on the Jews and other nonconformists to the Dutch Church, his demand they worship privately or not at all.

Soon Mill Street became the town's Jewish center. Once the community wrested the right—first withheld by Stuyvesant—to buy real estate, Jews settled here to be close to the docks, as most of the men were merchants with shipping interests. Decades later, the descendants of this community built North America's first synagogue on Mill Street, with a Succoth harvest shelter and a ritual bath fed from a pure spring. (A plaque marks the site.) Mill Lane, formerly Slyck Steegh, became Jew's Lane.

*R*etrace your steps back to Coenties and Pearl.

In 1662, just before the British invasion, Stuyvesant ordered cargoes of fill schoonered down the Hudson to make a "half moon of stone" for defending the Stadt Huys. The fortification was never put to the test. Not only did the British take the city without a shot, but gallingly went on to use the building as the new regime's City Hall.

☞ The gray lines on the pavement and the viewing window of the stone basement behind the Stadt Huys show us a glimpse of the tavern built in 1670 by the second English governor, Francis Lovelace, an inveterate trader who had the nerve to join his tavern to the City Hall by a walkway.

Except for parceling out land around the harbor to English cronies and indulging in some Anglicizing renaming, the new governor did little to change the town's Dutch mode.

☞ Note the **bronze plaque with a map** of the local shore-line in 1675.

The British started serious reform only when they retook the town after losing it back to the Dutch between 1673 and 1674. The idea prompting the innovations may have come from the concurrent overhaul in London, which was just undergoing the first (semi)coordinated improvements in its history following the fire of 1666.

To start with, the new administrators pushed slaughterhouses outside the city walls to enforce sanitation and regulated many winding streets. Next, they built a dock here to boost exports to the Caribbean. The new Great Dock extending from Coenties Slip formed one wing of a protected wet basin for ships; the other was the old Whitehall Street wharf.

After a long delay in what might have seemed a priority, the ruling establishment got around to mooting the idea of building an Anglican Church—the time lag perhaps due in part to the city's majority of low church dissenters. Upper class Anglicans had only recently begun to arrive from Britain as the town prospered.

One *big* change the British brought to New Amsterdam had to do with women's rights, or rather, the loss of them.

☞ Note the second, **smaller well** at the site dating from the first quarter of the eighteenth century. It belonged to a Dutch family, the Philipse, whose house stood nearby from the 1690s on. (They also owned the manor now open to visitors up in Tarrytown.)

The "founding" Philipse, originally a West India Company builder, had later made money investing in the "Red Sea" trade (read piracy) and had even turned his hand to counterfeiting sewant or wampum, the polished shells accepted by then as currency. The greater part of family money, however, derived from his wife, Marguerite Hardenbroek. (Note the different last names—as a rule, Dutch women kept their birth family names after marriage.) Marguerite Hardenbroek not only managed the estate up in Tarrytown but owned a fleet of ships and often sailed to Europe to supervise crossings.

Though Dutch colonial life (Vermeer again) is usually presented as interiors presided over by pink-cheeked hausfraus, most New Amsterdam women worked—often as tapsters or brewers. A Van Cortlandt daughter ran a brewery on Stone Street while still a teenager. Aside from holding jobs along with men, under Dutch law women were equally entitled to inherit and own property. Within a few decades the British conquerors had undermined this practice, not by fiat, but by example. By 1700 male primogeniture had become the norm, and male family members now acted as trustees for any land women managed to keep. Female poverty soared.

It's surprising, almost amazing to us, conditioned as we are to think of men as New York's "historical" property owners, to imagine women once owned a share of city real estate. (It's particularly hard to imagine it down here in this very male financial district.) A further thought on this is that few formal landmarks record women's history at a city, state, or national level. Only *3 percent* of the country's several thousand official landmarks have to do with women! (On the other hand, we are honored by the Molly Pitcher Comfort Station off the New Jersey Turnpike.)

W*alk south down Pearl to the northeast corner of Broad and Pearl. Stop on the corner and look up Broad Street.*

☞ This wide, swerving street lies on the bed of the canal the Dutch dredged out in 1656 from an underlying creek. ❼

In Dutch days, Brooklyn ferries and farmers' skiffs loaded with Long Island cabbage plied up here toward Wall Street. In winter when the waterway froze, people skated as they did in old Holland, the rich on metal blades, the poor on beef shin bones lashed to their shoes. As they had done at home, wealthy merchants built their houses along the banks: the bridge over the canal became a stopping place for swapping market news.

When the English reclaimed the town from the Hollanders in 1674, they obliterated this core Dutch space by filling the canal. Partly, they stuffed up the waterway because it stank from years of garbage. The effect, however, was to cut the heart out of Dutch spatial arrangements. Infill for the deed came from the excavated cellars of the many new houses under construction—the town's population now stood at almost five thousand people.

As the elite all wanted to live right at the harbor's edge and their numbers were expanding, shore padding was about to become an integral part of city life. (This is extraordinary when you consider settlers here were living in such a commodious new land.) In 1686 the city made this section of Pearl, known in those days as Dock Street, by sinking ships as cribs to hold deposits of rubble and scree. One rotted West India trade schooner from a slightly later fill—hull brimming with coral ballast from the Caribbean, gun-ports intact—was excavated recently at 175 Water Street.

In part, this street was opened to raise money to thank the resident governor, Thomas Dongan, for winning a charter of rights for the city from the duke. The governor's cash award was also a pay-back for his role in getting the duke to grant the city's elite a big new source of income. Through Dongan's intercession, His Grace had just turned over all vacant crown land here to a newly formed City Corporation, a coalition including locally elected aldermen. The City Corporation ordered this street made out of gratitude.

When the ground had consolidated, aspiring Englishmen hurried to live along the prestigious new stretch. Only a few Dutch merchants joined them, as the spatial dimensions of the British takeover had just begun to crystallize. Although some upper-middle-class Dutch merchants continued to live near the buried waterway on Broad Street, most middle- and working-class Dutch retreated farther inland at this time. It wasn't only ethnic separation that rose in the city then, but class divergence as well. As the corporation encouraged development of "waste" lands to benefit themselves, town spaces took on a sharper rich-poor division than before, though real segregation was yet to come, since many poor lived in alleyways sidled among the handsome brick mansions going up.

The canal at Broad Street was another effort to replicate old Amsterdam. The English filled it in.

☞ One of the houses, or rather a reincarnation of its old self, still stands. Cross the street to the former **De Lancey House, ❽** today's Fraunces' Tavern, on the southeast corner of the intersection.

Even as early British governors courted top Dutch merchants to ease their rule, they worried that the city's population remained preponderantly alien: English emigrants preferred neighboring colonies where land was cheaper and the political system more democratic. To serve as counterfoil, the governors encouraged Huguenots, Protestant refugees from France—and thereby pliant allies—to settle here. A fair number of them had money enough to afford house lots on Dock Street. Etienne De Lancey, who owned this house, was one such fortunate, his way smoothed by his wealthy Van Cortlandt father-in-law, who built this mansion for his daughter and Etienne in 1718. (A few top Dutch merchants were assimilating into the new elite through matrimony—or conversely put, a few canny immigrants were assimilating into brewery fortunes by the same route.)

☞ By the end of the seventeeth century, English-style housing such as this

Georgian mansion had begun to replace many old Dutch gabled dwellings. The new style's tenets are all illustrated in the De Lancey building—squareness, tall chimneys, steep-hipped slate-tiled roofs with ornamental balustrades and shallow dormer window, quoins (the decorative stones holding the brick at the corners), and, finally, long vertical windows and classical Greek treatment around the main door. One other characteristic of the style is the Flemish bond brick work. The sturdy weave (alternating horizontally and end laid bricks) is usually the tip-off of an authentic early building, but not here. Except part of the west wall, the house is a 1907 reconstruction.

The city's growing West India trade paid for most of these new dwellings. Ever since the 1680s New York had functioned as an agricultural supply depot for Britain's possessions in the Caribbean, with city merchants funneling upstate wheat and other staples down to the sugar plantations, fencing pirate loot, and buying and selling African slaves who had been "seasoned" (tamed) in Jamaica by British West Indian planters.

Even now, New York's colonial tie to the plantation economy is still visible along the East River shore. Domino sugar signs illuminate Brooklyn's skyline. Refining remains—in shrunken state—one of the city's few industries.

☞ Notice the relative proximity of the house to the river.

At first the building commanded harbor views and air, an important feature as disease rose in the port. By 1728, however, more shore padding had stranded De Lancey's residence one block inland, a ring of housing on Water Street walling it off from the river. Two years later De Lancey was forced to quit his home, a bare decade after settling in.

As the aldermen on the City Corporation exercised power over the town's common lands, they could dictate how city property was to be released and developed, so their private speculation grew ever more surgically exact. Not only did they and their friends get the land next to the shore, but underwater rights halfway to the high-tide line as well. If they chose (and they did), they could build wharves in the river or yet a whole new street on made-land. Real estate interests were on their way to becoming the power they are today.

Changes in land use intensified as shoreside commerce grew. By 1757 the De Lancey house had become a warehouse. Five years later Samuel Fraunces, a West Indian of French-African descent (again the Caribbean tie), bought the building and opened it as the Queen's Head Tavern.

☞ Walk north on Pearl Street, first glancing at the Federal style houses abutting the De Lancey mansion to the north. Unlike their neighbor, these warehouses—built for the purpose in the late 1820s—are original, not re-constructions. Continue north on Pearl until you reach Hanover Square. Noting the **periwigged and pigeoned statue** of another Huguenot, this one an appointed mayor under the British in the 1690s, walk through **Hanover Square,** a prestigious English enclave after Dock Street opened.

Captain Kidd and other pirates and privateers—officially sanctioned pirates—lived here to be near their ships. Along with local realtors, they were the city's aristocrats; in fact, the two careers often overlapped, as investing treasure in property was far sounder than burying it.

Just as city commerce was linked to the harbor, early journals were tied to ships bringing news from Europe. Hanover Square, whose eastern edge originally fronted on the river, was home to New York's first printing press. William Bradford opened his shop, "The Sign of the Bible," at Hanover and Pearl.

☞ The 1854 **Hanover Bank** (later, India House, a merchant shippers' club) at the foot of the square was also located here because of the harbor.

*C*ontinue north on Pearl to the intersection of **Wall Street and Pearl.** ❾

☞ As you exit Hanover Square, you will be passing through the site of the water gate in Stuyvesant's wall. Reconstruct through your walk how small the early city actually was—one-eighth of a square mile. The ground between Kapsee and the boundary gate, which in Dutch days clanged shut every night at nine, can be covered in fifteen minutes.

Despite the fact the British had started building beyond the pale, it suited them to keep the wall here until 1699, a vestige of medieval control. (Actually, though the financial community hushes it up in case of street name changes, the wall was not quite a wall at all. Rather, it was halfway toward being a "ha-ha," a stockade with a 5-foot deep, 12-foot wide ditch on the north.)

When the municipality leveled the palisade, all was set to make a fine wide boulevard, but trouble struck, or rather was revealed. The former Governor Dongan, it turned out, had bought up the parade ground north of the wall through a dummy company and already sold off the land for building lots. (It's fun to look at a city atlas and see the property Dongan amassed, Dongan Hills, Dongan Manor, and so forth. As well as owning 25,000 acres in Staten Island, the governor also appropriated the eastern third of the current City Hall Park as a vineyard after the Boston Post Road was cut through, the reason the park is such an odd shape. See the map for Walk 6.)

☞ Instead of the broad thoroughfare the new era citizens had expected, what they got was a 36-foot corridor, the narrow route we have today, straighter but otherwise not much different from the Dutch city's winding lanes. Look west up the street toward Broadway.

The same year it demolished the wall, the government started construction on New York's first real city hall at the junction of Broad and Wall. (Workmen packed rubble from the old stockade into the foundations.) As soon as it could shift, the government bureaucracy moved from the earlier shoreside taverns to the arcaded brick structure that resembled civic buildings going up in Britain's market towns. The days of running public life from smoke-stained taprooms were over.

Trinity Church, the new Anglican church (opened 1697), stood west of the hall at Wall and Broadway. If any one still doubted, the city was now irrevocably English. The intersection of Wall and Broad became British New York's political, religious, and economic apex.

Despite its unprepossessing width, Wall Street, now lit at night by oil lamps, became *the* desirable new address. Gentlemen scrambled to live in the blunt Georgian houses under construction.

☞ Still looking west toward Broadway, note the spired **Trinity Church** that centers the street.

The first Trinity Church was a small rectangular building with a miniscule entry porch, a surprisingly modest structure, considering its official backing. The governor allowed funds for the new church to be raised by taxing all citizens regardless of creed and also leased the Church a generous piece of property to develop for income.

More favors were to come. In 1705 England's Queen Anne gave Trinity another swath of land running from Broadway to the Hudson River, Cortlandt Street north to Christopher. The gift formed the basis of the parish's prodigious wealth.

From this time on, Trinity's power and wealth was, and continues to be, incalculable. (Partly, it is incalculable, as it is famously discrete about its holdings, preferring instead to talk about the quaint entitlements the church enjoys, such as the rights to any beached whales in New York harbor.) Just as an opening example of Trinity power is the fiat it issued in return for granting Columbia University its original downtown ground lots, a rule providing that only Episcopalians could serve as the university's president. This injunction lasted until the mid-1950s when Dwight Eisenhower (raised a near Mennonite) got the job through special pleading and a fluke.

The first sanctuary on the church's site faced the Hudson—the river still more vital than overland routes such as Broadway. After the building burned in the Revolution, the trustees built a new stone steepled structure in 1789 with money from Trinity's real estate leases. (It's never been proved, but some suspected arson by working-class dissenters resentful of the "English Church's" privilege.) As the neighboring stretch of Broadway was then becoming a more important thoroughfare, the trustees ordered the new incarnation turned to face the street rather than the river.

☞ In 1846, after the second church was pulled down as unsafe, the current church governors hired English architect Richard Upjohn to build the present structure and ordered him to move the foundation some tens of feet north of the old location. The goal now was to align Trinity's axis with Wall Street absolutely, make it not only face the street but command it.

Why was the transverse important enough over time to warrant this expensive geomancy?

☞ Look back again toward the East River, where the inflated tents hold tennis courts.

Wall Street in the British era had been mainly residential, but coffee houses had grown up at the river end for merchants overseeing their ships. The gathering spots had become so influential, the new dockage at the end of Wall Street took the name Coffee House Slip.

One of the commodities the merchants continued to trade was human lives. From 1711, the city's slave market stood at Pearl and Wall on the south side of the street on fresh landfill east of the former water gate. At its height, the slave population of the colonial town reached 20 percent; 32 percent, in agrarian Brooklyn. Whites were also sold on Wall Street. Among others auctioned at the market here were debtors, dependent women, orphans, and presumed vagrants. During their period of servitude these bond servants—mainly Ulster Scots-Irish, English, Welsh, and some Catholic Irish—were forbidden to go more than ten miles from the city, to buy or sell commodities, or to marry. The market lasted until 1762, when slaves and indentured servants began to be traded privately.

☞ Note the **Tontine Coffee House plaque** at the northeast corner of Pearl and Wall Streets.

After the Revolution, the city remodeled the English City Hall as the country's new capitol building, grandly renaming it Federal Hall. The conversion revitalized the street, which had burned during the war, as had much of lower Manhattan. Even after the Congress voted to move the capital to the Potomac in 1790 (to protect the legislature from New York's money men), Wall Street kept its prestige as a major bank had opened here when the war ended.

In 1792 merchant speculators built a brick coffee house, the Tontine, where the namesake office building stands today. (A tontine, incidentally, and somewhat lugubriously for a founding Wall Street institution, is an insurance plan whereby a group of participants allow the annuities to accumulate as each member dies, the final survivor receiving the whole.)

Ever since the end of the Revolution, when Congress, convening in Federal Hall at the other end of Wall Street, had issued $80 million worth of bonds to pay for the war debt, New York brokers had been meeting in the open air near this part of the street to trade securities.

The construction of the coffee house club was an effort to organize, sanitize, the uproarious speculation that followed. Twenty-four brokers, whose association became the nucleus for the later New York Stock Exchange, moved into the new quarters, set rules of conduct, and formally pledged themselves to give preference to each other. Their aim was to freeze out the more knavish speculators such as William Duer, a former assistant secretary of the Treasury who'd sparked a ruinous panic the previous year trying to fiddle the city's bull market through his insider knowledge—an early Boesky. The brokers called the document structuring their resolution the "Buttonwood Agreement," in honor of a tree near the site of their curbside trading. A button-wood (sycamore) tree in front of the present Stock Exchange at Wall and Broad commemorates the institution's street origins. (A cement tree planter in front of 40 Wall Street commemorates Ivan Boesky.)

***W**alk west on Wall Street on the north side passing the site of the Bank of New York at 32 Wall Street. The bank's **1797 corner stone** is incorporated into the modern building.*

Because of an unexpected boom after the Revolution, several more banks opened in the city within a decade. New York might have lost its role as the country's capital, but it soon would assume the lead as the nation's financial center. Most of the banks set up on Wall Street to be near the shipping that prompted their existence.

New York's recovery after the Revolution grew out of the mutual expediency of Britain and the port city, which proved stronger than mutual animosity. When the British departed, they'd destroyed New York's Caribbean trade and left it a wrecked town. Not long afterward, however, Britain's industrial revolution made it seek cotton for its mills, food for its workers.

From Dutch through English days and beyond into the dawn of the twentieth century, finance and the port were inseparable. This picture shows the busy docks at the end of Wall Street.

New York geared up to provide both, starting shipping lines to haul cotton from the south, digging the Erie Canal to fetch wheat from the western plains. Regular sailings from New York to Liverpool delivered the cargoes, returning with immigrants and manufactured goods from England.

Before the war New York had been a relatively small port compared with Boston, Philadelphia, and even Baltimore but by the 1830s businessmen exploiting the city's lynch-pin location had made it the nation's commercial hub. Mostly, the entrepreneurs were not native New Yorkers, but Connecticut and Massachusetts men come down to earn their fortune following the Revolution. (Families of Dutch descent, now retreated from trade into real estate, sourly called the successful interlopers a "codfish aristocracy.")

At first the new banks going up occupied old Federal dwellings such as the De Lancey House or new structures built to resemble private houses. This residential style—evoking the old way of doing business out of one's home—implied that banking was still a human-scaled business: the reference backward was to win people's confidence, much as today's banks use *forward* looking modernistic styles to gain people's trust.

By the end of the 1830s, portentous Greek Revival architecture had replaced Wall Street's domestic mode.

☞ Look across Wall at the **Merchant's Exchange, ⑩** (55 Wall Street), 1836–1842, on the south side of the street. This massive block-long structure, difficult to see in its entirety even from across the way, is the second exchange on this site.

For Sale,

A LIKELY, HEALTHY, YOUNG NEGRO WENCH,

BETWEEN fifteen and fixteen Years old: She has been ufed to the Farming Bufi- nefs. Sold for want of Employ.—Enquire at No. 81, William-ftreet.

New-York, March 30, 1789.

The first exchange opened here in 1827, urged by shippers who contrasted New York to other cities with gathering places "where . . . merchants may be as- sured of finding each other; and by having all brought together, may transact in a few minutes, the business, which if each were to seek the other at his counting-house, would require as many hours to accom-

Slave trading was an underpinning of New York's colonial economy.

plish." Not only did New Yorkers now need a place where merchants could meet, but they wanted to match, even outdo, European capitals. City guide books of the day glow with insecurity and ambition.

The merchants chose an institutional look, the English Palladian style, for their new center and crowned it with a dome. Even so, its builder-ar- chitect took care to meld the overall effect in such a way the structure would blend with the residential norm still dominating the street.

The great fire of 1835 that started near Hanover and Pearl burned the first exchange, along with 650 other buildings in lower Manhattan. Firemen on the 17-below-zero night fought valiantly, pouring brandy in their boots to keep the collected water from freezing, but eventually the great dome fell in, shuddering embers and masonry. (Currier and Ives' first print depicts this disaster.) Outside on the street New York's poor looted and chanted insults. Or at least they did until Marines arrived and restored order.

Undaunted, New York's businessmen rebuilt Wall Street, making it, in the words of the *Herald,* "a street of palaces . . . great, gaudy, splendid, Corinthian, scheming, magnificent, and full of all kinds of roguery."

This second exchange led the renewal. Within weeks of the fire, thirty men anted up the two million dollars needed to underwrite the block-sized edifice. It wasn't hard to raise the capital. By now, Wall Street held the greatest concentration of wealth and power in America. The merchants picked a Massachusetts architect, Isaiah Rogers, to design their new center. If you are here on a business day, enter to see the 72-foot high rotunda that echoes the rotunda in the first exchange.

☞ The earlier exchange had incorporated New England granite pillars on its Palladian facade. The new version used it exclusively. As more and more out-of-state businessmen arrived, a New England spirit, palp- able in mores and mortar, permeated the town. Granite was strong, hard to quarry, implacable, like the newcomers themselves. Or so the ethos went.

In the 1980s granite became the stone of choice for city businesses once again—for similar reasons. A new consideration in this dirty, less deferential era is that the polished material is graffiti resistant and stands up to acid fumes.

When this building opened in 1842 (the delay caused by the crash of 1837 and subsequent depression), the Stock Exchange moved in; leftover space rented quickly. Not every one liked the monolith that intimidates and overshadows the slender street even today. One visitor thought it "seemed carved out of a granite mountain." Another thought it vainglorious. "A New York merchant loses every year at least 32 hours ascending and descending the steps of the Exchange."

Admire it or not, after the 1835 fire the new mode spread almost as quickly as the flames that had engulfed the lower city. By 1840 Wall Street was barely recognizable. Stately Greek Revival buildings whose classical gravity was intended to lend dignity to banking enterprises replaced any Dutch and Federal houses that remained. Prints of the time show Wall Street as a little Athens of porticoed and pedimented banks. The only people in the pictures are tophatted business men. After the fire, residences, families, *women*, vanished uptown.

☞ In 1907 the building became a bank, and McKim, Mead and White added the Corinthian stories above the first cornice which conceal the dome, a one-time harbor landmark.

Continue west along Wall Street to **Federal Hall ⑪** on the northeast corner of Nassau Street and Wall.

☞ This Doric Greek Revival temple built as the Federal Custom House opened in 1842, the same year the Second Merchant's Exchange was finished.

Its architects were also (directly and indirectly) from New England— A. J. Davis and Ithiel Town, the latter, the man who changed the face of New York's harbor by introducing Boston's post-and-lintel mode.

Like the Merchant's Exchange, the Custom House's location here was the consequence of the continuing ties between "street" and port. When this building went up, duties on imports through New York's harbor accounted for two-thirds of the country's revenue.

Federal Hall National Memorial, the structure's current name, is a confusing anachronism that comes from its location on the site of the English City Hall, later revamped as the country's capitol building where Washington took his oath of office and Congress sat until New York lost its national role. Afterward, the old British headquarters became New York's City Hall (once again) until 1811, when the present version opened a short distance uptown. At that point, developers pulled down the *real* Federal Hall and sold it for scrap—this custom house going up in its stead several decades later. This account sounds confusing, but the intention of the patriots who misnamed this building for the old shrine was aimed to confuse, to expiate primal realtor sins, forge continuums where none existed.

Continue along Wall Street to the **Stock Exchange (1903), 12** at the corner of Wall and Broad.

By the twentieth century New York had left its mercantile underpinning based on import-export behind, and there was no longer reason to hug the harbor. Nonetheless, when they needed larger space for their operations, the governors of the new Stock Exchange still chose to build in this part of town.

☞ New banks followed the same (lack of) logic. Note the 1913 **Morgan Guaranty Trust Company, 13** formerly the J. P. Morgan Building, on the opposite corner of Wall and Broad at 23 Wall Street.

☞ Walk up Wall Street to **Trinity Church 14** on Broadway, feeling the rise as you go. Much of Broadway follows the island's high spine, the reason local Indians developed it as their north-south path.

This is also a good point to glance down to Bowling Green and re-sense the old city's tiny size.

It's hard to believe that it took New Yorkers as long as it did to move prestigious institutions beyond the old wall's perimeters. Even though the town's physical boundary had been demolished for more than a century and housing had extended north of the line, before the new City Hall went up, the old pale had still circumscribed civic thinking that constrained all-out growth.

Walk to the back of Trinity to see the cemetery's high retaining walls that rose close to the Hudson River before shore-fill swelled this part of Manhattan. Afterward, return to the front of Trinity and look down Wall Street to the East River.

CUSTOM HOUSE, NEW YORK.
DESIGNED BY ITHIEL TOWN AND ALEXANDER JACKSON DAVIS, ARCHITECTS.

The Custom House (opened 1842) on Wall Street illustrates the continuing tie of harbor and finance.

For the first time in years, there's a tie once again between the financial district and the city's harbor. A working dock operates at the foot of Wall Street, and bankers spend long hours at the nearby South Street Seaport. The dock, however, serves a dinner cruise boat, and the bankers are undergoing "attitude adjustment" at the seaport bars. Despite the fact that until recently, investors and city planners were behaving as if there was real reason for financial services to be down here, there is no cause at all. After the crash of 1987, 29 percent of offices stand empty. So do many apartments in the still unfinished Battery Park City (which you noted from the park earlier), built on fill in the early 1980s. New York officials make (rather quiet) trips to Hong Kong to search out buyers.

☞ If you look across the East River, you'll see a skyscraper capped with a green copper roof that dominates Wall Street from the far shore. It's Morgan Stanley's back office, relocated from Manhattan to Brooklyn several years ago to save money.

Though Morgan Stanley respected Wall Street's importance enough to stay close by and in fact went to the trouble of siting its new building to

command the street as Trinity had done earlier, its remove is emblematic of banks' satellite-age freedom. Today, institutions can locate wherever they choose. For several decades now, the city has been paying firms, including Morgan Stanley, to stay.

The all-powerful Episcopalian church, Trinity, molded Manhattan's development through its real estate holdings. In the 1840s when it was rebuilt the third time, trustees re-sited the church by ten feet so it would command the very center of Wall Street.

Ever since curbside trading here first began, New Yorkers have continued to imbue this physical street with numen. "The Street," as many who work here fondly call it, is at once transcendent, a collective history, a mindset that abstracts the physical ground, and a spatially tied place. We have granted the narrow transverse almost magical powers—the powers to keep the nation's and even the world's financial center tied to a geography from which it is now free. Will the ley-lines hold?

Recently Manhattan's southern tip has received an unwelcome testimony to its symbolic power in the form of bombings said to be done by "third world" saboteurs. No one would dream of bombing poor Inwood to the island's north.

2

South Street Seaport and Sailors' Snug Harbor
The Port and the Mariner

Subway: IND A, E lines to Broadway–Nassau Street station; IRT Lexington Avenue Express (trains 4, 5) and IRT Broadway–Seventh Avenue Express (trains 2, 3) to Fulton Street.

A good place to read this introduction is on a bench in the small triangular park at Fulton and Water streets.

In 1941 the WPA *Maritime History of New York* ended its doleful latter-day account of the port with the hope that artificial islands in the harbor serving as airstrips for seaplanes might allow the port to continue "in the spirit of its Dutch mariner forebears." The islands never materialized. Neither did the port's revival—at least, not in Manhattan. The 771-mile greater harbor still had 350 miles of dockland in the 1930s, but Manhattan's shipping had already begun to fade with the arrival of tunnels and trucking. Air traffic dealt a blow from the 1950s on. The 1960s brought containerization and deep-draft ships, which made smaller cargo vessels obsolete—along with Manhattan's finger piers. When Port Authority's container port at Newark-Elizabeth opened, New Jersey shipping, feared at the turn of the century, became reality. Though the greater metropolitan port of New York continues second in the country (Los Angeles is first), only a bare one percent of its shipping is under the American flag, only a fraction of its merchant marine American nationals.

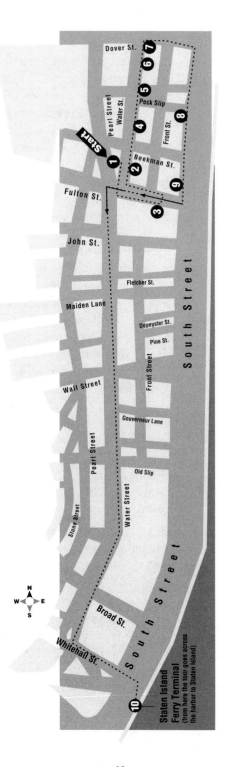

Start

Dover St.

Pearl Street
Water St.

Peck Slip

Front St.

Beekman St.

Fulton St.

John St.

Fletcher St.

Maiden Lane

Depeyster St.

Pine St.

Wall Street

Front Street

Gouverneur Lane

South Street

Pearl Street

Old Slip

Stone Street

Water Street

South Street

Broad St.

Whitehall St.

South Street

Staten Island
Ferry Terminal
(from here the tour goes across
the harbor to Staten Island)

N
W E
S

In the 1960s, as shipping and industry disappeared from Manhattan's rivers, developers beamed in anticipation of the shore's future recreational and luxury use. South Street Seaport had been on the descent to tourism since the 1880s, when shipping switched to the deep-water Hudson. Uptown curiosity seekers of the exotic—or the "real"—began to visit the fish market to savor its briny atmosphere, the reassuring energy of tangible goods changing hands.

In 1967, in a complex arrangement with the city and private banks, entrepreneurs turned the old East River port, long under threat of demolition, into a real estate and museum enterprise with the help of the Rouse Company, who'd already "rehabbed" Boston's shore market and Baltimore's inner waterfront. Of the 35 acres that the South Street Seaport Corporation leases from the city, roughly half have been restored. The other half holds fishing concerns and vacant buildings. The corporation would like to build residential complexes, but escalating property values (and landmark laws governing the height of buildings here) make this hard. In the meantime, much deteriorates. Ironically, many feel the old spirit of the port can best be felt in the rotting northern end rather than the preserved southern blocks, which project the generalized ye olde Williamsburgh mall(e) ethos of many American reconstructions. A Rouse is a Rouse is a Rouse.

Several years ago the *New York Times* reported on the nostalgic return to the seaport of an elderly sailor retired in North Carolina at the new Sailors' Snug Harbor. He'd come back, he said, because he was "a hedonist, an insatiate of sail." The shopkeepers regarded the old salt who wandered the boutiques, dazed at the port's change, with wariness bordering on fear.

☞ Despite the commercial thrust, there is a dedicated band at South Street who care deeply about presenting the past. One of them is Jack Putnam, the manager of the **bookstore** ❷ at 209 Water Street, across from this park. Though the book component of the store is shrinking as the imperative to sell *things* rises, I urge the walker to visit there before leaving. (Putnam also gives memorable Herman Melville walks in the port.) The site this little park occupies once housed another book store, the Edwin M. Blunt Book and Chart House, built in 1796. A sign above the store across the street recalls the cartographer, famed in his day, for the navigational maps he published of North America's Atlantic Coast, the West Indies, and parts of Central and South America.

After the Revolution the need for geographic knowledge ballooned as the young Republic, including New York, forged fresh trade links. Soon after the war, which had left the town in wrecked state, merchants were sending ships out on ventures as far as China, and the city was beginning its climb to national ascendancy. By 1790 New York's population was the largest in the country. By 1800 the harbor's tonnage exceeded that of its rivals, Boston and Philadelphia. In the 1820s Blunt ended his days writing "strangers'" guidebooks for the wave of businessmen on commercial pilgrimage here.

While mercantile New York was growing into the nation's leading seaport, the Common Council was supervising a rush program of landfill and wharf building. Shore hubbub continued even in the downturn before the war of 1812, when strife caused shipping to cease temporarily. Rich merchants continued to sink their capital into port improvement even though the harbor was clotted with anchored boats, unemployed men trod the waterfront, and soup kitchens doled out gruel.

Peter Schermerhorn, a relation (in-law) of the Beekman family who had owned property here since the 1720s, was one such developer. Buying the water lots east of Water Street in 1793 (where the present river end of Fulton runs today), he literally sank his capital by filling the block into its present shape,

Until recent decades New York's matchless waterfront was its reason for being.

completing the job in 1807. By 1811 Schermerhorn had finished building a line of office-ware houses on the south side of his newly minted land.

Soon after the row went up, Schermerhorn's friend, Robert Fulton, chose the wharf at the end of the street as the terminus for his new steam ferry route to Brooklyn, making the property more valuable still. (Fulton had tried out his ship back in 1807, chugging up the Hudson belching smoke "like a devil going up the river in a sawmill." There were other competitors, but Fulton had backing. One beaten inventor drank himself to death.)

After the end of the war of 1812 and the reopening of the Atlantic sea lanes, New York prospered once again, or at least the port in general prospered. In 1818 Jeremiah Johnson, a woolens importer, started the first regular sailings to England from an anchorage near Peck Slip a few blocks north of here. As well as gaining the lead on trade with Europe, city shippers also captured control over southern cotton and, soon afterward, when the Erie Canal opened, the nation's western trade as well. (Seaport merchants had promoted the canal's construction with this end in mind.)

Fleets of lighters off-loaded deep-draft ships, stevedores dragged carts, drays hauled granite blocks squealing and sparking along cobbles, sidewalks spilled with tackle from neighboring ropewalks. Caulkers, sailmakers, sawyers, riggers, brass founders, shipwrights, carpenters, wheelwrights joined the carters, longshoremen, and merchant's clerks in the shoreside welter.

River-front activity was so tumultous that longshoremen, often seamen moonlighting between voyages, were sometimes knocked off piers. As most couldn't swim, fatalities were high. One of the first projects of New York's Humane Society, the city's earliest organized charity group, was the installation of resuscitating machines along the dock front. The Rube Goldberg bellows-and-syringe contraptions inflated waterlogged lungs and blew "life-giving" tobacco smoke into the victim's bowels.

*W*alk east on Fulton Street to Schermerhorn Row. ❸

It's hard to sense the old uproar from the prim remains of Schermerhorn's counting houses on Fulton Street. An important feature of the row evoking the port's hectic pace is now gone. Once, exterior staircases, used to avoid the crowded ground floor, led to second floor "counting" rooms where Dickensian clerks on high stools penned manifests in plumey script.

☞ Schermerhorn's buildings, copied from counting houses in London and Liverpool, were built as warehouses and merchant offices. The four-story

View of New York Harbour.

Flemish bond brick buildings with pitched slate roofs (concealing wheels for winching cargo on exterior hoists) represented a new type. Until then, most buildings combined residence and work space. We'll see some examples of the earlier type at the north end of the seaport.

For two centuries forests of masts circled the downtown shoreline; from the 1870s on, steam traffic reigned for nearly one hundred years. Today, Manhattan's wharves are almost silent.

By the time this row went up, the waterfront's moil had started driving wealthier merchants inland to live. The separation of home and job beginning to characterize the city in this era caused many more changes, including the way families functioned. In the colonial economy men and women had worked together under one roof. Now, upper- and middle-class women stayed in the house supervising chores while their husbands walked to their seaport offices.

☞ The first aspect of Schermerhorn's row to catch the eye is the mass of brick. New fire laws, dating from 1766, required brick wall and slate roof construction in most built-up parts of the city. (Many flouted the rule. Brick was still expensive and hand-made, molded in mahogany frames imported from Central America.) The next thing you notice about the buildings is that down near the South Street end of the row, the brownstone window lintels crook rakishly out of plumb. As Schermerhorn never intended to move from his marine supply shop on Water Street but planned to rent this space to other merchants, he'd cut corners and rushed them up on landfill that had only partly consolidated.

If you were putting up something for your own use, you'd take pains it was well done. As society grew more anonymous, developers paid less attention. The decline of workmanship in these offices, probably the first in New York built just for speculation, reveals the breakdown of skills—and social relations—that was to worsen over time.

W*alk back to the benches in the park at Fulton and Water to read the remainder of the introduction.*

In colonial days apprentices who contracted their labor for a specified number of years had been considered junior family members living with their masters until they'd completed their contracts and hired themselves out as journeymen. After that, the theory went (and generally the fact), they would save enough to found workshops of their own and carry on the process. After the Revolution this training cycle short circuited. Some master craftsmen did quite well with the change, usually succeeding because of an ability to adapt, plus a skill for bargaining. Stephen Allen is a good example. Allen, whose workshop is now absorbed in the Square Rigger Bar at 186 Front Street, was an apprentice sailmaker during the Revolution but ended his training at age sixteen when his Tory master left New York. Though he ran into some opposition from other journeymen, as he'd not finished his full apprenticeship, by the 1790s he'd opened his own shop and sailmaking loft. Eventually, he became a well-to-do merchant and later, mayor. Allen kept some ties with the working class, but many others who merged with merchants and lawyers to become the city's new business middle class stopped minding about their staff and began cost-cutting labor practices. Those who weren't able to rise in the new open-ended society gradually lost a sense of control and stake in what they were doing.

When personal ties between classes began to erode, sailors were the hardest hit, all the more vulnerable because they were among the town's poorest in the first place—few who could choose took on the hard life. (This accounts for the high number of African American sailors, who formed a quarter of the crews.) At sea, ships officers kept the sailors in hand through increasingly brutal treatment. Aside from mutiny, crewmen had only one recourse—jumping ship. If they left in foreign ports and got caught, they could be arrested. Despite this, it happened often, as captains sometimes ran their vessels like floating jails.

The wary reaction of the present-day South Street mall operators to the old insatiate of sail from North Carolina is not new. From the beginning, city dwellers were suspicious of, if indebted to, sailors. Floggings at sea could make sailors conform, but there were no such sanctions in the town itself. "Jack-ashore" was thought both dangerous and credulously childlike, always a potential source of trouble. The first city ordinance on record in 1638 banned immoderate drinking and barred sailors from sleeping on shore. The proper place for seamen, whom Dutch New Amsterdammers called *hetgraw*—"riff-raff," was on ships, not land. The liminality of seamen, their radical propensity and global ties, made landsmen uneasy.

In 1741 New Yorkers accused sailors of involvement in a plot supposedly hatched by African Americans and Jesuits to burn New York. The gathering place of the "plotters," whose guilt was never proved but resulted, nonetheless, in scores of executions, was a riverside tavern. Landsmen feared these "low groggeries" where shipmates met the town's spindrift population of loose women, African Americans, and Irish immigrants.

In part, seamen's reputation for trouble grew from their resistance to forcible seizure as crew. During the French and Indian wars, British privateers prowled the harbor, kidnaping men off of boats and docks to serve them. In 1766 a captain who had been press-ganging sailors came ashore in a barge. It was a one-way trip. Throngs of seamen overwhelmed the party and burned the craft in City Hall Park as an example.

☞ In today's experience of city space, the seaport and City Hall have nothing to do with each other, but in fact, as the spires of the **Municipal Building** to the west of Water Street remind us, they are a stone's throw away and once were intimately linked.

Stone's throw is the right metaphor. During the Revolution sailors played a lead role in demanding independence from Britain. Ship captains who'd kept ties with seamen and longshoremen served as the tie between councils of war and the Revolutionary mob.

After the war American sailors continued to use their collective oppositional skills. Between 1785 and 1835 many sailor-led strikes swept the city. (The word *strike* itself is a nautical term. In 1768 mutinous British sailors decided to "strike" or pull down sails to cripple commerce.) In the beginning the men used a mix of old ritual tactics they'd employed in the Revolution as well as direct intimidation. In 1802 sailors fighting for a pay raise paraded in military parody up and down the seaport's wharves "with drums beating and colors flying." Two white sailors calling themselves commodores led the white battalion. Two African American "commodores" led the black sailors' troop. When some crewmen refused to join the fray, they went further and boarded a sea-ready ship, seized her documents, and dismantled her rigging. As time passed, the direct, often violent, approach grew more common. It was unemployed mariners leading a rally for jobs in 1808 that hastened City Hall's long delayed construction: the pressured mayor awarded the men work carting materials—the first WPA project in the city.

Usually, however, sailors turned their unhappiness and alienation against themselves. The northern end of Water Street grew infamous for drink and dissipation. In 1864 a sanitary inspection counted 500 liquor stores and saloons in this district, with seamen providing 75 percent of the custom. By now the area, once the city's most elegant, had become a sinkhole of "tenement house rot," epidemics, and social disease.

From the mid-nineteenth century on, the majority of Water Street buildings served as boarding houses. Some were respectable, the sort where counting house clerks, both single and married, could live without the cost of setting up their own households. Most were not. Sailors taking rooms here were pawns to the men who ran the houses. Proprietors plied them with women, liquor, and credit—until they colluded with crew-short captains to ship them out. Then, after pocketing the man's advance salary, the boarding house keepers called their debts, or, not uncommonly, Mickey-Finned the sailor (drugged him senseless), snatched his remaining cash, and dumped him on an outward bound ship. If it was a whaler, it could be a three-year journey.

*W*alk north up Water Street to the newly built **Seamen's Church Institute** ❹ at number 243. If you can, take time to visit the organization (founded in 1834) to learn about its programs and tour its model ship gallery. Hours are Tuesday–Saturday 12:00 P.M. to 5:00 P.M.

Many viewed the hard lives of the seamen with concern—both for the men themselves and for the problems their dissolute ways caused society. Soon after the Revolution, Congress had passed laws governing the treatment of sailors on land and sea, urging a change from punishment to pa-

ternalism. These measures had done little but place tentative limits on the degree of exploitation sailors suffered. Private institutions also opened to address mariners' social plight, though not their economic woes. Among other reform groups were the 1792 Mariners Friendly Society, the 1801 Sailors Snug Harbor, the 1807 Marine Benevolent Committee, the 1811 African Marine Society, the 1817 Pilots' Charitable Society, and the 1821 New York Nautical Institution.

> The mariners who served the shipping lived even harder lives than most of New York's poor. Ships were floating jails; the shore, a sinkhole of drink and disease.

In 1829 the American Seamen's Friend Society, a national association of the "wise and the good" (headed by my grandfather in the 1950s), began the Seamen's Bank for Savings to help sailors hold on to their money. ("When I woke up next morning, I had an aching head, my gold watch and my pocket book, n'my lady-friend had fled. . . . Singing, oh, Annie, my dear Annie, oh you New York girls, can't you dance the polka. . . .") A few years later the society founded the town's first boarding house "of good character" and soon afterward, hostels and libraries in ports round the world. Aside from caring for sailors' social and religious welfare, the association also fought for legal reforms including an end to shipboard flogging (finally outlawed in 1850).

It was New England merchants, migrants to New York at the end of the Revolution, who started many of the organizations, including this Seamen's Church Institute. The newcomers had moved here to make money and wanted a ruly, God-fearing work force that would be a stay against "shipwrecks, cargoes destroyed, lives lost as a result of superstition, drunkenness and misconduct. . . ."

Serious missionary revival efforts began on Water Street in 1812. (The date probably is owed to worsening social problems, as the port's war embargo savaged shore workers' lives.) Five years later the Marine Bible Society began making calls, seeking out sinners in their "lurkin' places" and holding nightly prayers on ships at anchor. Female charities raised funds, hoping "in the forecastle of every ship, hymns will replace lewd ballads."

The Seamen's Church Institute itself began as a floating chapel off Pike Street.

*C*ontinue north on Water Street to **Peck Slip,** ❺ site of the first seaport market.

Developers filled this old water berth in 1817. The next year Jeremiah Johnson's Black Ball packet line began its regular trans-Atlantic service from a dock at the end of the former slip. Conditions on this line were even tougher than most, as the regular sailings forced ships to leave in all weather. First mates on the Black Ball line were notorious for their violence—their bent for giving sailors "belaying pin soup"—beatings on the head with wooden dowls. The mutinous song "Blow the man down, Johnny, blow the man down," whose cheerful melody belies the homicidal refrain, is thought to have come from the hard-used sailors on this fleet.

☞ Many of the buildings still fronting the old slip were provision stores—some carrying luxury foodstuffs, coffee, tea, spices, liquors along with flour from western state granaries. Smokehouses here supplied ships the standard crew fare for long voyages—dried meat, hard tack, and canned stews, the latter an invention popularized after the war of 1812. Sailors supplemented this numbing diet with any fresh catch they could snare, booby birds, bladder-wrack, and flying fish. (The buildings along the south side of the slip are in sad melt-down condition because of the Seaport's development arrangements.)

In 1989, the New York City Board of Estimates voted to extend the South Street Seaport historic district (drawn in 1977) by one block up to Dover Street near the Brooklyn Bridge. The move stymied five city banks, who had hoped to develop the land into a fifty-story high-rise. The Peck Slip block is one of the few sites still eligible by city law to receive the development rights created to compensate the banks for surrendering their mortgage liens on this property. While debate continues, buildings rot.

☞ We are about to see the oldest surviving building at the seaport, whose dereliction rivals, surpasses, even these. To get an idea of what the 1773 Captain Joseph Rose House once resembled, look across Peck Slip to the pitched-roof **Federal house** on the northeast corner (45 Peck Slip.)

K*eep walking north to the* **Rose House** ❻ *at 273 Water Street.*

☞ Astonishingly, two realtors bought this building wreck at auction in 1989 for $325,000. At one point they hoped to rehabilitate the hollowed out, semi-roofless, tinned-up structure with a ground-floor store and offices above. Not surprisingly, they later withdrew their deposit. If, by a miracle of renovation, the old derelict—whose brick fronting, wooden sills, brownstone belt courses are original—had been salvaged, the gentrification would have been *re*gentrification.

In the eighteenth century this was a choice quarter of the port. The neighborhood was still passably fashionable when New York served as America's capital in the months after the Revolution. George Washington lived in a rented house, the first presidential mansion in America, near the base of the Brooklyn Bridge.

Debilitation began when commerce intruded a shade too much, never mind that it was the resident merchants themselves who brought it on through their billowing trade. Captain Rose, the merchant-seafarer who built this combination house and store (he sold goods of all sorts wholesale and retail), decided it was time to leave in the early 1790s, just before the city started to build Front Street on new landfill to the rear of his home. Ever since retiring from his Caribbean import trade (his specialty, Honduran mahogany), Rose had moored his brig, the *Industry,* at a wharf behind his kitchen garden. Now, aside from having to suffer the depredation of work crews, the chaos of construction, he would be marooned, his boat dry-docked.

Many of the captain's friends left with him when he retreated to one of the new houses going up near the Battery. For some years Rose's son carried on an apothecary shop here, but by 1812 Rose Jr. had also departed, and the building became a boarding house with a ground-floor shoe store. Seamy gave way to seamier. By the 1860s the house held a dance hall some called a "slum of moral putrefaction."

In certain blocks of Water and nearby Cherry you could buy whiskey or beer at every address. Several dozen of these places also featured dance halls and brothels under the same roof. The two were generally synonymous, as prostitution was central to port life. Most of the whores were young women alone, but some were the wives of sailors abandoned for years because of their husbands' long voyages. Veneral disease came with the job. By now, one of every six New Yorkers over fifteen had a venereal disease. Alcohol was the usual nostrum.

Aside from drinking and sex, blood sports were the main lure of shore leisure. Since colonial days, animal fights had been big draws for rich and poor in New York. By the mid-nineteenth century they had become exclusively a poor man's show. In the 1850s the old Rose house featured a "bilious green" oval pit, owned by an Irish immigrant, Kit Burns. The ten-by-six-foot "theater" holding tiers of circular benches rising to the ceiling seated up to five hundred bettors. (The numbers are hard to imagine in a house this size.) Among other spectacles, dogs fought rats brought in by neighborhood children who got "growlers"—buckets of stale beer—in payment. Sometimes the contest was between men and rats, or dogs against dogs. If this didn't hold audience attention, for a twenty-five-cent tip the owner's son-in-law would bite off the head of a rat.

In 1868 a renewed fit of revivalism hit Water Street. Even ex-seminarian John Allen ("the wickedest man in New York"), who ran a brothel farther up the block just above the Brooklyn Bridge, held daily Bible readings for whores and patrons. Burns also jumped in, offering the Rose-house "theater" to a reform-minded pastor for daily prayer services. It turned out to be a hoax, however, or rather, a come-on, as Burns had hoped to rent out his place, not donate it cash free.

The moral trajectory, nevertheless, was there. The year following the religious rally a minister bought the Rose-Burns house as a home for magdalenes (prostitutes.) Within the first five months one hundred "fallen women" who wished to repent—or possibly just to be fed—took lodging here.

The problem of poverty and reform is complex. Some converts were grateful for the break in the self-destructive, if temporarily comforting, spiral of drink and promiscuity that missions offered. Others resented outsiders' moralizing.

> Life was hard for women at the port also. While some earned "honest" livings, many were caught in the sorry sex trade serving seamen.

One reform effort that came from below and still does good work in the city (while some of the more paternalistic institutions have quit the field) is Jerry McAuley's Water Street Mission. The charity, begun down here in the 1860s by an old salt who saved himself from alcoholism, now operates on Lafayette Street behind City Hall. For a pledge of temperance during one's stay and attendance at a fellowship meeting, today's homeless get a free night's lodging and a hot meal.

*W*alk north on Water up to the looming Brooklyn Bridge (1883). At 279 Water Street (the corner of Dover) note the **Bridge Cafe. ⑦** If it's open, enter the listing, tin-roofed restaurant that now serves City Hall and Wall Street clients.

This 1801 wood structure opened as a grocer's store and residence. In the mid-nineteenth century it housed Monell's bar, where the habitués were so unruly one of the barmaids, Gallus Mag, bit off the ear of an annoying customer.

Next to sex and drink, blood sports were the main pleasure of shore life.

Turn right on Dover Street and walk two blocks to South Street. Turn right and head south back toward the other end of Peck Slip. The building on the southeast corner (116–119 South Street) is the **Meyers Hotel,** ❽ *a gleaming tin-and-mahogany trove holding an active saloon and restaurant. Enter through the glass-paneled corner door etched with flower baskets.*

By mid-nineteenth century the seaport catered to commercial travelers from all over the country. Edward Meyers, a liquor dealer, converted this building, designed by John Snook in 1873, into a hotel serving South Street's sailors and transients. A decade later Annie Oakley hosted a party here to celebrate the opening of the Brooklyn Bridge. The fete was one of many heralding the seaport's touristic future. From now on, this part of the waterfront became a curiosity center for uptowners beginning to take guided tours to celebrated downtown "danger" spots. (The Bowery and Chinatown were two other favorites.)

South Street's decline had begun in the 1860s with the gradual change from sail to steam. Steam freed ships from their earlier dependence on favorable eastside winds. Also, the bulky freighters needed the Hudson's deeper channels. Soon, the network of rail connections from the continental United States and the grand scale of the Hudson River piers marginalized the East River even more.

*W*alk south on South Street past the **Fulton Fish Market** ❾ *(94–103 South Street).*

The seaport's survival was owed to the Fishmongers' Association, formed at the time shipping here started to fail. (Their office at 124–144 Beekman Street is a Victorian beauty, crusty with terra-cotta cockles and starfish.) As shipping merchants left, wholesale fish dealers moved into the empty warehouses.

The present thriving if troubled fish market is the fourth on the site—the first opened in 1822. It's a private operation where the day's catch is trucked in (sadly), and retailers come to buy. Despite the absence of ships, a dawn visit down here to watch the sales and eat breakfast is still as much fun as earlier sight-seers discovered.

It wasn't just the seaport that languished in the 1860s, but American, particularly New York, shipping itself, as it remained tied to sail far longer than its European counterparts. Some South Street shippers had tried as early as 1838 to convince New York fleet owners that the future of ocean navigation lay in steam. They'd also tried to persuade the government in Washington, but it, too, was obdurate, refusing, unlike the British government, to grant subsidies. No one in America wanted plodding steamers when they could have faster, svelter clipper ships. The 1849 gold rush added even greater force to the urge for speed. Even the canny A. A. Low firm (headquartered at 161–171 John Street) was seduced by clipper madness, sacrificing cargo space and certain future gain to the swiftness—and beauty—of sail. This was one moment in America and this city when romance, not money, ruled. Local (and national) shipping never recovered.

The Civil War finished it off. From this time on, foreign firms gained insurmountable leads. What shipping remained unimpaired from the war took foreign flags. Increasingly, foreign seamen were hired for crew as they accepted harsh conditions, low wages. From this time on, Britain and her Cunard line ruled supreme. The nineteenth century closed with foreign bottoms importing 90 percent of goods through New York and exporting 94 percent. Most of the scant U.S. shipping that remained plied no farther than Cuba. Fortunately (for us), U.S. coastal trade continued American by law.

World War I brought a brief port rally, and Washington, under the gun, as it needed mariners for its defense effort, finally passed laws banning abuse and sanctioning the sailor's right to quit ships. At war's end, however, few men signed on, as pay remained abysmal.

☞ The somewhat motley **ships moored at South Street** (though mostly non-New York craft) serve to illustrate the wane of New York and American shipping.

The four-masted bark, the *Peking,* wound up her days carrying nitrate—bird droppings—which, by the turn of the twentieth century had become one of New York's main cargo items. Today's chief export is waste paper; the second, plastic garbage.

☞ It's worth the small admission price to the ships to get a sense of the cramped living conditions crewmen suffered even in relatively recent times. The ticket also allows you to enter other museum indoor shows. By 1996 there should also be an exhibit of port life at 12 Schermerhorn Row. Telephone (212) 748-8600 for hours and days.

Turn right at Fulton Street and walk west toward Water Street. You are retracing your earlier steps by Schermerhorn Row (point 3 on the map).

Until now, this tour has sketched the rise and fall of the South Street port and the hard lives of the seamen who served it. The next segment, easily done on the same day and for contrast's sake recommendedly so, goes out to Staten Island to an asylum planned in 1801 for the care of "aged, decrepit and worn out sailors." Today the estate is called the Snug Harbor Cultural Center.

Walk south on Water Street and turn left on Whitehall to the Staten Island Ferry Terminal, where a boat leaves every half hour for Saint George. The bottom-level floor of the ferry, outdoors at the rear, is the best place to experience the churn of the engine and the view back to Manhattan. The trip takes thirty minutes and the roundtrip fare costs only 50 cents. Allow at least three hours for the excursion, start to finish.

☞ On the trip over to the asylum it's interesting to look at the harbor islands and to reflect on their use over time as welfare sites.

The sailors' home at Snug Harbor was a paradisaical version of other nineteenth-century institutions. Earlier, in colonial America, municipal methods of caring for the urban poor featured outdoor relief, boarding by wealthier families, and, toward the end, town almshouses. To greater and lesser degrees, impoverished men and women remained part of the urban social fabric. (Actually, the municipality's first line of defense against indigents was exclusion, not allowing their entry in the first place. New York, of course, could not readily do this, as it was dependent on fresh labor.)

From the 1810s onward, society and municipalities steeled their feelings about the poor, came to think of them as "other" and to blame the poor themselves for poverty. In part, the inuring was a response to new religious tenets holding individuals responsible for saving their own souls and selves. Before this, people believed predestination ruled. The growing spate of immigration aggravated New Yorkers' judgmental mood.

By the 1820s a drive started to remove any poor who posed a problem. Insulation, that much more absolute than simple isolation, was seen as the solution to poverty, criminality, and illness.

In 1828, the city bought Blackwells Island (now Roosevelt Island) for $32,000 to house the city charity hospital, workhouse, and penal and lunatic institutions. "Separated on either side from the great world by a deep crystal current, [it] appears to have been divinely arranged as a home for the unfortunate and suffering, a place of quiet reformatory meditation for the vicious." Randall's Island soon held a potter's field, city almshouse, and House of Refuge for juvenile delinquents ("These almost infants . . . cunning and adrift").

Staten Island was an obvious target. In 1831 philanthropists built the Sailor's Retreat, a marine hospital caring for seamen with general disabilities and disease, on its north shore. Up until then the city had looked after sailors arriving from foreign ports with yellow fever, smallpox, and typhus. (They covered costs with dues collected from the men.) Mariners suffering illnesses considered less threatening to the public wandered the streets.

In 1844 Randall's Island got the city's new almshouse, along with a nursery for poor children where infant paupers were taught the "habit of labor." The next administration moved the almshouse to Blackwells Island, later adding the Blind Asylum and the Hospital for Incurables and Convalescents to the institutions already located there.

In one stroke, society "protected" social misfits and was protected from them. In 1850 some local residents of Staten Island who didn't feel they were sufficiently protected took the precaution of burning the locality's quarantine hospital. After this, in 1872, the city made artificial islands in

From the 1820s the city's elite thought the answer to crime, vagrancy, and disease lay in insulating "threats to society" on New York's harbor islands. This print shows one of the many institutes planted on Staten Island.

the lower bay to house many of the afflicted. The city forgot the lesson. Some of Staten Island's recent urge to secede comes from what it sees as "NIMBY" (not in my back yard), dumping on their island.

In the 1930s the new prison on Rikers Island received the prisoners from Blackwells Island. (The latter was renamed Welfare Island in hope of upping the moral tone of the "sin-steeped pile.") The use of offshore isolation has continued into our day with the prison barge and Hart Island's potters' field, where city workers stack AIDS babies underground in tiny coffins like safe-deposit boxes.

Robert Randall (no relation to the island), the merchant seaman who bequeathed the asylum for sailors in 1801, did not think of isolating the complex on Staten Island. His will ordered the charity built on his 21-acre Manhattan farm near what was to become Washington Square. His family, however, contested the bequest for three decades. By the time it was probated in 1828, times had changed. The era's hardening social philosophy plus the rising values of Greenwich Village land persuaded Randall's trustees they would be true to the spirit, if not the letter, of the will if they changed his wishes around a bit.

The eight trustees (including, ex officio, the mayor, the president of the Chamber of Commerce, the chancellor of the State of New York, the president of the Marine Society, and the senior ministers of the Episcopal and Presbyterian churches) won permission from the state legislature to build the institute outside the city. A few years later the trustees bought a 131-acre farm at Staten Island and arranged to build and maintain an asylum with income from the Greenwich properties. City life was too depraving, the trustees said. The remove to an island would be for the sailors' own good.

More recently, Staten Island was found too depraving or, at least, the trustees found the cost of operating the aging facilities there too prohibitive. In the 1970s the charity got legislative permission to sell both the Greenwich Village property and the Staten Island asylum. The sailors were shunted to North Carolina, where the home continues today, reputedly poor, despite the astronomical ground rents the trust had earned over time from its Washington Square property.

Much of what's left of the Staten Island complex is landmarked. (It lost many buildings, including a panopticon hospital and an 1890s baroque church resembling a mini-St. Paul's in Rome.) The New York City Landmarks Preservation Commission and the late Jackie Kennedy Onassis saved what remains. Arguments continue over the enclave, now housing various cultural institutions. Some want to renovate the estate as it once was; others want to turn it more completely into an exhibit space. The word *sailors* has been dropped from the name, and at least one spokesperson for the arts side has inveighed against ghostly salts with parrots intruding on their center.

Get off the ferry on the upper level and take the S40 bus from ramp C to Richmond Terrace. It will drop you across from the estate's west gate. The grounds are open daily, noon to dusk, the buildings Wednesday–Sunday 12:00 P.M. to 5:00 P.M. Telephone (718) 448-2500.

☞ On the side of the road where you get off, you can see traces of a waterfront landing overlooking the Kill van Kull oil tanks.

At first the governors ran the asylum fairly loosely. Seamen were allowed to take day trips into Manhattan on the asylum's ferry, which stopped here several times a day. Souring views soon changed that. "Idleness," social thinkers said, spoiled the men. Rules grew tighter, outings rare. Several oral histories record the satisfaction inmates took in escaping to Manhattan—sometimes by rowboat. Like many mariners who preferred the raunchy possibility of land perils to shipboard tyranny, some of the sailors here longed for the stir of the port, despite its depradation. (Incidentally, shoreside and shipboard conditions were so hard that the first wornout and decrepit sailors here were a sorry crew in their thirties and forties.) The trustees lectured the inmates that the purpose of the remove to Snug Harbor was to keep them from temptation—that if suasion failed, a wall around the estate might be necessary. *Paradise,* a Persian word and concept, means "encircled by walls."

☞ In 1842 the estate got this 7-foot-tall **iron fence.** It was not just an ordinary railing, but designed by an English architect who'd planned the aristocratic Cumberland Gates of London's Hyde Park.

***M**ake your way through the* **West Gate,** *a straightforward affair compared with most entrances here.*

Because of the wealth of the Randall endowment, asylum inhabitants (two thousand at peak) enjoyed more luxury than any other wards of charity in America. The insulating impulse, however, remained the same. Most governors of Snug Harbor, including Herman Melville's brother, who ruled the home for seventeen years, ran the institution with shipboard severity.

In keeping with the day's belief that it was demon rum that depraved the poor and disabled them for work, the number-one house rule here was a liquor taboo. Snug lore says that most of the entryways to the estate were built at off-center angles, as the sailors believed the alignment kept bad spirits from following them. From 1874 on, newly built gate houses where guards body-checked entrants for liquor certainly kept *hard* spirits from following. (An aside here is that in the 1840s, self-pledged abstainers set up the township of Temperanceville, a real estate-cum-teetotalling venture on the other side of Staten Island—the site, of course, picked for the moral powers ascribed to insulation.)

A*fter you are safely inside, turn east (left) to the lawn facing Kill van Kull in front of the* **grand, porticoed buildings.** *Noted architect Minard Lafever designed the central hall in 1831, the others followed.*

Among other establishments, an asylum for "aged, decrepit, and wornout" sailors opened on Staten Island in the 1830s.

In 1837 a European visiting Snug Harbor said, "seen from afar this little town appears magnificent. One would take it for a large city built by the Greeks or the Romans, so great is the number of its columns." Even now, the Greek temple ensemble is magisterial, a world away from the gritty seaport.

A*fter appreciating the buildings from this vantage point, I suggest you check in with the Visitors' Center to pick up its literature and maps and see its photo essay on the asylum. After you're finished, use the map to find locations on the estate. Some buildings may be shut, but you can peer into windows. The center also offers guided tours.*

☞ The **photo exhibit** of inmate life here is moving and informative. The pictures of the men (all white, almost invariably clad in formal suits and hats) are shown endlessly waiting. Waiting on benches for a bell to ring them to meals, waiting for prayers, waiting for morning "crockery brigades" when they emptied their chamber pots. (The sailors called the corridors Shinbone Alleys as prefects hit their legs with canes to keep order.) Having seen the photographs, you will sense the long halls come alive with gaunt men sitting patiently, staring, rustling, listening for the bell.

The bell controlled life here. If the sailors defied routine—missed a meal or a compulsory work stint—they could be "tabooed." The word, which at Snug Harbor meant losing various privileges, including outings and tobacco, made its first appearance in this country at the asylum.

Along with intemperance, the Victorians ranked "vicious" idleness as poverty's root cause. Officials at Snug Harbor dealt with the vice by ordering compulsory yard work and craft production. Unless the governor denied them the "privilege" for disciplinary reasons, the sailors could sell their weaving and ship models for pocket money. Like their brethren in the city almshouse, the sailors also picked up funding by selling their vote in the local elections. The practice continued until 1903, when the court declared that New York law did not permit "wards of charities" to vote.

The third cause of poverty, in Victorian eyes, was a lack of religion. This, too, was dealt with here—in quantities. Until the turn of the century the asylum held compulsory Protestant services in the **estate's chapel.**

☞ Far more evocative than the chapel (newly renovated as a theater) is the **Administration Building's Main Hall,** where asylum chaplains held morning and evening prayers until the chapel opened in 1855. The room is designed in the shape of the cross and exudes metaphors of sea and salvation. Stained-glass windows radiate seascapes of lighthouses, one showing the guiding polar star that keep ships on course, while the parquet floor holds an inlaid nautical compass to catch other drifters.

Ministers here were wont to preach sermons comparing the asylum to a "dry dock where men had come to refit for their onward voyage full of quicksands, concealed rocks, whirlpools and yawning gulphs. There may be a darker, severer, and more terrific storm, and a more awful warring of the elements still in reserve for you, than any through which you have passed—you may yet be hopelessly wrecked and left to sink into the deep and unfathomable abyss." "The holy pilot," however, stood ready to guide all those who sought his aid.

☞ The most moving illustration of the Victorian asylum principle is the mural surrounding the glass lantern dome rising above the center of the hall. It is a painting, at once boastful and innocent, of the estate's aristo-cratic iron fence. At Snug Harbor, even the sky is enclosed.

☞ The guardians of all this were the governors. The governor's house has been pulled down, but you can get an idea of their comfortable life-style by looking at the **doctor's quarters** (1846) still standing near the west gate. The asylum doctors competed with the governors for power and perks and had comparable residences.

Virtually all governors here came from upper-class, Protestant back-grounds. Thomas Melville, the novelist's brother, was one of the few ex-ceptions. His father had failed in business when an epidemic struck the port, suspended business, and kept creditors from renewing his notes. His bankruptcy forced both Herman and Thomas to sea—Herman miserably so, as recounted in his autobiographical *Redburn*.

It was Governor Melville's déclassé status, not the charges against him for stealing food and supplies, that made the trustees consider firing him near the end of his long stint. When the end came, Herman was almost as sad as his brother. He had loved to ferry out here for holiday dinners. The prosperous household presided over by his sister-in-law, the daughter of the asylum doctor, and the thirty-room house staffed by eight servants salved his pride. Like his brother, he'd never recovered from his father's fall in society.

Thomas Melville's successor, G. D. Trask, *was* from a prominent fam-ily and for a long time survived press exposés of his "cruel and brutal treat-ment" of Snug inmates. (The sailors leaked the stories to the news because the mayor ignored their complaints.) The patrician Marine Society de-fended Trask, claiming him as one of their own—a gentleman beset by a "wicked piratical element" among the institute's men. Eventually, the trustees did retire him under a cloud.

☞ Near the turn of the century somewhat more progressive thinking brought easier times and increased recreation. In 1892 the estate built this spectacular **Music Hall,** which is soon to reopen with performances.

Radios made their appearance in the oak-paneled reading room of the **library.** Old photos show the sailors quite cheerfully plugged in to crystal sets by earphones. The entertainment was an improvement over earlier fare—devotional literature picked by clergyman trustees. In the library's basement the "Monte Carlo Room" opened up for card playing, even modest gambling.

What remained lacking, among other freedoms (including a long interim from 1903 until the 1930s when inmates were denied the vote), was the opportunity for a heterosexual sex or family life. It was only near the end of the asylum's existence here that a few wives were allowed to stay at the **Matron's House.** Though the men's bedrooms look cozy enough in the photograph exhibit, they were strictly single sex.

Comparable to other Victorian charities, Snug Harbor was gently, even idyllically run. The regimentation of life, however, aimed to ensure control through de-individualization. The bell system, the vast dining halls, the waiting rooms, the mass graves the sailors were made to dig for winter casualties every fall before the ground froze over, all reduced the inmates to anonymity. Even records of death were kept in the aggregate. In 1891 the chaplain noted the year's fatalities as follows: "The sum of their ages was 6,981 years, giving an average of 66 years, 5 months and 2 3/4 days." The graveyard remains today to the rear of the estate behind a suburban complex, Randall Manor.

☞ Another related site, now the headquarters and gift shop of the Staten Island Botanical Society, is **the old morgue,** an evocative building with white tile walls, low hanging lights, and mahogany laying-out tables—a marvel of sanitized luxury.

According to Snug lore, Robert Randall is buried with a fifteen-year-old mulatto girl under a **statue** memorializing him—the only reprobate officially allowed in this strict sanctuary. Officially is as officially does. Despite the asylum's effort to conform its inmates, it is the ineffable, cranky, individual presence of the old salts that still animates the ghostly elegance of Snug Harbor today. Whatever they wish, the artists in residence here are going to have to share space.

After visiting the art exhibits and the several first-rate institutions at Snug Harbor (including Staten Island's Children's Museum), you might stroll past the asylum staff houses now being renovated for artists connected with the center. The **row of miniature mansarded houses** *is beguiling.*

☞ On a sunny day I like to sit and watch the ducks clamber around the pond near the doctor's house where retirees used to sail model boats. The pond must have seemed a child's puddle after behemoth-filled seas. When Snug Harbor still served as an asylum, visitors remember old men, fists screwed up to their eyes as telescopes, scanning far horizons.

To go back to the ferry terminus, take the S40 bus from the estate side of the road near the west gate. Busses run every twenty minutes or so.

3

The Lower East Side
Immigration from Past to Present

Subway: IRT Lexington Avenue Local (train 6) to Canal Street.

Start at the oldest surviving built site in the city, the **Jewish Graveyard ❶** *on the embankment above St. James Place (at the southeast end of Chatham Square between Oliver and James streets). One of the benches below makes a good spot to read the introduction.*

New York has always been a multi-cultural, multi-ethnic town. Ambivalence about its pluralism dates to the start. As far back as 1643, a visiting Jesuit priest noted eighteen different languages and claimed the city was on its way to becoming an "arrogant babel." The Sephardic Jews who opened this cemetery in 1682 arrived soon after the priest took his count and made his cutting judgment.

Peter Stuyvesant had greeted the Jews, ragged refugees from a former Dutch holding in Brazil, with hostility. In part, his attitude reflected the fact the newcomers had arrived without means of support; in part, it came from ingrained intolerance—the close-minded son of a small-town minister scorned most religions other than that of the Dutch Reform Church. In particular, the governor loathed Quakers, Jews, and Lutherans, in that order. Despite Stuyvesant's prejudice, most members of these communities eventually "made it." Success came for various reasons—the cosmopolitan attitude of Amsterdam's West India Company directors, the immigrants' collective struggle, the individual acumen of new arrivals, and, finally, the port's underlying open-endedness—if you were white. The circumstances of the involuntary immigrants from Africa (mostly by way of the West Indies) grew steadily worse in eighteenth-century New York. (See Walk 10.)

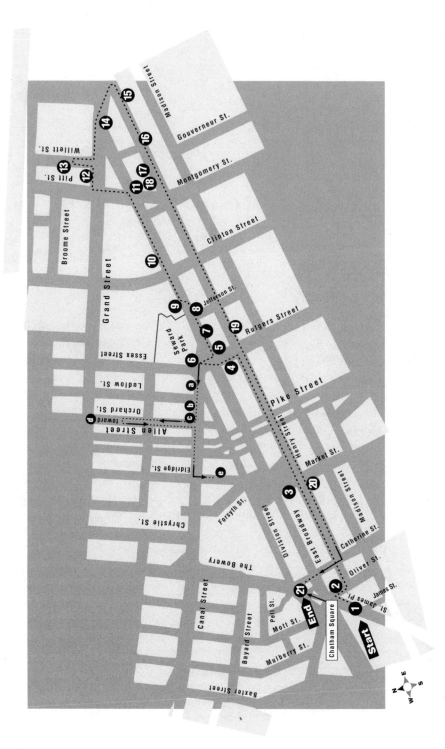

☞ This green graveyard was Shearith Israel's second cemetery; the first has never been located. Its placement at the old town's outer edge shows the continued marginalization of the Jews at the time it opened, despite the community's economic gains.

One grim index of wealth was slaveholding. In 1703, 75 percent of Jewish families were able to afford to own slaves, as opposed to 41 percent of general city households—a telling statistic, even allowing for the skew in figuring because of the small number of Jews in New York at the time. By the time of the Revolution, Jewish merchants were among the city's most prosperous. Haym Solomon, a New York businessman and broker, loaned much of the money used to finance the independence struggle. The mossy crypts above hold the remains of several other well-off patriots, including Benjamin Seixas, a founder of the New York Stock Exchange.

While prejudice entered into it, as today, it was mainly economics that shaped public attitudes toward newcomers in the city. During boom periods entrepreneurs were greedy for new labor; in lean times many feared and demonized arriving immigrants. In 1692 a local lawyer decried the city as having "too great a mix of nations." In 1785 the New York State Council denounced the "most fatal evils" that immigration would surely bring. As naturalization was a state's right between 1776 and 1789, New York's Federalist Party tried to mandate a twenty-one-year period before residents could even apply for citizenship. Fortunately, the opposing party—later the Democrats—overturned the statute and returned the wait to the five-year stretch. When the federal government assumed responsibility for naturalization, this same struggle was to recur at a national level when the conservative ruling party passed the harsh Alien and Sedition acts in 1798 designed to keep out French and Irish radicals. These, too, were overturned, and despite the uncertain welcome, America, and New York in particular, remained an immigrant magnet.

The city still is a world refuge. Today more than two million New Yorkers are foreign born, and 42 percent of all births are to immigrant parents—the highest proportion since the turn of this century. Many Lower East Side blocks have a population that is well over 80 percent foreign born, which raises the question as to why this neighborhood, often called America's gateway, has been an immigrant hub from the early nineteen hundreds on.

Garment work is one continuum drawing settlers; so, until recently, were low rents.

This walk first explores the area in Indian days and its development before and after the Revolution, then continues its (rough) timeline through Irish, East European Jewish, and, finally, present-day Chinese settlement.

Before starting out, we need a geographic definition of just *where* the Lower East Side is—though it's hard to provide, as the term changes. ("Where's the Lower East Side?" my walkers often ask, sometimes querulously. "*This* looks like Chinatown.") Today, the area is usually considered to extend from Chatham Square to 14th Street, the East River to the Bowery. The blocks immediately above Houston Street where 40% of the population is Hispanic, largely Puerto Rican, have been formally (and beguilingly) christened "Loisada," a Spanglish variant of the name. The section that this walk covers, Chatham Square to Grand Street, now has a largely Chinese population, but Jews, African Americans, and Hispanics also live here.

First, a look at the area in early times.

The Canarsie Indians kept a campsite, Nechtanc, at the far eastern hook of today's Grand Street and wore a path down to the Collect Pond (today's Foley Square north of City Hall), where they traded with other tribes. When the West India Company built its string of farms on the East Side, it absorbed part of the path into its new farm road, the Bowery.

In 1642 a party of New Jersey Indians took refuge at the Nechtanc camp from their northern enemies, the Mohawks. Despite the alliance they held with the Dutch, the governor ordered the group slaughtered as they slept. The victims were mainly women and children. Fearing reprisals, the government made a buffer zone above the town's settled tip near today's Chatham Square. Not surprisingly, it planted the town's most disposable residents there—recently freed slaves.

Following a slave uprising in 1712, the British canceled African American land rights and repossessed the farms the Dutch had granted the manumitted slaves—among other factors, the Indian threat was now long gone. Having retrieved the land, the government leveled the hills around the present-day square and sold off the tracts. For another century and a half, landless blacks continued to live in this "out-ward" or farther down in the sixth ward near the Collect Pond.

By the 1730s the hook at Grand Street—rechristened Crown Point, later Corlear's Hook—had become a popular picnic spot and swimming beach. South of the point, boatyards lined the East River shoreline down to where the Manhattan Bridge stands today. Despite the shipyard activity and real estate stirrings near Chatham, the bluffs above the beach (the topography is long erased) remained rural. Soon, however, two big landlords, the Rutgers and the De Lanceys, would shape the high ground.

In 1728 a second-generation Dutchman, Harmon Rutgers, bought 97 acres between today's Division Street and the East River; his land ran from today's Chatham Square to Crown Point. Rutgers' purchase was part of a general real estate frenzy at the time. Within the next two decades, one hundred families would own most of Manhattan's Hudson and East River shorelines. (Relatives of Rutgers got a vast parcel west of Broadway at bargain rates on condition they'd drain the swamps around the Collect Pond.) Unlike the English estate owners they emulated, New York's gentry bought land for profit as much as for prestige and refuge from port epidemics. Harmon Rutgers grew barley on his Lower East Side farm for his downtown brewery.

When Harmon's son Hendrick inherited in 1753, he left his father's house at today's Chatham Square and built a mansion half a mile to the north near present-day Jefferson Street. (East Broadway grew out of the private road linking his house to the Chatham area.) Soon afterward he platted lots for development at the southern end of his property. Trinity Church had just begun leasing out its acreage, and Rutgers was one of several landowners quick to follow suit.

In 1765 the brewer's heir worked out a joint strategy with his neighbor, fellow developer, and family in-law, Lieutenant Governor James De Lancey (a son of the Huguenot immigrant who owned the brick house on Broad Street that became Fraunces' Tavern; see Walk 1). De Lancey Jr.'s estate ran in crooked swath from present-day Division Street up to Houston, a large chunk of it valuable shore frontage.

To keep control and ensure an up-market operation, the two friends agreed they wouldn't sell outright but would stick to a policy of ninety-nine-year restricted leases compelling tenants to build "good brick" houses. Settling their estate boundaries along the line of a rope-walk factory making tackle for the East River shipyards, the developers opened a new thoroughfare, Division Street, to formalize the demarcation.

De Lancey was first off the real estate mark. A decade before the Revolution, long-lease tenants on his land had built 112 homes, and he had surveyed and charted a great square, modeled after Georgian enclaves in London, to attract yet more householders. It was to be New York's first planned enclosure, as Chatham had begun life as a convergence point rather than a formal creation. A map from 1766 shows the envisioned square approximately between today's Hester, Broome, Eldridge, and Essex streets—the center of De Lancey's estate. The plan never materialized as the war intervened and the Tory family lost its land after independence. Nothing down here except a long track running through his property, present-day Delancey Street, shows even a glimmer of the realtor's grand design. (The ancestral name itself is wonderfully democratized from the French, "de-Lanc-*cee*" to our "Duh-*lanc*-y.")

After the war, officials divided and auctioned the forfeited estate. The new proprietors then sold off small plots or rented them out to workers who were beginning to leave the seaport as prices soared near the docks. To maximize their investment, the new developers packed in dwellings and streets—the same mean streets that characterize parts of the Lower East Side today.

In contrast, Rutgers' property evolved in the up-market manner originally intended. (He'd been on the right side in the Revolution.) Though Hendrick's son, Henry, made over *four hundred* deeds to lessees soon after inheriting the property in the 1790s, he banned rear houses on his

Two big landlords, the Rutgers and the De Lanceys, shaped the Lower East Side in the eighteenth century. De Lancey planned to build a great square like the ones opening in London but fled town after the Revolution. (He'd been on the wrong side.) Developers packed his part of the neighborhood with the same mean streets we have today.

grounds, as these airless back-lot buildings, common by now in the city, attracted poorer tenants. He also required his lessees—merchants and shipbuilders who'd moved north as new streets opened—to build brick houses at least two stories high and 36 feet wide. (That's 11–13 feet wider than most latter-day New York rowhouses.)

***W**alk north on St. James Place to the* **Baptist Mariners' Temple ❷** *on Oliver Street, originally the Oliver Street Baptist Church.*

☞ Note the marble plaque above the church door and its date, 1785, the year the founding Baptist group here was organized. This 1844 Greek Revival temple by Minard Lafever is the third incarnation of the church to stand on the site. The original Baptist congregation sold off this great chocolate church, its brownstone spaltering from lack of funds, as a mission in the 1860s. The lighthouse bell dates from the time it served as a seamen's church, or bethel.

Today, an African American congregation worships in the main body of the church and, in time-honored tradition, immigrants hold services in the basement. (The present group is Chinese.)

Henry Rutgers was a generous man who gave away a quarter of his annual income; he was also a shrewd entrepreneur who donated some of his property to further his real estate ambitions. The gifts to church groups, who were required to build within a certain period, were come-ons legitimizing neighborhoods, attracting upper-middle-class settlers. Rutgers' loss-leader offer was good for Protestants only. (Nowadays, in a turnaround, churches are seen as bringing real estate down as they might offer offensive social services such as feeding or lodging the poor. Suburbs often rally to fight new church openings.)

☞ Look across the street at the northeast corner of Henry and Oliver streets. The turn-of-the-century P.S. 1 grammar school stands on a plot Henry Rutgers gave the city in 1806.

The deed stipulated that if a school ever ceased to exist here, the land would revert to the Rutgers Presbyterian Church. Since the time the first school went up, the site's been used accordingly.

After the Revolution when immigration multiplied, Rutgers was among other New Yorkers who founded the Free School Society, the forerunner of the city's public school system. Previously, New York's churches had sponsored education; now the elite wanted institutions designed to assimilate newcomers and prevent the formation of a large pauper "criminal" class common to European cities.

New York's Free Schools followed the British Lancastrian method of teaching, which that industrializing country had devised to mold children into a pliant work force. To keep order in the classrooms of 300 children (down from the 500 typical in Britain), monitors used negative reinforcements, including suspending children in iron cages, manacling them, and anchoring thirty-pound logs across their shoulders. Despite such incentives, schooling here was not entirely successful. Many children did not attend, and the boys were prone to slip away to nearby rope-walks, the equivalent of today's video arcades for juvenile loitering.

*C*ontinue north (actually, northeast) along Henry Street. Continue up to Market Street to the **Sea and Land Church** ❸ on the corner of Market and Henry.

Here Comes, There Goes the Neighborhood: This southern end of Rutgers property went (and continues to revolve) through more cycles than most in the city. Because of the riverfront shipyards, the shore end of Market was notorious as the town's red light district from before the Revolution. In 1813 Connecticut-born poet Theophilus Eaton, one part civic booster, one part critic, wrote:

> Now traveling East and turning round
> We tread the most licentious grounds
> East Georgia Street, now Market called
> Where men and maids become enthralled
> in infamy and foul disease. . . .

Five years later Henry Rutgers deeded lots here for a church to improve this precinct as well as the blocks below. The maneuver worked.

☞ Note the elegant Federal house, circa 1824, on the north side of Market Street at number 51.

☞ The Dutch Reform congregation built its new Georgian sanctuary in local fieldstone. The hand-hewn beams, sawed at a nearby shipyard, still span the nave. The original slave gallery also stands in the rear. It's an odd feature, as Rutgers, who worshiped here and had his funeral service at the church, was an active abolitionist.

By the late 1840s, the gentry moved away from this neighborhood as the Irish spread north from the old Five Points area back of City Hall, which had been an immigrant stronghold since the 1820s, also the center of the city's garment production. Sermons at the Dutch church resounded with calls to fight "the adversary of souls and geography . . . the continuing emigration of the more substantial class of church members uptown." One of the few remaining worshipers was the Rutgers nephew who'd inherited the last scrap of family land on the Lower East Side—two city blocks near Jefferson Street. (Toward the end of his life, his uncle, like other realtors, had switched from leasing to selling plots outright.) As time passed, the nephew and his sisters became the district's lone gentry residents. By now, coal yards, swill milk factories, and barrel makers surrounded the old Rutgers manse, its gardens "gloomy as a grave."

The year after the nephew's death in 1865, the original congregation sold out. A seamen's mission, the Church of Sea and Land, moved into the church, which had once charged annual $5,000 pew rents, on a chapel basis. Dancing was "tabooed" at functions but a "melodeonist" played hymns to entertain the men. Today, a Chinese Presbyterian congregation worships here.

It's hard today to get a sense of the region's tie to the river, but earlier on, the waterfront was a key reason Rutgers' gentrification effort couldn't hold. In part, our difficulty in making this imaginative link between the Lower East Side and the shore is the consequence of the tall public housing projects lining the water and the barrier of the FDR drive. In part, the difficulty stems from the fact the river itself has been dead for decades, a graveyard of car parts and paralyzed fish. (The city is cleaning it again, but there are still no ships.) In the past century, water transport defined local jobs, culture, and residents.

*C*ontinue along Henry Street under the Manhattan Bridge, passing **Mechanics Alley.**

Here, throngs of shipwrights once walked to the nearby boatyards, and "ribs of ships, tall masts with block and tackle dangling from ropes" hemmed the shore. At first the caulkers, sawyers, axmen, carpenters, blacksmiths were Yankee artisans who lived near their jobs in two- and three-family dwellings and boarding houses on filled marsh. By the 1830s many were immigrant Irish. As trade expanded, the boisterous shorefront culture inevitably seeped up from the streets along the river to the highlands of Rutgers' property.

*K*eep walking up along Henry, noting the **old tenements at numbers 39 and 41.**

☞ Sailors and shipyard workers probably lived in these post–Civil War rooming houses whose figureheads of prow-breasted women (look above the door) were calculated to lure mariners.

*C*ontinue on to Rutgers Street.

☞ **St. Teresa's Church ❹** on the west side of Henry Street was formerly Rutgers' Presbyterian, and, like the first two churches, stands on the realtor's land.

The Presbyterians built their original church here at Rutgers' invitation in 1798 and put up this schist replacement in 1841, only two decades before they pulled out. While prosperous "old family" residents had stayed on in these blocks longer than at the southern end of Rutgers' property, they also were beginning to see themselves as a beleaguered island of respectability.

In 1851 the church's pastor lamented the dozen or so Protestant churches already fled north and pled for missions to combat the "appalling vigor . . . rife and active" of heathenism on the Lower East Side. Comparing the neighborhood to the Sandwich Islands, he complained that demography had changed so much by now, "the adherents of a single community of errorists equal in numbers all of the evangelical denominations among us." The newcomers, he continued, brought the "big increase in crime recently come to this community." The gentry was not guilt free, however. They were to blame, the minister said, for their "excessive sympathy for the criminal which would make him victim of society's wrongs, not the responsible author of his own deeds."

Sadly for the Presbyterian churchgoers, this congregation was forced to take Errorist money in 1862 when it, too, finally sold out and moved north. No Protestant buyers were forthcoming.

By the 1840s poor Irish moving out of the old Collect Pond area, an immigrant hub since its in-fill after the Revolution, had entered Rutgers' fief. Initially, this church was upscale Presbyterian but sold out to "Errorists" in the 1860s.

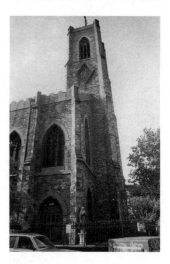

☞ The church reincarnated itself as St. Teresa. Inside, donor plaques recall the names of Irish shore workers and seamstresses who once worshiped here. Outside, the schedule for masses shows the church now serves Hispanic and Chinese congregations.

The next section of this walk deals mainly with Jewish immigration to the neighborhood from the 1880s onward.

Turn left on Rutgers Street and walk toward East Broadway. Look across Rutgers at the **Wing Shoon Restaurant** ❺ *on the northeast corner of Rutgers and East Broadway.*

☞ The restaurant with its curtain of ducks is a node of change. It used to be the Garden Cafeteria, a Jewish intellectual haunt. Once, Leon Trotsky and journalists from the nearby *Forward* debated the future here over black, sugary tea. Reportedly, there are murals of the old Hester Street pushcart market under the present formica paneling.

Jews had lived on the Lower East Side since the 1830s, when German and Austrian communities settled around Chatham Square. By the next decade there was enough Jewish presence in this neighborhood and the port ward below here to warrant their demand for a change in the Christian-based school books used in local public schools. (The city denied the petition.) While wanting a more empathetic curriculum for their children, the Jews were not religiously communal and lived in relative integration with German Christians just above Grand Street in Kleindeutschland. They did, however, build up one ethnic specialty. German Jews owned most of the retail stores along Grand Street and the nearby garment contracting lofts that supplied them. (The Seligman Brothers, latter-day bankers and philanthropists, were among other store owners on the thoroughfare, then the city's up and coming commercial strip. B'nai B'rith was organized at their cap shop at 450 Grand Street in 1843.)

In the late 1870s a colony of Polish Jews from a German-speaking province settled near Grand Street, as many of them were tailors hoping to enter the needle trade labor pool, still an Irish and German preserve. Russian and East European Jews emigrating to New York a few years later came to this neighborhood, drawn by the magnet Polish settlers, relatively affordable rents, and the chance to work for the German Jewish contractors supplying the Grand Street stores. (I witnessed this clustering process in the 1970s when a small community of Sikkimese and Tibetans formed in Providence because of the presence of a lone Sikkimese scholarship student

The Lower East Side has been
the center of the needle trades
from Irish days through the
Jewish era into present-day
Chinese settlement.

at Brown University.) As Irish and Germans found somewhat better jobs, the new arrivals took over much of the city's garment trade. Or rather, the trade, a vicious, underpaid, cruel way of making a substandard living, took over the newcomers.

In the thirty-three years between the assassination of Czar Alexander II and the outbreak of World War I, about one-third of East Europe's Jews left their homelands. Some left to flee bloody pogroms, some to ease lives that had grown intolerable. America was in everybody's mouth; even children played at emigration, the wretched, exhilarating shift of self to an unknown shore. By the late 1880s this part of the Lower East Side grew so crowded the population density rivaled Bombay's—700 bodies to an acre.

The crush and stench on arrival was shocking. Dream landscapes of lost countries couldn't buffer the loom and sting of dark tenements, hurrying streets, and choked work lofts.

*B*efore walking farther up East Broadway to Grand Street, you might want to take two diversions, first along Canal Street to Eldridge, and then north on Essex to Grand.

*T*o make the journey down Canal Street, walk west (it seems like south), passing the lacy white marble **Canal Theater,** ❸ a silent movie house (on the right-hand side of the street between Essex and Ludlow).

Dancing in the Lower East Side's many social halls (one for every two and a half blocks) was a respite from workaday life for many young people, despite parental disapproval. So were the early movies shown in storefront nickelodeons—five cents admission.

This elegant theater dating from 1920 was one of several local picture palaces that continued to show silent films ever after technology enabled sound tracks, as the visual focus allowed immigrants speaking different languages to enjoy the shows. Since the film-makers didn't have to worry about microphones, the actors could move around at will, hence the free-form comedies and madcap chase scenes. In later years, movie making was to become an immigrant, specifically an East European, specialty. Several major Hollywood producers who had grown up down here made films that spread the Lower East Side "old" neighborhood into American myth and consciousness, along with the promise you could always "make it" in America if you tried. President Ronald Reagan invoked this image of the Lower East Side as a "spring-board" when he spoke at the 1986 Statue of Liberty centennial to reinforce one conservative notion that new Americans could (and should) rise without government help.

Continue west on Canal Street across Ludlow Street.

☞ The L-shaped **funeral parlor ❻** on the northwest corner used to be a benevolent organization, the Independent Kletzker Brotherly Aid Society, opened by friends from the same Polish hometown.

Jewish peddlers made full use of the neighborhood's streets, just as do today's Chinese residents.

While newly arrived individuals certainly needed wit and courage to succeed, most couldn't have survived without a collective support system.

The twin entrances to this single building accommodate two funeral parlors, one Italian, one Chinese. Today, as in earlier times, ethnic groups still prefer their own arrangements for Eternity.

Since colonial times New York has had old-country associations to buffer the outside world, extend credit, provide aid in times of distress and death. The first association was a Scots charitable society begun in 1744, which, among other help, gave needy single women looms so they could support themselves through weaving.

Arrangements for death were thought to be even more important than for life, and ethnic groups, including Jews, formed their own burial associations to assist members with funeral expenses and to buy cemetery plots. Some assimilative adjustments may be possible after emigration, but Eternity is not one of them. Recent immigrants in the city continue to maintain most of the institutions that comforted earlier arrivals.

☞ Note the separate Italian and Chinese wings of the present-day funeral parlor. Well-wishers held services here for the drowned men from the *Golden Venture,* recently scuttled off Rockaway.

Continue one block farther on Canal Street to Orchard Street, which took its name from the De Lancey family's cherry groves.

☞ The tall **Jarmulovsky Bank** on the southwest corner of Canal and Orchard opened in 1896, replacing an earlier version. Jarmulovsky's architects designed this high-rise building to impress the neighborhood, attract depositors. Sadly, someone has just torn down its emblematic cupola.

Though many immigrants kept their savings in joint credit pools like the Kletzker society, when they grew more Americanized they switched to banks, usually owned by someone from their own community. Appearances to the contrary, this bank had weak reserves and collapsed after several runs on it in 1914. Rather like financial institutions of today, the bank had frozen its assets in real estate investments that had crashed in value and couldn't be liquidated easily. Enraged victims gathered in front of Jarmulovsky's apartment, forcing him and his family to flee across neighboring roof-tops.

☞ Influential German architects, the Herter Brothers, built the **tenements** ⓒ on the northeast corner at 45 Orchard Street. The yellow glazed terra-cotta Stars of David were a come-on, designed to draw Jewish tenants.

It worked. The decor, plus unusual amenities (baths and stoves), ensured full occupancy and high rents that gained the landlord a 20 percent return on equity—twice the average.

*I*f you have time, you might like to continue a bit farther north. Turn right and walk to 90 Orchard Street—the **Lower East Side Tenement Museum**. ⓓ Telephone (212) 387-0341 for hours.

The museum runs interpretive programs on various immigrant streams. In the future, each floor of the 1863 landmarked walkup will reconstruct the living space of families from different countries—a breakthrough, as most outdoor sightseeing has to do, perforce, with male space, since women have commanded so little public sphere. (Exceptions to this on the Lower East Side were the street strikes led by housewives, including the "Ladies' Anti-Beef Trust" revolt when women marched on butcher shops and torched meat with kerosene. Another exception were the settlement houses—a phenomenon the tour will explore later.)

*R*etrace your steps to Canal, then turn right and continue west across wide Allen Street (the site then, as now, of immigrant commercial sex) to Eldridge Street; turn left to the Khal Adath Jeshurun Synagogue, known informally as the **Eldridge Street Synagogue** ⓔ at 12–14 Eldridge.

The same Herter Brothers who designed the Star of David tenements built this temple in 1886–1887, the first and finest erected by East European Ashkenazic Jews on the Lower East Side. Before this time, most New York congregations had used converted buildings for worship, and the few expressly commissioned synagogues, mainly uptown, belonged to Sephardic and German congregations.

☞ Today, the Eldridge Street Synagogue is being restored. In 1991, the public, most of them uptowners, joined in a group effort to clean up the sanctuary, sealed for the past half-century. Even veiled by dust, the amber-lit sanctuary is one of the city's treasures. To arrange a visit and learn about the synagogue's programming, call (212) 219–0888. Also, you can attend prayers in the basement chapel, which has held services since the synagogue opened.

In the temple's glory days when deli entrepreneur Isaac Gellis was its first rabbi, the cheapest seat rented for $200. The costliest seats near the ark belonging to men such as Jarmulovsky the banker fetched a staggering $1,000. Other congregations muttered enviously about the splendor here and the temple's renowned cantor, who earned $5,000 per year.

Many Jewish congregations set up in old rowhouses, but some built beautiful new synagogues.

☞ The building's elegant Moorish Romanesque architecture *was* intended to impress, if not to provoke jealousy. (Well, perhaps just a little.) Today, its cascading terra-cotta front still dominates the street.

The arrival of Moorish synagogue design in the city is a story with interesting twists, the invention of a tradition. Before the mid-nineteenth century architects had designed the few commissioned synagogues to hold the ark in the east, but in other ways they conformed them to whatever style was prevalent. From the 1850s on some German Jewish congregations in America broke with the dominant Christian Gothic mode of architecture and began to use Moorish symbology "reminiscent of their Eastern origins" (a blurry link back to the Mediterranean). Paradoxically, the Moorish style was also an assimilated form, as exotic orientalism had become the rage of romantic European and American fashion. More paradoxically, the Shearith Israel congregation led by Sephardic Jews whose ancestors had fled from Spain and Portugal (hence closer to the genuine Moorish tradition) shunned the decor as too threateningly close to home. Despite some Ashkenazic congregations' and rabbis' aversion to the unfamiliar Moorish design, others valued it for its modishness. Glamour won the day, and, gradually, congregations including this one adopted the style.

If German Jewish taste influenced this congregation's choice of Moorish architecture, it didn't impinge on the synagogue's orthodox philosophy. Rabbis and congregation here stood united against reformed Judaism—the Americanized synthesis embraced by many middle-class German Jews who'd moved uptown.

***R**etrace your steps back to Canal Street; turn right onto Canal and walk back to the corner of Essex.*

***I**f you would like another mini excursion, turn left and walk north on Essex to Grand Street and back again. (This side trip is not marked on the tour map.)*

☞ These few blocks are a memory-scape of old world stores. Some of the shops appear un-self-conscious, but the overriding sensation projected here is artful quaintness, franchised ethnicity for tourists. (Gus' Pickles actually has a boutique at South Street Seaport.)

Census counts record that over 93 butcher shops, 112 candy stores, 43 bakeries, and 58 book shops belonging to East European Jews had grown up on the Lower East Side by 1890, a mere decade after mass settlement had started here. Today, most have shut because of Chinese competition and ebbing Jewish custom.

***O**nce you have regained the intersection of Essex and Canal, follow along to East Broadway in front of **Seward Park** to resume the main segment of the tour. Be mindful, however, as sad drunks often gather here.*

☞ Reformers carved this square out of densely packed tenements in 1899. Soon afterward, the playground opened. **❻**

Uptown reformers thought confined, ruly play spaces would safeguard the children of the new Jewish immigrants and also make them more orderly, less threatening.

Children, particularly teenagers, took to the streets to gain autonomy from their parents and a degree of individual space. At home, most shared not only bedrooms with their brothers and sisters but usually cots as well. The playground in this park was one of many in the city promoted by Jacob Riis, a progressive photojournalist from Denmark. The impulse driving Riis and other urban activists of the day was complex. In part they hoped that recreational areas would improve children's health and keep them safe from street accidents. In part they hoped the fenced, patrolled grounds would safeguard the city by coaxing children off of public thoroughfares, taming them through organized games. Juvenile street life was seen as the enemy—"not a symptom of poverty, but a cause," said one reformer. Many parents, afraid of losing control over their children, agreed.

W*alk across the street to the **Jewish Daily Forward (Forverts) Building,** ❼ 175 East Broadway.*

East Broadway was the district's grandest thoroughfare, and neighborhood intellectuals often used an honorific for it, "Ulitza," the Russian word for street, that was much grander than the common Yiddish term.

One of their group who would have stuck to Yiddish, the more populist language, was Abraham Cahan, a socialist immigrant from Lithuania who erected this building in 1911 to house the newspaper he'd started fourteen years earlier. The ten-story building rivaled Jarmulovsky's bank as the tallest on the Lower East Side—its size befitting the journal's importance as the neighborhood's principal voice. At night, neon lights blazed the *Forward*'s name toward these blocks in Yiddish. On the building's far side (facing Brooklyn, home to more native-born New Yorkers) a light track spelled out the logo in English. At its peak circulation in the 1920s, 200,000 subscribers read the journal. Today it continues uptown, shrunk to a Yiddish-English weekly. Size notwithstanding, it is doing interesting things, most recently serializing Philip Roth's latest novel.

One of Cahan's main planks was his fight to end garment work abuse, rife since the 1820s when Irish and German immigrants formed the first labor pool. By this era, most production had moved out of households and into sweatshops—the editor's primary target of reform.

As well as lobbying for better job conditions, the *Forward* also counseled its readers, predominantly women, on how to make the new world home. Readers wrote in questions to the "Bintel Brief" ("Bundle of Letters") column. Many dealt with generational differences. How much freedom should a daughter have? Should she "date"? Wear makeup? Attend the nickelodeon movies opening in the neighborhood?

The paper's most popular column, copied by other Yiddish journals to boost circulation, was a "Rogues Gallery," a column featuring pictures of missing husbands and fathers who'd fled the stress of supporting their families in the new world. Unthinkable as it may seem today, absentee Jewish fathers were a leading plague of immigrant life here. The phenomenon raises questions about the role of poverty in family structure. Perhaps the current generalizations about today's absentee fathers would benefit by historical context?

W*alk up East Broadway to the yellow brick building—the* **Educational Alliance ❽**—*on the northeast corner of Jefferson Street and East Broadway.*

At first, German Jews who had been living near here for generations in Kleindeutschland were shocked by the newcomers' poverty and frequent dysfunction, frightened also the East Europeans would threaten their middle-class, assimilated status. Both German Jews and German Christians fled the Lower East Side for houses going up in Harlem and Yorkville.

Within a few years the German Jews recovered, and though they didn't return here, they grew emotionally and charitably involved in immigrant life, anxious also to direct the newcomers in sociable (tractable) ways that would keep them out of dissident politics. In 1891 they founded this Educational Alliance, an organization formed from the merger of earlier Hebrew aid society, technical school, and library. The institute ran summer camps and arts classes as well as English and civics programs designed to promote assimilation. Classes here became a model for citizenship courses in public schools.

☞ Look up at the top of the building, where you can see a wire fence enclosing a roof-top playground. The trustees put the yard there partly because of space constraints, partly because they shared Riis' and other reformers' fear of the street and wanted strict confines for the newcomers' roving children.

If you have time, be sure to visit the ground-floor picture gallery honoring "graduates," who include Jan Peerce the opera singer, Mark Rothko the painter, and others who went on to transform America's art and politics. Pick up a current events calendar to see how the alliance reaches out to new Lower East Side residents through its programs and services, which include day care for the children of working mothers, most of them Chinese.

***W**alk back across East Broadway to the* **Seward Park Library, ❾** *an early branch of the public library system on the west side of the street.*

Andrew Carnegie, the immigrant (Scots) steel czar of America, bequeathed the facility in 1910, one of many libraries the millionaire gave to immigrant neighborhoods on the condition the community match his grant. Carnegie's goals for the newcomers were the same ones motivating the founders of the alliance—uplift and assimilation.

☞ The bloated Georgian structure, too grand and space wasting for a library, looks just like Carnegie's uptown mansion—which, conversely, looks just like a public institution. The same architectural firm designed both buildings.

Many adults who grew up on the Lower East Side attribute their real education to after-school sessions here. Old pictures show lines of youngsters (mostly boys) snaking around the library. So many young readers came here, the library had to add a roof-top garden space for the overflow. Librarians say the current population, mainly Chinese, are as keen to read as earlier generations but get half the chance: for years budget cuts have slashed opening hours to a minimum.

*C*ontinue on the west side of the street to the **Bialystoker Center Home for the Aged,** ❿ at 228 East Broadway.

☞ Notice the Hebrewized English script on the petite skyscraper. The frothy, set-back building is an Art Deco charmer, the miniaturized epitome of New York's good life at the time it went up.

In fine weather old men and women sit in the adjacent garden chatting, their faces turned toward the sun like frail moons. The remaining Jewish population down here is an elderly one. After the Manhattan Bridge opened in 1909, many Jews moved to Williamsburg and Brownsville in Brooklyn. More exoduses followed in the 1920s when the Bronx and farther suburbs opened up.

This old people's home, an example of a home country group helping its own diaspora, has its own synagogue. (It is not related to the nearby Bialystoker Synagogue on Grand Street. There seems to be no love lost between the two—perhaps an example of old country grudges carried over in the new world.)

☞ A mural on the north wall of the homely adjacent annex montages East European Jewish history on the Lower East Side.

Possibly because of the neighborhood's almost sacral place in American mythology, successive residents have developed a strong historical consciousness, a stark contrast to most other parts of the city. Community institutions ranging from Yeshivas to the Chinatown History Project hold exhibits, and schools make neighborhood history a curriculum staple.

*C*ontinue walking on the west side of East Broadway toward Grand Street.

☞ Look across the street at the row of faded Greek Revival houses with wrought-iron railings and wood porticoes on the blocks between Jefferson and Montgomery streets. Some of the old dwellings now serve as storefront synagogues and Talmud Torahs, or scripture schools.

At first this country was deemed so godless no Russian rabbis would come: East Broadway was often the scene of disputes between Orthodox and socialist Jews. Realizing the need for solidarity, the *Forward*'s Abraham Cahan was one of the few to try to bring the groups together. By the turn of the century, however, more than five hundred synagogues and religious schools had opened on the Lower East Side.

Today only a few centers remain open, among them the half-dozen or so on this avenue, most of which belong to the Hasidic order, a sect with branches in Poland (the Lubavitch) and in Hungary (the Satmar.)

☞ Note that the rabbi's name on the door plate is invariably followed by "from Sassow" or some other town.

The congregations, who come from the same corner of Europe as their rabbi, or whose families did, enjoy the homogeneity and refuse to merge even if membership dwindles. Recently, while the sect itself is growing, the number of observants on the Lower East Side has been falling as Hasidim leave for Brooklyn.

☞ When the congregations depart, new Chinese entrepreneurs adapt the old houses to condos. Note the pink marble veneer on some.

☞ At the **Martin Luther King Park** ⓫ (off of Montgomery Street) look across the street to your right (or cross over if you wish) to see the sagging white-columned porch visible above a garden wall. It's the back of the Nurses Settlement (known as the "noices"), now the Henry Street Settlement, founded by Lillian Wald in the 1890s.

A German Jewish banker, Jacob Schiff, paid for this house and its neighbors on Henry Street. (The tour will pass the fronts in a minute.) Showing the continuing ambivalence of uptown Jews toward the new immigrants, Schiff helped out on condition his tie remain secret. Despite his demand for anonymity, the banker stayed closely involved, checking Wald's work every week and keeping a close eye on the neighborhood in general. Among other control measures, he hired agents to watch the Christian agencies down here to curb the evangelizing going on.

On muggy nights Wald and her coworkers slept on this porch to breathe. As the name "settlement" tells, the nurses working here broke with the earlier tradition of charity workers who had just visited—more like raided—poor neighborhoods. The new breed of volunteers on the Lower East Side (there were several other settlement houses) lived among the poor, a proximity allowing empathy and fostering a new understanding of the structural (i.e., not moral) failures underlying much poverty. The volunteers' physical sacrifices were considerable, as most were young women from sheltered backgrounds. Wald's own parents were leaders of upstate German Jewish society.

Despite the hardships and the danger of disease (TB was rife), many women exulted in exploring their own selfhood as well as the neighborhood around them. Remarkably (to today's middle-class New Yorkers afraid of crossing spatial and class lines unless it's to get a brownstone), they seem to have felt at home in the streets, or perhaps just invisible, protected by their uniforms and the authority they wielded. One source of strength the women drew on was the close bond, often homosexual, that most settlement workers enjoyed—a sorority offering refuge from the poor they served as well as respite from patriarchal families uptown. This female bonding and shared living was asexually paralleled by the women of the neighborhood, whose close quarters and common troubles also generated a strong—if occasionally quarrelsome—support system.

Lillian Wald, a beloved reformer, didn't live uptown like earlier charity workers, but started her Nurses Union on Henry Street, sleeping on this porch in hot weather.

Veer left on the Samuel Dickstein Plaza up to Grand Street. Note the rise at Pitt and Grand, the rump of old Mount Pitt, once a bulwark in Revolutionary defenses, leveled after the war. Cross to the north side of Grand Street.

☞ The **modern brick colonial building** ⑫ at 466 Grand Street houses the cultural center of the Henry Street Settlement. The handsome **theater** next door features local playwrights. Telephone (212) 598–0400 to learn what's going on.

At Grand and Willett Streets loop half a block north on Willett to see the **Bialystoker Synagogue.** ⑬

☞ The fieldstone Methodist Episcopal Church built in 1826 opens toward the river, as the waterfront was still the neighborhood axis when the building went up. Later, in 1905, when the Jewish congregation moved in, the river orientation posed problems. Traditionally, Jewish worshipers face the tabernacle in the east of the synagogue—the direction of Jerusalem. This church's awkwardly spaced entrance (for Jewish rituals) is a reminder of the pitfalls sometimes inherent in adapting buildings. Recently, an Hispanic painter has renovated the temple's old murals, including a fanfare vision of Jerusalem.

Unlike most Lower East Side synagogues today, this congregation is still active, thanks to the Jewish retirees living in the nearby Sidney Hillman, Seward Park, and East River Houses.

*R*eturn to Grand Street and, turning left, walk toward the intersection of Grand and Henry.

☞ The gaudy red brick and white stone building on the southern side of Grand Street (311 East Broadway) holds one of Manhattan's last remaining **Mikvehs, ⑭** or Jewish ritual baths, attended by orthodox women (and very occasionally by men).

Usually synagogues are built with tubs whose source of water theoretically must be clean, either from a pure spring or a rooftop cistern. In this neighborhood, however, most synagogues were converted storefronts or churches, so a public ceremonial bath was essential. A practical advantage of the baths—if they were sanitary, which, despite the ideal, was not always the case—was their service for people living in waterless tenements.

☞ Note the carved initials "A.T." above the door honoring Arnold Toynbee, an early English reformer who tackled the industrial revolution's urban woes in London. Before becoming a bath, the building had held a settlement house.

☞ The Amalgamated Clothing Workers of America opened the **Hillman Houses** across the street in 1951. The crutches, ace bandages, and Dr. Scholl's foot pads in the ground-floor pharmacy underline the age and frailty of residents. The thriving Moishe's Bakery next door is more cheerful.

Twenty-one years earlier, the union had built its first housing down here with the twofold aim of providing decent shelter for its members and investing workers' dues for income. Despite efforts at controlling overhead, original rents at the project cost $12.33 per room per month, $8 more than most Hook residents paid at the time.

☞ If you look a bit farther east along Grand between Henry and Madison Streets, you will find several old Federal houses remaining on the south side of the street that go back to the early nineteenth century. (Their ground floors are now converted into stores.)

Housing and fresh air had been a problem on the Hook since the first boatyards here. In 1832 local employers, appalled at the death rate of craftsmen, petitioned the government for intervention in the crowded neighborhood. The Committee on Public Lands turned down their demand for a public park as too costly for the most affected local owner, industrialist James Allaire, to absorb. A park in this working-class neighborhood could yield only limited return in raised rents, and, furthermore, the manufacturer needed the shoreline for his boiler works. In 1833, perhaps out of relief that the park decision had gone in his favor, Allaire built one of the city's first tenements close to his foundry on Water and Corlears Streets, not far from here. In theory, the tenement was a step forward for his workers, as until then they'd lived crammed in carved up single-family houses like the ones just noted.

Ten years later, another Hook leader, this time a shipyard owner, built ten five-story tenements near here on 25-by-100 foot lots. Each had twelve to twenty-four apartments. Unfortunately, instead of improving the quality of life, the cramped spaces in these "model tenements" legitimized poor housing and crowded conditions. By the 1890s Hook tenements on 25-foot plot lines commonly held one hundred people, the number rising in the following decades.

*A*t the intersection of Grand and Henry, turn south (right) on Henry Street.

☞ Construction on the **Vladeck Houses,** ⓯ the first government housing in this part of the Lower East Side, began in 1940 after a struggle.

Despite wretched Hook conditions, the original (non-union) plan for neighborhood development was intended to bring riches, not reform. In 1929, when the city announced it was planning to rim Manhattan with a new arterial highway, the Regional Plan Association and the Lower East Side Chamber of Commerce announced their proposal to tear down slums and build luxury high rises that would attract "high class" residents like

Housing has been a problem on the Lower East Side for almost two hundred years. This Vladeck project, begun in 1940, was this neighborhood's first government-sponsored low-income project.

those moving to Sutton Place along the river uptown. Proposed inducements here included a yacht basin.

Lower East Side settlement houses and other opponents fought the poor's ouster, though not their upheaval. Architect Andrew Thomas, who'd just built the model Dunbar Apartments in Harlem, offered designs for relatively low-cost housing between the Manhattan and Williamsburg Bridges, a project that would have entailed demolishing 135 city blocks.

In the end the poor won (sort of) through no fault of their own. First, the new Midtown riverside enclaves such as Sutton Place temporarily met luxury needs; next, the stock market crash and depression derailed any further thought of high-end construction.

In 1934 the New Deal created the Public Works Authority to channel federal money for low-income residential development and slum reconstruction. In fact, nothing happened despite the Henry Street Settlement's lobbying. Though the settlement got some funding for its cultural and recreational center (just seen on Grand Street) no grant arrived for housing.

What Henry Street did get, however, was President Franklin Roosevelt's ear. (Almost certainly through Eleanor, who had worked in a Lower East Side settlement house before marriage and developed her sense of mission here.) In 1939 the government finally announced this subsidized housing project.

Despite the efforts of an enraged Lower East Side Chamber of Commerce to block the enterprise by reviving their earlier plan for luxury housing (they even picked a fine old neighborhood name to lend patina to their alternative model), the Vladeck project, not "Rutgerstown," won the day. The 1,771 apartment units that went up here were low cost, affordable to some if not all area residents.

A few years ago there was another victory for affordable housing, or so it seemed. When Edward Koch was mayor, he called for big-time realtors, particularly the Lefrak firm, to erect luxury housing on city-owned land bounded by Delancey, Grand, Clinton, and Norfolk Streets. The bid flouted the guidelines set by the current Lower East Side board requiring local developers to build one unit of low-cost housing for every unit sold at market rate. Only 20 percent of the proposed Lefrak housing would have been low- and moderate-income units. Lower East Siders, angered by displacement, fought the project and won. The spring of 1994, however, saw a new round of struggle over the still empty site, this time, ironically, between the Orthodox Jews of the Grand Street co-ops, once themselves the beneficiaries of low-cost housing, and Puerto Rican activists. While the Jewish groups say they want market-rate investment as the Lower East Side already has 15,000 low-income units, progressive Jewish leaders in the Lower East Side Joint Planning Council, a coalition for housing, accuse the Orthodox community of racism. Meanwhile, the latest plan by a private developer calling for 600 upscale apartments, a park, and a multiplex cinema that would "pay for itself without public funds" is up for approval under the pro-privatizing Mayor Rudolph W. Giuliani regime.

W*alk south to 290 Henry Street,* **St. Augustine's Church,** ❻ *formerly All Saints.*

The next three locations are a dip back in time, too important to skip. The rest of the walk that proceeds down Henry Street, retracing some of the route we have taken earlier, will look at the Lower East Side through Chinese immigrant eyes.

☞ The rubble foundation of this stocky church includes debris dredged from nearby Mount Pitt when the city leveled that hill after the Revolution.

For New Yorkers this continuum is like sitting on the lap of someone who sat on the lap of Lincoln. The visceral thrill must be hard for visitors from ancient cities to understand.

☞ The main interest of this 1827–1828 sanctuary opened for the local shipping elite lies in its interior. If you can, pay a visit inside to see what was designed as a slave gallery the same year New York abolished the last vestiges of slavery. Denial through architecture! If you call ahead (make sure to give a donation), it may be possible to visit the cramped gallery, virtually a crawl space, to sense what it felt like to be a slave looking down at services through a transom. Or, later, to be a freed black and still to have to sit apart. (Imagine singing hymns from behind a screen.) Today, the church's congregation is black and Hispanic; note the vivid statuary of saints—Episcopalianism at its outer limits.

Some of the African American congregation from the nearby housing projects are relatively recent migrants to the area. Some, however, may well be descended from the community who lived in shacks on neighboring Madison Street after their farms were repossessed in the eighteenth century. The condition of the free blacks in this neighborhood was so dismal that missions opened here from 1796 to sermonize ghetto dwellers—"Sabbath breakers of the vilest class." Epidemics caused by filth and overcrowding (often in unlit basement rooms) killed off large numbers of the population from the same period. One reason reformers were so opposed to street life was they saw streets as the "path" through which children carried contagion from "fever nests" into middle-class neighborhoods.

Continue south along Henry Street.

☞ The **firehouse** ⓱ on the west side of Henry Street, with the radiant sunburst capitals on the pillars flanking the doors, once housed the "Americus," the volunteer fire company served by William Tweed, the city's political boss in the late 1860s. Note the tigers on the modern engines which the Tammany Party, New York's Democratic arm, adopted as its emblem in honor of Tweed.

The resident firemen, like others in New York, are fonts of local history and take great pride in their own institutional past. Tweed ran with the machine here, along with a crew of Irish volunteers. So many politicians developed their power base through firehouses that the phrase "machine" politics (taken from the old fire engines) became synonymous with Democratic politics.

Originally the building was a residential brownstone but got remodeled in 1854 for its new function. It was the most elegantly appointed firehouse in the city—gilt-framed oils, tasseled lamps, Turkish carpets. In the 1880s the building received another makeover as well as the (extant) stables for horses. Hand-drawn machines were now a thing of the past.

They may be back. Recent cutbacks have stricken this firehouse and closed others in the neighborhood. The firemen here are angry and articulate.

☞ The dainty **Federal houses** ⑱ (263, 265, and 267 Henry Street) next door to the station, with their dainty fan windows, Ionic framed doorways, and delicate iron work, belonged to Lillian Wald's Nurses Settlement.

When Wald moved into the genteel houses built for rich doctors in the 1820s, they had long since been cut up into warrens of rooms. Today, the old dwellings still serve the nonprofit Henry Street organization, which continues to operate from here, offering legal aid, day care, and geriatric programs as well as lobbying for social change. Unlike Wald's day, only the director and the social workers at the Henry Street shelter live at the settlement; many of the other staff members commute from Queens and the suburbs.

Keep walking south along Henry.

☞ You'll see recent changes on the west side of the street. Several Greek Revival rowhouses are being reclaimed from the poor they have served so long.

Those houses being *restored* belong to "Yuppies." Those being *refaced* belong to new Chinese investors. Today, the real force of change on the Lower East Side is Asian money. Chinese have lived down here since the 1820s, when Far Eastern sailors had rooms at the river end of Market Street, but racist immigration laws kept the population small and for decades essentially male. Since the end of the restrictive quotas in 1965, Chinese have poured into the neighborhood from Hong Kong and the People's Republic of China. (For their part, most Taiwanese have bypassed Manhattan and gone straight to middle-class enclaves in Flushing.) In 1960 there were fewer than 20,000 Chinese in New York. Now Chinatown alone holds 150,000 souls. The old Chinatown was six acres squeezed near the Manhattan Bridge; current demographic projections say Chinese will have settled the blocks up to Delancey Street by the year 2000. Resultant land pressures raise rents far beyond old-timers' reach, and suffering rises in inverse proportion to investment.

☞ Only a minority of the newcomers are wealthy; most are laborers, drawn by sweatshops, who live like the old-generation Chinese, squeezed into decrepit walk-ups. They do their best to make them home. At 14 Jefferson Street, between Henry and East Broadway, note the Victorian "ears" on the window lintels. Someone has painted the ears, a favorite nineteenth-century decoration, gold to resemble the finials of Chinese temple roofs that ward off evil.

☞ Another building just above the northeast corner of Rutgers and Henry streets, **a rowhouse now a Buddhist temple,** ⑲ also charts neighborhood change. By the late 1850s this Greek Revival building, put up twenty years earlier, would have held a dozen or more families. Over time the dwelling, still adorned by its wooden portico and scrolling iron banisters, sheltered Irish, then East European Jewish immigrants. Today, it's painted yellow and red—monks' colors—and houses a Buddhist temple dedicated to Kuan Yin, the Chinese goddess of mercy.

☞ The gray building nearby at **154 Henry Street** is actually two early rowhouses that got merged long ago. During the period of heavy Jewish migration, the structure served as a synagogue annex; now it's a Buddhist center for the elderly.

You'll pass many older people in the streets nearby. Grandmothers, small as lanterns, lead children along the crowded pavements caring for them until their mothers return from work, as earlier immigrant grandparents tended their children's babies.

☞ Today, the building's exterior is a palimpsest. Note the red painted rim-around the top roundel of one Moorish window dating from the Jewish era. The current residents have transformed it into an auspicious Chinese moon door.

Inside, tables in the basement dining rooms, still showing the rough foundation stones of the old houses, hold styrofoam rice bowls. Blue-robed nuns oversee the meals, paid for by slide-scale contributions. Upstairs in a hall, once the site of Jewish services, worshipers bow before an altar graced by images of Sakyamuni, the historical Buddha.

Continue walking south on Henry Street past the **New Chinese Condo Tower** ⑳ at the southeast corner of Henry and Market Streets.

Even after the 1987 crash, Far Eastern investors opened 500 new and rehabilitated condos here in a two-year period—the average price in many, $375 per square foot. Recently, a cold-water tenement near Chatham Square sold for $4 million. Chinese housing advocates struggle to stem the displacement caused by new money. Despite the ideal and occasional reality of a flexible family that absorbs needy acquaintances, homelessness is growing, and the Lower East Side holds the city's first Asian American shelter. A few years ago, when the Chinatown Planning Council opened twenty-six units of low-cost housing on Grand Street, 3,000 applications poured in.

☞ Many Chinese immigrants pay exorbitant rents to sleep rotationally in bunk-bed dorms. The tenements they call home are often as brooding and shadowed as the one in the rear lot between 21 and 23 Henry Street, on your right. (You can see it by peering through the narrow alley gate.)

In pre-electricity days families doing garment work in back houses often sewed in semi-darkness, as candles were beyond their means. Today, garment work continues in buildings like this, fluorescent lighting making longer hours possible.

***C**ontinue to Catherine Street, the southern boundary of Harmon Rutgers' property (the street is named after his wife).*

Because of new Chinese money, land on Catherine Street now costs as much as Fifth Avenue footage. The flash local money coupled with poverty makes gang life alluring to many newcomers here, especially the young. Today's Lower East Side gangs have dress codes and territorial names reminiscent of those belonging to immigrant youth in the 1820s. (Flags embroidered "Canal Boys" shrouded the coffins of the Vietnamese youths shot dead in a publicized incident several years ago; poignantly, the lettering

Originally, seamstresses sewed garments in dark, unventilated homes. In the 1860s production moved into sweatshops, where it remains, by and large, today.

was in English.) Some of the reasons prompting the gangs are familiar—rootlessness, a human urge to bond, a need to express and subsume one's self in dramatic ceremonies, and, finally, greed—a wish to share the city's gold. In this case, the gold is drug and protection money. Although there are similarities between the nineteenth-century and the latter-day gangs, one big difference is the rise of violence—guns are now common.

It isn't only gangs that vie for power. As in early days, politics among the varying groups, often seen as homogeneous by outsiders, divides these immigrants along lines of partisan strife brought from the homeland.

Turn right and walk west on Catherine Street to **Chatham Square,** *the southern end of the Lower East Side and the start of the Bowery, the old West India Company road that once beveled through the farms laid out by Peter Minuit. From this point on, the walk will mainly indicate generic, rather than specific, institutions as the neighborhood spins with change.*

☞ The **Confucius Statue** in flowing metal robes presiding over the north end of the square does not please all the local Chinese.

The memorial to the sage—a traditionalist who resisted social change—irks immigrants from the People's Republic and some working-class Chinese of all descent. The statue's presence is owed to the early dominance of a conservative elite in Chinatown, who benefited from years of close ties between the U.S. government and Chiang Kai-shek.

Recently, the emerging tussle over which group will shape the neighborhood has moved into rivalry over parades. For decades conservatives from Taiwan have celebrated their national day near Mott Street in the center of Chinatown. In 1994 immigrants from the People's Republic demanded a similar march to mark the anniversary of the Mainland nation's founding in 1949. Police, however, allowed this group only a peripheral parade route through the neighborhood, prompting pro-Mainland factions to claim that the local precinct was under the sway of the Taiwanese Nationalists. For their part, the police argued that they were simply trying to buffer the route from the concurrent San Gennaro Festival in Little Italy, which backs up on Mott Street.

☞ **Sweat shops:** Many of the six thousand illegal work lofts that have returned to the city in the past decades rim this square. Some buildings have so much steam puffing out of vents they look like vertical Toonerville trolleys.

New immigrants on the Lower East Side often live in an underground economy; that is, they work in unlicensed, untaxed businesses. Today, as the city government and unions grow less able to keep control, this "underground" economy is up, down, and all over.

The seamstresses in these shops work more than sixty hours a week and get paid less than the minimum wage (usually $9,000 a year). Most have no overtime pay, no job security. As in earlier times, employers and workers usually come from the same ethnic background, but unlike the Jewish era on the Lower East Side, when East Europeans used their ethnic strength to organize unions, today's shop owners have managed to turn ethnocentric politics against their workers. The Chinese, they tell outside reformers, prefer to be left alone. The International Ladies' Garment Workers' Union (ILGWU) has been trying to give adequate wage and work protection (some say not hard enough), but it's weakened by foreign imports and the flight of industry. *Homework,* that innocent word touted by former President Reagan, is back in fashion, particularly in the fashion business.

☞ **Restaurants:** Food services are Chinatown's other big employer.

Chinese restaurants initially grew out of the public kitchens opened to serve the bachelor society created by immigration laws allowing only Chinese laboring men to enter the country.

Activists who try to organize the hundreds of local restaurants are daunted. At this point, thanks to the power of local management and a weakened mainstream labor movement that has been slow to accept minorities, only one restaurant down here is unionized. The result of the exclusion is that most waiters in Chinatown get only $200 a month, including tips. Earlier immigrants were also ghettoized, but life is harder for the Chinese now because of racism and the decline of blue-collar jobs—the only ones viable for non-English speakers in the city.

A new factor also enforcing ghettoization is today's tight legislation governing work and visas. Chinatown's many undocumented immigrants are at the mercy of the gangs bringing them here—a plight dramatized by the wreck of the would-be immigrants on the *Golden Venture,* which was run by a smuggling enterprise reputedly backed by Taiwanese "investors" in Flushing.

☞ **Benevolent societies** ring the square. Among them is the Cuban Chinese Benevolent Association at 9 East Broadway.

Although traditional associations serving those with the same family name, occupation, or home village can do some good, young Chinese community organizers feel they can also be parochial, keeping immigrants from allying with wider (and more effectively democratic) institutions.

☞ **Banks:** Note the glossy glass shaft of the **Ka Wah Bank** at East Broadway and Catherine Street. Compare it with the American-built bank across the street to the north, miserably disguised as a Chinese temple.

Thirty or more firms have opened in the Lower East Side in the past two decades, following the cash flow from Asia. The majority are Asian institutions channeling Far Eastern money; the others, branches of mainstream institutions hoping for a share in the market.

Like the condo activity here, the plethora of banks seems anomalous in the midst of Chinatown's poverty. Sometimes outsiders tend to confuse local residents with the "model minority" Chinese in Flushing (who are largely Taiwanese), but a quarter of Chinatown's population (mainly Cantonese, and more recently, Fujianese) live below the poverty level. Fully 71 *percent* of residents here have never finished high school. It is an odd replay of the old "uptown-downtown" divisions of earlier immigrants. These days, however, the boroughs have taken the place of Manhattan's upper reaches. More strangely, the old-time Chinese settlers are the struggling poor; many of the newcomers, the wealthy professionals.

So why isn't the neighborhood more depressing? Or, to an outsider, depressing at all, for that matter, but rather the opposite? Despite the hardships, the guttering housing stock, exploitative work conditions, internal crime, outside racism, it doesn't seem Reagyanna-ish to say that the Lower East Side retains a vitality that has characterized it over centuries. Or, on second thought, a more correct assessment might be that the vitality of the *immigrants* down here continues unabated.

As one weaves through the vendors who've replaced the old pushcart peddlers, passes newsstands selling ten different Chinese-language papers, measures one's step to zither strains billowing from music stores, it's apparent the Chinese are at last inhabiting the neighborhood on their own terms. Or at least, somewhat more so. Only a short time ago Chinatown was forced to present itself as a charming comestible for visitors, complete with Oriental chickens that played tic-tac-toe and souvenir Buddhas that looked like Elmer Fudd. Today, sheer numbers are bringing power. Perhaps one day soon even the name itself (an outside designation) may vanish along with the pagoda telephone booths, and it will simply be called the Lower East Side.

Today, the city still offers possibility despite its near desperate condi-tion. Seeing the myriad faces of people from all corners of the world who call themselves New Yorkers causes the heart to twist with hope and pride. And worry. Possibility, whose root meaning is power, today has come to mean chance.

4

reenwich Village

Subway: IND A, C, B, D, E, F or Q lines to West 4th Street. Exit at
West 3rd Street door.

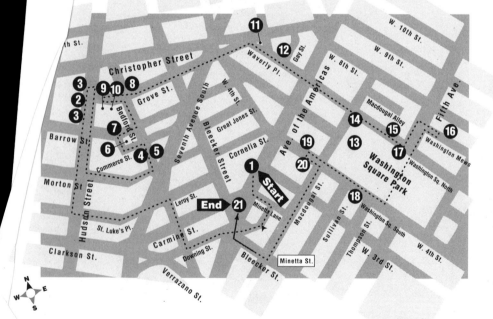

Today "the Village" is considered to run from Houston Street to 13th Street, Washington Street to University Place. In fact, this territory includes several neighborhoods that grew up quite separately. Until this century Washington Square wasn't thought part of the Village at all. The term *Village* itself came into use only at the turn of this century. The name *Greenwich* (after a London suburb) grew common in the 1690s but referred just to the area above Christopher Street, west of Sixth Avenue.

To start, we're going to look at the district near the river that became an artisan stronghold in the eighteen hundreds. Afterward, we're going to cross to Washington Square, developed at mid-nineteenth century as a merchant enclave. Last, we will go a few blocks south of the square to a neighborhood that became an Italian immigrant center in the 1880s and, later, a Bohemian preserve.

*A*t the West Fourth Street subway stop, exit at Third Street on Sixth Avenue and walk one block south down Sixth (renamed Avenue of the Americas). ❶ Cross to the east side of the avenue here and enter Minetta Lane. Follow the short strip until it runs into Minetta Street, then turn right on Minetta Street. Recross Sixth Avenue (west) and walk west on Downing until you reach Bedford. Turn right (north) on Bedford until you come to Leroy Street. Turn west (left) here to cross Seventh Avenue South. On the west side of the avenue, Leroy Street becomes St. Luke's Place. Follow along the place west past the park to Hudson Street. Cross to the street's west side and walk north (right), until you come to **St. Luke's Church** ❷ between Barrow and Christopher.

Enter the complex through the gate just north of the church, walk straight ahead, and then turn left and walk behind the church until you reach a path to the garden, a lovely, sheltered spot to rest and read the following introduction. In truth, this will be the second introduction. The winding streets you have just traveled provide the (literal) grounding for any Greenwich Village account.

Geography in New York is not usually destiny, for we shape sites to suit ourselves, but it was more important here than most parts of the city.

The little Minetta Brook that molds much of the neighborhood rose in hills near 23rd Street, then slanted south through marshland that would become Washington Square. Next it twisted down latter-day Macdougal and a coil we call Minetta Street—the road skewing parallel streets, bewildering walkers, and angering cab drivers. (That is, unless they happen to live in the Village and have absorbed the tangle into their body-brain.) Actually, it's wrong to use the past tense for the Minetta. It still courses under

The twisting Minetta Brook made streets and property lines in Greenwich run peculiarly. Big landowners in Greenwich resisted the 1811 city grid and kept the neighborhood as they wanted until they were ready to market it on their own terms.

the weight of streets. You can see its remarkably clear bubble in a glass tube in the lobby of 2 Fifth Avenue.

Tobacco bloomed in the brook's fertile basin. Hackensack Indians from New Jersey who kept a camp near the foot of Gansevoort Street grew the weed around their west river landing cove they called Sapokanikan. (When Henry Hudson sailed by looking for the northwest passage, some natives rowed out from the settlement offering "a great store of very good oysters," which the diarist recorded "they bought for trifles.") Even before leaving for New Amsterdam, Peter Minuit's successor, Wouter Van Twiller, managed to claim tobacco land in the area for himself. Later, the property Van Twiller christened Bossen Bowerie—"farm in the woods"—became the ex officio estate of future governors.

Several Greenwich roads result from the Dutchman's land grab, as his grant came with the proviso he maintain all existing tribal footpaths for incoming European settlers. One of the tracks to the north of here became Christopher Street. The city melded another into Greenwich Avenue and the short east-west blocks of Astor Place. In 1828 engineers straightened part of this cartway into what would become Washington Square's North Row.

In the 1640s the West India Company gave land here to municipal slaves they'd just granted a circumscribed freedom. In what was to become standard pattern, the "Negroe lots" all sat in swampland, in this case along the banks of the Minetta. The newcomers built a connecting dike, known through the eighteenth century as the "Negroes' Causeway," to navigate from one side of the brook to the other. A portion remains embedded in the section of Minetta Street between Bleecker and Minetta Lane.

During the same decade several Englishman moved to Greenwich's more hospitable acreage to open ambitious tobacco plantations. New Amsterdam's administrators blamed the hamlet's heterogeneous population for the independent spirit it showed. Even when Indian reprisals swept Manhattan, the government couldn't make settlers here move south inside the Wall Street palisade.

In the main, administrators left Greenwich to itself until the next century. Change came when the British crown and its local surrogates began granting waterfront property to their favorites. In 1705 Queen Anne gave Trinity Church the tract stretching from Broadway to the Hudson, Cortlandt to Christopher Street. Thirty years later the City Corporation awarded a swath north of Trinity's property to Peter Warren, ex-privateer, naval hero, and consummate crony who already owned land here, extending his estate until it ran north from Christopher to 21st Street. After the Colonial Assembly met at Warren's house to avoid a downtown epidemic, several other members fell under Greenwich's wooded spell and also started buying property as summer retreats.

The estates lasted until after the Revolution, when owners cashed in on the need for land at the town's northern rim. For some time Trinity had been leasing the southern end of its tract to craftsmen priced out of the East River dock area. (Trade there had grown so dense, even wealthy artisans were forced to go.) Now, Greenwich property holders copied the church and started leasing out land to developers, who subleased the plots in turn to sailmakers, butchers, and carpenters for building houses and workshops. Speculation spun so high between 1785 and 1815 that Manhattan's land prices rose an astonishing 750 percent.

By the 1790s developers had bought all the neighborhood's big estates and started laying out streets. To hasten progress, Trinity offered a strip of land near the river for a new north-south road, Hudson Street.

Aaron Burr was one of the new investors. In 1797 he leased Trinity property north of Canal and filed a map plotting the holding into 25-by-100-foot lots for New Yorkers who were just beginning to filter north of the (Canal Street) stream still dividing the city. Burr planned to level a steep hill on the grounds and then cut Vandam, Charlton, and King Streets through the property. (His successor took up the project.)

That same year, the state prison opened at the foot of Christopher Street, stirring development flurries at the north end of Greenwich. Enough houses grew up around the new jail to support a local market. Despite the new facility, the year after the jail opened, New York's Mayor Richard Varick was still complaining about the town's "laggardly" oyer court and crowded jails. "All our System is calculated to increase the Number of

Vagabonds, Rascals and Convicts in our City and will do so, until such fellows can again be soundly flogged 39 lashes twice or thrice." Prison population surged as the veterans of the War of 1812 turned to crime to ward off poverty in the face of rising rents. In 1828 swelling land values and overcrowding sent the facility upriver to Ossining. By then, conditions at the jail had grown so bad, critics charged it as "a most prolific mother of crime."

But I've gone ahead of the story. Let's return to the teens of the nineteenth century, which saw a bitter battle in Greenwich between the city government and local real estate holders. Though the municipality had forced most New York realtors to adopt the new city grid plan of 1811, landowners in this area balked, holding out for development on their own terms. When investigative commissions accused them of "blocking" New York's "larger good," the landlords responded in broadsides denouncing the plan, accusing the grid mongers of imposing a leveling sameness. It was a class, as well as an aesthetic argument. To put teeth in their defense against the "ill judged attack upon private property," the property owners set dogs against city surveyors foolish enough to try to chart local streets. The anonymous pamphleteer turned out to be local land power Clement Moore, the son of Trinity's rector, more known for "A Visit from St. Nicholas" than for rogue politics.

In the face of the wealthy opposition, the City Council backed down and extended the grid only to the blocks east of present-day Sixth Avenue. Moore and his confederates went on to develop land here and in Chelsea as they'd (damn well) planned.

By 1821 Moore and another local realtor, Don Alonzo Cushman, were ready to build. The city had just linked Greenwich to downtown Manhattan by vaulting over the old canal. Moreover, after a decade of petitioning, Trinity had finally agreed to finance a local church. Renters always followed the steeple.

Another event sped local settlement—yellow fever. The full name of the church Trinity sponsored here was, is, St. Luke's in the Fields. The latter referred to the semi-rural nature of the area when the church's foundations went in, the former evoked Greenwich's historic role as a health haven: Christ's disciple had been a physician and later the patron saint of healing.

Ever since 1702, when a wave of "Barbados distemper" swept New York, epidemics had multiplied as the city grew. From early on, escapees had gone to Greenwich, where river breezes sluiced the air and tracts of sandy high ground (the Minetta bog notwithstanding) provided drainage.

Most important, compared with downtown, there was hardly any population. From the start, Manhattan's tip had been a dense hive, a ripe target for disease. During successive epidemics small pox rarely crossed the creek dividing Greenwich from downtown, yellow fever never did. In 1793 the semi-autonomous board of health the city had formed to combat epidemics advised buying the swamp at latter-day Washington Square as a free cemetery for the poor. They were just in time.

Two thousand people died in the summer of 1798, the year after the new graveyard opened.

In the next big scourge, 1803, New York copied Philadelphia, which had coped better in similar disasters, and pitched 5,000 tents in Greenwich for the working class. People who could afford to made their own provision. Aaron Burr's real estate venture gained from the influx of wealthier fever refugees during this epidemic, as afterward many bought his lots. This was an ironic or unfair turn. To some degree, it was Burr's other venture, the Manhattan Water Company, that had aggravated, if not caused, the epidemics in the first place. Burr's company—the city's only commercial water source—had skimped on the job, compounding the town's already grave sanitation problems. A sideline banking business, allowed by a fine-print clause in his contract with the city, proved far more lucrative. Later, the banking avocation turned into Chase Manhattan. The name "Manhattan" recalls the old water scheme.

In the 1805 siege one-third of city residents, all who could pay, fled Manhattan's tip for Greenwich. Wagons and people on foot blocked the roads. A contemporary wrote, "only poor mechanics, small grocers, draymen and blacks" were left in the lower city. Those poor who could not come were blamed for being "guilty of wanton exposure of their life."

Once again, the city pitched tents here from the river to Broadway. On this occasion the city provided for 10,000 refugees. The demand for local housing was such that an onlooker wrote, "where yesterday you saw nothing but green turf, tomorrow you behold a store. By night as well as by day the saw is heard . . . the village begins to assume the appearance of a town."

Banks and public offices moved up to "solitary Greenwich" to serve their regular clients. (The Bank of New York had already bought property during the fever of 1798 on what came to be known as Bank Street and had run its business from here during several other epidemic seasons. Some say the street took its name from this; others disagree and claim it is named after a surveyor.) The 1805 visitation was severe enough that stringent quarantine regulations suspended shipping. Economic activity ceased. According to a traveler, "Visitors roam untrodden downtown, silence, solitude . . ." Business closures as well as disease felled the town's more marginal residents.

In 1822, the summer St. Luke's Church opened, an even worse epidemic swept the lower city. That summer the church's bell tolled ceaselessly for the downtown dead and dying. Once again anyone who could leave the city did. Only doctors and dying were left south of the barricade the municipality staked out along Chambers Street down near City Hall. Watchmen sprinkled lime on the streets; weeds grew up through the paving. Rather like Daniel Defoe's plague-ridden London, officials forbade New Yorkers to enter the sealed section of the lower city. This time, the upper class was more than usually frightened. In the past epidemics had hovered around the immigrant stews near the South Street port. Now disease had infested the relatively protected lower Hudson shore as well.

Builders put up lodging here so swiftly that a wooden boarding house for 300 tenants went up during a single weekend. Those who could make money from the refugee boomtown did. Aside from the thriving Greenwich contractors, small boys hawked plain pine coffins for four dollars—an outrageous profit margin.

"Black" frost at the end of that October ended the siege, but as Greenwich and lower Manhattan had grown together with the vaulting over of the canal the year before, many middle- and upper-class refugees elected to put down permanent roots. Several banks, insurance companies, coffee houses, and auction houses stayed behind to serve the new colony.

W*alk back out of the garden to Hudson Street. First, be sure to stop and look around the church if it happens to be open.*

☞ St. Luke's trustees built the **brick rowhouses** ❸ flanking Saint Luke's as rental property in 1825. The child of Trinity, the mother of real estate, was not going to be left out of future land booms. Today only half of the original row remains, and the houses are considerably altered. Originally, they were two and a half stories high with pitched roofs and dormers.

Our walk will now go back to look at the neighborhood as it first developed in the decade after the Revolution and onward in time.

C*ross Hudson Street to the east and turn south toward Morton Street. Turn left and walk east on Morton to Bedford Street, then turn left (north) on Bedford to Commerce Street—a name given after the 1822 epidemic that brought downtown business to Greenwich.*

☞ The **Isaacs-Hendricks House** ❹ at the southwest corner of Commerce Street and Bedford is the oldest surviving house in Greenwich. It went up on the subdivided Elbert Roosevelt estate in 1799, the same year the street opened. First, look at the Commerce Street side of the house and its back garden. Though built for a merchant—an unusually high status occupation for Greenwichites at the time it went up—the dwelling began life as a simple frame structure. Its brick facing on Bedford is an addition from 1836 when land grew more valuable and owners improved their houses accordingly. (The third-floor studio dates from 1928.) Originally, the house was freestanding, with a horseway leading into the rear yard. In 1873 the owners built a sliver residence in the old carriage entrance. See 75 1/2 Commerce Street, at 9 and 1/2 feet wide the narrowest house in the Village and famous for its larger-than-life inhabitants. Poet and character Edna St. Vincent Millay lived here in the 1920s.

The house's first owner, a Jewish wholesaler, Joshua Isaacs, suffered bankruptcy and sold the house to his in-laws, the Hendricks, a wholesale merchant family who also had a sideline copper business. (They traded with Paul Revere and later sheathed the first trans-Atlantic steamship, the *Savannah*.) Hendricks Senior, Shearith Israel's president, had died in the 1798 epidemic when he'd stayed downtown during the hot weather to attend Rosh Hashanah services at the Mill Street Synagogue. His sons had personal reasons to value Greenwich as a health haven.

☞ The house across the street at **70 Bedford Street,** ❺ dates from 1807. Later, like the Hendricks dwelling, it too got a third-story addition. In other ways also the building is similar in scale and sensibility to its neighbor. Its original occupant, however, was an artisan more representative of early Greenwich settlers than the grand Jewish merchants across the street. John Roome, who built the house, was a sailmaker and may well have bought supplies from the Hendricks, who sold duck sailcloth from Russia, among other wares. Note the brownstone belt course above the ground floor that once held Roome's manufacturing loft. Until the late 1820s when land prices rose out of sight, most artisans in Greenwich worked in their yard or their home.

☞ Roome also moonlighted as a crier of the oyer court—the court hearing cases on highway robberies, larceny, forgery, and fencing stolen goods. One of his jobs for the justices, who meted out punishments ranging from public whippings to hangings, was overseeing the delivery of prisoners to the new Christopher Street jail.

*If you cross Bedford and walk farther along Commerce Street, you'll see some **little Federal houses**, 16–18 Commerce, that stand on land Aaron Burr bought for speculation (this short side trip is not shown on the map). The houses went up in the 1820s. Burr did not live here, albeit one building has a misleading plaque.*

Return to Bedford and continue on Commerce toward Barrow, following the street's coil.

Despite the 1820s influx, Greenwich's old street pattern west of Sixth Avenue kept the area from being merged as an indistinguishable part of the city. The skein of streets and the landlords who owned them blocked the north-south throughways that were, quite literally, avenues of change in the rest of town.

☞ A prosperous milk dealer built the **twin brick houses** ❻ linked by a walled garden in 1831. They're Federal structures that got bonneted with mansard roofs in the 1870s.

The first owner was one of Greenwich's artisans and purveyors who'd managed to join in the speculation fray. By now even middling craftsmen like John Roome owned several rental properties in the vicinity. At the time these houses went up, land values had risen to the point artisans had to get involved in the game to afford living here. Most humbler people, including the women weavers aided by the Scots Benevolent Society, were already long gone.

☞ Before leaving this corner, note the 1852 **Empire Hose fire company** ❼ at 70 Barrow Street, its winding staircase still faintly visible through the large windows.

The volunteer company owned "Mankiller," the city's most powerful engine, envied by other firehouses, as it could spray 137 feet over the top of a "liberty pole" in the phallic water games the fire "laddies" liked to play at the end of a rousing conflagration. Volunteer companies such as this were the last strongholds of lusty working-class culture in a rapidly constraining age.

Walk along Barrow to Bedford; turn left and walk to Grove Street, a street ceded to the city by Trinity in 1809 and opened in 1811.

☞ The **frame house** ❽ on the northeast corner of Grove and Bedford at 100 Grove Street, belonged to a sash maker, Thomas Hyde. Hyde built the freestanding clapboard house in 1822. The current Greek Revival door replaced the original Federal entrance in the 1830s, and the third-story addition came in the 1870s. Despite change, the house is still more satisfyingly "olde" looking than the Isaacs-Hendricks residence.

In unremitting disinformation, guides tend to call it "the oldest house in Greenwich Village." Locals—their patience tried by numbers and noise—sometimes critique walking tours uncharitably.

Sash making is not something one thinks about today. (That is, unless you happen to own a landmarked house, in which case the bill for a replacement sash replicating the wood original as mandated under a recent city landmarks law can run you hundreds of dollars.) In the Federal period, however, windows were important architectural elements. Delicate panels with classical trim flanked doorways; graceful windows—often fanshaped—above the entry completed the ensemble.

Even without architectural fads, Hyde got plenty of commissions. The year he moved here, 1822, was the watershed summer when fever refugees caused a tide of local construction. Hyde worked in the **shed at the back of the compound.** His combined work and residential unit was one of the last of its kind in the city. Rising land values made the arrangement uneconomic; changing modes of production and growing alienation between master craftsman and apprentices made it impractical.

Separation became the norm as production expanded. Master craftsmen moved away from shops and stopped providing living space for their assistants. By the late 1820s, only a few artisans still controlled the real estate they once had used for their trade. From now on, workers had to travel quite long distances to their work sites. (The process had started earlier in Europe, giving rise to the word *journey,* as "day" or "jour" laborers walked long miles to reach their jobs.)

As the status of junior craftsmen fell with the growth of the free labor market, the fortunes of wealthy artisans such as Hyde

Most craftsmen who'd built their houses and workshops here after the Revolution (note the building on the left) were priced out of the neighborhood.

rose proportionately. Not only did the sash maker make money, but he went on to become assistant alderman, a post positioning him to earn still more.

*T*urn left on Grove from Bedford and walk a short distance west on Grove to the **Federal houses** ❾ at 2–10 Grove Street.

St. Luke's builder, James Wells, who put up these houses on Trinity land between 1825 and 1834, was another craftsman to benefit from the changing order and ensuing building boom. (By now, two-fifths of the city's artisans worked in the construction trade.) After rising through church ties and his own enterprise, this one-time carpenter became an important builder-developer in Greenwich and Chelsea, later entering politics as a city assessor. Like Hyde, he wound up a local alderman. (Wells' realtor firm survives in the same neighborhood today as Wells and Gay-Stribling.)

☞ This block is one of the first planned complexes in the city, as Wells designed the houses to complement the rental houses the church owned on Hudson Street and ordered the tree planting (hence Grove Street's name) to evoke St. Luke's garden.

Sycamores graced the house fronts, but the rear of the houses held an architectural feature soon to disappear in the city—back yards designed for messy domestic work. At the time these dwellings went up, most residences were still being built with the old amenities—if that is the word for rather unpleasant catch-alls. The (extant) yards of this row held privies, woodpiles, pumps, smokehouses, washtubs, vegetable patches, and barrels for salting pork and rendering lard. Inside the houses, cellars and ground-floor back rooms provided more work space for other household tasks, including spinning and weaving.

Upper- and middle-class wives were still doing a lot of heavy household work in the 1820s.

In the 1830s when manufactured cloth swept the city, home production ended and many middle-class women—the sort who would have lived in these houses—had few chores other than attending children: even this was mediated by maids. The city's new Greek Revival houses, which we'll see in Washington Square, reflected the changed life-style.

Before heading east to the square to look at the quarters of the merchant commuters who arrived there in the next

decade, let's first note how the other half lived after the divisive shift occurred in work and class.

These dormered 1820s Federal houses had rear yards for messy domestic chores. Note the dwellings' modest size, their unassuming facades.

☞ **Grove Court,** ⑩ 10–12 Grove Street, a gore of buildings set back on Trinity land, was an early tenement known as Mixed Ale Alley (perhaps because of a mixed-race tenantry?).

As land costs continued to climb in the 1830s and laborers could no longer build their own homes, most crowded into carved-up single-family houses. New York at the time had only a few multi-household residences (tenements) for despite the need, builders avoided the work, as luxury housing brought more money. An entrepreneurial butcher put up this effort in 1853–1854. Its location here among the wealthier houses was unusual for the period.

***W**alk east on Grove to Seventh Avenue. Cross the avenue and continue east past the little park to Waverly Place. The walk is now entering the orbit of the "Village," which took its character from the merchants who settled in Greenwich from the late 1820s on.*

☞ The theatrical **brick building shaped like the triangle site** ⑪ it occupies opened as a clinic in 1832. Unlike most old buildings in the city, it still bears a signboard, "The Northern Dispensary," announcing its original function. The date reads 1827, as householders wanting a place to send their servants for free medical treatment had organized it a few years earlier in temporary headquarters. It was the first public building the newcomers established, a reminder of the health concerns prompting them to move here.

At a deeper level, the merchants had really come to Greenwich to flee the poor, who by this time were seen as virtually *causing* the epidemics in their "haunts of obscure riot and low debaucheries. . . ." Up to the near past, even though there had been a rough delineation of class zones in town, the polarities had been blurred by the many workers and unemployed poor who lived canted around the better homes.

During the 1830s the square's elite met at the dispensary to plan Greenwich's incorporation and to found the Greenwich Savings Bank.

For 158 years the clinic stayed open, providing free service. It shut in 1986, unable to pay the stiff fine mandated by the city's Human Rights Commission when resident dentists refused to treat AIDS patients. Today, various groups contend for its use. Some want it opened as a nursing home for AIDS sufferers; others, to make it a diagnostic center for breast cancer.

*K*eep walking east on Waverly Place to **Gay Street,** ⓬ a crooked lane on the left, originally an alley-way lined with stables, that runs through to Christopher Street on the north.

It was private horse power plus the new horse-drawn omnibuses plying the city (1831) that made Greenwich's development as a commuter enclave possible. Early householders on Gay Street—named after a contemporary abolitionist—included black coachmen in service to the new merchant colony. (Blacks had continued to live in the neighborhood since Dutch days, the densest settlement still down near the original farm grants at Minetta Lane.)

*C*ontinue east to Sixth Avenue, the neighborhood's commercial spine from the 1830s on. Cross the thoroughfare, then stop to look one block down from here at the Doric-columned church on 4th Street on the far side of the avenue.

☞ The Irish contractors and masons constructing the handsome houses going up east of Sixth Avenue built **St. Joseph's** in 1834. Its imposing size and trend-setting Greek Revival architecture tell us it cost considerable money.

With a single exception (Henry James' grandmother), money was not enough to allow Irish into Washington Square except as masons or domestics. Sixth Avenue, where the Irish lived over their stores or brickyards, was the one immigrant strip in the neighborhood.

As much as the western part of Greenwich came to be called "the American ward" because few new immigrants lived there until the end of the nineteenth century, Washington Square also grew up as a Protestant "American" bastion. (Minus, of course, the black American Protestants who were not invited in.)

In theory, one could say both the majority of artisans near the Hudson and the incoming Washington Square merchants came from WASP backgrounds, but the two groups came from entirely different social strata. This is a glaring example of how the acronym WASP does not serve. It has come to imply only *elite* white Anglo-Saxon Protestants and also begs the question of Dutch and Scots descent.

If the new square residents had a tie, it lay not to the west but to the east, where luxury houses were being developed in Astor Place and Lafayette Place for members of the same caste. In the 1830s the city officially divided Greenwich into two wards.

This public clinic erected in 1832 shows the health concerns prompting Greenwich's development as an upper-middle-class suburb. The city was pushing north at this time anyhow, but epidemics speeded the phenomenon. At a deeper level, the merchants' move to Greenwich was to flee the downtown poor, whom they blamed for the epidemics.

Continue walking east to **Washington Square.** ⓭ *If you feel like it, take a seat on one of the benches and sense the square's presence. We'll step back a moment in time to see how the enclave developed.*

Land here was originally marsh, fed by the Minetta Brook that still runs beneath the ground. (Local trees here do well because of the underlying streams. At least one of the trees is three hundred years old.) In colonial days the hummocky swamp was thick with wild fowl, a favorite spot for hunters.

In 1793 the city planned a more urgent use for the waterland—a mass grave site for the bodies of paupers and fever victims. In the general upgrading following the Revolution, the municipality bought and drained the marsh as a potter's field. Early nineteenth-century guidebooks refer to the trenches of bones furrowing the square. A recent excavation during the park's renovation uncovered skeletons of more than 22,000 bodies interred between 1799 and 1826. As late as 1965, Con Ed workmen found crypts with burned coffins and swags of tattered yellow shrouds—the death uniform of yellow fever victims.

The gravedigger Daniel Megie lived in a frame house on the south side of the field at Thompson Street. He doubled as hangman for the state prison on Christopher Street. The potter's field also did double duty as execution ground; Megie hung his victims here. The hangings were public, an old crowd-pleasing tradition inherited from England. The Christopher Street prison even bore the grand old name "Newgate."

☞ The **elm in the park's northwest corner, ⑭** one of the city's oldest trees, served as gibbet. Sadly for ghouls and tour guides, in 1992 the Parks Department cut the mighty gallows limb where felons had swung almost to the year this ground became a residential square. New York lore has it that General Lafayette was honored by an invitation to watch the hanging of twenty highwaymen here on his visit to the United states in 1824–1825. I've not been able to verify this, but if it happened, the hangings would have been among the last on this site.

By the third decade of the nineteenth century, change around the square had become exponential, speeded up like a Disney nature movie. In 1818 the city laid out the south side of the square-to-be at 4th Street. In 1826 developers raised handsome new Federal style townhouses along the street, and the municipality landscaped the old potter's field and execution ground into a "public place and military parade ground." The seeds of conflict were already inherent in the double designation. One year later the city opened Washington Square North.

When work on the parade ground and public place ended, the town celebrated. Festivities resembled the old yeoman republican assemblies on the Fields (present-day City Hall Park) before the Revolution. Cooks roasted several bullocks and 200 hams. Someone counted kegs spaced out to form "a quarter mile of barreled beer." The collective celebration harked back to Yankee artisanal custom and before that to Elizabethan English tradition. But society was reconfiguring. By 1829 the "parade" ceased to be reserved for the general public, and city guidebooks were already describing its surrounds as one of the town's most select sites.

In the two years since the ground opened it had gone from an accessible gathering spot for the public including artisans from the western part of Greenwich to an elite preserve for the city's merchant class. (The contest over whether squares were inclusive or exclusive spaces began in the west in Paris in 1611 when the king of France took the Medieval and Renaissance concept of a public piazza and turned it inside out by making a closured residential square for the nobility. The public-private nature of New York's squares has been cause for dissent through today.)

In retrospect, the old-style inaugural celebrations seem rather sad, elegiac.

The development of the potter's field as a square, of course, was a realtor and municipal strategy designed to raise the area's value.

In New York the ceaseless leveling of natural eminences posed challenges for developers trying to make preeminent residential spaces. Paradoxically (naturally), they themselves were the people behind the erasures. Unlike Brooklyn Heights, where realtors were shaping an elegant enclave at the time Washington Square was upgraded, Manhattan had few remaining natural features to deploy against commercial intrusions. The rigid grid plan added to the problem. It was left to landowners and builders "to create vistas of respectability" through architecture, private covenants (rules guiding development), and modification of the city street plan.

In contrast to a decade earlier, when the city had been trying to force the grid on Greenwich landowners, by the late 1820s the city government was sympathetic to the real estate developers and gentry householders who wanted elite street-scapes. Except for Madison Square, begun slightly later, the opening of New York's squares and places such as Leroy, University, and Waverly Place all date from this time. It was no coincidence that municipal finance had just shifted from rents and fees collected from public properties to taxes on private property. To raise the tax base, the City Council even granted cash awards as well as concessions to luxury developers. It was public tax money that transformed the old pauper's burial ground at Washington Square.

As historian Elizabeth Blackmar notes, the trend at this time toward enclosed residential blocks was so powerful the municipality only slowed down when it grew obvious that more cul de sacs would threaten vehicular circulation.

One of the casualties of this square's escalation into an elite city space was the last will and testament of a local landowner, Robert Randall (an "honest privateer"). When Randall had died in 1801, he'd bequeathed his 21-acre estate to indigent sailors as a retirement home. The will stipulated that the land should never be sold and must always be used for needy seamen. (See Walk 2.) As Randall's family managed to stall its probate in court, the deed was executed only in 1828, by which time the trustees judged the property far too valuable for the old salts. Packing off the men to a luxurious asylum in Staten Island, they leased out the North Row property. The Greenwich acreage yielded so much rental income that the charity became the wealthiest in America.

North Row: ⓕ Washington Square residents shared social and business ties as well as proximity. Several of the tenants were related, and many had moved uptown together from homes on lower Broadway and State Street. The men were bankers, merchants, and shippers. Only one was a manufacturer, though Stephen Allen, risen from sailmaker to mayor, became a lessee in 1835. Most families came from New England or Scottish backgrounds, a common bond being the Presbyterian Church where both groups worshiped, as the New England contingent lacked a Congregational church in Manhattan. (The church, now another denomination, still stands at 81 Christopher Street.)

Henry James has engraved the square in our memory as the bastion of "old New York," but just a few of its original residents had been born in the city. (James himself, born near, but not *on* the square, was something of an outsider, the reason he was such an exquisite snob. His background was upper-middle-class Protestant Irish by way of upstate New York. His grandmother, who, unlike James, did live in the enclave, was the daughter of an affluent green-grocer.)

☞ The **large Federal mansion** at 20 Washington Square North, now serving as a Catholic convent, went up in 1828, the first house on the North Row. Originally, the house was freestanding; the rest of the row followed several years later. Notice the brick work on the west of the facade. Sharp-eyed people on my walking tours have pointed out the different construction here, the result of the replacing of an old carriage-way once running through to the back of the house with infill.

The majority of the North Row houses were put up individually, but friends often worked out their plans together, and a single person, Samuel

Thomson, builder of the first Custom House is *thought* to have designed the whole row. Considering how important the development was at the time, it's odd no one knows for sure. The case for Thomson grows out of his connection with Snug Harbor, the fact that he held several leases on the North Row, and that he had bought and resold the east side of the square to New York University. Also, most of his work was in the same Greek Revival style of these houses.

☞ Look east across the park at the New York University buildings.

The earliest university building here was an English Collegiate Gothic structure.

North Row residents conceived and funded the institute that opened in 1833, and residents here remained the university's largest donors through the 1850s. At a base level, the founders hoped a cultural center here would anchor property values. Their more philosophic aim was to create an alternative to the conservative Episcopal university, Columbia. Unfortunately, at first NYU didn't bring the kind of panache its organizers hoped. Instead, it caused just the kind of trouble square residents had come here to avoid. Or worse.

The founders had chosen white marble as the stone for their project. Marble (some called it limestone) had been popular in the city ever since the state had moved Newgate upriver to Ossining (Sing Sing) in 1828 and put the prisoners to work digging out the Tuckahoe quarries. The jail also made the men dress stone for fireplaces, building veneer, and architectural trim, which prison authorities then sold to city contractors.

☞ Note the marble steps and lintels on several North Row houses.

In 1833, when NYU made a deal with the state to buy prison-cut marble, local stonecutters rioted against the master mason who'd arranged the supplies. The use of prison labor enraged them as yet another assault on artisanal traditions already in decline. As violence grew, the city called out the Twenty-seventh Regiment (later known as the Seventh). The clash occurred just outside the square at Broadway and 4th Street, but the workers also threatened dwellings here, so troops camped on the green for four days and nights to protect householders. After all was done, NYU continued to use the prisoners' stone as well as the bricks left over from the North Row. Two Gothic pinnacles of the old university carved from the offending marble remain at Washington Square South.

National Guard ~ 7th Reg! N.Y.S.M.

The square was intended to shelter its residents from city turbulence. It didn't work well initially—soon after the North Row houses went up, labor riots protesting NYU's use of prison stonecutters swept the neighborhood. (See NYU in the background.) The regiment shown marching on the square camped there for a week to defend local householders.

***S*troll along the North Row to look at the houses we've been pondering.**

Today, NYU owns many of the buildings. Originally, those to the east of Fifth Avenue were on long lease from the Snug Harbor estate. It was only in the 1970s after the Snug Harbor trustees got legislative approval to overturn Randall's will and sell the property that the university was able to buy outright. If residents of the square founded NYU in part to ensure local property values, current Village residents consider the university something of a loose cannon because of its constant push for space. (For its part, NYU feels hemmed in and envies colleges with real campuses.)

☞ Dozens of covenants—building do's and don'ts—protected this look-alike row from anomaly. Nuisances were screened out, plot frontage mandated, and building materials prescribed. Note the height—all the houses had to be at least three stories high. In contrast to the 1820s when three-fourths of New York's new buildings (such as the Federal dwellings on Grove Street) were two stories tall, in the next decade one-third of new structures going up had three stories or more.

The hike in land prices made larger houses necessary to guarantee a return. Private cisterns, coal-burning stoves, and gas lighting grew de rigueur for the same reason. Buyers now required the new amenities partly for convenience sake, but also because they viewed internal improvements as a capital investment that would raise their houses' value.

Like the square, upmarket houses built in the 1830s were designed to be sanctuaries— note the deeply recessed door of this North Row house. Also see the cramped window under the cornice that belonged to a maid's room. Heavier immigration at this time brought a crop of foreign servants, and new houses going up provided special(ly awful) spaces for them.

As much as governing covenants codified these buildings, the row's homogeneity was also due to the wish of individual householders to present a common facade. After all, the protective covenants were a main reason people moved here. By a circular process, the melded blockfront, grander than the sum of its parts, became the day's stylistic ideal, a declaration of social solidarity.

☞ Note the row's unifying elements, the (successful) effort to add dignity to the first-floor parlors with full-length windows and graceful balconies. The wrought iron fences have repeated motifs, often honeysuckle (anthemion), obelisks, and lyres. The flush cornices are rather elaborate. Number 21 is especially fine.

On the other hand, I sometimes think we make too much of the North Row. Taking Londoners around the space is a deflating experience.

☞ If it's possible to enter a NYU building with some plausible excuse, do so, to experience the modest elegance inside. As much as the various facades conformed, the houses' floor plans and interior details also resembled one other. Fitted out with carved mantles and gilt bronze chandeliers, the spaces are simple and decorous. The people who lived here were wealthy, but not the sort of tycoons who would soon build houses on Fifth Avenue.

To better appreciate how row householders spent their days, I recommend you make a side trip, when you can, to the Old Merchant's House Museum at 29 East 4th Street. The 1832 dwelling is in a different architectural mode (late Federal), but the life-style of its inhabitants, both servants and owners, was similar to that in these houses. The museum is open Sunday–Thursday, 1:00–4:00 P.M. Telephone (212) 777–1089.

Popular wisdom says the Greek Revival style came into favor because of the period's fascination with ancient Greek democracy plus an empathy for a recent Greek revolution against Turkey. Supposedly, America's democratic republican sensibility following independence found its objective correlative in the mode. I myself find Greek Revival buildings, except for the small rural carpenter versions, deliberately imposing, rather coldly patriarchal.

☞ The deeply recessed double portals framed by Doric or Ionic columns were partly just style. The emphatic demarcation of inside and outside, the stress on thresholds, however, also reflected the growing stresses of the city, the "flying squadrons of murderers, housebreakers, footpads, forgers and swindlers," as one overwrought New Yorker wrote. Real and psychological needs now drove middle-class families to take shelter in their homes. Much as the square without was built as a class preserve, the houses themselves were built as temples dedicated to a sanctified idea of nuclear family.

By the 1820s, upper- and middle-class people saw households as more than just lodgings—or work places, which they continued to be in poorer circles. Gentry houses now became bastions of civilization, cradles of morality, an inwardly turned alternative to the rough, competitive world of commerce and politics. A caveat to this is that the houses also did serve worldly ends. Dinner parties here produced advantageous deals. The addresses themselves served as business credit. The interior architecture of the new residences accommodated the expanding ritual of dinners and teas even as front parlors such as the ones in these houses provided neutral spaces for receiving acquaintances and strangers, a buffer zone protecting family privacy in the rest of the house.

Despite the masculine appearance of the house fronts, the interiors belonged to the women, as the recent emphasis on dwellings and the grow-

ing idealization of family gave upper- and middle-class females new cultural authority. This was the era when middle- and upper-class women were put on pillars and into the confines of "home," a phenomenon that continued until recently and is already mourned by some.

During the day the square became a mini woman's domain—a socially created safe space with a preselected society of all the right people. Wives called on each other with their children, leaving cards—a new invention—if their friends were out. The children also became playmates and commonly intermarried in later life (another class and economic advantage of living here).

Sequestered in houses behind porticoed facades, North Row family life became the intensely private, child-centered institution it remained until recently. Wives on the square ruled during the day, as their husbands commuted downtown to work.

It's no coincidence the idea of Christmas as we know it—a densely private affair centered on children— began in this era. It's appropriate that the realtor-reverend, Clement Moore, who kept Greenwich out of the leveling grid, was the author of the poem embodying the new sentimentalized version of the holiday. Before this, New Yorkers did not particularly celebrate Christmas. New Year's Day, marked by open-ended public visiting, was the big event. In the 1830s when society grew less deferential, more raggedly fungible, the open-house custom began to fall away, replaced by today's family-centered rites.

A host of invisible servants made the new domesticity possible. Before the 1820s, households that could afford it had been supported by slaves or poor relations who lived mingled among the household as familiar dependents.

☞ Look up at the cramped attic space below the cornice lines of the North Row houses that supplanted the pitched roofs of earlier Federal houses. Numbers 4 and 5 offer a good example. (The word *attic,* new to the American lexicon, was a salute to the supposed Greekness of the style.) Note where recent conversions have been made to add a little more ceiling height to what was originally almost a crawl space. The attics held the first rooms *made* for domestics. Contemporary real estate newspaper ads ballyhooed these new self-contained servants' quarters.

From 1800 to 1850 domestic labor formed the city's largest employment sector. The phenomenon had two causes: slavery had been scaled back and finally outlawed in 1827; European immigrants arrived en masse and needed work. When the ladies of these houses visited one another, much of their talk, generally complaints, was about the servants (usually three or four) who worked for them.

In the main, domestics were Irish or American blacks—the latter still working in service, as they were excluded from skilled crafts. Yankee girls, who'd "helped" in similar households before the Revolution, now refused service, preferring almost any other job to positions where they were on twenty-four hour call. Incoming immigrant women also hated the life and quit when they could. "Intelligence agencies" for recruiting servants flourished. Stealing discontented maids from one household to another grew rife: employers started a society "for improving the character of domestic servants" to address the problem, or, rather, the effects of the problem.

*W*alk north up Fifth Avenue (laid out in 1824 from the square to 15th Street). Turn right into **Washington Mews.** ⑯

Like much of the North Row, Washington Mews began on long lease to NYU from the Randall estate. The little houses on the north side of the mews opened as stables for square families. The ones on the south side were put up in 1930 on the back gardens of North Row houses.

This stable complex was a city first. All the male householders here commuted downtown. From the late 1830s on, virtually no people of standing lived in lower Manhattan: the island's southern tip now held only daytime businesses and full-time poor—the beginning of inner city abandonment.

Forty years later the wealthy began to abandon this neighborhood also, when shipping moved from South Street to the Hudson River, bringing first Irish, then Italian shore workers to the blocks south of the square. At this time, developers pulled down the subdivided wood houses near the Minettas belonging to African Americans and put up the present tenements. Many old inhabitants joined the white elite in uptown flight. Among other black congregations to move north was that belonging to St. Benedict the Moor, a Catholic sanctuary on Bleecker, organized by African Americans in the 1830s. The old church now became Our Lady of Pompeii.

The shift marked the beginning of the end of the square's relatively long run as a genteel bastion. (See Walk 5 to contrast what happened east of here in the luxury enclave around Astor Place.)

Even though some stubborn families on the square's north, that much further from the immigrants, clung to their homes a bit longer, change came here, too. As early as 1884 the owners of 3 Washington Square North altered it into a studio complex later housing Rockwell Kent and Edward Hopper.

*W*alk back to Washington Square Arch. ⑰

In spite of the effort of some guidebooks to make a case for an unbroken Greenwich literary and cultural tradition going back to the early nineteenth century, early creative sorts here were the opposite of the latter-day Bohemians. People like architect A. J. Davis and painter Samuel Morse, who roomed at NYU after the 1837 crash forced the university to rent out space, have more to do with the merchant elite than with the Bohemians arriving at the turn of the twentieth century.

Henry James, of course, is the most famous intellectual associated with the square. His parents took him abroad just after his birth in 1843, but he made a flying visit to his grandmother, Mrs. Walsh, when he was two. Though the lady died soon afterward and the house went out of the family (it's now demolished), James obsessively recreated both dwelling and neighborhood in his fiction. "The Square," he wrote, "has a kind of established repose which is not of frequent occurrence in this long, shrill city . . . a riper, richer, more honorable look . . . the look of having had something of a history."

When the novelist returned from his self-imposed European exile for a brief visit at the turn of the century, the square's new monument maddened him. James loathed the unmoored quality of the "lamentable little Arch of Triumph" and the (mis)association of progress it lent the enclave.

James was right. Despite the fact that today, Washington Square Arch, designed in the imperial Beaux Arts mode by Stanford White, has become *the* emblem of both square and Village, it stands for everything the square was designed to resist. The arch's prototype, a wooden effort put up in 1889 just north of 8th Street, had been more appropriately placed, since it spanned lower Fifth Avenue, a conduit for traffic and flow.

When this second rendering went up, the battle for neighborhood stop-time was lost in any case. Many officials involved with the arch inveighed against putting the monument here not because of its wrong aesthetic, but because few but unworthy immigrants would ever get to see it.

The present arch (built in 1892) stands for progress and flow, everything the enclave was designed to resist. The arch in this picture, a prototype done a few years earlier, spanned lower Fifth Avenue—a more appropriate location.

Walk south across the park to glimpse places associated with Italian and "Bohemian" settlement in the Village.

This guide will just note a few. For a first-rate account of the period, I recom-

mend *Greenwich Village, 1920–1930* by Caroline Ware. Also useful is the Village chapter in Susan Edmiston and Linda Cirino's *Literary New York.*

Walk along Washington Square South to **Judson Memorial Church** ⓲ *on West 4th Street between Sullivan and Thompson Streets.*

☞ The man who paid for this tan brick church in 1892, Edward Judson, intended it to stand on the borderline between the remaining North Row rich and the South Square poor: it was one of several local missions founded by tense Protestants who stayed on. The sanctuary's Italian mode (Roman-Renaissance style interpreted by Stanford White) is ironic. Judson, whose father had been a missionary in Burma, founded it to *Americanize* Catholic immigrants through bringing them the Baptist word. Today, the church is much loved by locals and speaks *for* not *to* the neighborhood.

Walk west to the **brownstone** ⓳ *at 147 West 4th Street.*

At the turn of the century, young people from all across America came to New York in flight from small-town Victorian strictures. Many settled in the Village because of its low rents and "quaint" charm. Soon, the critical mass of like-minded youth shaped the district into a social and moral free zone. (For themselves, at least.) The conflation of the Village with liberated behavior became even more notable during Prohibition, when dozens of old Federal houses opened as speakeasies.

In 1918 writer John Reed, a central player in the "Bohemian" circle, rented space in this old brownstone, earlier home to William Cullen Bryant, for finishing *Ten Days That Shook the World.* Partying hangers-on in his home at Patchin Place made his own space untenable.

A **corner building** ⓴ (long gone) at 137 Macdougal Street housed the Liberal Club started by Reed's group in its more serious moments. Intellectuals with an activist bent met at Polly Halliday's eatery on the ground floor—among them were muckraker Lincoln Steffens, anarchist Emma Goldman, birth control pioneer Margaret Sanger, and publisher Max Eastman. Max Eastman's monthly publication, *The Masses,* achieved some political success as well as showcasing artistic talent, including painter John Sloan. The paper advocated workers' compensation, women's right to vote, free access to birth control information, and the formation of a world peace organization. The journal's influence forced mainstream papers to cover events they might not have otherwise. For example, when *The Masses* published John Reed's article on the Paterson strike, other journals followed suit. In 1916 *The Masses'* anti-war stance led to the repeal of its mailing permit and brought conspiracy charges against the editors and Reed. Though charges were dropped, the paper died soon afterward.

It was Reed's 1913 book *The Day in Bohemia* that made the young migrants consciously articulate their identity as *Villagers*. Reed had been the first to use the word, a coinage invented along with the concept, in many ways a coinage giving rise to the concept. To be a Villager, unfortunately, had little in common with being a local. The *Masses* circle managed to do considerable good for the world at large, but their personal lives were often inbred and insensitive to those outside the circle.

Despite the fact Reed wrote (in *The Day in Bohemia*) that all the world's adventure lay within a block of his house, and every foreign country within a mile, he and his friends showed scant feeling for the Village Italians. In theory they loved "primitives," but, with the possible exception of painter John Sloan, slight crossover occurred.

Caroline Ware points out that exchange was usually limited to food shopping (the locals thought the Villagers naive spendthrifts) and encounters at music programs held in Greenwich House. (The latter was a settlement house opened by Mary Simkhovitch in 1902 to help impoverished immigrants and blacks south of the square—a wretchedly poor area holding 928 souls per acre, several hundred more than the Lower East Side.) Greenwich House continues today at 27 Barrow Street.

One good the young "intelligentsia" did bring to the immediate neighborhood, if incidentally, was its part in saving old housing stock here from destruction. From early on small realtors began to cash in on the newcomers, remodeling the interiors of many old dwellings for multiple tenancy.

☞ It's fun to scan local buildings for evidence of Greenwich's "artistic" period, the glass-roofed studios cut into the pitched roof Federal buildings at the time.

W*alk south on Macdougal passing the* **Provincetown Playhouse** *at number 133, an erstwhile stable.*

Members of *The Masses* circle founded the theater, known for its house playwright Eugene O'Neill. Many productions here were self-referential, vaunting clique members, flaunting involuted love affairs.

C*ontinue walking south past the rows of ersatzly genuine Italian cafes, then swing right on Bleecker to* **Our Lady of Pompeii** *(at Father Demo*

Square) ㉑*, which inherited its first sanctuary from St. Benedict the Moor. Italian parishioners built this new, 1920s version in the homeland campanile mode.*

Although it took time for the new immigrant community to get enough money to shape local architecture, uptown tourists had been coming to the Village since the 1880s to soak up the "Mediterranean atmosphere" they found in its street life. By 1910, half the residents of the south Village were Italian born, and realtors were playing up the south Village's "Latin Quarter" identity (blurring Italians with "Bohemians") to promote sales.

Other estate agents drew on the Village's colonial past and made links back to the old hamlet of Greenwich. In the 1920s local residents began a committee to preserve some neighborhood landmarks, including the Isaacs-Hendricks house. Eventually, the Village's "olde" look even got exported uptown when builders there wrapped East Side brownstones in Federal veneers.

Despite discovery, and the Seventh Avenue extension in 1919, the Village remained somewhat autonomous until the 1930s, when the IND subway linked the neighborhood to the rest of the city. In this period many old rowhouses were torn down, replaced with high-rise apartments. Prices by then had grown as high as the buildings. Wits noted that the only writers left in the Village were those who could afford to write checks.

Today, no special talent bank resides here. NYU and the New School are in the Village but not particularly of it. The life-style, however, of non-Italians is mellower than in most city neighborhoods, "mainstream" culture more inclusive, diverse sexuality more celebrated.

Despite or because of the commodification that has ruled Greenwich for the last one hundred years, people still come from other parts of the city and the country to feel closer to something real. The realities, as the walk has shown, are various and changing.

5

The East Village

Subway: Lexington IRT (local) 6 to Astor Place.

I suggest reading the introduction on a bench fronting St. Mark's-in-the-Bowery Church, Second Avenue and 10th Street. To get there, walk from Astor Place to Stuyvesant Street and turn east, toward Second Avenue. Note the slant of the block, how the New York University dorm on the northeast corner of Third Avenue and Stuyvesant Street adjusts itself to follow both the street's angle and the regular city grid. Keep heading east to the triangle of church land. ❶

Realtors coined the term "East Village" in the 1960s to invoke Greenwich Village and turn tenements into a silk purse. Many locals still fight the upscaling designation and insist the neighborhood is the Lower East Side—or should be.

Spaces in New York are often contested, but this section is more so than most. The locality's most notorious struggle ground is Tompkins Square Park; the problem of who will live down here, however, is neighborhood-wide. Ironically, many of the activists who battle displacement are outsiders themselves, either drawn to the neighborhood because of its artistic and literary edge, or forced here because of rent hikes elsewhere.

In another irony, the realtors who conjured up a genteel name for the area had some history on their side—more than the decaying housing stock here would suggest. In the mid-1820s the blocks from Bleecker Street to Stuyvesant Street, from Broadway to Second Avenue were an elite precinct, a luxury enclave inspiring the upmarket development around Washington Square. But something happened. Within two decades the neighborhood gentry had cleared out, gone north. Even for Manhattan where change is constant, this was speed. What factors hurried the cycle? What hastened

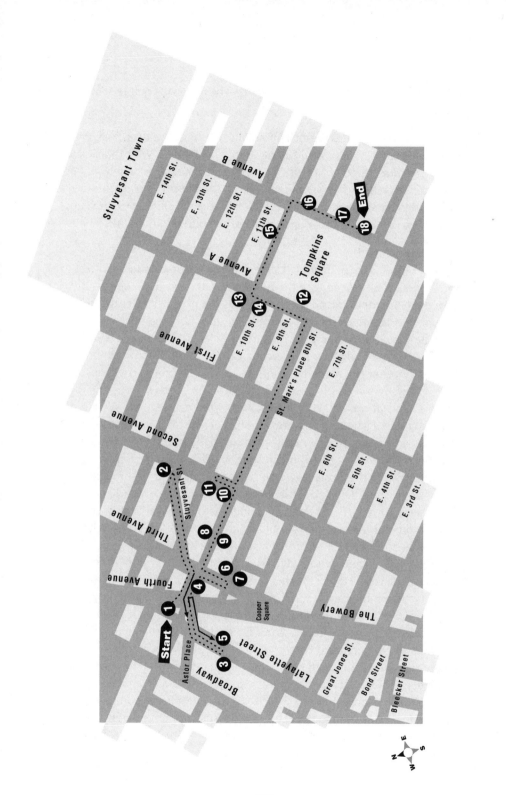

Stuyvesant Town

E. 14th St.

E. 13th St.

Avenue B

E. 12th St.

E. 11th St.

Avenue A

End

Tompkins
Square

First Avenue

E. 10th St.

E. 9th St.

St. Mark's Place 8th St.

E. 7th St.

Second Avenue

E. 6th St.

E. 5th St.

E. 4th St.

E. 3rd St.

Stuyvesant St.

Third Avenue

Fourth Avenue

The Bowery

Astor Place

Start

Cooper
Square

Broadway

Lafayette Street

Great Jones St.

Bond Street

Bleecker Street

N E
W S

125

the poor's arrival from the 1850s onward? The tour will explore some reasons.

☞ To start with the Stuyvesants: Originally, the block we're on was part of Bowery #1, the 120-acre farm belonging ex officio to the West India Company governor. In 1651 Stuyvesant privatized the land as a summer estate—the city's first. The present church (1799) sits athwart the site of an earlier Stuyvesant chapel. The governor's house stood close by to the southwest; Stuyvesant Street runs on the bed of the old road that linked house to farm.

Over time, Stuyvesant added land until the tract ran from 5th Street to 15th Street, Fourth Avenue to the East River. (In those days the East River flowed much farther inland. In some places the property extended to Avenue B, at others to Avenue C; beyond that, the shoreline is landfill.) Creating the estate turned out to have been a prescient move. Fifteen years later when the British took New Amsterdam, Stuyvesant lived out his semi-exile here. Fortunately, from his point of view, a few other Europeans had moved close by—otherwise, only a few African American farmers and their families lived in the neighborhood. These were manumitted West India Company slaves whom the government had given small plots between Astor Place and present-day Prince Street in 1644, in the hope the colony would serve as buffer against Indian attacks. (The half-free men were supposed to maintain a protective trench along Prince Street—roughly ten blocks down from here and farther west; little else is recorded.)

In part, Governor Stuyvesant had built the first chapel here in 1660 to attract more European settlers should trouble come. A few years earlier his farm's isolation had proved problematic. When Indian war parties raided the island, Stuyvesant's wife, Judith Bayard, had been here alone. The background of the conflict, like the theme of much of this walk, had to do with property. Some time earlier, an elderly tribeswoman walking down the Broadway trail near the Battery had stopped at a Dutchman's orchard to forage for peaches as the Indians considered fruit and shellfish a communal resource. The Dutch had other views, however, and she was killed. The resulting reprisal for the death of the old woman is known as the Peach War.

When the attack came, the governor's wife had not been able to get a single New Amsterdammer to come to her aid despite pleading, and she had had to *pay* ten men to travel uptown and defend her. Interestingly, no Dutch would help even for money; the men she finally persuaded were French Huguenots of her own background.

The chapel lent the hamlet a vestige of civility. A few downtowners moved up here—enough to warrant a school for local children, including the offspring of Stuyvesant slaves.

In 1692 Mrs. Bayard bequeathed the chapel to the Dutch Reform Church. In 1793 Peter Stuyvesant's great-grandson, Petrus, who'd just plotted the family property for sale, set about getting a better church to anchor his new real estate development. Stoutly Episcopalian, like most Dutch-descended New Yorkers by then, he donated the ground lots to Trinity. In return, Trinity promised to build. Despite the financing it received, **St. Mark's-in-the-Bowery** ❷ was independent from the start, the first Episcopal parish in the city to be separate from its sponsor.

☞ Today, the fieldstone structure looks swaggeringly rough hewn. Originally, it was stuccoed over, patterned to resemble marble. The spire is an 1828 addition by New Haven's Ithiel Town; the porch followed in the 1850s. Take time to explore the portion of the graveyard remaining after the 1816 opening of Second Avenue chopped off the eastern slope.

In 1803 Petrus gave St. Mark's more land for its cemetery on the proviso the family could bury its slaves for free. Among remains in the rather creepily mounded plot (it looks as if stirring skeletons buckle the grounds from below) are Stuyvesants, Fishes, Winthrops, Van Burens, Goelets, Schermerhorns, Iselins, Vanden Heuvels, and Lorillards.

After you've finished, retrace your steps along the street you came and walk to Astor Place. If you can, read the following before you go, or, better still, as you go along.

☞ When Petrus gridded his property, he mapped several routes, including Stuyvesant Street. The street is at odds with the regular grid pattern of Manhattan Island and looks skewed. In fact, it is the *only* city street laid on an actual east-west axis. The commissioner's plan of 1807–1811 aligned streets to the shape of Manhattan Island; the Stuyvesant family used the compass. Because of the family's power, the municipal grid left Petrus' roads unscathed.

☞ Stuyvesants and their in-laws built houses on the lots around the new church. Number 41, the **1795 Federal dwelling** diagonally across from St. Mark's, is one; number 3, an **1803 Federal house** on the north side of the street, a block farther west, is another. Note their pitched roofs, dormer windows, generous frontage, and Flemish bond brick.

Despite the development, the hamlet's population remained low. In 1807 only seventy parishioners worshiped here regularly, though more came in summers when fever swept New York's downtown.

In the 1810s dry-docks opened to the east nearer the river, but even so, Bowery Village remained a rural outpost for the next decade, and Westchester farmers and drovers bringing produce and cattle down the Westchester–Boston Post road used the hamlet as a way stop. (The route later developed as Third Avenue.) Cattle dealers held illegal cut-price auctions at an open market near today's Cooper Square. Heinrich Ashdor, a former butcher with ties to the stock men, kept a tavern catering to the trade.

Keep walking west past the **Renwick Triangle,** *a red brick and brownstone streetscape built in 1861 after the last Stuyvesant living here passed away.*

☞ The low stooped Anglo-Italianate row is generally, but not universally, attributed to James Renwick, Jr., the architect of nearby Grace Church. The upmarket development, a marked contrast to the rest of the neighborhood when it opened, was probably the result of its sheltered nook between the two churches.

Why had the gentry gone?

When you reach Astor Place, walk to the southernmost traffic island and look down at the north-south roads that belt into the neighborhood. Check the accompanying map, as it makes the near convergence of the Bowery and Broadway still clearer.

☞ A **stabile—a black cube titled the Alamo**—sits on the little triangle. The aptly named piece—it's a coincidence—marks the site where New York's bitterest class battle took place in 1849.

After the Revolution, two streams of cultures had grown north along the Bowery and Broadway, one working class, the other genteel. Originally the two streets and cultures were different but not oppositional. The Bowery was the city's yeoman spine—a street shaped by the presence of wealthy butchers, earthy men who hosted bull baiting and trotting races along the avenue.

Walk to the east side of Cooper Union building (number 4 on your map) and look down the east flank of Cooper Square that merges into the old thoroughfare.

The **small dormered houses** go back to the days when the Bowery was still a republican, working-class street. Its reputation—and reality—as the city's skid row came only later, in the 1890s.

***N**ext, walk west on Astor Place to Lafayette Street (formerly, "Place") and turn south (left). Lafayette Street will serve as a proximate study for the genteel spine, Broadway. (The latter is long since commercialized.)*

The realtor John Jacob Astor knew this area well through his elder brother, tavernkeeper Heinrich Ashdor. In 1804–1805, just before the city extended Broadway up to this point, he had bought a large tract above Great Jones Street, renting out some and leaving the remainder undeveloped during the War of 1812 and later depressions. (Astor had been buying real estate in bulk ever since the trade embargo preceding the War of 1812. Using money from his shipping and fur ventures, he took the new city grid as guide. While the new grid had started as a tool to facilitate housing for all New Yorkers, it had quickly become a speculator's handbook, as it advertised where roads would open. Astor outpaced the rest with ease. During the shipping blockade he'd lent money to distressed merchants, refusing all collateral but mortgages. Because of foreclosures, at war's end in 1815 he was well on his way to becoming "the landlord of New York," the richest man in town.)

By 1826, the blocks below here had become the city's finest residential zone, and it was time to act. Astor carved out Lafayette Place as a cul-de-sac extending his southernmost holdings.

☞ Pause in front of **Colonnade Row, ❸** 428 to 434, on the west side of Lafayette Street. (It's best to look from across the road.) Originally the row held nine houses unified by the monumental colonnade of Corinthian columns. Today, the ensemble is sadly shorn and runnelled with grime. Developer Seth Geer, who'd bought this plot from Astor, put up these houses in 1833 and fronted the row with the same material that had caused riots when he'd used it for the new New York University building in Washington Square that same year. The columns and facade, gleaming ghostly under layers of dirt, are Tuckahoe marble cut by prison labor.

The complex was attributed until recently (though the evidence is being reconsidered) to A. J. Davis, an upstate New Yorker of New England Congregationalist background and Boston training. At the time these houses went up, Davis was one of three influential architects recently arrived in New York City from New England. The others were Ithiel Town and Isaiah Rogers. It was no coincidence the three men appeared in the city

This elegant row went up in the early 1830s. Its decline followed the flight of local gentry after the Astor Place riots.

at the moment New York was separating, virtually segregating, into polarized rich and poor neighborhoods.

Astor's new Place was part of a larger realtors' effort at the time to circumvent the grid by making elegant enclaves and squares. The enclosures would ensure high property values and provide homogeneous, defendable neighborhoods—an increasing concern as immigrants flooded the city and the poor grew poorer.

Even the sleepy Bowery Village backwater had felt the threat of an underclass since the dry-docks had opened near the East River at 10th Street. In 1826 St. Mark's had started a Sunday school to shape up dock workers' footloose children, and a few years earlier, one of "the Spring Street Fencibles gang" had killed a local merchant on what would become Astor Place.

The professionalization of architecture came out of the same growing class divisions that prompted the enclaves. Earlier "architects" had either been unknown carpenter builders or—more rarely—men like John McComb, Jr., carpenter builders who achieved some reputation. The newcomers were Architects with a capital A.

In 1834 Town, who'd traveled through Europe with Samuel Morse looking at art, pleaded for a New York Academy of Architecture. (Town's library of classical styles was the first in America.) The new architects saw themselves as reformers who would shape the city's moral and political environment. In 1836 Town led New York architects in trying to start a magazine that would popularize the art as a "Godly reform, affect[ing] abolition, temperance and preservation of family unity." Interestingly, in view of the elaborate projects they undertook for wealthy developers, their homilies took aim at the city's growing nouveau riche rather than the poor.

☞ The architects might have preached against luxury and the "wolf of appetite," but their designs belied their words. The Corinthian pillared residences on Lafayette Place cost upwards of $25,000 apiece—the same hefty price as the houses on Washington Square North. They were the handsomest, most conspicuous rowhouses ever to go up in New York—a little bit of Bath in Manhattan.

The row's splendor, like the neighborhood's, was brief. By the 1860s the five southernmost dwellings had been converted into the Colonnade Hotel, an Astor scion's mansion now housed a restaurant, a neighborhood church held a boxing ring.

The recent architecture of separation, which was intended to defend, did the opposite here. One building actually exacerbated gentry flight.

In 1847 Astor, who owned the posh Park Theater at City Hall Park, announced he was building a home for the opera at Astor Place and picked Isaiah Rogers as the architect. (Astor had brought his protégé to the city a few years earlier to build the town's first deluxe hotel.) Rogers' theater, a boxy Greek Revival hulk, extended out toward the Alamo cube from the site where the District 65 building stands today.

The new auditorium was a departure. First, it specialized in Italian opera, an art form that was itself exclusionary. (Attendance was already seen as a badge of class solidarity—Washington Irving wrote that it was what kept him in town. "One meets all ones acquaintances at the opera, and there is much visiting from box to box.") Second, unlike other theaters, which up until this time had had pits with low-cost seats, the new-built opera house had none. The only affordable seats were in a truncated third-tier section where chandeliers blocked the view.

When the theater opened, play-going was more than entertainment to city dwellers, it was central to life. New York at the time held at least six legitimate theaters and sixty others showing skits and genre. Audiences were huge; the Bowery Theater alone (built 1826) held 3,500 seats.

Just as the Bowery and Broadway had not originally been oppositional, neither had earlier theater culture. Bowery programs staged Shakespeare as well as vernacular drama; the working class enjoyed classics as much as the gentry. From the 1840s on, the two separated. Walt Whitman, writing theater criticism for newspapers at the time, copied Edgar Allan Poe in considering Broadway the "art" street, the Bowery the "heart" street. He loved each of them but saw them as contradictory, unreconcilable.

The opera house was near the crossroads, the confluence of both.

Popular lore often recounts the riots at Astor Place as a tale of mobs rampaging for trivial reasons, a faction fight between fans of a British (actually Irish) tragedian actor, William Macready, and America's greatest actor, Edwin Forrest. Passions over actors' merits did run high in New York. The cause of this clash, however, was profoundly political—a cry of the heart against resurgent aristocratic influence in the city.

There had been precedents. Before the Revolution, the Liberty Boys had pulled down a theater near the seaport because British officers cheered a line considered offensive to America. In 1831 the removal of decorative eagles from the Astor-owned Park Theater sparked patriotic mayhem. The present mob's constituency, however, a combination of Irish and Yankees, was a first—one of the few occasions when the two came together in common cause.

Both sides sought the showdown, knew it was coming. There had even been a dress rehearsal. At the first performance demonstrators in the audience pelted the British actor with vegetables, while crowds outside jeered and stoned the theater. Despite this, most of the opera house trustees insisted that the play resume the next day. The second evening, when 10,000 workingmen roiled up the Bowery to the theater, the mayor called out the police, the militia, and the Twenty-seventh (later the Seventh) Regiment. Firing at

In 1849 the city's working class from the Bowery and the city's elite from Broadway (or, rather, their surrogates) clashed near the apex where both roads meet. The conflict sped the city's growing spatial and social split.

GREAT RIOT AT THE ASTOR PLACE OPERA HOUSE, NEW YORK.
ON THURSDAY EVENING MAY 10TH 1849.

point-blank range, they killed thirty-one people, critically wounding 150 others.

Burlesque shows and popular song commemorated "the Massacre Opera House" and "DisAster Place." By 1852 the opera house board shut its doors and opened a new theater, the Academy of Music, uptown on 14th Street. Soon, all but a few gentry had left for Union Square, the new elite sanctum. While to us the move seems only a small distance away from the old settlement (just one subway stop north), in those days an eight-block hike uptown was considered a trek into pioneer territory.

*S*troll east along Astor Place, back toward the Bowery, to the 1859 **Cooper Union Foundation Building, ❹** *the ungainly brownstone dominating the crossroads.*

The free, coeducational institute was a gift from Peter Cooper, the inventor who'd pioneered the first American locomotive. Students here got the equivalent of a college degree while learning "the practical arts and trades."

As a young man Cooper had run a grocery store near Stuyvesant Street. His introduction to the area might have come through Astor, who sold furs to his father, a hat maker. Possibly, his Methodist links brought him to the neighborhood, as a small community of that denomination had grown up here in the teens of the nineteenth century. In any case, Cooper kept the land he'd bought at Astor Place, even after he moved uptown. And upscale.

☞ Cooper Union's siting between the two streets, Bowery and Broadway, was deliberate. The philanthropist built his institute at this critical juncture and junction to mediate class divisions, induct young men and women into the respectable working class.

Cooper liked to stress the "union" aspect of the institute, saying he called it that for three reasons—the union of art and science, the Union of country at a time the Civil War was looming, and the "union of effort to make a republican government a blessing to *all*." (He wanted to put a huge sign proclaiming "UNION" on the southern front of the building facing down the Bowery. It was one of many ideas that others overrode. The inventor had endearingly checkered tastes.)

Cooper remained attached to the neighborhood's people all his life and set aside meeting places in the building for Bowery groups, including the butchers. The most celebrated public space in the building was the Great Hall, an assembly room intended as a forum for free speech. In view of the

Peter Cooper tried to mediate the city's class divide through his gift of a free arts and sciences institute for working-class youth, which he built near the juncture of the Bowery and Broadway.

clashes at Astor Place only a few years earlier, Cooper's gift of a platform for airing divisive issues is poignant. In likely reference to the riots, his architect put the hall in the basement to maintain crowd control, slow stampede.

☞ Go in and see the iron-pillared room if you can. Even better, go when something's happening. The hall is still a pivotal city forum.

Abraham Lincoln credited his speech at the Union in 1860, picked up by the national press, for his victory in the Republican nomination. Other speakers here have included Susan B. Anthony and Victoria Woodhull, who appealed for suffrage and women's rights in the 1870s, as well as Clara Lemlich, leader of the 1909 shirtwaist workers strike, and Emma Goldman. Though people from both the right and left have appeared in the Great Hall, the institute is most associated with workers and the left—despite Cooper's own aversion to organized labor.

☞ If you have time, explore the Union's other public rooms and special exhibits. Because of Cooper's scientific interests, the building brims with innovative technology. As a start, an iron beam framework—among the first used anywhere—supports the brownstone and brick walls. The concept, later translated into steel frames making skyscrapers possible, had occurred to Cooper because he manufactured rail track and understood how well it lent itself to other functions.

Once you're back outside again, walk around the building, noting the large plate-glass windows that once served as display cases for the ground-floor stores that subsidized the Union's upkeep.

☞ On the building's roof you'll see a circular shaft. Cooper designed this to hold an elevator but never lived to see one installed.

Today, Cooper Union remains more affordable than most comparable institutes in the country, even though it has started charging fees in recent years. (Some students are still admitted free, supported by ground rents from Union-owned property, including the land under the Chrysler Building that Peter Cooper bought when it was a shanty-studded lot.) Despite the relatively low tuition here, the student body has changed. Instead of the poor and immigrant New York youth Cooper had in mind, most present-day students are middle-class youngsters from across the country. The shift has forced the institute to look for dormitory space to house out-of-town pupils. In a vicious cycle, the need for dorms adds to the real estate pressure on the Lower East Side and spiraling rents. NYU remains the chief offender.

☞ Note neighborhood banners protesting both institutes.

The American Bible House was another reformist building to open here following the riots. From 1853, it stood just north of Cooper Union, where the Engineering Institute is today.

Just in case co-option into the respectable working class failed, the city gave money in 1856 for a new armory for the Twenth-seventh Regiment (later the Seventh) inside the Tompkins Square market at 7th Street and the Bowery. Normally, all regiments paid for their own drill halls. This was a gift, payback for the regiment's help during the opera house riots.

Return to Lafayette Place, to number 425.

One building near Astor Place that did not start as a reformist institution but became one is the **Astor Library, now the Public Theater, ❺** which was bequeathed by the realtor several months before the opera house melee.

☞ The southern wing of the Italianate brick and stone structure begun in 1849 is by German architect Alexander Saeltzer. The two wings are later additions.

.It was the developer's single public benefaction and came with constraints. In contrast to Cooper Union, which ran a reading room that stayed open until ten in the evening and offered a night school, Astor's library shut at four in the afternoon. After the 1850s this institution also extended its hours. Gentlemen of leisure were gone.

☞ Commercial buildings arrived in the neighborhood in the late 1880s when the city lengthened Lafayette Place south to link up with lower Manhattan. The Romanesque **De Vinne Press Building** at 393–399 Lafayette dates from this time and once held a printing company. The ornate, **column-ringed cast iron and brick building** at 404–411 Lafayette housed the Durst factory and men's clothing store.

In 1895 the Astor library shut, its collection merged with the New York Public. For twenty-five years it stood empty, until it became a soldiers' club at the end of World War I. For the next four decades it was home to the Hebrew Immigrant Aid Society. (Note the banner-sized initials H.I.A.S. on the building's north wall.) In 1965 the fanciful building seemed doomed, but a last minute reprieve saved it—one of the first city landmark acts. In 1967 the Public Theater opened here.

The next leg of the tour takes you over to Tompkins Square Park. A good place to pause and catch your breath before starting out is McSorley's Old Ale House, which opened in 1854 when the neighborhood metamorphosed. If you follow this suggestion, retrace your steps east past Cooper Union and the Bowery to Third Avenue; turn right and walk one block to 15 East 7th Street.

☞ **John McSorley's bar ❻** is one of the oldest survivals in the city. Memorabilia include a potbelly stove, gas lamps, a carved mahogany bar, and Peter Cooper's own drinking mug. (Despite his hope the Union's reading room would "lure" city youth "from the saloon and gang," Cooper was a regular here.)

The Irish had only a short run before this neighborhood changed into Kleindeutschland, "little Germany." Near the time McSorley's opened, Cooper wrote his wife, "Germans are driving the Irish from the field. Even groceries are passing into German hands. . . . Beer is replacing whiskey." Ger-

mans had been a big minority in the city since the 1820s, but heavy migration awaited the failure of the 1848 revolution in Europe. More settlers arrived in 1878 when the Berlin government smothered socialism.

> As the gentry left this part of the East Side, immigrants moved in—first the Irish, then the Germans.

Between the 1850s and 1890s, the Lower East Side blocks below Houston Street up to 14th Street, the Bowery over to the East River, grew into a German precinct. The community included about 20,000 German Jews and as many Protestants (along with some free thinkers). The far majority however, were Catholics, mostly from Bavaria and the Rhineland. All in all, there were 300,000 Germans in Kleindeutschland, making it the largest German city in the world other than Berlin or Vienna.

Housing grew so tight that despite the amount of good building stock, even skilled workers like shoemakers lived and worked in basements. The mass of little industries here, cabinetry, brewing, cigar making, and garment work (swollen by the Civil War need for uniforms), accounted for most of New York's manufacturing.

☞ Note **St. George's Roman Catholic Church, the Ukrainian Cathedral, ❼** across from McSorley's. This ambitious cathedral building dates from 1976 and reflects the Ukrainian community's latter-day wealth.

At the turn of the twentieth century, middle Europeans fleeing homeland dislocations—mostly the onset of a quicker paced market economy—

took the trades and housing Germans left behind when they moved up-town. Poles, Ukrainians, and Czechs settled the blocks below 5th Street. Poles and Ukrainians are still an important presence in the neighborhood, but the Czechs retreated up Avenue A to Yorkville after quarreling with the Poles. (They'd politicked with envoys from Russia, Poland's ancient enemy.)

In the late 1980s the cathedral used part of its money to put up a condominium, a tax-free venture that critics called a money-making scheme sure to hasten neighborhood gentrification. For their part, cathedral spokespersons argued it was not so much an investment as a boon for parishioners suffering rent hikes.

*W*alk back up to 8th Street (St. Mark's Place) and turn right (east).

☞ Note the wide sidewalks that show us it was planned as a gentry *place,* not just an ordinary street. Nowadays, vendors have taken advantage of the extra space. Milling crowds make it hard to stand still long enough to see the buildings. Several of the houses on the block date from the street's opening and form part of a uniform row constructed in 1832. Because the old houses have been so overlaid, it's difficult, and thus doubly rewarding, to distinguish them. The **disheveled hotel** on the south side of the street at number 4 has dormer windows and a derelict doorway arch, complete with splayed keystone, that give clues to its age.

Developer Daniel LeRoy, who built the city's first unified blockfront not far below and west of here, and author James Fenimore Cooper were among the street's gentry. A plaque at number 20 marks **LeRoy's residence.** Cooper's has none. A New York City value judgment?

☞ Look closely at the **blue building,** ❽ 21–25 8th Street, across the street on the north side. You can see by its several arched doorways that the structure is actually a conglomeration of several Federal dwellings joined together.

The German Arion Society merged the houses when the choral group moved in; after that, the clumsy building became the Polish national house, the Polish "Dom." Later, in the 1960s, when the East Village entered its "hippie" era, the makeshift house held the Electric Circus. Today, it serves as a drug counseling center and holds courses for urban homesteaders in wiring, carpentry, and masonry skills—useful for rehabilitating the abandoned tenements farther east of here.

☞ The buff brick building at 12 8th Street, stamped with a terra-cotta roundel of flags, opened in 1885 as the **Deutsch Amerikanische Schuetzen Gesellschaft, ❾** or shooting club.

☞ The association marked a change in emphasis of the New York German turnverein movement, a socialist association featuring athletics, riflery, and music, which had been a bastion against nativism (Yankee oppression) in the city from the 1830s until after the Civil War. When anti-immigrant prejudice declined (somewhat), the organization's purpose grew less defensive, more recreation oriented.

Walkers who are interested may like to make rather a long trek down to 64–66 East 4th Street to see the last verein building on the Lower East Side—a combination political hall, gym, and theater dating back to 1874. (East 3rd and 4th streets hold a host of ghostly German buildings guttering with ruined busts and faded sign-boards—the memory of memory.)

*W*hen you reach Second Avenue, turn up (left) to see the **Ottendorfer Branch of the New York Public Library, ❿** *135 Second Avenue (between 8th and 9th streets.)*

☞ German architect William Schickel designed the brick and terra-cotta building in a mix of Italian Renaissance and Queen Anne styles. The fiery building, strange in gray New York, still has the largest collection of German books in the city.

Oswald Ottendorfer, editor of New York's leading German-language daily, the *Staats-Zeitung,* donated the Freihaus Bibliothek und Lesehalle library in 1884. From the Civil War on, the *Staats-Zeitung,* founded decades earlier, had the clout as well as the circulation of a major English-language newspaper. Under Ottendorfer's paternalistic editorship the paper became the voice for most immigrants in Kleindeutschland.

Through his paper and the reform wing of the Democratic Party, Ottendorfer lobbied for the introduction of German culture and language in New York schools and an end to stereotyping the Germans in general. Middle-class Protestants preferred them to the Irish, but popular magazines still published withering articles and even nastier cartoons depicting the community as thuggish philistines.

☞ The patriarchal—if illiberal—editor also donated the **Stuyvesant Polyclinic ⓫** next door, known as the German Dispensary until World War I,

While German consumers led the way to New York's commercial culture, at first their free-wheeling enjoyment of life shocked middle-class Anglo-New Yorkers, who caricatured it in this illustration.

when it circumspectly changed its name. Early clients here were mainly garment makers suffering pneumonia and consumption brought on by the constants of their work—fatigue, cold, and bad ventilation. This building, florid with busts of European doctors and scientists, replaces an earlier facility also given by Ottendorfer.

*R*eturn to the intersection of Second Avenue and Eighth and cross the avenue, noting the **Orpheum Theater** on the east side of the thoroughfare, a remnant of the German-Yiddish rialto.

☞ Ukrainian nationalist clubs and dumpling restaurants make up most of the blockfront between 8th and 9th streets. The **Ukrainian Community Center** at 140 Second Ave once housed the German YMCA.

*C*ontinue walking along 8th Street (St. Mark's Place), crossing First Avenue.

☞ As you go east toward the river, much of the land becomes swampy and housing grows correspondingly poorer. This part of 8th Street, however, runs on hard, dry land, and consequently the buildings are a mix of good-class tenements and single-family Greek Revival rowhouses.

The Seventeenth ward of Kleindeutschland, where you are now, was the least industrial section of the neighborhood, the area between Second Avenue and Tompkins Square the most prosperous. While the wealthiest Germans, the brewers, had begun moving up to Harlem and Yorkville in the 1870s, many other comfortably off families stayed on in the better streets near Second Avenue and Tompkins Square. Most Germans moved north after the turn of the century. In part, they left for better housing and to escape new immigrants; in part, they left to escape the mass melancholia that descended on the neighborhood after the excursion boat sponsored by a German church blew up in the East River, killing over a thousand women and children. A statue of two youngsters in Tompkins Square commemorates the disaster, one of the occasions—which happen more than we acknowledge—when a whole community resonated with a common emotion.

☞ Notice the ground-floor stores in some of the tenements.

In German days, most storefronts held bakeries or tailoring establishments. Farther toward the river, tenement backlots held more noxious industries—cigar factories, printing presses, distilleries, and slaughter-houses.

*A*t **Tompkins Square Park ⑫** *I suggest you sit on a park bench while you read the following. When you are done, you might like to stroll around the park to look at its landscaping.*

From the start Tompkins Square was a precarious fulcrum between local gentry and working-class residents. In 1846 upper-middle-class-houses (still standing) opened on the square's north side—the high, dry end. The next year, tenements followed on the swampy southern rim, which had turned into a poor immigrant strip named "Rag Pickers row" after its scavenger residents. Rag and bone picking was becoming such a way of life that before long, gangs organized to control it, the seeds of our Mafia "carting" crimes.

To the northeast of the square, the blocks around the dry-docks located between 10th Street and 11th Street near Avenue C and D became Mackerelville, an Irish slum named after the bony fish the poor depended on. Some maps still show Drydock Street, now far inland, as the shore has been padded out over time. Until 1992 the Drydock Savings Bank recalled the old repair yards.

Present-day editorials about current strife in Tompkins Park often say the Stuyvesant family *gave* the 10 1/2 acres to the city. This is the story.

From 1826 to 1833 landowners in this area battled over development. The split lay between those who primarily owned property on the high, dry side west of Second Avenue and those holding bog to the east. (There was some overlap. Several owners, including Astors and Stuyvesants, held property in both places.) The conflict revolved around how improvement of the big marsh ought to be done and who should pay for what. Among other plans for the area, one promoted the idea of gouging 20-foot-wide canals along 6th, 9th, and 14th streets.

Naturally enough, the high and dry owners wanted to pay less for the necessary drainage and landfill, while the swamp owners—including Stuyvesants, Pells, Fishes, and Astors—wanted the venture done in a way that would distribute costs. The argument continued so long that the land lay fallow for two decades. Worse, during the delay other entrepreneurs had leveled all the hills around, making the prices for scree jump so high that developers would have had to cart rubble all the way from Brooklyn to fill the bog. In view of this, the swamp lords threatened to dump the property back on the city as not worth improving. The city council, sympathetic to developers since the late 1820s, took the point. In 1833 it anted up $62,000 of taxpayers' cash to compensate the landowners, in particular, the Stuyvesant family. Another $22,000 was set aside for filling and draining the muddy flat into a park.

The proceedings, of course, raised the value of all holdings surrounding the upgraded property. Tompkins Square Park opened one year after the purchase. Or, rather, it sort of opened—for the next decades the Twenty-seventh Regiment often preempted the publicly financed enclave for its parade ground. The military expropriation flew in the face of the era's social thinking. Ever since 1848 when Andrew Jackson Downing, an English landscape architect, wrote on the need for parks following the revolutions across Europe, urban reformers had demanded parks as "lungs" where workers could improve their health and (safely) ventilate social grievances.

The Astor Place riots in 1849 brought the argument home. Streets clearly were the enemy; parks, where behavior could be shaped and sanitized, the solution. In fact, the city plan of 1811 had provided a fair amount of space for parks, but private development had absorbed most of the space. By 1838, only 178 acres remained of the 450 originally set aside.

For many reasons, perhaps the leading one being the frequent claims on the park by the Twenty-seventh Regiment, Tompkins Square turned out not to be a venting place that domesticated the working class, but a space that politicized it. Many of the rallies here verged on riot. In 1857 local Germans protesting food prices stoned a bakery wagon. That very year, 15,000 unemployed gathered to assail the citywide loss of jobs and a swooping 30 percent rent hike. During the Civil War draft rioters overran the square despite the deterrent effect of Union troops bivouacked here.

In 1866 (the same year a shelter opened on Avenue A allowing the homeless to sleep on the floor) the city legislature authorized the permanent conversion of Tompkins Square into a single-use parade ground: until then, the Twenty-seventh had been the main beneficiary. Now, the government uprooted remaining trees and laid down asphalt (the better for marching) manufactured by a crony of Tammany Boss Tweed. A few years later when anti-Tweed groups took office, they scratched off the offending material, but the bias against locals continued. An exception came in 1870 when 50,000 Germans gathered in the square to celebrate Germany's victory in the Franco-Prussian War. Six hundred butchers paraded on horse back and 200 carpenters marched with axes; Luther's triumphal "Ein Feste Berge" swelled the air.

The square's worst turbulence, until our own era, occurred one icy January day in the 1874 depression when 10,000 jobless workers and their families gathered here to demand a public works program. Violence (as some would argue about the 1988 clash) came from the top down. The crowd, that "hydra-headed class" "ready to strike at all we value most," had convened here perforce following an injunction banning a march organizers had planned to lead to City Hall. Issuing the ruling just hours before the demonstration was due to start, the city backed its ukase with a massive police presence. The ensuing conflict between the workers who had been herded into this space and the police was later termed a riot, but the event was pure blood bath. Sixteen hundred foot patrolmen and mounted squads riding full gallop charged the crowd, cudgeling wildly, pursuing even as people scattered down side streets and hid in neighborhood stores. One horseman followed right into a grocery.

Samuel Gompers, then a youngster working in a local cigar factory, saw the bloody clubbing; later, he credited the "orgy of brutality" with determining him to start the American Federation of Labor.

The public demanded a review, but the gingerly probe by a hand-picked board, seen as sympathetic to the government, caused even more outrage.

THE RED FLAG IN NEW YORK.—RIOTOUS COMMUNIST WORKINGMEN DRIVEN FROM TOMPKINS SQUARE BY THE MOUNTED POLICE, TUESDAY, JANUARY 13th.—See Page 145.

From the 1850s on, green spaces were seen as places that would domesticate the working class, keep them from trouble. Tompkins Square Park, however, lent itself to struggle. Rallies and riots occurred here regularly.

Following the "riots," newspapers reported that the original "owners" were thinking of suing the city to recover their "gift," as the park had been "misused." (It's not clear whom they were blaming.) For a while, the city toyed with de-mapping the grounds, but things went the other way. Champions for the park came from two stratas. The first group was made up of urban theorists (*city planning* is too modern a phrase, but following the Civil War some professional men in various fields began to look at the city in a more totalistic way than had occurred until then). These men, whose motives were a mix of altruism and anxiety about keeping city peace, argued that civic order could be achieved, must be achieved, through spatial reform. The park's other defenders were German community leaders who campaigned vigorously for its local use, reform notwithstanding.

Eventually, it was the local regiment's decision to move uptown that made the long awaited "return" of Tompkins Square to the public possible. Not only did jeering youths make it uncomfortable for soldiers to drill here, but, in any case, there were hardly any wealthy left down here to protect. All in all, it was better to shift north to the Upper East Side, where people of the business class had just begun to settle.

In 1875 the city hired Frederic Law Olmsted, who'd codesigned Central Park, to redevelop the square as a true green. In theory. Despite its announced withdrawal, the Twenty-seventh still practiced here, so Olmsted could only play with the corners around the parade ground, not with the park itself. By the time the regiment finally did go in 1878 (the year after yet another mass job rally in the square), landscape architect Julius Monkewitz got the contract, as Olmsted had just been fired from the parks department in an intramural struggle.

☞ The new man redesigned the grounds with a $50,000 budget using Olmsted's style. The park, with its meandering paths and rustic summer houses, looked much as it does today—or, at least, did look like until the recent tear-up. Many of the park's trees date from the late 1870s. Perhaps not coincidentally, the planting and picturesque landscaping created a patchwork topography that prevented large gatherings of people.

☞ "The changing of Tompkins Square from a sand lot into a beautiful park," Jacob Riis said, "put an end for good and all to the Bread and Blood riots of which it used to be the scene, and transformed a nest of dangerous agitators into a harmless beer-craving band of anarchists." By 1883 reformist groups ringed the square as if it were a dangerous animal. Many were Protestant associations such as the Boys Club, the St. Mark's Memorial Chapel, and the Children's Aid Society. Some were bottom-up immigrant associations intent on shaping the destiny of their own communities.

The Kitchen Garden school begun in 1882 stood at the corner of St. Mark's Place and Avenue A, the German street known for its beer halls, oyster saloons, and groceries. The name was a mean reference to kindergardens, which the Germans had newly introduced to the city. The school, run by the Wilson Industrial School for Girls, the female wing of the Children's Aid Society, instructed immigrant tots from the age of five onward. They didn't teach play; however, but traditional female skills such as cleaning and laundering with 30-pound irons. Society still needed servants but found them harder to get as industry expanded. In 1860, 42 percent of German women were in service; in 1880, only 17 percent.

The Harriman family (forebears of Averell), railroad and upstate real estate tycoons, got the idea of starting the Boys Club after a visit to the Wilson School. The aim was to, yet again, "woo boys from the saloons and the streets." The manifesto continues at the organization today, although drugs have replaced saloons. (Today, the street, is, in fact, a double enemy, as drugs are sold outside on public corners.)

It's interesting to contrast the energy Victorian intellectuals drew from city thoroughfares (see Walk 8) with the countervailing idea that streets were a dangerous incubation ground for the poor. "The street is all surface," Riis said, pleading for parks where children could "root" themselves in a positive way. "Nothing grows there, it hides only a sewer." Flaneurism, the bourgeois male avocation that had developed in the 1830s, was literally a one-way street. (Even though the word *flaneur* meant "idler," "loafer," it was respectful, affectionate, with a built-in acceptance, like calling a confirmed sociopath a "scalawag" or "rogue.") Middle-class men felt entitled to their "privileged gaze"; working-class boys out of their area—or even at large *in* their neighborhood—were seen as dangerous usurpers. Today, police are still trained to notice immigrant or racial groups who come out of "their" neighborhoods and walk Midtown avenues. Imagine a black man in poor clothing running through a "good" neighborhood. How many people would assume he was a jogger?

***W**alk north on Avenue A to the* **Boys Club of New York** ⓭ *at 10th Street and Avenue A (287 East 10th).*

From 1876 until 1900, when the Harrimans bought this corner and put up their own building, the Boys Club operated out of the Wilson School basement. In 1918 the club added an annex with one of the city's first indoor swimming pools; it still stresses athletics even though its constituents have changed. As the Tompkins Square Park area has gentrified, the boys who are members no longer come from the immediate area. Most live in the subsidized housing projects over on Avenue D.

☞ Across the street from the Boys Club, on the southwest corner of 10th and Avenue A, stands the glowing **brick and terra-cotta church** ⓮ (by James Renwick Jr.) that once housed the St. Mark's Memorial Chapel, an 1883 Stuyvesant beneficence replacing an earlier mission donated by that family.

(The Stuyvesants remained big landowners down here through the 1930s, when they hired Frank Lloyd Wright to build *four* skyscrapers on the grounds of St. Mark's Church—a preposterous and mercifully unrealized scheme.)

When this mission opened, the relations of St. Mark's with the neighborhood were problematic. Locals dubbed its Benevolent Institute—the nucleus of Columbia's Teachers College—the "Malevolent Institute." In recent decades the church has been a champion of neighborhood needs, the agent of many solutions.

*Walk east on the north side of the square to Avenue B, passing **the Italianate houses** put up in the 1840s for upper-middle-class families but soon
subdivided for poor immigrant tenants. If you have time, you might enjoy a
visit to the **Carnegie Library** ⓯ at 331 East 10th, which keeps a file of clip-
pings on the park as well as a library of books in East European languages.
When you reach Avenue B, turn right and walk south to 143 Avenue B, the
Christadora House ⓰ at the corner of 9th Street.*

☞ The condo, which rests on floating plates, takes its name from a charity
home given by a philanthropist at the turn of this century. The present
Deco high rise replaced the older residence in 1928. Originally, the upper
stories held dorms for women; the middle part, offices and schoolrooms,
the ground floor, stores that supported operating expenses.

At the opening, the presiding city commissioner praised religious
agencies as the needy's only source of help other than the government:
"You could always count on them."

But it seems you can't always count on them. In 1947 the settlement's
sponsors, memorialized by a logo in the lobby "love thy neighbor as thy-
self," sold out to the city. Despite the effort of local groups to buy the building as a community center during the period it stood empty, the city sold
the building in 1976 to a developer for a meager $62,000. Soon afterward
the buyer "flipped" it. (A flip is a rapid resale, often one of a series—a commonplace practice in the 1980s boom era.) In 1982 entrepreneur Henry
Skydell bought the high rise for $1.3 million and resold it in 1985 for a
$2.2 million profit. Since then, the building has become the emblem of un-
friendly gentrification in the neighborhood. During the 1988 riots, demonstrators came here to break windows and stave in the door with an improvised battering ram.

Keep walking south on Avenue B to the next block.

☞ The 1886 dun pile with the gabled cornice was the **Children's Aid Society's Boys Lodging House** ⓱, sometimes called the Newsboys and Bootblacks Lodging House. Local tenement lords, including the Astor family,
contributed: Calvert Vaux, Olmsted's long-time collaborator, designed it.
(Both men were friends and fellow thinkers of Charles Brace, who founded
the CAS in 1853.) Note the terra-cotta monogram, C.A.S., and the date.

The solidly built hostel—it has fireproof materials and rich oak interiors—is one of half a dozen or so commissions Vaux received from the soci-

Reformers such as C. L. Brace, founder of the Children's Aid Society, started many institutions to shape up (or ship out) immigrant youth. Brace intended the News Boys and Bootblacks Lodging House on Tompkins Square to keep children off the streets, inculcate a sense of purpose.

ety. Another Vaux building done for the the society, an industrial school, still stands on 6th Street between Avenue C and Avenue D.

As Brace deeply opposed long-term institutional living, this building provided only overnight lodging. Its upper floors held dormitories; the middle floor, school rooms; the basement was set aside for games. (Children's need to play, or perhaps just *boys'* need to play, was a new concept Brace had discovered on a trip he and Olmsted had made to Germany. The source was ironic, as most of Brace's constituents here were German youngsters.)

Some children came to the house on their own to get a bed, entering through the basement door on 9th Street, where superintendents doused them with Larkspur, a stinging disinfectant of the day. Like the Boys Club, which still charges a small fee, the CAS asked a few cents' entry on the theory that it made the boys self-reliant. For ten cents extra the children could rent a curtained nook. A major tenet here was to encourage respect for money—how you could earn it, save it, spend it.

Some boys didn't come on their own, but were brought in, rounded up by patrols coordinated by telephone dispatchers, a new technology the CAS helped popularize.

Brace, author of *The Dangerous Classes of New York and Twenty Years'
Work among Them,* was a pioneer in modes of removing (underclass) children from the street. The activist's raft of ideas ranged from providing lodging houses such as this to building up rail-served suburbs in Westchester
for whole families. His best-known scheme was the mass deportation of
city children to the Midwest. (About five thousand boys and girls a year left
New York over a forty-year period. The Astor wife who helped finance this
house personally paid for 13,000 youngsters to leave town.) Brace's friend
Olmsted also worked to get the urban poor resettled elsewhere. Parks were
ameliorative, but the West was *so* much better for them. In 1858 the
Catholics themselves turned to emigration schemes, both to circumvent
Brace's roundups and because they, too, thought the city a dangerous ma-
trix.

Despite its overbearing attitude, the CAS, to its credit, looked into the
reasons why children were on the streets and worked for change, a different approach than many organizations, including the Boys Club. In Brace's
time the CAS made 55,000 investigations of child abuse cases and successfully prosecuted 18,000 of those in court within a sixteen-year period—impressive figures, given today's judicial logjam.

☞ Note the Star of David on the 8th Street pediment, which dates from
1925 when the East Side Hebrew Institute moved in.

The Hebrew Institute stayed until 1976, when they abandoned the
building as not worth trying to sell. The abrupt departure was a telling index of neighborhood decline, if rather surprising as uptowners had already
started moving down here. The following year the Friends of Calvert Vaux,
a co-op association of middle-class Manhattanites, bought the structure
from the city.

W*alk south to 8th Street to* **St. Brigid's Church, ⓲** *which stands across
from the Children's Aid Society on Avenue B. Irish dry-dock workers, the
majority parishioners when it opened in 1849, helped to build it.*

☞ If you are able to enter (usually Sundays only), be sure to see the ceiling of the nave, its resemblance to a ship's hull.

Originally, conservative clergy ran the church and its pastors sided
against their congregants during the Civil War draft riots. Now, St. Brigid's,
home to the city's largest Hispanic congregation (and painted yellow to
look like adobe), leads local activism. For years, the church's ministry has

worked to end neighborhood displacement and mediate conflict over the square.

In August 1988, 440 police attacked, some say counterattacked, demonstrators in the streets around Tompkins Park opposing the 1:00 A.M. curfew requested by middle-class newcomers in the neighborhood who wanted both the park's homeless settlement and the nightly rock music here gone. (The music, itself, was part of the East Village's history, a vestige of the counterculture scene grown up in the 1960s when rents were truly low.)

Most agree the face-off was ignited by youthful punk wanna-bes from the suburbs come to absorb the remnant hippy ethos here, but many of the participants in the melee had conflicting agendas. Reportedly, the crowd's constituents changed during the course of the several-hour battle that grew out of a fairly violent demonstration. (The youngsters had thrown rocks, bottles, and powerful firecrackers at the police before the latter answered with force.) Later, as the police response flared into police brutality, more locals with an activist, pro-human rights (and ergo pro-homeless) bent, joined in.

This poster blames the police, but the problems behind the 1988 Tompkins Square clash were complex—and were owed, in part, to struggles over neighborhood housing.

The characters involved in the foray and the larger struggle for direction down here were as various and contrary as the city itself.

First, there were the 150 or so homeless in the park who had been knocked out of their living quarters by real estate hikes or personal problems. Second, there were the East European groups who have been in the neighborhood since German days. People of this community, who own shops and homes between Second Avenue and Avenue B, are essentially conservative lower-middle-class men and women who have worked hard for a living. (As many of the players and issues remain the same today, I'm switching to present tense.) The East Europeans dislike both the punk youngsters and the working-class Hispanics, who now form a majority in much of the neighborhood from Avenue C eastward toward the projects. They also aren't fond of the artists and Yuppies (read displaced middle-class New Yorkers) who have been pushed into this area by rising rents in the rest of Manhattan. The Yuppies and artists (some of the latter recent arrivals, some with roots going back to the 1960s), in turn, dislike each other and are divided over the homeless in the park, some supporting their rights, others complaining the tent city prevented its use by other neighborhood residents. The Yuppies and the artists also have mixed opinions about the political "radicals" who have taken over some of the locality's abandoned buildings now owned by the city, which they occupy as squatters. These latter also are not a homogeneous group. Some say they are mainly making a social statement; others claim real need. For their part, the homeless are divided about the squatters, many saying they have little sympathy with the mainly white, formerly middle-class group that have come to be known as the "anarchists." Meanwhile, slightly farther east (and so far not part of the turmoil around the square, though part of the larger housing conundrum in New York) is the predominantly black population in the city projects. Last are the drug dealers, whom presumably nobody likes. (Somebody must! They're still around.)

Debates over the police action or brutality continue. As time passes, the meaning of the riot has also changed, with the homeless issue virtually superseding the dispute over music rights. Despite the deepening of the riot's significance, most local activists fighting to save low-income housing in the neighborhood, are sorry the affray and its aftermath have become so prominent. The larger battle, they posit, is general displacement on the Lower East Side and the dominance of New York's real estate interests that allows it.

Local and other community workers believe that the city has earmarked this area for gentrification no matter what. They warn it was no coincidence the police sweeps on Avenue A happened the same year the developer flipped the Christadora for $3.5 million. Some in the force themselves are not happy to feel they are being used as the strong arm of realtors. On the other hand, they have little sympathy for the punk element in the various set-tos, whom they see as spoiled, irresponsible middle-class youth.

At the end of April 1989, in a heroic effort to reconcile opposing interests, St. Brigid's hosted an open-mike conference for all the neighborhood. Many voiced their thoughts on how the park should be used. The common thread underlying the differing opinions was a fear the city government would take the park out of their hands through relandscaping and other machinations.

The same month as the public conference, the city knocked down one of the tenement houses it owned on 9th Street between Avenue B and C, saying it wasn't safe. Many in the community felt they also purposely destabilized the tenement next door (occupied by squatters) so that they could demolish that building, too. Rallies protested what some saw as the municipal intention to turn city-owned in-rem land over for market development. As the government owns several hundred parcels of real estate here, which they have seized for back taxes, city decisions will shape the East Village's future.

In 1989, under new bans on sleeping in parks, Tompkins Square Park was "swept," the homeless routed. At the same time, the city redoubled support services in a park building where volunteers provided medical aid and counseling. Some Lower East Side squatters marched with banners in protest, but other local residents, sick of tents and worried for their children, hailed the "cleanup." A few years after the turnout of the homeless drug abuse, prostitution, and crime were still thick on three sides of Tompkins Square, though gentrification began to take hold on Avenue A.

As the number of homeless grows, more and more public spaces get shut or loaded with constraints.

Except for a small sports area, the park itself remained shut for "renovation" until September 1992. Today, the curfew is still in effect and argument continues. In Greenwich Village a small fenced park at

Sheridan Square is kept locked all day, rather like a zoo for landscapes. It is called a "Viewing Park." Perhaps this is the wave of the future.

Depending on how tired you are, you might like to walk back to the subway at Astor Place via 10th Street so you can look in at the Russian herbal baths at 268 East 10th. The baths, opened in 1892, are the last to survive in the city, an evocative sensorama of the old Lower East Side. Alternatively, a crosstown bus, #M13, will take you back west on 11th Street toward the subway.

6

Irish History in Lower Manhattan

Subway: IND A, C, IRT Broadway–Seventh Avenue Local (train 1) or
Express (trains 2, 3) to Chambers Street.

The Irish were the first immigrant group I began to study when I came back
to this country. My father's family, Anglo-Catholics whom I'd never met,
had come from County Sligo, a source of shame and dismay to my Yankee
grandparents, who raised me. Naturally, I wanted to learn more.

Start at **St. Peter's Church** ❶ *at the southeast corner of Barclay and
Church streets. If it's a good day, I suggest you sit on the church steps to
read the following introduction.*

From the seventeenth century on, Irish men and women from all backgrounds drifted to this country and city. The following account includes all
categories of emigrants here, though as prejudice grew, some later called
themselves other nationalities. The roster is a litany, more a threnody, of
Ireland's loss, America's gain.

Ulster Presbyterians were the first to come in great number, when the
British government let the Anglo-Irish foreclose on their farms. The industrial revolution hastened the outflow, causing blacksmiths, carpenters, tailors, and weavers to sail as indentured servants. Some came on independent contracts with employers here; others were imported by New York
businessmen for auction at the Wall Street market.

Religious constraints as well as economic needs drove much of the
Presbyterian emigration. The sect had more autonomy than Catholics, but
Anglican Ireland repressed it nonetheless. The second-class treatment con-

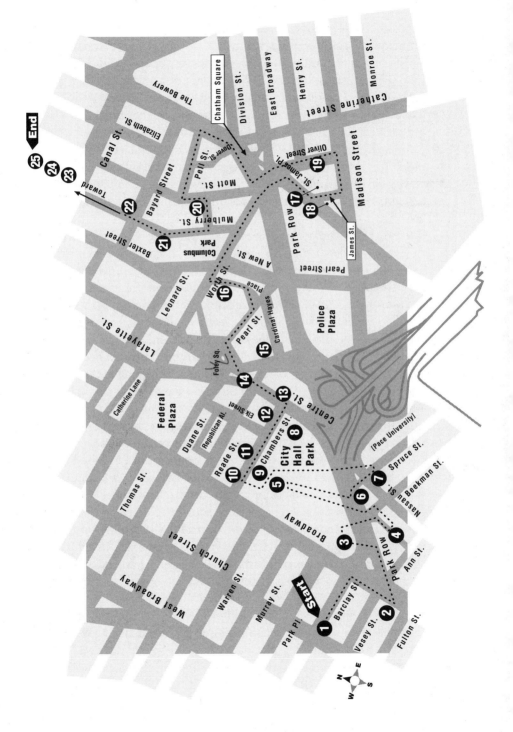

155

tinued before the Revolution in New York, where Anglicans from Trinity Church marginalized the new Scotch Irish Presbyterian Church (founded in 1716) as far as it could. The two factions built up opposing parties: Trinity-Tories, Presbyterians-Whigs. The two also formed separate cultural institutions: Trinity, Columbia University; Presbyterians, the New York Society Library and eventually New York University. (Trinity Church is a site featured in Walk 1.)

Surprisingly (at first glance), another early group to emigrate here were the Anglo-Irish, who served Britain as its surrogate ruling class in Ireland. Despite the privileges the British government granted the ascendancy Irish, it withheld true political rights. This policy drove their proxies abroad or to rebellion.

Quakers were a third group to leave. They sailed seeking trade and because they, too, suffered religious intolerance at home. New York's Irish Quakers included Thomas Eddy, who founded the Free School Society, and merchant shipper Robert Murray. Murray, whose family name is memorialized in Murray Hill and in downtown's Murray Street, was one of the New York Quakers who controlled the Cork–New York import-export trade. By the time of the Revolution the business was so brisk, one of every ten boats entering New York Harbor was Irish, mostly carrying cargoes of beef, butter, and potatoes as well as wool and linens. Immigrants rode in the crawl space between decks. It was this export trade and the British policy behind it that reduced the Irish peasantry to near single-crop subsistence.

A fourth group to emigrate were descendants of Anglo-Catholics who'd fled Cromwell's Ireland to France in the seventeenth century. These Wild Geese—so-called because of their migration—arrived in New York with General Lafayette to join the Revolution. One of them, William Constable, Lafayette's chief aide-de-camp, founded and led New York's first St. Patrick's Society in 1784.

Methodists descended from Palatine Germans who'd tried for three generations to make a go of life in Ireland were yet another group to leave. In 1776 they organized a church down on John Street, a few blocks below here. (You may wish to make a side tour to this church, which was rebuilt in 1841 but still holds woodwork by its founder, Philip Embury.)

Surprisingly, until you know that before the Revolution the same bigoted legislation oppressing Catholics in all British dependencies governed here, the one Irish community that didn't come in any number was Ireland's Catholics, who formed 75 percent of the homeland population. They had no civil rights and scant religious freedom in Ireland, but America before independence was no haven. Like most other American colonies, New York banned the religion. In fact, for many years taking Anglican communion was the cardinal desideratum of naturalization—an under-researched subject—particularly given that if people did *not* undergo this rite, they were technically unable to own property. (Did Jews, for instance, take communion? Was the law always honored in the breach?) Incidentally, speaking of church-state ties, when I was having immigration troubles in the mid-1970s, having lost my citizenship, I was asked by some in Congress to produce a letter from my minister testifying on my behalf. It was *very* clear they did not mean a Buddhist priest.

Of those few Catholics who did come to New York, many joined the Episcopal church; Trinity's cemetery holds numerous pre-Revolutionary graves bearing Gaelic names—presumably of Catholic origin. After the Revolution, life got better for most Catholics—to a degree—as the federal government repealed the ban on priests and legalized the sect.

Two foreign legations, the Spanish and the French, gave money toward buying this site from Trinity and building St. Peter's, the town's first Catholic church. Irish immigrant Cornelius Heeny, rich from his partnership in furs with John Jacob Astor, was another donor. (The two men had started as beaters, combing through pelts, picking out ticks and fleas.) Unlike his associate, who chose speculation over soul-salvation, Heeny devoted his life to good causes. The benefactor is up for sainthood now and would be Brooklyn's first. The move to canonize Heeny, a New Yorker unknown to most city residents today, reminds us of the varying foundation myths different groups construct to frame the story of their locality and ethnic heritage.

For protective coloring, architects designed the first St. Peter's in assimilated Federal style. Despite the repeal of laws against Catholicism, growing conservatism following the Revolution, and a hardening mood against outsiders begged caution. (In 1806, the same year the law requiring new American citizens to renounce foreign ecclesiastical princes, that is, the pope, was abolished, anti-Catholic riots shook parts of the city.) In any case, there was no traditional architecture to draw from. For centuries Britain had outlawed church building in Ireland.

☞ This somber Greek Revival building constructed between 1836 and 1840 is the second St. Peter's. It resembles other buildings of the period—among them the Merchants Exchange and Federal Hall on Wall Street. The bankerish prosperity of this church was misleading—calculatedly so. As much as earlier Catholics had tried to look "American," now they were trying to look prosperous, as if they'd "arrived." The two soon were to become conflated.

While a few individual Catholics were doing well when St. Peter's went up (such as its architect, John Haggerty), overall, most were not. By the time this church opened, its parishioners had run up a debt of $135,000, on which they paid 7 percent interest—a fortune at the time. Showing how grave the situation was, the parish even sent a fund-raising priest to *Ireland,* although the 1840s potato famine was already under way.

The church *had* to sell. The (secret) buyer was Bishop John Hughes himself, the head of New York's Catholic church, who wouldn't be shamed by having the building leave diocesan hands. In 1841 Hughes began an umbrella association to cushion the financial burden of all city parishes. Within fifteen years he succeeded not only in paying off debts but also in opening dozens of charities and schools and tripling the town's Catholic churches.

☞ Note the plaques on the church's exterior front wall. The hagiography is another example of foundation myths—or selective memory—at work. The majority of markers here honor Irish New Yorkers. One tablet honors the Irish-staffed Sisters of Charity, who worked out of this church, teaching in the city's parochial schools and tending the sick in cholera epidemics. Another honors the seventeenth-century governor Thomas Dongan.

After the Revolution the French and Spanish legations had helped to found St. Peter's, and a Cuban, Father Varela, had nursed the church in the 1820s; by Hughes' day, however, the Irish had full control, not only of St. Peter's but of the city's Catholic hierarchy as well. Even French and Spanish Catholics, let alone the more recently arrived Germans, were forced to split off from the "mainstream" church to found their own parishes. Aside from the doughty Irish-born Hughes, another reason for Irish dominance was their English language. British rule in Ireland had eroded Gaelic. Many immigrants arrived here knowing only their conqueror's tongue.

***W**alk east on Barclay to Broadway, turn south (right) to* **St. Paul's Chapel** ❷ *on Broadway and Fulton Street.*

☞ Note the **granite obelisk** in the south corner of the cemetery (near Fulton Street) carved with an entwined Celtic harp and Old Glory.

The martyr Robert Emmet may be one of Ireland's chief heroes, but his elder brother, memorialized here, is mine. After the British executed Robert in 1803 when they quelled the second wave of the United Irish rebellion, begun a few years earlier, Thomas Addis Emmet endured and continued to work for Ireland and its diaspora. ("Oh, Hope," said an Emmet descendent, unimpressed by my argument that the Greek word *martyr* means to bear witness, not to die, and that it is harder to live for a cause than to perish for it, "imagine being drawn and quartered.")

Following the failure of the latest uprising, the senior Emmet hurried to Paris to enlist French aid. Failing, he left for New York, helped by two second-generation Irish Americans he'd met in Paris—DeWitt Clinton and Robert Fulton. (The latter had been lobbying the French government to try out his newly invented torpedo in the cause of Irish freedom.) Both men were to remain Emmet's lifelong friends: when Clinton became governor, he made Emmet—a lawyer—the state's attorney general. The newcomer was lucky for the patronage. Before the Revolution, Americans hadn't scorned the Irish, just Catholicism. Now, ethnic as well as religious preju-dice combined in a vicious anti-immigrant sensibility. Emmet himself was able to become a citizen only as Clinton had helped reverse a law—aimed at Irish and French "radicals"—that had raised the naturalization waiting period from five years to twenty-one. It remains at five today.

In 1817 Emmet and Dr. William MacNevin, a Catholic United Irish-man (also memorialized in St. Paul's churchyard), started an immigrant aid society with Emmet its first president, MacNevin succeeding him. Among other accomplishments, the two friends (and in-laws) set up a free em-ployment bureau and arranged to buy Illinois farmland for Irish to settle.

The time when the two men arrived in the city was the height of non-sectarian Irish solidarity at home and in America. Emmet and his comrades in arms, Wolfe Tone and William Sampson, were Protestants of English de-scent. Nonetheless, they and other Protestant Irish joined their Catholic contemporaries in fighting British rule. In New York Emmet and his law firm were known for pro-bono work defending Catholics. When he died—in court, pleading a poor Catholic's innocence—the city closed its offices to honor him; ten thousand mourners followed his cortege.

W*alk up Broadway to the north side of the graveyard. The* **obelisk to Dr. MacNevin** *inscribed in Gaelic and English is a look-alike of Emmet's and stands near the railing in corresponding place of honor.*

The 1865 monument commemorates the activist surgeon who founded the College of Physicians and Surgeons and headed the city's cholera board in 1832, a dreadful epidemic year. (The main victims, Irish

poor.) As political funerals and memorials often do, MacNevin's honoring
here served as a nationalist rallying point—at least, a secret one. Fund-rais-
ing for this obelisk was part of a laundering operation run by the Fenian
Society to gather money for guns. At the time they were collecting for the
monument, the group planned to invade Canada and ransom the captive
country back to Britain in return for a free Ireland.

Not all American Irish supported the group or the scheme devised at
the Fenian's Union Square headquarters. The Roman Catholic church hierarchy, for one, opposed the movement. Despite the clerics' disapproval,
the U.S. government, including Secretary of State William Henry Seward,
and probably President Lincoln himself, backed the Fenians with money
and sponsorship in return for Irish enlistment in the Union Army. At least
they did until after the failure of the operettic war to capture Canada. At
that point the government promptly double-crossed the plotters and arrested the leaders when they returned to American soil.

*C*ross over to the southern end of **City Hall Park.**

☞ The city built the **fountain ❸** at the park's southern apex to celebrate
the arrival of the town's first decent water supply in 1842.

William MacNevin had been the project's main lobbyist, since the
city's sanitary horrors had aggravated, if not caused, recurrent epidemics.
Money, not compassion, eventually won. The 1835 blaze that destroyed
lower Manhattan and bankrupted fire insurance companies assured the
scheme. As it had done earlier when it sponsored "Clinton's ditch" (the Erie
Canal), the city recruited some of the (Croton) aqueduct's construction
crew directly in Ireland. Other navvies came through St. Peter's Church,
which ran a labor exchange specializing in *sober* workmen. (The aqueduct,
once the scene of bloody riots as laborers suffered appalling treatment, offers a fine level walk from Tarrytown down to the city.)

*C*ross east from the park to Park Row and peer down **Theater Alley, ❹**
which runs just behind the row between Beekman and Ann streets. This
was a serviceway running at the back of New York's premier theater, "The
Park."

While most male Irish immigrants worked in construction, most
women labored in the garment business or as domestics. Many, however,
became prostitutes. By the 1850s more than a third of New York's whores
were Irish—a figure consonant with mass migration and poverty. (About

the same ratio of inmates in the almshouse behind City Hall were also Irish, despite church efforts to care for its own poor.)

New York's theaters were major centers of commercial sex, their third tiers virtually given over to assignations, and whole bordellos emptying out for performances. This back alley served the women who arrived through the Park's back door—a coy bow to propriety. Later, when the city cracked down on prostitution in the theaters and middle-class women started to attend in greater numbers, the third tier became the "family circle."

***C**ross back into the park for a look around the 1811 **City Hall**.* ⑤

Despite the fact most earlier Ulster Americans had come from modest backgrounds in Ireland, wealthier only by degree than later Catholic arrivals, by the 1840s they'd begun to call themselves "Scotch-Irish" to avoid the stigma of newcomers fleeing famine. As New York's Irish immigration continued to grow, the former group opted to become pure Scots, or Scotch. Since the co-architect of this elegant French Georgian building, John McComb, Jr., was descended from Ulster parentage, his background also got recast through the familiar route, first Scotch-Irish, then Scotch neat.

The Saint Patrick's Friendly Society founded by Ulstermen after the Revolution had never been democratic. At this juncture it became even more of a withdrawn, patrician club, and many wanted to close it down all together. Members of the Murray family were the single clubmen to contribute to immigrant charities in New York. Others sent only sparse relief to Ireland itself.

In colonial days Ulster immigrants and their descendants were proud to be Irish. As immigration grew, men like John McComb, Jr., co-architect of City Hall, called themselves Scots-Irish, later, Scotch neat.

***C**ross the road east of the park once more and stroll along Park Row, the city's journalistic hub from the 1830s to 1900. (Sorry for the criss-crossing, but it serves the chronology.) Pass the 1889* **New York Times Building** ⑥ *on the north corner of Park Row and Spruce Street, then walk east for one block to Nassau Street.*

☞ The early skyscraper on the corner of Spruce and Nassau is the **American Tract Society Building,** ❼ designed in 1896 by R. H. Robertson. The building's size, its up-to-the-minute Romanesque style, and its prime location in the city's newspaper center tell us it was important in its day.

Just what *was* the Tract Society? As immigration grew, views on charity hardened until moral reform was in, welfare out. Gospel distribution was seen as the most efficacious means of preventing pauperism. Middle-class Protestants frightened by industrialization, rapid urbanization, and, most of all, the flood of arriving strangers, founded the New York City Tract Society, an auxiliary of the American Tract Society, in the late eighteen twenties. It was only one of many voluntary associations formed at the time to "stabilize" the city.

Tracts were the mass media of their day. From its onset through the 1860s the Tract Society raised money to print millions of pamphlets, which it gave out free to assimilate newcomers. (Catechism, later a Protestant cause for reproof to Catholics because of its absolutism, was largely a new world institution, deployed to withstand Tract Society missionizing. In Catholic Europe it had never been particularly important.) After the 1860s, the society grew somewhat more secular and engaged in charity work and social reform. Nonetheless, its moralizing persisted.

Retrace your steps (once again) back into City Hall Park to the **Horace Greeley Statue** ❽ on the east side of City Hall.

One of the saddest moments to do with Irish history and the park happened in the summer of 1863, when draft riots rent the city. Originally the Irish had been quick to join the war, even signing on in Ireland itself, where the Union government (and the Confederates) opened recruiting stations. In this country army centers by the docks inducted immigrants just off of boats. Shamrock-flagged Hibernians formed several brigades, most notably the Sixty-ninth—the Fighting Irish. In the war's early years, troops camped here at City Hall Park before leaving for the front.

As might be guessed, New York's upper echelon was not so keen to sign up, and once it became plain it was going to be "a rich man's war and a poor man's fight," the Irish lost their taste for volunteering.

In July of 1863 Lincoln introduced the draft. Overwhelmingly, the draftees were poor and immigrant. Moreover, should a rich man happen to get called, he could buy his way out for $300. The Irish exploded. Rioters ransacked arsenals, recruiting depots, and transport and communication lines. They also lynched blacks. As well as deeming abolition the root of the Union's problems and fearing blacks as economic competitors, some (though not all) Irish also held toxic racial prejudice.

From early on crowds filtered into City Hall Park to demonstrate against the pro-war journals among the newspapers here. One target was the *Times,* then in an older building on its present site.

The nearby *Tribune* (now gone) offered an even bigger lure, as the crowd considered the paper's editor, Horace Greeley, the leading journalist promoting slavery's end. Greeley—himself of Irish descent—was an ill-chosen enemy. Long active in Irish welfare, he'd given to relief both at home and abroad. He'd also aided emigration schemes ("Go West, young man"), as he felt the Irish poor and others had more hope on farms and suburbs. In contrast to many of his peers who essentially wanted the underclass out of the city at any cost, Greeley genuinely seems to have had immigrant well-being at heart.

True to form, the editor kept his compassion even mid-riot and ordered the *Tribune* to remain pacifist. In contrast with the *Times,* which at the first sign of trouble hooked up a boiler contraption to shower intruders with scalding steam and armed itself with cannon and Gatling guns, the *Trib* did no more than barricade its doors with bales of watered paper. Matters soon left Greeley's hands. By the next day, federal government troops manning howitzers had taken up positions in all buildings ringing City Hall Park.

After a week, the riots stammered to a halt. Aside from the firepower brought in—including Navy gunboats circling the harbor—one factor bringing an end was Tammany's conciliatory pledge to pay the $300 dollar exemption bonds for all draftees. Bishop Hughes also intervened, though lukewarmly and latterly. His actual role is still obscure, though most of the city's Catholic churches were cowardly; quick, unbidden, to serve authority by offering rolls of parishioners' names and addresses to the draft board.

The embroilment cost the city millions of dollars worth of property and took 105 lives. (At the time, most observers ventured figures ten times greater.) No New York riot has approached it again for violence and destruction. From this time on, the Protestant elite, who'd more or less ceded local governance to an increasingly Irish-based Tammany, pledged themselves to recapture the city from the "brutish Hibernian law of unrule."

W*alk north of City Hall to the* **Criminal Courthouse,** ❾ *finished in 1872. It's better known as the Tweed Courthouse because it went up under the* *aegis of William Tweed, Tammany's "boss" from the late 1860s to the year this building opened.*

As it happened, Tweed himself was of middle-class Scottish (from Scotland) extraction but had risen to power through an Irish political base, drawn mainly from city fire companies. (He's often mislabled as Irish for the same reasons McComb, Jr., is claimed as a Scot.) Even though Tammany had started as an anti-immigrant organization, by the 1860s the Irish voting block had become so important to its success that pliant judges were accused of naturalizing tens of thousands of new arrivals on the eve of an election. In 1864 just short of a hundred thousand immigrants were given papers.

This building cost the public $12 million and is considered a monument to Tammany corruption. Probably $11 million of the construction budget was unnecessary. One infamous bill for a minor plastering job came to $46,000. Exposure of the scandal was the spark leading to Tweed's downfall.

☞ In recent decades this courthouse has been in sorry shape, but in 1990 the city hired contractors to repair and clean it. (No costs published.) On weekdays you can look inside the ground floor and sense the sallow ornate atmosphere that reeks deals and "squatulation"—a Tammany term for dishonest, as opposed to "honest," graft.

☞ Another famous Tammany project is visible from City Hall. Irish contractor-engineer William Kingsland planned the **Brooklyn Bridge.** Irish navvies under John Augustus Roebling constructed it.

*W**alk north of the Tweed courthouse to Chambers Street and cross the road, noting the* **Marble Department Store, ⑩** *built in stages from 1846 on by Ulsterman Alexander Turney Stewart.*

More than two thousand people worked for Stewart's enterprise. In the two floors beneath the lower cornice, Irish seamstresses stitched the bulk of the dresses sold here. Immigrants in the Five Points area to the north sewed the remainder in their homes. The emporium, however, was destined to stay open just fifteen years. When the wealthy of this neighborhood moved uptown (in great part to flee the growing Irish presence), Stewart turned this venture into a wholesale outlet and warehouse for his new operation at 10th Street and Broadway.

HARPER'S WEEKLY

A JOURNAL OF CIVILIZATION

VOL. XV.—No. 761.]   NEW YORK, SATURDAY, JULY 29, 1871.   [WITH A SUPPLEMENT. PRICE TEN CENTS.

Entered according to Act of Congress, in the Year 1871, by Harper & Brothers, in the Office of the Librarian of Congress, at Washington.

TRUCKLING TO THE MOB.

THE MAYOR TO THE ORANGEMEN.

BRAVO! BRAVO!—NEW YORK, JULY 12, 1871.

Growing Irish political influence was too much for some. After the downfall of the Tweed ring in 1871, Protestant reform groups (shown here as the whip-lashing lady) took back power in the city government.

*W*alk east along Chambers past the empty building once the **Emigrant Industrial Savings Bank,** ⓫ *an offshoot of the immigrant aid society begun by Emmet and MacNevin in 1817, resurrected in the 1840s by Robert Hogan, a New York doctor.*

☞ This grand Beaux Arts structure opened in 1908 with earnings the bank had accrued from deposits over the decades since its founding.

New immigrants used the Emigrant to funnel money for relief back to Ireland and to bring family members over here. Despite the perception of many native Protestants that the Irish were a permanent underclass, in fact Irish across America managed to remit over $65 million between 1848 and 1865. The figure is startling, particularly as most depositors were working people, Stewart's seamstresses among them.

*K*eep east along Chambers Street past the grand **Hall of Records** ⓬ *(1899–1911) and turn left on Centre Street across from the* **Municipal Building,** ⓭ *the Beaux Arts city government annex built in 1914.*

The office's northern end rests on pylons sunk more than a hundred feet deep in the old Collect Pond, a filled lake that once stood roughly between White, Bayard, Elm, Canal and Pearl Streets—a two-mile circumference. Sluggish outlets ran to both rivers along latter-day Canal, James, and Oliver streets.

Because of this neighborhood's high water level, local courthouses hold heavy duty pumps in their basements. When workmen drill to repair pipes, they often tap into springs from the buried pond, which served the colonial city as its reservoir. Maps show that part of the lake still stood undrained after City Hall opened in 1811, even though the government had planned to empty it ever since the end of the Revolution, as the potteries, breweries, tanneries rimming the pond had long since made the water poisonous. When the city finally did get around to sluicing off the dregs, the land remained bog. New buildings going up on the pulpy landfill buckled and cracked. Freed blacks and impoverished Irish immigrants inherited. (It's tempting to think the word *slum* grew out of the topographical "slump.")

*Y*ou can feel the descent as you continue north on Centre Street into the square, a solemn hollow of courthouses built on the fill. ⓮

The city cut Centre Street through in the late 1820s as partial slum clearance. The southern link, which didn't run down to Chambers as it does today, was then Collect Street, the northern section, Rhynders (a co-incidental aural twin of "Rynders," the legendary gangster chief who ruled Five Points a few years later). In the end, the city extended the road through the middle of the old pond-slum southward and rechristened the whole stretch Centre Street.

*C*ontinue walking north on Centre across Reade. On your right you will pass **St. Andrew's Church ⓑ** *(tucked down a bit on a plaza bearing its name.)*

The 1950s brick building descends from an 1842 Roman Catholic parish on this site, Carroll Hall, that used to host predawn masses for Catholic printers in nearby presses.

One of the congregants at the old church was Moses Humphrey, an Irish compositor and part-time fire laddy whose persona was drawn on by several playwrights for "Big Mose," a fictional hero embodying the city's new working-class culture. Four or five plays celebrated this urban Paul Bunyan who could throw a street lamp as if it were an Indian club and swim round Manhattan Island as if he'd just stepped into a bath. These plays codified an ethos that has represented New York down to our own day. Even the so-called Brooklyn accent is, in fact, a derivative of the accent established in the various Bowery theatres at the time Big Mose held center billing.

*T*urn east (right) from Foley Square on Pearl Street (just south of the New York County Courthouse) and walk north up Cardinal Hayes Place to **Five Points. ⓖ**

Until recently there was still a pivot of roads here, whose tangled intersections gave the neighborhood its name. Today, a thirty-story federal office building occupies the site. While digging the building's foundation in 1991, construction workers turned up spectacular remains of early industries and residences. Instead of preserving the find as the city's omphalos, builders paved it over, in contrast to the nearby Negro Burial Ground unearthed at the same time during the excavation for a federal courthouse.

Unlike African Americans (who had the inherent sanctity of cemeteries on their side), the Irish were unable to organize an effective protest group or did not care to, as most live outside the city and, furthermore, are generally ashamed of Five Points history. (This is my impression drawn from watching suburban Irish Americans respond to a first-rate slide narration of this neighborhood made by the American Social History Project.)

Unlike black New Yorkers, the Irish had come as "free" immigrants, but they were equally slaves to poverty and, in fact, lived intermingled with

African Americans here in Five Points. There was also a considerable degree of interracial marriage, a countertruth to the race-hate the Irish showed during the draft riots.

Most families lived pressed into Federal houses intended for single families, occasionally as many as 120 men, women, and children to a building. Others huddled in old industrial piles, including a former brewery at the northeast corner of today's county courthouse. The yawing structure, converted to barracks housing, held a thousand free blacks and Irish in conditions so squalid it became an inverse source of pride to New Yorkers in the 1840s and 1850s, a boast to out-of-towners. (New Yorkers still take satisfaction in how awful things are. When CNN asked me to compose an "ideal" city tour for President Gorbachev during his last trip to America while still in office, every friend I consulted said he ought to see rush hour in the subway, polluted this and that, and so on. Not one person suggested anything positive.)

Up until the 1840s, city guidebooks had boasted innocently about New York's institutions. Now writers became obsessed by the divisions of the town—both in terms of space and class. From this period, books on the city grew increasingly melodramatic, Manichean. The middle-class authors' obsession with dichotomies sprang in part from their own vulnerability to the economic and psychic flux besetting the era, their longing for old certainties. Titles played off sunlight and shadow, daylight and dark, high ground and low. Five Points was the cynosure of submergence, the most intoxicatingly rank of all. "Journalistic" accounts went mad with underground imagery, conflating living in low ground and basements with debased morality, inferior norms.

Some truth glinted through the accounts of subterranean life in Five Points. Many of the city's poor (more than 29,000 in one survey) slept in windowless cellars at the time; this neighborhood was no different. The pond ooze here, however, made underground life harder to bear. At night before bedding down, residents ran ropes across the cellar floors to keep their heads above water.

As the city grew more divided, brave souls in missions such as the Tract Society felt obliged to cross lines—not just to enter neighborhoods but to penetrate dwellings themselves. Since the 1830s, middle-class women had been visiting homes down here to preach the gospel and mainstream American values. (The word *household* will not do. It was *homes* the visiting ladies were after.) As the home came to be more and more sanctified, increasingly seen as the matrix of morality, the women's' ardor for intrusion grew.

By the 1840s some reformist incursions with prurient undertones had become frankly voyeuristic excursions, particularly as outsiders other than the mission ladies came to see life here for themselves. Visitors, primed to believe the worst, were brought down to Five Points to see the low "viciousness." Charles Dickens gratified his hosts by pronouncing the slum far worse than any in London. His book, *American Notes* awarded five stars to Five Points, definitely worth a detour, as "all that is loathsome, drooping and decayed is here." (Local denizens returned the compliment by incorporating the writer into their cosmology. A "dive" the writer had visited later called itself "Dickens' Place.")

> Poor Irish often occupied cellars and swamp. Critics conflated the sunken terrain where immigrants lived with their (supposed) low morality, debased customs.

Male authors, whose disposition to see life here melodramatically was greater than the ladies whose judgments had been somewhat tempered by familiarity, delineated the small neighborhood into a lapidary array of villainy. Each cranny was picturesquely designated. Even the old brewery itself (rumored site of "horrid" miscegenation and shallow graves holding the victims of "nightly" murders) was divided into captioned terrains. One large room was the "Den of Thieves," another chamber, "Murderer's Alley."

NEW YORK CITY. — "DOING THE SLUMS" — A SCENE IN THE FIVE POINTS.
FROM A SKETCH BY A STAFF ARTIST. — SEE PAGE 247.

Uptowners had been coming to Five Points since the 1830s, first as charity workers, later as tourists of the exotic and dangerous.

So much interest centered on this symbolic (and real) site of decay that a group of Protestant women reformers adopted the theatrical middle-class mode of seeing Five Points and aided their charity by conducting guided tours through the old brewery before tearing it down to build a mission. The women's replacement of the wretched brewery with an evangelist institution, incidentally, is an early example of occasional female power in remodeling the city's built environs. Although it's easy to make fun of the lurid leanings and soi-disant benevolence of the propertied classes at this period, even to scorn their sense of entitlement in telling others how to live, something even worse has happened in our day, when, with rare exception, the middle class lacks almost all concern for the poor save constant fear. The idea of entering most poor city neighborhoods, let alone poor households, would never dawn on us, but not because we have become any less patronizing.

☞ If you look north, you can see the Art Deco stepped-back version of the Tombs Prison still on its original Centre Street site. Like its predecessor, erected in 1837, it stands on solid land that had been an island in the Collect.

Despite Five Point's rot and crime, which had outraged many New Yorkers almost since the land had been filled and occupied, despite the endless demands of investigative committees for a jail and police station down here, reform was slow. Interested parties blocked change. At Common Council meetings the neighborhood's liquor retailers argued that profits from the existing setup raised property values all around. It was not just themselves and the gentry families and Trinity Church (owners of long-term leases here) who stood to gain from the status quo, they argued, but the City Corporation itself, as it reaped tax money from the local "sin" trade. This debate went on for decades until the municipality eventually razed much of the slum and carved out Foley Square near the turn of the century. Needless to say, the ousted slum dwellers were left to fend for themselves.

Even now, scholars are not sure how justified the Points' reputation for violence and dissipation was. One factor arguing against the most lurid accounts is that although unemployment was a constant problem, many of the area's residents, men, women, and children, worked in the garment business and presumably couldn't have been as depraved as fancied. (The rector of the Five Points Mission, whose salary was paid for by uptowners, quit his assignment to open an industrial school, saying the locals needed work, not uplift.)

Five Points' critics were right about one thing. Life here *was* raucous and public if not particularly vicious. Street drinking, fighting, carousing, flirting, all veered wildly from the genteel Protestant ideal of domestic privacy. In hot weather many families never went inside at all, even to sleep. Death caused by falling from rooftops was frequent enough that police complained that they lost too many duty hours writing up the incidents.

Parts of life here were fun, or could be; New York's working class came from all over the city to visit Five Points' dance halls, saloons, beer gardens, and theaters. Even if guidebooks generally ascribed wickedness to these, probably most were relatively innocent, forums for the new urban leisure culture being shaped by youth here. Among others who enjoyed outings to Five Points were the young women working as maids in Protestant households. When they headed out the door on their days off, draped in high fashion, employers were infuriated but had no choice but to let them go. Not everyone was so welcome—when poaching clerks or gentlemen occasionally crossed terrain and entered the neighborhood looking for sex, Five Points youth commonly banded together to beat them up, warn them off.

Immigrants and uptowners viewed public space in completely different ways. For example, Irish households depended on pigs for profit and food, and let them roam the streets. The establishment found the straying animals hazardous pollutants and ordered round-ups.

***W**alk east on Worth Street; cross Park Row to St. James Place, then turn right and walk one block south to **St. James Church** ⑰ on James Street. (The Place is also called Ancient Order of the Hibernians Place, after the benevolent society founded at the church.)*

☞ By the time St. James opened in 1836, the area was long industrialized: remains of one of the neighborhood's old breweries are embedded in its foundations. Like St. Peter's Church on Barclay Street, this church was designed in upmarket Greek Revival style. (Or at least its brownstone front was expensive—notice the cost-cutting fieldstone side walls.) The architect may even have been the sought-after Minard Lafever, who did the sailors' asylum at Snug Harbor (see Walk 2). The results of the outlay were predictable. When the church opened, its debt was so big it couldn't afford to pay interest. St. James has just undergone major reconstruction as the ceiling of the nave threatened to collapse. Once again the church is in debt and paying interest on loans for repairs. If you can, please help!

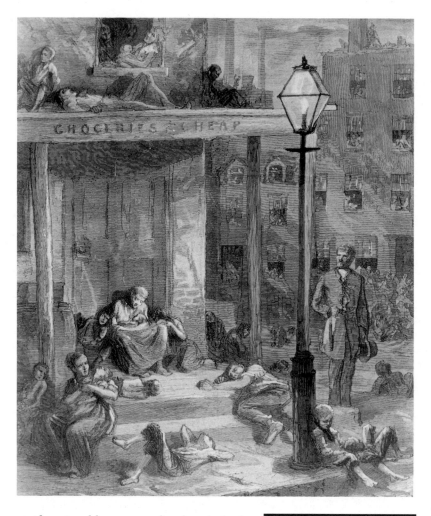

GROCERIES & HEAP

☞ If you're able to enter the church, look up at the newly refurbished ceiling with the four-leafed shamrock pattern. More shamrocks lattice the altar where the Fighting Sixty-ninth brought their colors to be

Outdoor life in Five Points shocked middle-class Protestants.

blessed before joining action in the Civil War. The church windows also preserve Irish priorities. Two "national" saints, Saint Brigid and Saint Patrick, hold place of honor outranking the apostles.

For decades St. James was the font of local social work. Priests from St. James cared for cholera patients stranded in the port on quarantined Irish boats. (Several priests died, having caught the devastating disease from their patients.) They were also in the forefront of the Catholic temperance movement, a bid to end alcohol abuse without the imperious, reproving attitude some Protestant reformers showed.

When this church opened, nativism was on an upswing in the city. Protestants opened a mission in a building across James Street, where they bull-horned propaganda and stashed their windows with baubles for local children.

Since the main conflict between denominations was the school question, inevitably St. James got dragged in. The Free School Society in New York City, dating back to 1806, used a bigoted curriculum denigrating Catholic beliefs. (Some Protestants at the time called the Pope the "Whore of Babylon.") Despite the fact that St. Peter's had opened a school in 1800 and there were several others, most Catholic children attended the Free Schools, as alternatives were few after the state ended its aid to church schools in 1824. Most of the decisions leading to the citywide parochial school system were worked out here and at Carroll Hall.

Because of pressure from Catholics, New York's legislature passed a bill in 1842 diluting the control (and Protestantism) of the Public School Society, the successor and clone of the old Free School Society. At this point, government schools became ward schools and grew somewhat more sensitive to local beliefs and customs, but Bishop John Hughes pressed ahead with his plan for a separate system in any case.

☞ The Gothic **red brick schoolhouse** ⓲ (1856) on the corner across from the church is one of the city's first parochial institutions.

The Sisters of Charity instructed the girls here, the Christian Brothers from Ireland taught the boys. As the number of immigrant children grew, some went to Catholic schools, others to those run by the ward. (The latter were more sympathetic by now, not just on account of the recent reforms but because second-generation Irish women staffed many classrooms.) Ironically, today, most children who attend parochial schools are not Catholic but Protestants of color. As Catholic money has left for the suburbs, the system is hurting, and the city government worries that this useful adjunct to public schooling may falter if not fold. The diocese is closing many schools.

*W*alk on James Street toward Madison.

☞ The ground floor corner of the old tenement on the corner of James and Madison, now holding a bodega, once housed an Irish saloon and grocery store.

Most likely its proprietor was also creditor to the people who lived in the building. If good-hearted, he would have provided for his customers during lean periods; if mean-spirited, he would have landed them in stranglehold debt. Often, the store owner functioned as a local political power as well: Tammany used these neighborhood businesses to carry out its agenda, control its turf.

☞ Enter the store (it would be polite to buy something) and try to experience the space as the male preserve, the political and social club, it once was. (And still may be, as bodegas themselves are highly politicized institutions.) Notice how sharp the corners actually are—this is the ne plus ultra of corner stores.

*T*urn left along Madison Street and walk to the building at mid-block, **47 Madison.**

☞ The two-story Federal dwelling, which belongs to St. James, is a good example of the worker housing built after the Collect fill, the same sort that was later subdivided to hold scores of tenants.

*C*ontinue to the corner at Oliver Street.

☞ If you look one block farther up Madison to Catherine Street, you can just barely make out an old church and rectory on the corner founded in 1853. The building now holds a Chinese Methodist Church, but up to 1987 it had a sign reading "old Five Points Mission." Presumably, this was a survival of one of the Protestant missions founded in this neighborhood long ago. Could it have been related to *the* Five Points Mission?

*T*urn west (left) along Oliver Street and walk along a row of **modest brick houses ⓳** belonging to St. James.

☞ Note the plaque on one of them announcing that Al Smith, social reformer, New York governor, and 1928 Democratic presidential candidate, lived here as an adult.

Smith had grown up farther down near the seaport, but he'd served as altar boy at St. James and studied at the church school. Smith's widowed mother had managed to pay the fees for him and his brothers and sisters by doing umbrella piecework at home and later running a grocery. His father, a cart driver, had died young. On average, teamsters, virtually all of them Irish, died within ten years of taking on their job—cart horses expired after four. Many Irish families were headed by widows, and New

York's Irish theater often drew on stock figures of powerful Irish mothers, a pre-quel to stereotypical Jewish mothers, who were strong for many of the same reasons.

*K*eep walking west on Oliver Street until you come to Chatham Square. Then zig-zag your way northwest across the square to the Bowery, the grand old thoroughfare once sharing honors with Five Points as matrix of New York's new working-class culture. Walk north to Pell Street, then turn left (west) until you come to Mott Street. Turn left and walk south on Mott until you reach the **fieldstone church** ㉒ at the corner of Mosco. The street sign for Mosco has been missing for some years.)

☞ In the 1850s St. James' twin parish, the Church of the Transfiguration, bought this 1801 Georgian church from Yankee Protestants. Over the years the church served Irish, then Italian worshipers, and now a Chinese congregation. You can follow the progression on the donor plaques near the door. Today's student body at Transfiguration's school is mainly Buddhist.

*T*urn right on Mosco Street. The steep incline to Mulberry Street draws you back down into the sunken Collect Pond area. The **bend in the line of Mulberry** ㉑ (as well as Baxter and Mott) follows the old Collect shoreline.
 The name "Mulberry" came from a tree-planting effort begun after Independence to support a native silk industry. (Planting trees then was big, a way of showing patriotism and faith in the new Republic, rather like today in Israel.) By the 1840s the street had turned from silk to sow, according to economic indices. After Five Points was razed, this section of Mulberry Street, the famous "bend . . . stewing in its slime," had replaced it as *the* city emblem of immigrant congestion, malfeasance, even murder. (Any streets lacking line of sight are always more dangerous.) In the late 1880s reformers demanded change. A decade later, by which time Italians had long replaced the Irish, who'd moved north to Yorkville, the city cut Columbus Park out of the packed tenements. "Light has come in and made crime hideous," rejoiced Jacob Riis, whose pictures of the Bend's misery had done much to win the conversion. When engineers refurbished this roadbed after making the park, contemporary accounts reported they found three feet of compacted garbage. Over time, the debris on Mulberry Street had matted as hard as macadam.

☞ Speaking of macadam, you can notice some cobblestones on Mulberry Street that predate the Civil War. After the war the city rarely used them again for surfacing. Like the Paris Communards, draft rioters had thrown cobblestones, the weapon of the poor, Irish confetti.

*W*alk north along Mulberry Street.

The various immigrant groups who lived along Mulberry kept their county as well as country connections alive. Irish from Kerry lived on one part of the street, Irish from Sligo on another. Nowadays, the Italian and Chinese do the same.

*C*ontinue north to the second parking lot on your right along the Mulberry Bend.

☞ Look inside (on the right-hand side of the yard) at the **double tenement.** A rear dwelling lies shadowed behind the street-front building. Imagine the darkness when the adjoining tenements on the parking lot still stood.

Until the late 1880s, the shared yard between the two buildings would have been full of privies. Tenants would have had to carry water for bathing and cooking up the tenement stairs.

*K*eep north on Mulberry Street, passing on your right the 1890s school on the corner of Bayard Street, ㉒ its armory architecture showing the environment period planners thought suitable for immigrant children. Continue ahead through the remnants of Little Italy pastiched among the Chinese stores and restaurants. (At this point, your route is no longer shown on the map.) Turn left (west) on Grand Street and walk two blocks to Centre Street.

☞ Since the boom 1980s, the domed and pillared **police station** has housed expensive condos. It opened in 1909, an example of the Progressive movement's effort to create a reform environment by erecting imposing monuments.

The idea didn't work very well. The police force, for one, was rife with corruption at the time. A tunnel under Centre Street leads from the station house to a walnut-paneled tavern on Grand Street, now the Osteria Romana restaurant, once a haven for on-duty officers. Drink was the least of it.

Hibernians had served in New York's Finest in growing numbers ever since 1765, when a Constable O'Sullivan was killed on the job. When this station house opened, the police force was still predominantly Irish. Despite the loss of Irish American clout in city government, starting in the 1930s, with Mayor La Guardia's administration, many still work on the force today. Most, however, commute from Rockland County or Long Island, as working-class hopes dim in Manhattan and only the wealthy and poor remain in town. (The gentrification the condoed police building has brought to this working-class neighborhood illustrates the point.) To gain more representation in the service, black and Hispanic city residents are lobbying for city residency requirements.

*R*eturn to Mulberry Street and continue north to Prince Street.

In 1809 clergy laid the foundation stone for **Old St. Patrick's Cathedral** ㉓ on land St. Peter's had originally bought for a cemetery. The site was so far from town, wild foxes prowled the grounds. By then, New York's population of 90,000 included 13,000 Catholics. A second church was overdue.

*A*fter circling the property, absorbing the whole complex, walk east on Prince to the old cathedral's Mott Street front.

☞ Joseph Mangin, the co-architect of City Hall, designed the structure. It was his first effort at Gothic, one of the first times the style appeared in the city. His awkwardness shows in the ungainly result.

The interior, refurbished in Victorian pallor after a fire, is glum. The most interesting memento is the pastoral genealogy by the front door, a list of church priests and city prelates, including John McCloskey, the country's first cardinal, enthroned here in 1875. Mortuary vaults in the crypt are also fun to visit, though visits are hard to arrange. If you wish to try, you should call well ahead and make a contribution in thanks for the church's trouble. Telephone (212) 226–8075.

☞ More than anything else, it is the grounds of the old cathedral that tell a story. The salmon brick walls ribboning the compound once served as the church's first line of defense. Note their height.

During the 1830s and 1840s fathers and sons armed with shillelaghs and blunderbusses stood guard at night to ward off nativists, working-class Yankees who feared and loathed the Irish newcomers. City newspapers fanned the anti-foreign, anti-Catholic flame. Samuel Morse, civic leader, artist, and inventor, wrote a series of newspaper articles claiming that American Catholics were planning to snatch the Louisiana Purchase for the Hapsburgs.

The high walls around Old St. Patrick's Cathedral saved the church from Yankee nativist attacks in the 1830s and 1840s.

Morse used a pseudonym. Another journalist writing on the subject did not bother. Walt Whitman editorialized in the *Aurora* that he regretted that one effort to dynamite old Saint Pat's Cathedral resulted in nothing more than broken windows. He also regretted that "Dagger John" (Bishop Hughes) hadn't been blown up as well.

Next time you go by the "new" St. Patrick's Cathedral on Fifth Avenue, notice the stone carved Stars and Stripes near the left front door. It was put there to parade patriotism, to prove that Catholics were not just "Paddies of the Pope." During the decades this church was under attack, Protestant gangs climbed the spires of other Catholic churches, tore off crosses, and planted American flags. This fearful climate lasted until after the Civil War.

Today, the grounds are so peaceful it's hard to believe the earlier violence. Bird hush, bird song. Sparrows hop among mossy headstones (shown tilting even in Civil War–era prints.) Wood pigeons sob in the trees.

☞ As you leave the cathedral, make sure to look at the large brick **Federal building 24** on Prince and Mott graced with dormers and a delicate fanlight door. From 1817 a wood-frame orphanage stood on this site; in 1834 this grander version opened, run by the Sisters of Charity.

New York's Irish took their flags to be blessed at the cathedral before sailing to fight in the Civil War.

Given immigrant mortality rates, the orphanages were vital. From the middle of the last century the Children's Aid Society had been sending Catholic orphans out of the city to Protestant homes in the Middle West. If some of their effort might have been well intentioned, the results were often tragic.

☞ One need only glance north up Mott Street to see the kind of (literal) *effrontery* New York's Catholics had to endure even after the Civil War. Note the pretty **terra-cotta building** ㉕—a Calvert Vaux creation—directly across from the cathedral's front door. It once housed the ward industrial school opened by the (unofficially, but very, Protestant) Children's Aid Society in 1888. Though in theory, and possibly reality, the school was useful, placing it at the church's very gate was contemptuous spatial politics, a nervy cultural ploy.

Today the old orphanage houses a church school begun soon after the cathedral itself opened. Most of its current students are Chinese, the neighborhood's present-day majority population. A number of Italian children, whose grandparents succeeded the Irish, also attend, but now many commute down from the Bronx where the community has by and large relocated.

These waves of immigration are the city's continuity. For the past two decades, until the recent recession slowed the flow, tens of thousands of Irish emigrants have once again poured into the city, mainly to Queens. People in the west of Ireland say they have trained themselves to think of New York as an overseas county. Otherwise, it hurts too much.

7

Brooklyn Heights
Victorian Bastion

Subway: Lexington Avenue IRT line 4, 5 and IRT Broadway–Seventh
Avenue Express (trains 2 and 3) to Borough Hall (Brooklyn).

In the nineteenth century some in Brooklyn presented the city as an urban Arcadia, despite countervailing reality. This walk will look at the impact of topography and myth in shaping a sense of place.

Start at **Borough Hall** ❶ *(Remsen and Cadman Plaza West). You might like to sit and read the introduction on one of the plaza benches in front of the old hall, or on the building's steps.*

I'll start by defining Brooklyn in relation to Manhattan. Not only is this way of proceeding (so irritating to Brooklynites) historically correct, but it is the reason that from the 1830s on Brooklyn's realtors and other boosters went to such extremes to individuate their city.

In Dutch days Brooklyn served as Manhattan's agrarian hinterland and as such was far less densely settled than its commercial counterpart. Under the English it remained a conglomeration of slave-served farming communities, joined in 1683 as Kings County. Because of its conservative rural atmosphere and the continuing power of the Dutch Reform church, Dutch influence survived here far longer than across the river. After the Revolution, when Manhattan began its lurch toward national importance, Brooklyn stayed much the same.

An exception was the landing area around the shore at the foot of Cadman Plaza (old Fulton Street), where a ferry had served Long Island farmers since 1642. After the war the hamlet—Brooklyn's link to New York—burgeoned as Manhattan's seaport prospered. Under the lead of small

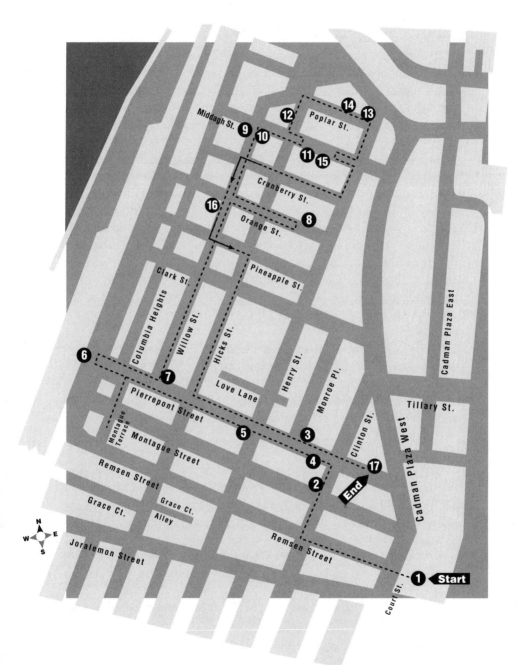

Middagh St. **9** **10**

12 Poplar St. **14** **13**

11 **15**

Cranberry St.

16 Orange St. **8**

Clark St.

Pineapple St.

Columbia Heights

Willow St.

Hicks St.

Henry St.

Monroe Pl.

6

7

Love Lane

Pierrepont Street

Tillary St.

Montague Terrace

Montague Street

5 **3**

4

2

Clinton St.

17

End

Cadman Plaza East

Cadman Plaza West

Remsen Street

Grace Ct.

Grace Ct. Alley

N
W E
S

Joralemon Street

Remsen Street

1 **Start**

Court St.

entrepreneurs—affluent butchers and master craftsmen of Yankee and Irish Methodist stock—a cluster of houses and businesses grew around the landing. (See the Fulton section of Walk 8.)

In 1784, 100 families who'd moved en bloc from New London, Connecticut, founded an industrial hamlet just east of the river settlement grandly named the City of Olympia. The newcomers got the land, confiscated from Dutch Tories, at bargain cost, paying for it with almost worthless army pay certificates they'd bought from hapless Revolutionary veterans.

One of the new township's mainstays was boat building. The Navy Yard is a descendent. In 1801 two brothers, Sam and John Jackson, sold their shipyard to the federal government and developed the adjoining property for worker housing. They called the new housing estate Vinegar Hill after a pivotal battle site in Ireland during the 1798 United Irish rebellion against Britain. (The name continues in a neighborhood housing project abutting the Navy Yard.) After the revolt's failure, the Jacksons banked on thousands of Irish emigrating, and events proved them correct. The speculators met the boats, found the men shipyard jobs (for which they raked in commissions), then off-loaded their housing plots on the newcomers.

The settlement at Olympia was so closely linked to Manhattan's trade, virtually its industrial park, that the same year the Jacksons sold their boatyard to the government, Olympians proposed building a bridge across the river. Bridge Street, near the Brooklyn end of today's Manhattan Bridge (where the river runs at its narrowest) dates from the unrealized scheme. A few waterfront streets also mark the Olympians' New England origin—among them, Adams and Plymouth.

Unlike the industrialized area to the northeast, the high ground of Brooklyn Heights, a shelf 80 feet above the river, remained farmland even after the Revolution. Industries, however, rimmed its base. One belonged to Philip Livingston, a member of the grand Livingston family (invariably referred to in Brooklyn hagiography as "the Signer," since he'd endorsed the Declaration of Independence). Livingston the Signer was also Livingston the Distiller. He kept his gin mill down at the foot of Joralemon Street.

One could say that gin was the elixir that brought the Heights into being. In 1802, anticipating New York's post-Revolutionary boom, a New Haven man, Hezekiah Pierpont, bought Livingston's distillery. His product did so well, others soon copied it, forcing Pierpont to diversify into real estate. (Real estate ran in Pierpont's blood—his grandfather, a Congregational minister, had pocketed the remaining common lands in New Haven as part of his parson's prerogatives.) In contrast to the founders of Olympia who had seen the Heights as an intractably negative feature, "too difficult to raze," Pierpont saw the elevation as an asset he could sell. Over the next years young Pierpont accumulated much of the southern Heights, until his property ran from today's Cadman Plaza West to the river, Remsen Street north to Clark Street. (He got the northern stretch between Pierrepont and Clark only near the end of his life.)

At the time Pierpont began, assemblage was relatively easy, as the Heights held only seven farms—large tracts, ripe for consolidation. Furthermore, as he had plenty of money from his wife's family who owned swaths of land in northern New York, he could wait for values to rise before reselling.

The prospective buyers Pierpont had in mind were men like himself—upper-class merchant-entrepreneurs of New England background. After the Revolution tens of thousands of young men, both comfortably off and poor, were leaving southern Massachusetts and Connecticut for upstate New York or the city, the former setting forth to enter New York's infant shipping trade, the latter, of no interest to the realtor, fleeing impoverished farms.

All Pierpont lacked for his suburb was access, a regular and speedy ferry service to Manhattan. He never doubted that the men who bought his plots would live here but work in Manhattan. Some consider Brooklyn Heights to be the first suburb in America. Others argue since it follows a grid and consists mainly of row houses, it is not a suburb at all. The debate is a semantic quibble. The term is used here in the sense that the neighborhood was primarily developed as a residential dormitory for commuters.

In 1814 the transport Pierpont needed arrived in the form of Robert Fulton's steam ferry. (The well-connected Pierpont had met and adopted Fulton as a protégé in Paris.) With the promise of dependable transport, Pierpont began to plot the property.

Plot and counterplot. Pierpont had rivals with an alternative vision. Just as Pierpont appeared on the scene, the Hicks brothers, scions of a local Dutch artisanal family, inherited land in the northern end of the Heights closer to the ferry landing. They wanted to develop the land for Brooklyn-based middle-class artisans, the sort who already lived along the old ferry road and down at the shore. (The Hicks family were Yankee Dutch stock, containing farmers, a hat maker, and a ferry captain nicknamed "Hicks the Spitter" because of his habits.)

The Hickses planned to carve Heights land into small lots packed with frame houses. Pierpont postulated wide streets and generous brick houses loaded with covenants. Above all, he wanted no industry or the poor who came to serve it. Pierpont was not against industry per se (witness his distillery), but it had to be down by the waterfront out of sight. His zoning impulse was widely shared at the time by his peers in Manhattan and elsewhere.

In Manhattan, which had less defensible topography than the Heights, the move toward spatial and class division took the form of making exclusive residential squares. Here, despite Brooklyn's commercial boom hiking land in Red Hook (just south of the Heights) to several thousand dollars an acre in the 1830s, the high ground remained free of the commercial ravening that constantly routed Manhattan's gentry. In the Heights householders and developers were in charge of their space.

In contrast to New York, where the wealthy would hold residential ground for a generation or so before fleeing the commercial energies they themselves had set into motion, residents in Brooklyn Heights could peer out at their winged ships in the harbor while ducking shorefront gore and grime. Prints of the era always show Heights householders high above their waterfront warehouses looking out *over* aestheticized river traffic.

Pierpont's vision prevailed over the Hicks brothers'. Among other moves, the newcomer hired his own surveyor, who drew up streets to his liking for a fee of thirty-five dollars and later managed to get himself made street commissioner.

By the time Pierpont died in 1838, his fief at the southern Heights was well on its way to becoming an exclusive commuter enclave. Eventually the Hickses packed up, and much of the northern end of the Heights also developed in an upscale manner, though some modest worker housing survived.

This walk will chart the transformation of the Heights from its artisanal origins at the northern end into the rarefied residential neighborhood it became.

(Obviously, to show this development, it would have made better sense for our route to go from the northern end of the Heights southward instead of the reverse. Unfortunately, the southern Jay Street subway stop is a better station than the sometimes problematic one at High Street. Lo-

cal folk not dependent on subways might try to reverse the itinerary and walk it from end to start.)

☞ The location of Borough Hall, Brooklyn's old City Hall (1836–1849), is the first matter to consider. Hezekiah Pierpont sold the government a tract of land to accom-

modate the new civic structure (and grace his holdings.) The Greek Revival building is not spatially related, however, to Pierpont's residential enclave. Neither is it spatially related to Brooklyn's downtown business district to the east, which grew out of an early settlement node on the road to central Long Island. The building's purposeful axis toward the amorphous space of today's Cadman Plaza makes no sense at first. It seems marooned—that is until you realize the hall faces the old ferry hamlet and sits astride the once vital farmers' road.

The building's architect, Gamaliel King, himself fits the profile of the gentrifying age. Until 1830 King had been a grocer, afterward a carpenter, and finally a builder-architect. When work began on the building, the aim was to make the new civic structure resemble Manhattan's City Hall, finished more than two decades earlier. Whatever her sister city had, Brooklyn wanted. Even heads of state who paid respects at Manhattan's City Hall were obliged to make courtesy calls here.

☞ Unfortunately, during its long construction span the structure wound up ponderous Greek Revival, not elegant French Georgian like its ideal in

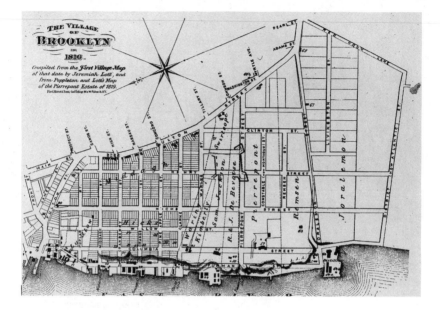

After the Revolution two factions struggled to develop Brooklyn Heights in their image: the Hicks brothers wanted a yeoman community like the one at the ferry; newcomer Hezekiah Pierpont wanted a posh commuter suburb for Manhattan merchants. Note the crowded allotments at the Hicks' end of the Heights.

Manhattan. By the time the construction was truly under way, the earlier style had long passed. (The clown hat cupola is a turn-of-the-century replacement for a smaller wood version.)

It wasn't mere ego that drove most of Brooklyn's elite to demand city status for the town. New York had bullied Brooklyn ever since English rule. Not only did New York control ferry access to Brooklyn but it even owned the shoreline here. (In 1748 maddened Brooklynites torched New York's Corporation Tavern, which that city owned on the Brooklyn landing site.)

After the Revolution, Manhattan's aggression continued despite efforts at symbiosis by entrepreneurs like the Olympians. In the 1830s New York's stance grew tougher still. Its realtors were enraged by the middle-class outflow to Brooklyn—so was the City Council, which had recently made property taxes its main base of revenue. In 1834 Brooklyn circumvented Manhattan's opposition to getting a charter as an independent city by making an end run on Albany. Local activists called for a city hall to celebrate the achievement, as they wanted their hard-won sovereignty made visible through stone.

Despite Brooklyn's new status, which kept it from Manhattan's maw, its battle with the city across the river continued over ferry rights, and the corollary entitlement to open landing sites on the Brooklyn shore. Fearing new suburbs and further middle-class emigration, Manhattan blocked both options as far as it could. (Only a few lulls broke the tension. One such reprieve came in the 1830s, when Manhattan allowed Brooklyn two more ferry boats patroniz-ingly named the *Olive Branch* and the *Relief*.)

The one-sided competition continued until the consolidation of 1898. At this time Brooklyn, Manhattan, Staten Island, most of Queens, and remaining indepen-dent sections of the Bronx joined into New York City. (By this time the majority of Brooklyn's elite saw merger in their interest, as they thought it would speed development here.)

Brooklyn's City Hall (now Borough Hall), built after Brooklyn became a chartered city, showed off the town's hard-won independence from Manhattan.

☞ The Romanesque hulk at the far end of this plaza is the **1891 post office,** opened just before Brooklyn's surrender of city status. Its size reminds us that at the time it went up, Brooklyn was America's third largest city.

***W**alk west on Remsen Street, then turn right (north) on Clinton Street to Montague Street, once Pierpont's private access road for his property and named for an aristocratic in-law.*

In 1853 Manhattan allowed a ferry landing at the foot of Montague and a boat route connecting Wall Street. From the Civil War onward, the street held Brooklyn's cultural institutions and, soon afterward, its financial ser-vices.

☞ Note the nine-story **Brooklyn Real Estate Exchange** at 189–191 Mon-tague, an 1890 building now (de)faced over, and the cluster of palatial banks near the corner of Clinton.

Today Montague Street is still the "strip," the one penetration of down-town business and "outsiders" into the domestic sanctity of the Heights. (The presence of the Jehovah's Witnesses, a big exception to this formulation, is addressed at the end of this chapter.)

☞ If you loop down the street, you will see many bow-front windows standing empty. Because of rent rises here in recent years, numerous independent shops have shut, and chain stores moved in. With the advent of the new Manhattan projects scheduled to open nearby, property values will go higher still.

☞ Note **St. Ann's and the Holy Trinity Church ❷** on the northwest corner of Clinton and Montague streets (1846) by Minard Lafever. The windows by William Jay Bolton, dating from that same year, are the earliest examples of American stained glass.

Originally, St. Ann's had stood down at the waterfront in Olympia. By the 1830s, as the Heights developed and the shoreline grew blighted from industrialization engendered by the New Englanders themselves, descendants of the Olympia settlement moved up to the Heights. Their churches, including St. Ann's, followed.

Today the name and settlement of Olympia are forgotten. In great part the memory loss was deliberate. Olympia, founded as an industrial, commercial entrepôt, did not fit with the "city on a hill" imagery Heights realtors and newspapers developed for their fief.

The rarefied, reified identification came in two stages. Hezekiah Pierpont didn't tinge the argument for suburban life with a moral dimension, but, rather, stressed the suburb's access to Manhattan without its problems—crime and disease. (In 1822, yellow fever in New York was so severe that incoming European ships skipped the seaport and landed only at Greenwich Village and Brooklyn—a big boost to both settlements. You will see many houses on your walk with plaques dated 1823.)

By the late 1830s when Hezekiah's son Henry had inherited the property, a moral corollary—Brooklyn's probity compared with Manhattan's wickedness—had been added to the formulation. (See Walk 6 on Irish history and the guidebooks of the era viewing city spaces and classes as pitted in Manichean struggle.) From this time on, Brooklyn realtors portrayed their holdings as free of the vicious poor and vicious nouveaux riches that sullied their sister city. Developing a panoply of nostalgic images, they presented Brooklyn as a place where one could live as "one's father had lived" before the fall.

VIEW OF NEW YORK.
FROM BROOKLYN HEIGHTS.

For almost one hundred years Brooklyn became known as "the city of homes and churches," "the city of moral earnestness known to people everywhere." Many noted church architects, including Richard Upjohn and Minard Lafever, who designed this church, chose to live in the pious domain. Lafever even taught Sunday school in Red Hook, a poor area to the south.

Unlike Manhattan, where the wealthy had no natural enclaves, Brooklyn Heights (in the foreground) provided defendable high ground for making a residential bastion.

*C*ontinue on Clinton to Pierrepont Street, then turn left to see the **First Unitarian Church ❸** at the northeast corner of Monroe Place and Pierrepont.

☞ This tremulous Gothic structure dates from 1844, a year before its architect, Lafever, went on to build the church on Montague Street.

From the beginning of its suburbanization through today, Brooklyn Heights has stylized itself after its "Puritan" New England roots. In fact,

Heights founders actually shed New England baggage rather easily. Unitarianism, planted here by New Englanders in 1833, was already a step away from Calvinist orthodoxy. Unlike earlier Puritan Congregationalism, the denomination encouraged entrepreneurial thinking. By this time some New York Yankees had not only switched to the less demanding Unitarian sect but even given up the Puritan tradition altogether, joining its old foe, the Anglican church, paramount in New York since British rule.

Hezekiah Pierpont was among those who switched to the denomination offering social and economic mobility. His son, Henry, even founded an Episcopalian church (on Hicks and Grace Court). The Pierponts, incidentally, went the whole route, laying claim to an ancestral title in England and for good measure adding the extra aristocratic French "re" to their name that's used on street signs today. The effort at (re)ennobling failed, but Anglicanism stuck.

☞ The house at 116 Pierrepont Street, across from the church, is a good example of the Greek Revival residential style popular here from the 1830s through the 1840s. Note the sanctuary mode. The pilasters on the sides of the door give depth: one has the feeling of going from the outside into an inner protected space.

Suburbanization began at the same period as the impulse for a cloistered family life. The process was complementary. The idealization of the family, particularly the wife, as preserver of virtue created the climate for residential enclaves and vice versa.

The idea that the wife stayed in Brooklyn and the husband went to do battle in the big city was so profound, it extended even to death. One tombstone in Greenwood, Brooklyn's great Victorian cemetery, comes in the shape of a brownstone. The deceased (a woman) stands on the steps of the house waving good-by to her husband. The top-hatted man, paper tucked under his arm, is caught in motion. He's half turned toward the commuter horsecar, half toward his wife. He waves behind him with a baffled expression. Well might he be puzzled. Though in reality, it is his spouse who has departed, she, nonetheless, must iconically stay put.

Because more than 70 percent of Heights men commuted to Manhattan for work, the daytime Heights became a woman's domain. Unlike Manhattan, where genteel women commanded only their own homes, here womanly "virtue" became the community ideal. Woman had more influence as consumers also—at least, of images. Unlike Manhattan, where upper-middle-class wives read their husbands' male-oriented papers (with social notes tacked on), whole Brooklyn magazines and journals, including the *Eagle,* grew up pitched primarily toward genteel women. The papers expanded Brooklyn's female identification until it passed the point of simple identification and grew to be characterization—Brooklyn itself becoming female. "She [Brooklyn] has never kept evil company or late hours or indulged in any dissipation. . . ." "Like a good woman she offers little to the chance visitor impelled to come by idle curiosity and nothing to the roué. . . ."

Matters, of course, were more complex than the passive images bestowed. Brooklyn's elite women made good use of their community power. In 1864 Heights women raised a remarkable sum of money for Union Army hospital supplies at their Brooklyn Sanitary Commission fair. Its leader, the feisty wife of Brooklyn's great engineer, J. T. Stranahan, staved off concerted efforts at a male takeover, and local realtors credited the event with putting Brooklyn on the map.

Another deliberate oversimplification the papers and realtors made was conflat-

Upper-class women in the Heights shaped the community's images—in this print, local ladies dress up as colonial New Englanders to raise funds for the Union Army.

ing the rarefied world of Brooklyn Heights with the City of Brooklyn as a whole. The image selection that excised Brooklyn's immigrant slums, poverty, and industrial blight, only slightly less dire than Manhattan's, was perpetuated not just for Brooklyn Heights' readers but for the middle-class Manhattanites the boosters sought to woo.

Because of the hidden nature of poverty and industry here and the gentry's entrenchment on the Heights, the Arcadian freeze-frame had a long run.

☞ Note the Romanesque facade on the Greek Revival house next door at 114 Pierrepont Street. The fashionable styles laid one atop the other marks an elite presence here over generations.

☞ Enter the **Brooklyn Historical Society** ❹ to see the exhibits in the History Gallery, the wood-paneled library, and adjacent ladies' retiring room or "fainting parlor." Telephone (718) 624–0890 for hours Tuesday–Saturday and for the cost of admission.

This association joined commercial institutions in fostering images designed to forge continuums. Whitman called it making "a conscious contract with the past," which he set out to do in his sentimentalizing pieces on Brooklyn history for the *Eagle*.

In 1847 local residents began a chapter of the New England Society to celebrate the pure "Puritan" background of the Heights' founders. The impulse was sharpened by the fact that by now foreign-born Brooklynites below the citadel almost equaled the native-born Yankee population. Thirty years later, in the face of still further immigration, the New England Society reinvigorated itself with the help of a national body, the New England Pilgrim Society, which lent beleaguered WASPS around the country morale and aid-in-kind. Here, this took the form of Plymouth rock reliquary, a claim on the past, as moon rocks were a claim on our future.

Heights residents built this structure in 1878 to house a library and picture collection of local material, the self-preserving impulse prompted, in part, by the historicizing activities of the recent national Centennial. One hundred-odd years later, members here voted to change the name from the Long Island Historical Society to its present designation. After a decline, Brooklyn, or at least this part, was once again highly fashionable, grander than Long Island. The change-over provoked a battle royal—Heights residents still take naming and self mythology very seriously.

☞ George Post designed the society's building in a thick cake of brick and terra-cotta trim. Note the heads over the door. Among other attributes, the Viking represents virility, Nordic background, and the shipping business—a profile of the Heights' best men. The Indian, by then safely dead, represents early American legitimation, the illusion of continuity. (Heights histories, then and now, like to place the suburb in a continuum starting with Iphetonga, a Canarsie camp on the river bluff.)

Brooklyn's Genealogical Society and New England Society still share board members with the BHS, and the genealogists continue to meet here. Today, however, the Historical Society interprets all of the borough, and the new History Gallery, which opened in 1989, exhibits chunks of Plymouth Rock as part of a timeline that includes West Indian carnival dresses from Bedford Stuyvesant and aluminum samovars from Soviet immigrants in Brighton.

*C*ontinue along Pierrepont toward the river (the numbers descend), passing the **Behr House** ❺ on the southwest corner of Henry and Pierrepont.

☞ The charmingly florid mansion, built by a sandpaper tycoon in 1890, is an exception to the usually sober dwellings on the Heights—more akin to houses going up in Park Slope at that period. Even during the excesses of the "Belle Epoque," Heights residents prided themselves on their "New England" restraint. Note also the generous frontage mandated by Pierpont of the (altered) **Greek Revival houses** farther down the block, across the street, at 86, 87, 60, and 58 Pierrepont Street.

Lewis Tappan, the New England shipping merchant, lived in number 86. Lewis and his brother Arthur introduced the Greek Revival building style to New York when they hired Connecticut's Ithiel Town to design their seaport store. The Tappans were leading voices of the antislavery movement. Because of the Abolitionist presence on the Heights (there were anti-Abolitionists as well: one church split over the issue), modern-day activists here are often compared to the earlier idealists. At least they were at two out of the two civic meetings I've attended in the Heights—one an antinuclear rally, the other a gathering to halt high-rise construction on the piers below the citadel. On both occasions we gladly accepted the mantle.

*C*ontinue on Pierrepont to the **Esplanade;** ❻ note the marker near the flagpole commemorating "Four Chimneys."

Until recently, it has been an important underpinning of community faith that Hezekiah Pierpont moved into Philip Livingston's house, which was supposedly located here. Successive chroniclers followed this geomancy, a fib devised in the nineteenth century by Brooklyn historian Henry Stiles to establish dynastic succession. Recent "scholarship" suggests that the Signer most probably lived down near his gin mill on Joralemon Street. The debate rages hot and heavy in a local newspaper, which also, incidentally, uncritically republishes Whitman's elegiac, highly suspect, columns on Brooklyn history.

☞ The 1951 esplanade covering the Brooklyn Queens Expressway shows Heights power. In less influential areas to the south, Robert Moses' highway rifled through neighborhoods, rattling all, ruining some.

Hezekiah Pierpont first proposed a promenade along the bluff in the 1820s. His plan to provide local residents a strolling place and raise the value of his riverfront properties failed, thwarted by realtors with nothing to gain. A second try by son Henry in the 1840s also lost, this time as outlying taxpayers perceived the plan as a special-interest venture for which they would pay. (Walt Whitman, rallying working-class Fort Greene residents, led the second round of opposition, as he wanted a park in *his* neighborhood.)

☞ The view is so splendid here, it's enough to sit (or walk) and think of nothing special. Before leaving the Promenade, however, note the piers below—a source of contention that has filled the Brooklyn Heights newspapers since shipping ended in the 1960s.

☞ In 1986 the city government and the Port of New York Authority, who own the 80-acre area of shoreline, piers, and water slips, proposed developing the site. Their plan, a conSPIREacy of high-rise condominiums and office towers, appalled local preservation groups. Since then, the Brooklyn Heights Association, the Brooklyn Bridge Park Coalition, and some Brooklyn officials have stayed the project, proposing a park and recreational marina that would protect the view. The outcome is still being contested in a series of court battles. In 1993 in order to circumvent local pressure groups, the city government took the piers out of the control of the Brooklyn Heights (vicinity) district and awarded stewardship to the industrialized district farther south. In autumn 1994 the Heights won the latest go-round as the Port Authority was persuaded to sell the piers to the New York State Urban Corporation, which is sympathetic to low-rise development.

To some degree, Heights players brought the piers problem on themselves by relentlessly defining themselves as a prestigious residential district and showing little empathy for a working waterfront. Though Heights dwellers tend to be an estimably civic lot, at the open session I attended about the future of the docks the discussion was narrow, the issues seen entirely as a problem of high to low. How would development affect the Heights residents and their view? Would there be crowds, noise, people coming through on their way down to this new development? That evening, this was early on in the conflict, the Citadel and Perimeter mentality was so strong, not a mention was made of how various development strategies might affect the neighborhoods abutting the Heights to the south where a (somewhat) commercial shorefront struggles on. The recent victory reflects the eventual decision of the movement's leaders to form a wider alliance.

Walk back up Pierrepont Street to Willow Street, first making a minute detour south (turn right) to see the two **brownstone mansions** *on Montague Terrace.*

Richard Upjohn built the Renaissance Revival houses in the 1850s. The Low shipping family, who pioneered the China trade, owned the house at number 2. Low in-laws, the White family, whose fortune came from furs, owned the look-alike residence at number 3. Henry Pierpont's house stood where the children's park is today.

Turn left on Willow Street from Pierrepont and walk north.

This is the road the Hicks brothers opened in 1818 at the northern end of the Heights. Despite backing by the Brooklyn Village trustees, the Hicks were able to run it only this far, as Pierpont wanted to protect his long block fronts. The road picks up again as Willow Place at Remsen Street, the southern margin of Pierpont's fief.

The route from here to our destination at Poplar Street encompasses some lovely streetscapes. For walkers who would like a more detailed sketch of the houses along the way, I suggest Clay Lancaster's *Old Brooklyn Heights* and Gerard Wolfe's *Guide to the Metropolis*. This tour will just point out a few.

☞ The exquisite **Federal dwellings, ❼** 155, 157 and 159 Willow Street on the right-hand side, go back to the late 1820s. Number 159 lost its pitched roof when a story was added. A baker owned the large renovated wood **Federal house** at 104 Willow, on the west side of the street. (The clapboard

facing shows it was built before Pierpont bought this section of his holdings. He would have mandated brick.) The house went up in 1829. A
decade later, even many wealthy tradesmen had been pushed out of this
end of the Heights for Manhattan-oriented commuters. As you continue
north, note the elegant fences and stoop railings that front most houses
here.

The district's ironwork, both wrought and cast, was prized then as
now. By the mid-nineteenth century it had become a target for thieves in a
rash of robberies besetting the Heights, and developers bought the fenced
fences for new buildings going up in the Fort Greene and Clinton Hill areas. Most Heights householders blamed the burglaries on the Irish Bridies
who worked for them as maids, or, rather, they blamed the women's longshoremen boyfriends, whom they were certain used the girls to breach the
citadel. In fact, the citadel was breached from within, as we shall see.

A*t Orange Street, turn right to Henry Ward Beecher's Congregational
Plymouth Church, now* **Plymouth Church of the Pilgrims.** ❽ *(And therein
lies a tale.) To visit here, you must either come to a Sunday morning
church service, or call (718) 624–4743 to arrange a visit.*

☞ Before entering, mull the building's exterior—the simplicity of the barn-
like structure designed by Joseph Wells in 1849 to replace a slightly earlier
version that burned. (The portico is a post–Civil War addition.) The plain
style is in the right tradition for a Congregational church.

☞ Its predecessors, Puritan meeting houses, did not have spires: the buildings were not considered sacred. New England's sanctified, steepled
churches came *after* Episcopalianism had routed, or subverted, Puritan orthodoxy. (Though I know this to be a fact, picturing a steepleless New England throws my internalized calendar image out of kilter. Steeples are to
greens as needles to compasses.)

☞ In the Close, note the **Statue of Beecher,** the Connecticut minister who
preached here from the year the church opened until 1887. Shown with
the Reverend is "Pinky," the mulatto girl whom the minister sold in mock
auction to raise his congregation's consciousness about slavery.

Beecher also raised money for rifles known as Beecher's Bibles to aid
the free-soil movement in Kansas but was not, in fact, a true abolitionist.
He often pontificated that the system was a better form of living for blacks,

as most couldn't manage their own lives. He didn't care much for dark skin either—Pinky was virtually white, according to the painting of the child that hangs inside the church hall. Despite these nuances, a Plymouth hand-out records there is a church tradition "which cannot be documented" that slaves seeking freedom in Canada were often hidden in the tunnel-like structures beneath the church, and "Plymouth has been called the Grand Central Terminal of the Underground Railroad."

At the time of the war Beecher was the most important person in the nation next to Lincoln. He earned as much salary as the President—$22,000 yearly—and doubled this by writing and lecturing. He also earned enviable residuals by endorsing products ranging from laxatives to hore-hound throat drops—the latter a favorite item for ministers to sponsor, as their sermons lasted three hours minimum.

Many of Brooklyn's preachers had celebrity and product identification, but no one held a candle to Beecher. Several thousand worshipers attended Plymouth each Sabbath. The city ran special "Beecher" ferries on Sundays to bring over the New York contingent, giving Manhattanites a shot at re-demption. (One of the leitmotifs in Beecher's sermons was "Who owns the city of New York [Manhattan] today? . . . The Devil owns the city.")

In our own day Henry Ward Beecher represents the embodiment of Heights distinction and fixity, a position as ensconced as this statue. In his own time Beecher grew controversial. Sensationally so. The migrations of another Beecher statue down on Cadman Plaza charted the rise and fall of the preacher's reputation. Originally sited in front of City Hall, the statue was exiled by the municipality in the 1880s following the preacher's trial for adultery with one of his parishioners' wives. It's still down at the far end of the plaza near the Post Office, but there's a rumor it's slated to come back to the original site. All is forgiven, or rather, forgotten. A library of material has been written about Beecher and the scandalous case that held America spellbound.

Before his trial Beecher had preached that love should be predicated on an indi-vidual romantic and sexual basis, not on conventional social norms. If people of

Despite the preacher's attunement to changing times, Brooklyn Heights' myth portrayed Henry Ward Beecher as the embodiment of Brooklyn's old "Puritan" values—a contrast to Manhattan's venality.

Beecher's new Telephone connection

Instructing all his lady hearers to buy the NEW AMERICAN SEWING MACHINE, 244 WABASH AVENUE.

high degree (not the Yankee lower class or immigrants) developed an attraction through an elevated plane of understanding, the affinity could take sexual expression outside of marriage. He called the phenomenon "nesting." Of course, the trial made much of this, and he was forced to recant. The trial ended with a hung jury and Beecher salvaging his job and some, though not all, of his reputation.

A recent book by Altina Waller, *Reverend Beecher and Mrs. Tilton: Sex and Class in Victorian America,* suggests why public interest was disproportionate even for a trial as titillating as this one. She suggests that the public fastened on the preacher because he precisely (and charismatically) reflected general societal change. Instead of being the custodian of principles or the bestower of beliefs and values (the way he's presented today), Beecher was, in fact, a sensitive *receptor* and popularizer of mood shifts already under way. More a chameleon than a rock.

Beecher's ministry here and the controversial trial yield truths about this Brooklyn neighborhood that don't jibe with Heights lore, past or present. (In fact, the church records of many local congregations reveal fierce social and doctrinal struggle—a stark contrast to the smug "city of homes and churches" apotheosis.) To track Beecher's case we must compare earlier Congregationalism with his interpretation.

Before Beecher's preaching, to be a Congregationalist was a matter of some hardship. You couldn't belong to a church casually: go for the music, skip the sermon. Up until the 1850s you had to pledge 10 percent of your property to the church and conform to rules governing your home and habits as well as your spiritual life. It wasn't only the Calvinist God who was judgmental. Church officials could also weigh you and, if they found you lacking, drum you out of the church and, by extension, society.

In the 1850s, however, a demand for a gentler system, a more comforting religion welled up. Many churchgoers postulated the idea that God was within, not a patriarchal Sky God modeled on figures such as Beecher's own father, a brimstone preacher and tyrannical parent. The new demand was for what Beecher called "a gospel of love," a concept he popularized at Plymouth Church. The teaching was completely at odds with the traditional Calvinist doctrine preached in the other local Congregational church, the Church of the Pilgrims, half a mile south at Henry and Remsen. (The two churches merged in 1934, any suggestion of a schism long buried.)

The Church of the Pilgrims, opened in 1844 by New Englanders on the Pierpont side of the Heights, also had a celebrated minister, the Reverend Richard C. Storrs, known, poor man, as the Chrystotem of Brooklyn, "the

Christ carrier." Parishioners at Storrs' church were both old school believers and old guard society, quite different from Plymouth's congregation.
Both preacher and worshipers here stood fast for tradition. Members of the
Church of the Pilgrim were outraged but fascinated by the doctrinal and social changes Beecher was popularizing at the other end of the neighborhood.

Despite the fact that some Heights residents today use Plymouth
Church to emblemize the safe pieties, the old-fashioned virtues and un-
changing New England underpinnings of Brooklyn, the opposite was true.
The congregation here who tended to be from the outer fringe (though not
the foot) of the Heights were, indeed, New Englanders. They were not,
however, the shipowning elite New Englanders represented (then as now)
as forming the basis of early Heights society.

Worshipers at Plymouth were largely displaced country boys frightened by their migration to the city, tremulous from lost ties. Though city
dwellers today live in a deracinated world, we are secure or at least experienced, compared with these young people who had little to prepare them
for the dislocations they suffered in the nineteenth century. Beecher's
church was essentially a singles church serving an anonymous new society
that has continued til our own day.

☞ If you can enter the church, you will find that although many guidebooks characterize the interior as classical New England style, the pulpit
area is more proscenium stage than Calvinist lectern and reflects Beecher's
new-age interactive preaching. To raise his eye contact quotient, Beecher
tore out the fixed pulpit and used a chair (preserved in the Historical Society), which he moved around the podium while addressing his audience.

The church used the pews here differently also. In the old Puritan tradition handed down through the Congregational church, seating had followed a fixed social order. More important people sat in the front pews,
less important in the back. Even after the custom of pew rents began, people continued to sit according to community rank. (For many years in a sophisticated protocol rivaling India's caste system, Yale University, a Congregationalist college, seated students according to their fathers' rank.)
Beecher's church broke the system wide open. Some other churches also
sold pews, but the widely advertised auctions here were unprecedented,
the hierarchy raucously up for grabs.

☞ Before leaving the church, note the side windows depicting pilgrims in
the wilderness made for the sanctuary between 1907 and 1909, a decade
after the New England Society's second big promotion in this part of Brook-

Beecher's Plymouth Church, often called a pillar of tradition, in fact brimmed with innovations—spatial and theological. Note Beecher's proscenium-style stage, which allowed interactive sermonizing.

lyn. The formal title of the series is "The History of Puritanism and its Influence upon the Institutions and People of the Republic."

It was a case of ghost dancing—or its visual equivalent. At the period the windows were installed, definitely *non*-Puritan sorts were beginning their assault or ascent on the Heights. Some have been unkind enough to suggest that the wilderness was intended as a metaphor for the "new" Brooklyn.

☞ The windows at the rear of the church above the choir stalls celebrate church-related personages. One shows Beecher looking piously up to heaven. Another shows Lincoln, who worshiped here as president-elect and became Beecher's patron. (A visit here had become a must for luminaries visiting New York, one of the two things a notable did, along with scheduling an appearance at Cooper Union.) On the other side of the Lincoln panel, a window honors Beecher's sister Harriet Beecher Stowe, Emma Willard, and several more strong ladies. The unusual bow to women alludes to Beecher's role in the suffrage movement but, more primarily, reflects the power of females in defining Brooklyn Heights' hagiography.

*R*eturn west on Orange Street to Willow and turn right; walk north to Middagh Street, passing **Beecher's house** ❾ at 22 Willow. Turn right on Middagh.

The street name commemorates the Dutch farm family who bequeathed this end of the Heights to their nephews, the Hicks, at the beginning of the nineteenth century.

☞ Be sure to see the **dormered Federal house** ❿ at #24 Middagh (the corner of Middagh and Willow) with the exquisite doorway framed by the most delicate Ionic columns and leaded glass panes. The building with its willow-swept back garden and peaceful street-front is solace for urban eyes.

What makes the houses in the Heights and several other Brooklyn communities so compelling is the neighborhood's totality. Unlike Manhattan, where an odd landmarked house usually stands in a pastiche streetscape, the Heights has nearly six hundred houses of pre–Civil War vintage. In 1965 the Brooklyn Heights Association successfully fought for and won the status of Historic District from the New York City Landmarks Preservation Commission, the first such designation in the country.

☞ The small structure in the back yard beyond the willow probably began life as a craftsman's shed—a common arrangement before work and residence separated in the 1830s.

The building's early date and its location at the artisanal end of the Heights (plus its similarity to the workshop of the sash maker William Hyde in Greenwich Village from the same date) make this a strong conjecture. There is no conclusive evidence, however, and Heights residents prefer to call it a carriage house, as it once served that function.

*C*ontinue walking east along Middagh Street.

☞ The **clapboard dwellings** at 25 and 27 Middagh, dating back respectively to the late 1820s and early 1830s, housed artisans and seafarers. They are much altered and stripped of detail, but keep the scale of the originals. The homely spirit of the street is quite different from the Pierpont-ed suburb to

Brooklyn had had an industrialized shoreline ever since the 1790s, but Heights residents ignored the waterfront hubbub (which provided their incomes) and pretended their enclave was an Arcadian oasis.

the south, and you can feel the pull down to the waterfront, despite the expressway barriers walling the neighborhood off from the ferry landing.

*C*ontinuing east on Middagh; cross Hicks to see several frame buildings, including the **1827 Greek Revival wooden house** ⑪ with the white portico at number 56.

From 1822, paint factories down at the ferry landing churned out white lead for the Greek Revival vogue. The color white is a good vehicle for looking at the role of construct in shaping spatial reality. Today, because of New England's urge for Greek classical styles, which lasted from the 1820s to the 1840s, white is so thoroughly associated with New England that we sometimes think of the northeastern states as being a quilt of milky villages. Like the steeples, it's a consciousness imprinted in our minds through years of received images on calendars and Kitsch—the images, of course, being pumped out all the more ferociously after factory smoke became New England's truly representative shade from the mid-nineteenth century on.

Early colonial houses, in fact, were not white at all, but barn red, mustard, and smoky blue. It wasn't until the Greek Revival mode arrived that buildings got painted that color, the bleaching the result of the Victorian mindset that couldn't imagine Greek temples as anything but eternally white, certainly not as the savagely bright structures they'd originally been.

***R**etrace your footsteps on Middagh to Hicks Street, noting the tall institutional-looking brick building at 65 Middagh, a* **public school** *put up in 1846. Turn right and walk north on Hicks toward Poplar. Halfway down the block on the west side you will pass a little alley flanked by two* **frame houses,** ⑫ *numbers 40 and 38.*

☞ If you look up the stretch you will see the houses have long rear extensions and that the one to the south of the ally has a side porch. The back quarters of the two houses are their original sections, built in the 1790s. The side verandah at number 40 facing north toward the ferry road was once the front porch. At the time this house was built, the ferry landing, *not* the view across the river to Manhattan, was the neighborhood's fulcrum. The parts of the houses that front on Willow were added only in the 1840s when the ferry hamlet was something to be shunned.

As shoreside commerce prospered, so did urban blight and social breakdown. From the teens of the last century, civic leaders around the landing and lower Fulton Street began institutions aimed at controlling Yankee working-class boys and Irish immigrant children. In 1816 they started the Sunday School Union and in 1838 began the union's first annual parade. Celebrations took the form of marching Protestant children invasively through the city. (By 1926 the Brooklyn *Eagle* reported 100,000 participating children in a line of march spanning an incredible fifty-two miles. For years, Brooklyn was the only borough to have an official holiday. Now it's extended to Queens and called Brooklyn-Queens Day: grateful students home from school have no clue to the origin.) In 1824 local industrialists founded the Apprentices Library on Henry and Cranberry, which eventually grew into the Brooklyn Museum. In 1858, a decade after the last of the few remaining Fulton Street middle class had moved up to

Protestants marched their Sunday school classes through all parts of town. Until immigrant Italians arrived and started their own processions (albeit within their own neighborhoods), Catholics kept a far lower profile.

the Heights, the municipality took still firmer measures to guard the pale and opened an armory on the site once housing the library.

***C*ontinue north on Hicks to Poplar; turn right and walk east toward Henry Street.**

☞ Poplar Street was the front line of the boundary separating the residential Heights from the industrial ferry area. Protestant churches maintained missions here to secure the zone, contain, if not convert, local working-class boys—many of whom worked at the newspapers that had been located on Fulton Street since the end of the Revolution. Plymouth Church opened **Poplar Hall** ⓭ at 173 Poplar on the north side of the street near the time the armory went up—a different approach to the same "problem." Note the name in the pediment and the little flowers carved above the arched windows—Henry Ward Beecher's symbol. (Female parishioners always kept a bunch on his podium.)

☞ Catholic charities, sick of Protestants patronizing their youth—and concerned for the children's welfare as well—built their own dormitory, social center, and job exchange here two years after the Plymouth mission opened. The striking **red and white brick building** ⓮ at 157 Poplar is the second incarnation and dates from 1883. (Note the sign between the second and third floor crediting the Children's Aid Society as donors. Presumably, the Brooklyn Catholics borrowed the nom de plume of the Manhattan institution as a deliberate rejoinder to that organization. *This* C.A.S. was an entirely local and Roman Catholic operation.)

Often, people called this newsboys' home "the orphanage," with reason for the correlation. Despite local realtors' portrayal of Brooklyn as health personified, compared with Manhattan, periodic bouts of cholera and yellow fever devastated the city throughout the nineteenth century. In 1846 a cholera epidemic killed almost seven hundred people, 99 percent of them poor immigrants who lived, as usual, in the low-lying swampy areas. The wealthy occupied the Heights not just for the view but for their lives as well.

*C*ontinue east on Poplar to Henry Street.

☞ Here you can find an **1834 clapboard building** (64 Poplar) on the south side that is attributed to Walt Whitman and his carpenter father.

The younger Whitman had worked at the newspapers down on Fulton Street from age eleven, and although Heights lore claims the poet today, he was very much on the lower class and topographical gradient—only a cut above the newsboys.

*T*urn right and walk south (back up the slope) one block to Middagh; turn right (west) again toward the river (you will be walking toward the part of the street where you have already been), passing a **tenement with fire escapes** ⓯ at 68 Middagh on the south side of the street.

When the first subway arrived here in 1908 followed by the Manhattan Bridge the next year, the Heights grew vulnerable for the first time to an immigrant flow from Manhattan's Lower East Side. This tenement next to the Catholic parish house dates from the era the gentry started to leave and the poor began their march on the lower Heights. It still has tubs in the kitchens.

The nearby Catholic Church of the Assumption of the Blessed Virgin Mary, which owns the rectory next to the tenement, moved up here from the shorefront when construction began on the Manhattan Bridge. Until Assumption set up here, Catholics had been kept off the Heights, with a single exception. (The exception is Saint Charles Borremeo, a presence dating to 1851. Even fairly recent accounts of Brooklyn church history, providing minute details of Protestant lineages, record startlement at its arrival, saying it "sprang up like a Minerva out of Zeus' brow.") The priest at the church owning this parish house is pleased at his growing congregation and teases that he will see that Brooklyn Heights becomes "Assumption Heights."

Nineteenth-century Heights religious selectivity applied even to some Protestant churches. In the 1860s the Methodists, still down by the river near the ferry landing, made an effort to move their church up the slope. Henry Ward Beecher descended to stave off the upstarts. "It is your purpose, I believe," he told assembled churchmen, "to erect a great Methodist Church somewhere on the Heights. I am sorry for it and would recall to your minds in this connection the fable of the snail and the lobster shell. Beware of the devil of respectability and don't be afraid to be common. My fear is that you will attempt to make a big magnificent popular church. My prayer is that God may defeat you."

A decade later, a Methodist minister refusing to surrender the idea used military analogy. "With a good leader and fifty thousand dollars in your treasury you can storm and capture Brooklyn [Heights] as General Wolfe did the heights of Abraham in Quebec. . . ."

From this point, work your way south toward Pierrepont Street by zig-zagging between Henry, Hicks, and Willow streets, enjoying the varied rowhouses, churches, and the blue slate sidewalks that buckle up over the roots of ancient trees.

☞ At Hicks and Cranberry you can see a fine crossroads with old gambrelroofed houses dating back to the 1820s. Number 68 Hicks housed a grocery store and a tavern; number 59 Hicks diagonally across the intersection was the residence of a barrel maker. Satisfyingly, they have not been gentrified. One houses a laundromat, the other a veterinarian's office.

All through this part of the Heights you will be passing some of the many properties belonging to the Jehovah's Witnesses (more formally, The Watchtower Bible and Tract Society of New York). ⓰ Ironically, this low church evangelical group now is the largest institutional presence on the Heights. Consummate outsiders, the Witnesses started off their Bible distributing operations near Fulton Landing in 1909 (actually, on the site of the old Olympia), and began their publishing mission at the base of the Heights a dozen years later. Today they own $186 million worth of property on the citadel as well as down on the rim. Opinion is divided over the sect. The late Brooklyn historian, landmarks preservationist, and Heights resident Elliot Willensky admired the group for its upkeep of housing stock and the stabilizing influence of its members' constant street presence. Others are rigid with disdain for the fundamentalist religion itself, the semi-communal life-style of its adherents, and, not least, the fact that the group pays no property tax. Relations, as one might imagine, hit a low in the late 1980s when the Witnesses tried to build a thirty-four-story residence on Columbia Heights, the premier street along the Heights that faces the river. (Losing the skirmish, they have just opened a tower down on Sands Street near the water.)

At Pierrepont Street, turn left and walk east to the **Morgan Stanley Office Building, ⑰** One Pierrepont Plaza.

Though the Brooklyn Heights Association won its fight to stop the Witnesses' first high rise, it lost the struggle against Morgan Stanley's clunkish spire, which opened in 1986, helped along by Mayor Ed Koch.

☞ Notice that the structure has more blank walls than windows. The bank built it for their secretarial back-up staff, who need computer space and do not rate views. The firm's executives (still in Manhattan despite threats of relocating to Connecticut) have vistas at their headquarters.

Mayor Koch and Brooklyn's borough president leaned on the bank, and the city paid it cash, to locate its back offices here. On paper, the project made Brooklyn, New York's second-poorest borough—measured by per capita income—look better statistically. In reality, many people are not so sure. Some say the office projects (several more are forthcoming) will merely bring Manhattan's problems—raised rents, congestion, tacky service strips—across the river. They doubt that jobs for Brooklyn's unemployed blue-collar workers will follow. Critics also fear volatility, as the projects are pegged to Manhattan's financial services. Will there be a need for them in recession times?

From the 1840s on, developers projected Brooklyn as Mrs. Faust, the well-brought-up lady wife of dynamic, uncouth, money-grubbing Manhattan. Now it looks as if the borough is being cast as the secretary of the powerful executive.

8

Whitman's New York
From Soho to Fulton Ferry

Subway: BMT Broadway line or IRT Lexington Avenue (local) 6 train
to Canal Street.

I tramp a perpetual journey, (come listen all!)
My signs are a rain-proof coat, good shoes, and a staff cut from
    the woods,
No friend of mine takes his ease in my chair,
I have no chair, no church, no philosophy,
I lead no man to a dinner-table, library, exchange,
But each man and each woman of you I lead upon a knoll,
My left hand hooking you round the waist,
My right hand pointing to landscapes of continents and the public
    road.

O public road, I say back I am not afraid to leave you, yet I love
    you,
You express me better than I can express myself,
You shall be more to me than my poem.
                                        —"Song of the Open Road"

Shoulder your duds dear son, and I will mine, and let us hasten
    forth,
Wonderful cities and free nations we shall fetch as we go.

I find it fun to walk this route with friends and take turns reading aloud
from *Leaves of Grass*. On the other hand, it's also sweet to take the open
road alone, reading as you go. Be careful, though, of traffic along Canal

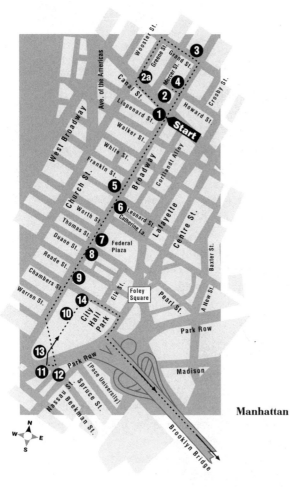

Manhattan

Brooklyn

Street, the likelihood of pick pockets ("the trottoirs everywhere close-spread, thick tangled").

Start on the corner of Lispenard Street ❶ (one block below Canal) and Broadway. (There is a parking lot where you can stand out of traffic and read the introduction.)

Lispenard Street took its name from Rutgers in-laws (see Walk 3) who bought 70 acres of swamp from the British Crown and drained it before the Revolution. From 1809 to 1819 the city channeled the rivulets that ran river to river under Canal Street in a drawn-out, contentious project. The aim was to empty the dregs of the Collect Pond to the east and mop up remaining marsh.

Walt Whitman was born in 1819, the same year the digging of the canal—which eventually gave the street its name—ended.

In early times the mesh of hills and bog made the area around Canal Street hard to reach from lower Manhattan. Few bridges spanned the stream winding under the present street. Peter Cooper (born 1791) remembered crossing the water on a log as a boy.

In the eighteenth century, settlement was light. The land mainly held small industries, including a tannery and, interestingly, given the cast iron buildings to come, an iron foundry. After the city paved Broadway up to present-day Astor Place in 1809, development accelerated. Residences proliferated on Broadway and Spring Street, an east-west transverse not far north of here. When the canal's stench and the town's expansion forced the city to vault the ditch in 1821, builders raced to build blocks of housing. (The waterway was never filled. A few years ago, a portion of the roadway at the Hudson end of Canal Street caved in, revealing the stubborn stream below.)

By 1835, when Whitman arrived in Manhattan at age sixteen to work in the city's printing trade, the Federal houses built here following the canal's covering had already begun to be demolished or transformed for trade. Twenty years on, when the poet published his first edition of *Leaves of Grass* celebrating this neighborhood, retail stores and textile warehouses abounded. Remaining residences such as the—still extant—Federal dwelling at 149 Mercer Street commonly held brothels. New York book stalls sold a popular guide to Mercer Street bordellos advertising "fair Quakeresses," "accomplished señoritas," and "Creole dazzlers." Whitman wrote: "The prostitute draggles her shawl, her bonnet bobs on her tipsy and pimpled neck. . . ."

Whitman had been born in West Hills, Long Island, to a farming family with long ties to the region. His father's ancestry was English Quaker, his mother's Dutch. This rooted "American" lineage and the self-conscious patriotism of his parents (they named three of their sons after Washington, Jefferson, and Jackson) were among the influences eventually leading Whitman to create an American myth. (Rather, *the* American myth.) Paradoxically underlying this conscious impulse, the goad driving the poet to distill a quintessential American ethos was not the certainties he knew, but the flux and loss around him.

The first change Whitman experienced was his move to Brooklyn at age four. Farms were failing, Brooklyn, still a village of 8,000 but about to take off as Manhattan's residential suburb, offered work or the promise of work. Whitman Senior became a carpenter and small contractor in the housing trade. Young Whitman added to the family income by serving as a printer's apprentice at Fulton Landing, the hub of Brooklyn's newspapers. In 1835 he got a job as a printer's assistant in Manhattan on Printing House Row. During the next four decades Whitman spent much of his time, except for a short stint in Washington, shuttling between Brooklyn and Manhattan. In 1873 he retired to Camden, New Jersey, his retreat due partly to health but more to soul weariness. During Whitman's forty years here, New York City had grown from a comprehensible artisanal town of less than 125,000 to an overwhelming metropolis of 1 million. By the time Whitman died in Camden in 1892, Manhattan and Brooklyn held more than 2.3 million people between them.

Whitman's life spanned New York's growth from a Jacksonian town to a modern metropolis.

Whitman called New York the city of "orgies, walks and joys." He is the urban walkers' poet, our patron. (Male) boulevarding, mingling with the masses, *seeing* together, was a new phenomenon both here and in Europe when Whitman came to the city in the 1830s.*

*Poet Theophilus Eaton, who wrote *Review of New York, or Rambles Through the City* in 1813, is an isolated forerunner who walked all parts of Manhattan's settled tip, seeing kinetically, and using latter-day Whitmanesque terms such as "thronging" to describe the city's (proto) coursing humanity. Eaton's dates are important—the city had just begun its sharp spatial and class divide at the time, providing the diversity essential for "flaneuring"—an entitled tour through diverse zones.

Before this time the poor had made the streets their home, an extension
of their crowded houses, but few are recorded (consciously) observing street
life as theater. At an upper level, until now, the fashionable had not wandered
far afield but promenaded on circumscribed thoroughfares to see and be seen
by their peers, acknowledging slightly familiar faces ("nodding acquaintances") with a bow. The new mobility was made possible in great part by the
joining of city streets after the Revolution when the municipality hitched
many short links together. Before then, streets were considered gathering
places rather than conduits for flow. For example, the old colonial pumps
were right in the middle of Broadway and other avenues; shopkeepers advertised themselves as "John *in* such and such a street."

As demography changed and the city compartmentalized, bow
changed to blur. If Whitman had a gesture, it was not a bow, but a distant
wave. As he moved about to absorb "our million hued and ever changing
panorama" he saw it all "as a kind of half dream, saluted by drivers in passing." In the 1830s the growing anonymity of the enlarging city made this
new voyeuristic way of experiencing possible: the intensifying velocity and
density of urban life made it desirable, both for pleasure and for gaining a
restorative sense of the whole.

By the way, New Yorkers still walk more than any other people in this
country, and many don't know how to drive—a weird American subcul-
ture. Another point is that it is not true that New Yorkers do not give each
other eye contact, particularly now that middle-class "respectable"
women* are also allowed to flaneur—a fairly recent entitlement. There is
probably more eye contact here than any other place outside of Italy. On
the hoof at least, every person is fair game for novelistic and erotic surmise.
It is only when *not* on the move, in a fixed, usually enclosed, space that eye
contact is anathema. One more point is that flaneuring as a privileged city
game may end as poor neighborhoods turn desperate and also as the poor
continue to transgress boundaries and enter rich neighborhoods—a recent
phenomenon born from homelessness. Classic flaneuring was defined as
privileged males crossing boundaries. When poor men did it, it was, is vagrancy, or worse (See Walk 4).

A second factor altering the urban way of seeing in the 1830s was
the horse-drawn omnibuses that had started operating in New York a

---

*In the past, "unrespectable" women's perambulations were not aimless saunters, but
purposeful walks for procuring men. "Respectable" women's perambulations were purposeful
walks for procuring goods. See Walk 9.

few years before Whitman arrived. The poet-observer was as addicted to riding as to walking. Sitting up top with the coachmen, Whitman gained a perspective on the city streets and also developed a panoramic view, a kinetic sense not possible on foot, of how the city flowed together. Even today, a good way to see the city is from a regular bus. The vantage of height and magisterial pace are perfect for unobstructed gazing.

The events Whitman observed were physically and socially costly as well as exhilarating. Entire neighborhoods changed overnight in the welter of building and rebuilding. In 1842 Whitman wrote a news piece about a woman at the Baptist burial ground on Delancey Street armed with a loaded pistol defending her husband's grave against real estate developers. "A mob rioted in sympathy," he reported, but the "Divinity of trade prevailed."

Whitman had two strategies allowing him to experience city pain as well as excitement without analyzing causes. The first was cataloging at rapid clip. By sheer life force, his spirit triumphed over chaos. So did the city he constructed, at least in his

In his free time the poet rode omnibuses (introduced a few years before his arrival), which allowed him to see the city kinetically, as an entity.

poems. As much as present-day New Yorkers talk of "street energy" in a way that (until recently) could seemingly redeem, or at least soften, harsh circumstances, the energy Whitman absorbed on his rambles allowed him to find regeneration even in the darkest aspects of city life. The second way of experiencing that allowed Whitman to alleviate the grief he found, to obfuscate its sources, was empathy, becoming one with his subjects.

When writing prose about Brooklyn, his beloved childhood hometown, Whitman was far less cagey than in his poetry on Manhattan, which while seeming to celebrate flux and embrace "the all" in many ways looked back nostalgically to a harmonious—and rapidly passing—artisanal world. In his Brooklyn reporting Whitman set out to forge a "conscious contract with the past," constructing warps of filiopietistic landmarks and heroes. He also invented self-myths. His favorite was a highly unlikely tale about General Lafayette's return visit to Brooklyn in 1825. Whitman claimed the old revolutionary singled out his five-year-old self from a well-wishing crowd, swept him in embrace, and kissed him—an "event" the poet construed as marking his place in the nation's continuum.

The strategies worked—up to a point. Whitman stayed engaged in the urban scene longer than the preceding generation of writers, such as James Fenimore Cooper and Washington Irving, who'd retired fairly early in life to country estates. After the Civil War, however, Whitman also quit the city. Even before leaving, he'd written friends in Washington (1867) that he went around New York daily, "but I find the places and crowds and excitements—Broadway etc.—have not the zest of former times—they have done their work, and now they are to me as a tale that is told."

Walk north up Broadway to Canal Street and turn left; staying on the south side of the street, walk half a block west. Look one block farther along Canal, beyond the building billboarded "Uncle Sam."

☞ The **dormered Federal Houses** ㉚ on the north side of Canal, numbers 313, 317, 321, and 325, remind us of the period the neighborhood was residential. The crooked-chimneyed, pasted-over houses with half-hidden dormer windows date from a year or so after the canal got sealed shut.

Samuel Morse, inventor and painter, lived at 321 Canal in 1825. Like James Fenimore Cooper and Washington Irving, Morse was one of the city's establishment intellectuals, a world away from Whitman's deliberately marginal stance. Though the Century Association where Morse was treasurer had opened in 1847 to succor the town's "creative," Whitman was not a member. In fact, he consciously strove to overcome the elitist attitudes of earlier gentry writers such as Cooper and Washington Irving.

Perhaps his antipathy to the earlier writers owed not simply to their style but to some overlap of intentions. He would have scorned the link, but Whitman's effort to construct and redeem New York (and America) through his poems was in the tradition of Cooper and Irving, both of whom had earlier tried to contrive a picturesque mythology for the new world based on folklore and "nature" romance. (As a boy, Whitman had read "The Leather Stocking Tales" with pleasure.) Some of the poet's sentimental writings on Long Island, which he liked to call Paumanok, the native American name, are as forced as Cooper's Gothic effusions.

When Whitman arrived in Manhattan in 1835, Federal residences such as these lined Canal Street.

At this juncture, you should be roughly across the street from the **Arnold Constable Store,** ❷ *307–311 Canal, which is on the north side of the transverse near Mercer Street.*

☞ This Italianate department store, graced by arched windows and corinthian pilasters, went up in 1856. It is marble, one of the many grand commercial institutions that replaced the old brick residences here.

Boom and bust. Constable had joined Arnold after going broke in the depression of 1837. The city was due for another depression the year after this store went up—a killer, leaving 200,000 people without adequate support. As this store sold luxuries, it survived, while stores catering to middling sorts went out of business. It was this convulsive cycle that Whitman tried to transmute into sheer life force through his writing. The poet's gusto, at times orgiastic, at other times creaking with self-consciousness and self-will, was as famous in his day as ours. (One of the reasons that many sophisticates hate Whitman is his "enthusiasm," so deadly to an adolescent and the only aspect of the Good Gray Poet most curricula expose to high schoolers.)

Whitman's literary cronies of the day at *Vanity Fair* magazine spoofed Whitman's boosterism of New York's commercial energies and his spating, all-embracing judgment-free style.

I loaf and invite the Buyer
I am the essence of retail. The sum and the result
    of small profits and quick returns
All these things are of me, and many more also
    for I am the shop, and the counter, and the Till
But particularly the last.
And I explore and rummage the Till, and am at
    home in it.

***C**ontinue west along Canal to Greene Street and cross north. Enter Greene and look up the thoroughfare.*

☞ The street has stayed much the same since its rebuilding as a commercial district before and just after the Civil War. What's remarkable here is the continuance not only of form (the iron buildings were saved from destruction in the 1960s by the redoubtable preservationist Margot Gayle) but to some degree, its function. Despite massive Soho gentrification in the 1970s and 1980s, many textile warehouses remain. Note the signage.

By the 1830s, dry goods were coming to New York in such profusion that storage warehouses were jerry built and subject to spectacular collapse.

☞ On the northeast corner of Canal and Greene "Hollow Pavement" signs cautioning against parking motor bikes indicate **underground vaults.** Note the glass bubble surface covering the sidewalk. From the 1840s on, merchants built cellars under the pavement next to their stores to cope with the barrage of textiles inundating New York. The rounds of glass set in the pavement provided illumination below ground. Unlike most vaults in lower Manhattan and Brooklyn, this glass cover is in rare pristine state. Most have been macadamed over.

Also invaluable for holding the flow of goods were cast iron warehouses, introduced in the 1840s and the preferred mode by the Civil War. Developers, who, for whatever reason continued to build in stone, even copied the look of iron. Touch some of the buildings to make sure they are metal.

One of the city's cast iron structures that greatly popularized the form was the 1853 Crystal Palace exposition hall in Bryant Park, a copycat of a similar building and exposition in England two years earlier. The iron-framed glass-paned fabrication supported by a myriad of columns could (literally) hold tons of the era's new consumer goods under one roof—a dazzling debut for mass culture and consumerism. Whitman was so entranced by the building and exhibits he returned more than a dozen times, until officials assigned a detail of detectives (a new city phenomenon) to shadow him. The tall, rough-looking man made himself more suspicious by the in-your-face "bohemian" garb he affected.

"Around a palace, loftier, fairer, ampler than any yet,
Earth's modern wonder, history's seven outstripping,
High rising tier on tier with glass and iron facades. . . ."
—"Song of the Exposition"

Cast iron seemed a heaven-sent medium for the rapid expansion of New York's commerce. By the 1860s and continuing through the 1890s, the city's iron industry, grown out of bridge and greenhouse building in England, was third in importance after the dry goods trade and garment production. One attribute ascribed to iron (soon proved false when the Crystal Palace blazed, cracked apart, then melted) was its supposed fire-proofness. Iron's second desirable feature, its low cost, far cheaper than stone, stood the test of time. The third most crucial asset was the easy assembly iron allowed. Units of panels and arches could be mass produced from sand molds, given a primer of paint, then numbered and carted to the building site for construction. Non-English-speaking immigrants working under a foreman could put up buildings in a single day.

The era of replication both fascinated and repelled Whitman, who as a young man had helped his carpenter-builder father construct frame houses in Brooklyn. The same new technologies giving the poet, and other Victorians, optimism were also eroding the old artisanal order he idealized.

☞ Even names of well-known architects (John B. Snook, Henry Fernbach, Griffith Thomas, Isaac Duckworth) that the big New York iron works hired as in-house designers do not appear on buildings here. Only the logos of the foundries belonging to James Bogardus, Daniel Badger, and J. B. Cornell can be seen in the base blocks of many of these buildings.

Walk up Greene Street to Grand Street. Turn right and walk to Broadway.
Because of their dependency on southern cotton, New York merchants

By the Civil War, commerce had overtaken city neighborhoods the poet knew best, and cast-iron warehouses such as these replaced most of Soho's residential blocks.

initially opposed the Civil War. (The mayor even proposed secession as a free city-state so as not to get involved.) It was only after the attack on Fort Sumter in 1861 that the local elite and much of the rest of the town turned around. Many of the merchants who had earlier opposed New York's joining the war now profited from churning out supplies for the Union Army.

☞ During the conflict, the parking lot on the northwest corner of Grand and Broadway was the site of **Lord and Taylor. ❸** Brooks Brothers stood across the street on the northeast corner of Broadway. Both stores had immensely lucrative contracts for uniforms sewn by low-paid immigrant labor.

During the draft riots of 1863, Irish mobs sacked Brooks Brothers. Lord and Taylor managed to defend themselves, as their Yankee clerks marched down to the Arsenal and returned with howitzers. For months afterward rotations of Lord and Taylor clerks spent nights at the store sleeping on bales of dry goods, pistols at the ready.

Walt Whitman's brother George, who had joined the army and was then posted in Kentucky, wrote that the riot "was enough to make you shamed to be a Yorker . . . I would have went into that fight with just as good a heart, as if they had belonged to the reb army."

*W*alk south on Broadway to Howard Street; turn right (west) and note the stone buildings, 50 and 52 Howard Street, opposite the brick back of Arnold Constable across the street. This was the **New York State Soldiers Depot Convalescent Home and Hospital, ❹** opened for wounded Civil War troops on recovery leave.

Walt did not share his sibling's stomach for fighting. (Or syntax.) Some say his Quaker background and adversity to killing kept him from joining. Whatever the reasons, he spent the start of the war taking bizarre water

SACKING BROOKS'S CLOTHING STORE.

therapies, purges, and diets, including the new cracker regimen just invented by a Mr. Graham. It was as if he had to cure himself from some disease that was troubling the body politic. (The obsessive fitness culture prompted by Victorian anxieties resembles our own.) Whitman's solipsistic self-nurture at the beginning of the war contrasted with his earlier editorial and political ardor

Violence tore New York apart during the Civil War draft riots. Whitman's brother George, who had enlisted in the Union Army, wrote him that the riot "was enough to make you shamed to be a Yorker."

on pro-Union and Free-Soil issues. Like other Free Soilers, he respected states' rights and was against abolition but opposed extending slavery in states where it wasn't as yet established.

The poet's Free Soil stance was as much for whites, whom he thought were demeaned by the institution of slavery, as for blacks. Despite his self-proclaimed cosmic empathy, Whitman was racist toward African Americans. To back his prejudice, he drew on the sixth U.S. census statistics, which supposedly supported the conclusion that African Americans couldn't assimilate and was fond of citing the incidence of insanity and "idiocy" among free blacks—purportedly ten times higher than among slaves.

He often referred disparagingly to the many free blacks he'd seen begging as a child in Brooklyn—a likely occurrence at that time, as exclusion from trades was rife and African Americans had only recently (1809) won back the right to own land. Much of present-day Soho, for example, had been deeded to freed slaves in Dutch colonial days but repossessed after 1712.

> (Arous'd and angry, I thought to beat the alarum, and urge
> relentless war,
> But soon my fingers fail'd me, my face droop'd and I resign'd
> myself,
> To sit by the wounded and soothe them, or silently watch the
> dead;). . . .

> —"The Wound-Dresser"

Whitman finally bestirred himself after his brother was wounded in action. Moving to Washington where George was convalescing, the poet spent several years working in the bureaucracy and volunteering his time nursing. During this period he transmuted his anguish about the war into what would become the central spine of his American myth. Whitman credited his Washington period with teaching him "hospital wisdom," the ability to keep balance even when seeing wounds crawling with maggots. He already, however, had a morbid, if saintly drive for the avocation. Before the war Whitman regularly assisted in the wards of New York Hospital a few blocks down from here on Broadway and Duane Street.

Walk back to Broadway and turn right (south), keeping to the west side of the street, to 359 Broadway.

☞ Stop just south of the building and look up at the side wall. The top three floors of this 1853 structure, one of several daguerreotype studios on this block, served as **Mathew Brady's lab, ❺** portrait studio, and gallery when the building opened, until he shifted uptown a decade later.

When Brady moved here from lower Broadway, he had just swept the daguerreotypy awards at London's Crystal Palace exposition. Until several years ago there was a legible sign here in bold yellow lettering advertising the studio. It's gone now. The landlord painted it over because, it's rumored, he wanted to avoid landmark designation to build a sliver high rise. The review by the New York City Landmarks Preservation Commission was full of courtroom drama hinging on whether Lincoln had come here as Republican nominee for the portrait later engraved on the five-dollar bill. In fact, Lincoln went to Brady's uptown studio. Gratifyingly, the hearing was one of the first where arguments for saving the building revolved round the structure's social importance rather than just aesthetics. More gratifyingly, the building has recently won landmark status.

Like the poet, who wanted to find, to forge the American voice, Brady (a migrant to the city from upstate near the time Whitman arrived) aimed to cohere America through his images.

The gallery, now housing a sweatshop, once hung with portraits of America's great—old revolutionaries and their widows. Whitman, who titled one of his journalist columns "City Photographs," likened the room of embodied memory to "an immense Phantom concourse." During the Civil War Brady's photographs of Union Army soldiers and their sufferings in the field paralleled the poet's writing.

One outcome of the fluid age the two artists lived in was an increasing anomie. Many at the time commented on the growing sense that life was less real, or as Karl Marx said, "every thing solid melts into air." This amorphous feeling coupled with the rise of photography and the press led to the cult of celebrities—a new phenomenon. Much of Brady's success came from pictures of the famous he shamelessly sought and hawked.

Victorians used photography, a new art, as aid to self-invention or, at least, the self's sealant. From the 1820s on, Whitman constructed himself through photography on a regular basis. (Brady took some.) The several hundred photographs of the poet engendered a range of images that he manipulated to convey carefully chosen meanings of himself. In old age he promoted the bushy-bearded good gray poet picture that in recent years has contributed to his trivialization as a benign Santa.

Once dressing (and posing for photographs) like a Bowery fop in a "swaggy" posture, Whitman later switched after reading a George Sand novel. In 1847, after reviewing Sand's book about a carpenter Christ figure, he started dressing like the novel's protagonist in a working-class slouch hat, checked shirt open at the neck, and baggy pants tucked into boots. (This was the same outfit that made the detectives notice him at the Crystal Palace.)

With his name change to "Walt" when *Leaves of Grass* came out in 1855, Whitman was a new man, or rather, *the* new man.

In light of his father's craft and his carpentry apprenticeship as a young man, the dress is rather poignant. What once was unconscious now was costume.

Continue south on Broadway. At Leonard Street, stop on the west side of the avenue and look across at 346 Broadway, formerly the **New York Life Insurance Company building ❻** by Griffith Thomas.

☞ When it went up in 1870, a post–Civil War boom in land prices had led to the greatest speculative period in the city's history until our own. The immense building (huge even before the addition of several upper stories and a tower) is a good example of the expanding economy and gigantism contributing to Victorian malaise and its opposite, hubris. The money that built the structure came from the growing subscription to life insurance in an age that saw the breakdown of family ties and caretaking responsibilities.

Keep walking south along Broadway. The southeast corner of Thomas and Broadway, where the Jacob Javits Building stands today at 308 Broadway, is **the site of Fowler and Wells'** ❼ *Phrenological Cabinet and book store.*

Whitman distributed his *Leaves of Grass* through Fowler, who—remarkably to our specialist eyes—also served as his phrenology analyst. Like many modern writers, Whitman grumbled about the poor distribution Fowler and Wells gave his work. He *knew* it could reach wider audiences. It had some great reviews—he himself had taken the precaution of writing several glowing ones. This was perhaps wise, as other critics were not always so kind. The *Boston Intelligencer* called the collection a "heterogeneous mass of bombast, egotism, vulgarity and nonsense."

Whitman was a latecomer to the other service offered here, phrenology, the pseudo-science of revealing the client's personality by charting his cranial bumps and then improving the client's disposition and prospects by reshaping his cranium through massage. By the 1840s the practice had become the rage in American cities and countryside. The same angst that made photography popular prompted the fascination: in a confusing age the manipulation gave the illusion of control. At first Whitman demurred, but he became a fan after learning he had the skull of "a genius." His analysts noted, among other attributes, his propensity for adhesiveness or brotherly bonding.

Make a loop west (turn right) on Thomas and walk to Trimble Place halfway down the block. (This short side trip is not drawn on the map.)

One of the ways Whitman used the adhesive side of his nature was nursing at New York Hospital founded in 1771 between Duane and Worth Streets on the west side of Broadway. **Trimble Place,** named after a hospital chairman, marks the old ambulance entrance between the facility's two wings.

Traffic accidents were common in the surging city, particularly along frenetic Broadway. Many of the patients here were the teamsters Whitman loved, both abstractly for their "animal qualities" and individually for their company. One teamster in particular, Irish coachman Peter Doyle, whom Whitman had nursed in Washington, became his longtime friend. Whitman even chased ambulances—the only ambulance-chasing poet on record. The volume of admissions due to accidents was one reason for the indebted hospital's straits and its shift uptown.

In 1862 Whitman wrote in the *New York Leader,* "The hospital exists now on its own income—about 38 percent of patients are gratuitous, the U.S. pays 75 cents a day for soldiers." In follow-up articles he explained how the city had never helped the institution and how the state had quit its subsidy in 1857.

☞ In 1869 the cash-short governors sold the land (now soared in value), and developers cut Thomas Street through the grounds as a private thoroughfare.

Warehouses (by Griffith Thomas) went up on the north side between Thomas and Worth for the flourishing textile trade. The southern hospital wing lasted until 1870, but it, too, was dismantled when the real estate board complained that the building was driving down values in adjoining property. Trimble Place was preserved only to give the new warehouses light and air.

Return to Broadway and turn right (south), passing the **African Burial Ground,** ❽ formerly the Negro Burial Ground, on the eastern side of the avenue between Duane and Reade Streets. (Detour east on Reade past the new courthouse to see the protected part of the cemetery begun in the 1690s after Trinity Church banned even baptized African American congregants from being buried in its graveyard.) Retrace your steps and continue south down Broadway to Chambers Street.

☞ You will walk past **A. T. Stewart's Marble Palace,** ❾ where Mathew Brady clerked to support himself when he came to the city to learn photography.

Note the copper corner clock on the store's northeast corner advertising the "The Sun it Shines for All." From 1917 to 1952 the building housed *The Sun,* the city's first penny press, founded in the 1830s, and one of the many journals where Whitman worked. (In the poet's time it was located on Centre Street near today's Municipal Building.) It was new technology, particularly the Hoe circular press, that made penny papers like the *Sun* possible and built up huge circulation.

*W*alk south through **City Hall Park**, noting as you go the Italianate **Tweed Court House** ⑩ behind **City Hall**. If it's a warm day, sit down on the steps of City Hall for a rest and perhaps a sandwich before going on to ponder Whitman's relationship with the park.

From the 1830s through the turn of the century, this part of New York was the city's newspaper hub. The tie between media, harbor, and city government was tight; papers had to be near City Hall and had to have harbor access, as international news arrived by boat. James Bennett of the *Herald* (located to the south of the *Times* down near Ann Street, just south of the park) even developed a rail line to Montauk, Long Island, where he kept sloops that could race out to incoming vessels and get the scoop. (See Walk 6 for more about the newspaper district.)

The buildings we see now on the **old newspaper row** ⑪ (Park Place and the streets immediately behind) went up at the end of the area's run as the city's journalist center.

Whitman worked at almost a dozen papers along Printing House Row near City Hall.

(An aside here is that in 1893—the period from which most of these offices

date—the city had *nineteen* dailies plus scores of foreign journals. Today, we can barely support three major English-language dailies.)

***Y**ou may like to cross the park to see the row more closely.*

☞ Buildings of interest include: R. H. Robertson's **American Tract Society Building** at 150 Nassau Street; the 1889 **New York Times Building** at 41 Park Row (its third incarnation on the site); and the 1883 molded terra-cotta **Potter Building** at 38 Park Row, which once housed the *Press*. (Engineers deemed the material fireproof at the time. The site's earlier incumbent, the *New York World* where Whitman worked for a time, had burned to the ground.) The **1899 cupolaed building** at 15 Park Row once held the Associated Press. For a brief while, this early skyscraper was the tallest building in the city, one of the highest in the world. Its cupolas were the cynosure of the New York skyline.

Whitman's first job when he came to Manhattan, after finishing his apprenticeship in Brooklyn in 1835, was as junior printer at the *New World*. Like other papers, the *New World* kept printers on twenty-four-hour call. (The predecessor of St. Andrew's Roman Catholic Church near Police Plaza used to offer 2:30 A.M. masses for immigrant apprentices.) The long waiting hours gave Whitman time to read and write, and the journal published his first poems. But employment didn't last long. Six months later the fire that destroyed Printing House Row, along with much of lower Manhattan, forced Whitman and others out of work and out of town.

When he returned to the city in 1841 after five years' absence in Long Island teaching and "loafing, inviting the soul," newspapers had become big business. New York was on its way to becoming the information center it is today. Despite the expansion, journalism was still considered a trade, not a white-collar profession. (Even today some reporters like to keep alive the old brawn and brawl image handed down by late-night movies.) Though Whitman had "graduated" from printing to writing when he returned for a second stint here, the seven or eight newspapers he toiled for treated him as an expendable workhorse. Conversely, he was allowed to voice far more independent opinion than is imaginable today—with a few exceptions. One came early on when he was forced out of his first writing job at the *Aurora* just behind Park Row on Nassau Street. His articles on the school issue were so vitriolically anti-Catholic, even his extremist editor finally ordered him to turn more conciliatory or leave.

When Whitman quit the *Aurora*, he moved on to the *Democrat*, a Tammany paper published in the Tammany Society's own building near the Brooklyn Bridge where Pace University stands today. During his time there—he lived as well as worked in the building—Whitman wrote a temperance novel on commission for his ex-employers at the *Aurora*. *Franklin Evans the Inebriate* was so bad he later disowned it. His work for the *Democrat,* mostly lurid imitations of Edgar Allen Poe, then being published in the *New York Post,* was equally poor. (The two writers never met, though both worked in the city at the same time.)

If the new printing technology had created the capability for mass circulation, the journals' publication of foreign writers created the market. A favorite was Charles Dickens, published in the *World* and the *Tribune*. It was these novels that kept city pressmen on twenty-four hour call. The rage for European authors was so intense it created a backlash. Ralph Waldo Emerson led the demand for an American voice. Whitman followed. "America *is* a poem in our eyes: its ample geography dazzles the imagination and will not wait long for meters." Actually, half of Whitman followed. The other half reveled in world literature. Because of the book reviewing he did for papers, Whitman read and skimmed massively. Translations of the Upanishads, Homer, Goethe, and Sand were among the many influences for *Leaves Of Grass* he later took pains to hide.

W*alk along Park Row to the intersection with Beekman Street; turn left, then right into* **Theater Alley,** ⑫ *which served the old Park Theater.*

Whitman mingled high and low culture in his poems, but never resolved the duality he perceived to be a conflict. Particularly when he wrote about music, he was torn between what Poe called "art and heart" music, respectively represented in the city by Italian opera and touring New England folk troupes. Whitman's ambivalence extended to the theater.

By the 1840s the Park Theater on Printing House Row was at the classy end of the spectrum and some, though not all, of the Bowery theaters at the other. (Whitman liked the "urgent" audiences in the Bowery, "the common quickening and kindling of the spirit." The theaters there, he wrote, showed more democracy and had better "animal specimens" in the pit.) Whitman, a drama fanatic and newspaper critic, was a Park regular. After hearing Junius Brutus Booth on its stage, he wrote that it had been the greatest "revelation" in his life, that he had been "intoxicated with the human voice to the point of trembling." The spoken voice, he said, was "the underpinning of poetry."

Cross back over to the park and sit comfortably to read the following.

Aside from journalism and theater, politics is the other prism for seeing the park through Whitman's eyes. Even though he steered clear of analyzing the upheavals around him in his poetry, Whitman was a profoundly political man. When he lived at the Tammany building, as well as working as a journalist and playwright, he also lobbied on Free Soil issues, giving soapbox orations in the park. His language in these was direct, non-literary—in his own words, "come-day, go-day palaver."

For years Whitman was active on the Brooklyn Democratic committee—serving on councils and at one time acting as secretary. During this time he officiated at rallies, sat on reviewing grounds, marched in parades, and composed patriotic hymns. He remained a loyal party man until 1848, when he severed ties with the Democrats because he found the new ruling Democrats to be "opportunistic enemies of free labor."

Among civic struggles in which Whitman directly involved himself was the battle for the working-class public park in Fort Greene, Brooklyn. With notable exceptions (including his prejudice against Catholics and African Americans), Whitman was progressive for the day. Fanny Wright, the radical English leader of the Workingman's party, was one influence. Whitman had read her speeches and attended her lectures in Brooklyn Heights.

After quitting the Democrats, Whitman floated. He became a devotee of Lincoln but could never bring himself to be a Republican. The poet's first sight of his future idol, Abraham Lincoln, then president-elect, occurred just below the park on Broadway, when a crowd of 30,000–40,000 people stalled his omnibus as they gathered to gaze at the politician. Lincoln had not yet come out publicly for abolition, but New Yorkers still worried that the congressman was too apt to split the Union. Tension in the city over Lincoln's visit wound so high, municipal officials feared for his life. Whitman described the sullenness of the crowd, their "mask of silence," as they watched the president-to-be arrive at the Astor House Hotel just above St. Paul's Chapel.

The park was to see many more shifts of feeling.

After the war and Lincoln's assassination, the mood changed once again. In a vast cortege of crepe and grief, the president's body was carried down Broadway to lie in state under City Hall's rotunda. (You might want to read Whitman's ode to the fallen leader, "When Lilacs Last in the Door Yard Bloom'd," before moving on.)

Whitman wrote in his notebook about the procession: "All Broadway is black with mourning—the facades of the houses are festooned with black—great flags with wide and heavy fringes of dead black, give a pensive effect—towards noon the sky darkened and it began to rain. Drip, drip and heavy moist black weather . . . Lincoln's death—black, black, black as you look towards the sky-direction."

☞ Whitman's descent over years from optimism to somber watchfulness has an objective correlative in park structures. Several of Whitman's poems, including one celebrating the Atlantic cable, whose success was feted at City Hall, have to do with new technological breakthroughs, the thrill of connection. Once, the poet apotheosized the 1842 Croton water fountain ⓭ at the southern end of the park as being the concrete expression of the poem he wanted to write.

By the 1870s the same inventions that had been greeted in the 1840s were increasingly viewed as controlling, dehumanizing. Or at least their owners were seen that way. The Victorians' initial ecstasy with modernity, their sense that technology was made for people rather than the reverse, short circuited. In the wake of the harrowing Civil War, rampant corruption, and general drift, Whitman and others grew depressed, occasionally despairing. In 1871, just before suffering a stroke, the poet published *Democratic Vistas,* a bleak look at America's future laced with

Lincoln's death was a blow to the poet, who left the city for good in the 1870s, demoralized and ailing.

melancholy over the haplessness of the many, the concentration of capital
in the hands of the few.

☞ As much as the fountain at the park's southern apex serves to illustrate
Whitman's new age hopes, Boss Tweed's **Criminal Courthouse** ⑭ at the
northern end of the park serves to emblemize Whitman's later doubts.

The same year *Vistas* came out, the courthouse (which had a cost over-
run of $11 million out of $12 million spent) went up. Tammany's enemies
hailed it as a monument of corruption. In many ways the scandal surrounding the building illustrated democracy's failure, or at least its weak-
ness.

A year afterward Whitman suffered a stroke and withdrew to New
Jersey.

*T*he next part of this walk takes us over to Brooklyn. Cross over Centre
Street to the bridge (begun in 1872 just before Whitman left for Camden).
Take care to stay on the left of the center path as you walk over to avoid
bikes. Be sure, however, to stop and look at the "sparkle and scud" of the
harbor and river, as well as back at Manhattan.

Whitman, sensibly, preferred the nature-framed sea view of Manhattan as opposed to the prospect from the grid. In *Specimen Days* he wrote of
gulls, "those daring, careening, things of grace and wonder, those white
and shaded swift darting fish-birds . . . ever with their slanting spars, and
fierce, pure, hawklike beauty and motion" and Manhattan, "rising out of
the midst, tall topt, ship-hemmed, modern, American, yet strangely oriental, V-shaped Manhattan, with its compact mass, its spires, its cloud-touch-
ing edifices group'd at the centre."

*T*ake the first exit off the bridge on the left. After you get down the stairs,
turn left, then left again, then walk to your right past the bridge foundation
(inside which is a small museum), slowly proceeding down **Fulton Street** ⑮
toward the river.

This old road continues inland to Jamaica, where it once served Long
Island farmers, including Whitman's grandparents. The ferry operation at
the foot of the ancient track, built on a Canarsie trail, went back to 1642,
when a boatman stayed on call for farmers carting produce to Manhattan.

From early on, the busy landing spot (Brooklyn's closest spur to Manhattan) accrued markets and slaughterhouses where butchers dressed meat
bound for New York. By 1815, the year the street got named Fulton in

honor of the steam ferry entrepreneur, a cluster of taverns, small factories, and newspaper publishing houses had located here. Most of Brooklyn's few thousand residents lived close by the hamlet. Its trustees incorporated it as a village shortly after the new ferry service opened.

During the early nineteenth century the butchers were the leading men of the settlement, wealthy men, whose physical size also lent them command. (Even kings were first chosen for their bigness.) Everit Street down near the water honors one civic worthy; Doughty Street, another. These men, who worked when butchering was respected as "an art and mystery," provided the basis for Whitman's idealization of artisans—the Republic's heart of oak.

What Whitman factored out of his idyll was that already by 1816— eight years before he moved here as a child—the noxious industries around the landing, and the unruly work force they spawned, had led to such urban blight and social "breakdown" that the local gentry had begun Sunday school missions to tame the gangs of disaffected youth who "roamed" the streets. Or at least to keep them indoors.

Fulton Ferry and the nearby Brooklyn waterfront was Whitman's matrix, and he had more in common with the working-class people here than with the gentry merchants beginning to settle the Heights. By the time of his family's move to Brooklyn in 1823, they had fallen down scale in the rapid expansion of capitalism, and despite their old "American" lineage, which made the poet so proud, they were living quite precariously.

The first house the Whitmans took was down on Front Street close to the river near the Fort Greene Navy Yard. A year later they moved for the winter to Cranberry Street above here on the northern flank of the Heights. Within months, they'd returned to the shore at Johnson Street, the beginning of a series of relocations, as Whitman Senior lost house after house, unable to meet mortgage payments. Except for one more brief stint on the Heights, the family was rooted here. Until he quit at age eleven, the poet attended public school at Adams and Concord near the water.

The social importance of these high and low topographical coordinates is important and has cropped up before. (See Walk 7.) Heights dwellers today often cite Whitman's occasional attendance at St. Ann's Sunday school, where he went for its free lunch, as their link to the poet, since the church now is located there. In Whitman's youth, however, it was still down at its original site near the river. (Later as an apprentice, Whitman occasionally did worship on the Heights—at the Dutch Reform Church on Joralemon—where he soaked up biblical language while resisting the content.)

When Whitman left school, he went to work as an office boy for a lawyers' firm on lower Fulton Street. Through the kindness of his employer, who lent him books—Walter Scott, the Arabian Nights, J. F. Cooper—he became an omnivorous novel reader. Like the other young apprentices who made the neighborhood nervous, he also spent hours exploring the shoreside shipyards, rope-walks, distilleries, glass works, and lead factories.

☞ Just above the south side of Fulton Street, note the red brick newsboys' home standing on the edge of the Heights **⓰** (151 Poplar). A Catholic charity organization built this Venetian Revival structure to house orphan newsboys, who worked and often lived in the streets.

Whitman, considerably, but not absolutely, more secure in economic terms than the newsboys in the home, got his first job in journalism at age eleven, composing for the Jacksonian *Long Island Patriot* on Fulton. The next year he left to work for the Whig opposition paper, the *Long Island Star,* also located here, where he stayed until 1835, when he graduated as journeyman printer and left for Manhattan.

Before departing for "the city," as Brooklynites say even today, Whitman helped his father constructing houses.

☞ A frame building dating from 1834 still stands close by here at 64 Poplar Street (also see Walk 7). The earnest clapboard house, typical of the houses the Whitmans worked on, can be glimpsed through surrounding buildings from the Fulton Street vantage. It is attributed (not documented) to the Whitmans, father and son.

> The preparatory jointing, squaring, sawing, mortising,
> The hoist-up of beams, the push of them in their places, laying
> them regular,
> Setting the studs by their tenons in the mortises. . . ."
> —"Song of the Broad-Axe"

One of the many joys of Whitman is the exact craft language he uses. Though his poems sentimentalize and extend the artisanal period well after its decline, the words come from his bone.

*S*troll farther down the spreading road to the river.

☞ The **brick buildings ⓱** on the north side (numbers 7–23) of Fulton went up in 1835 after the new Brooklyn city government widened the street.

Before leaving Brooklyn for Manhattan to work in newspapers, Whitman may have helped his father, a carpenter-contractor, build this house on the Heights' north slope.

(The village had been incorporated as a city the previous year.) The granite Greek Revival storefronts and leaning canopies of the buildings that once served saddlers, harness makers, lard renderers, coopers, boarding-house keepers, and Irish packet ship agents look as they appear in old prints of the bridge opening. That is, they did until recently, when the garish neon-lit pizza shop opened. The **gray building (1–5 Fulton)** ⑱ began life in 1836 as the Franklin House Hotel and dining saloon. The four-story brick structure was originally Greek Revival but got Italianized or, rather, Italianated in the 1860s. Next to the hotel is a stable from the same period, which probably served travelers bringing their horses over on the ferry. Notice the winch and hoist bracket over the loft door for lifting hay.

In the days when the neighborhood still had a mix of wealthy artisans and a poor working class, the hotel's second floor held a ballroom with a French dancing master who taught quadrilles to local children. The dancing had a short run. By the 1840s, most affluent people down here had moved to the new rowhouses going up on the Heights.

☞ Look at the **Eagle Warehouse** across the street, a fortressy structure that stands on the site of the printing plant belonging to the *Brooklyn Eagle,* a paper founded in 1841 by a conservative Brooklyn civic leader. A scrap of the old press is said to remain at the back of the 1893 warehouse on the northeast corner of Doughty and Elizabeth. (I've never been able to find it.)

The paper lasted until the 1960s and at one point even had a branch in Paris. (Imagine Brooklyn commanding that respect today.) Whitman edited the journal from 1846 to 1848 and for years remained a frequent contributor, writing some of his most memorializing local history here. Among other idealizations Whitman perpetrated through the *Eagle* was Brooklyn's harmony and equality. Statistics don't bear him out. Historian

Edward Pessen calculated that in 1841, 1 percent of the population, the new merchant commuters to Manhattan, owned at least 42 percent of the wealth. The overwhelming majority of these fortunates lived south of Fulton, crammed on the Heights inside a square mile perimeter.

Like many other journalists in Brooklyn at the time, Whitman's regressive stylizations not only solaced his need for stasis, but consciously or unconsciously promoted Brooklyn's powerful real estate interests, which represented the city as an Arcadian haven. The "littlest," "quietest" pitch worked. Despite Manhattan's best efforts to thwart development, by mid-nineteenth century, Brooklyn horsecar companies had twelve lines converging at Fulton Ferry to link the sprawling new suburbs growing up. The 1861 Brooklyn City R.R. Company's office, a horsecar enterprise, still stands at Furman and Fulton, near the old ferry landing.

☞ It is exhilarating to sit at **Fulton Ferry Dock** ⑲ next to Barge Music and read "Crossing Brooklyn Ferry." If you have brought food, stay on through the evening for a memorable view of the river, the bridge, and Manhattan.

> It avails not, time nor place—distance avails not,
> I am with you, you men and women of a generation, or ever so
>   many generations hence,
> Just as you feel when you look on the river and sky, so I felt,
> Just as any of you is one of a living crowd, I was one of a crowd,
> Just as you are refresh'd by the gladness of the river and the
>   bright flow, I was refresh'd,
> Just as you stand and lean on the rail, yet hurry with the swift
>   current, I stood yet was hurried,
> Just as you look on the numberless masts of ships and the thick-
>   stemm'd pipes of steamboats, I look'd.

*W*hen you're done, I suggest you walk next door to the River Cafe, ⑳ *where there are usually cabs, or you can telephone for a car service to take you back up the Heights to the subway.*

9

Ladies' Mile

Subway: IRT Lexington Avenue Local (train 6) or Express (trains 4, 5)
to 14th Street–Union Square.

A good place to read the introduction is on a bench at the south end of Union Square near George Washington's statue. The elevation gives a lofty view down Broadway and other link roads. ❶

Union Square, originally called a "Place," a less formal, less designated space than a square, began its historical life as a potter's field. It remained as such until 1831, though the commissioners of the New York's first planning grid had mapped it as a park twenty years earlier.

In 1831 private realtors led by Samuel Ruggles (early biographers always call him "Ruggles of Gramercy Park," as if he were a boy developer in an adventure series) persuaded the City Council to underwrite landscaping here. Architects patterned the ellipse within the square, a fenced park with four gates that shut at ten P.M., after the Place Vendôme in Paris. Ruggles, who eventually built himself a house on the square, took a detailed interest in what he saw as "his" venture, and for his part eventually contributed London sparrows—a first in the city—and bird houses. Some bird houses still hang in the trees here, related or unrelated to the originals.

The political climate favored Ruggles and other wealthy investors at the time, as the council had just begun intensive support for real estate improvements to raise the city's tax base (and help their own sort of people). The same year the city backed this upgrading, it adopted other preserves, including Gramercy Park, another Ruggles venture, and Madison and Tompkins squares. Developers had already started putting up Washington Square's north row, an enclave soon linked, at Ruggles' behest, to Union Square by the gentry corridor University Place. (The reader might like to

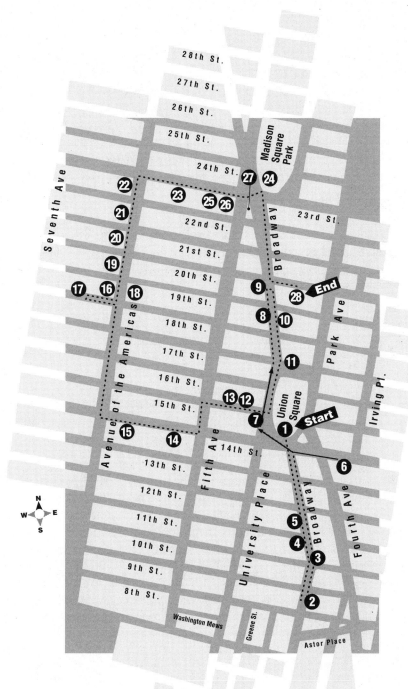

look at the Washington Square section of Walk 4 and at the section on Astor Place's gentrification in Walk 5 to contextualize happenings here.)

In 1834 Ruggles leased several lots on the east side of this publicly financed enclave and built a row of four-story Greek Revival houses in the Boston bow-fronted mode. Some good examples of this type remain on the north side of 16th Street between Fifth and Sixth avenues. A windfall for the developer came after 1849 when the wealthy moved from Astor Place following the riots there. For the next fifteen years Union Square became home to fashionable New Yorkers.

☞ Follow George's gaze down Broadway. For most of its years since 1856, the equestrian figure stood in a corner of the square facing north, the direction of the city's growth. It got turned around in the 1930s in a park re-landscaping effort designed to boost crowd control following mass job rallies by the unemployed.

Union Square might have become the new center for the town's elite, but it was never a bastion. Despite Ruggles' best efforts, the many roads spinning into the hub militated against efforts to make Union Square an absolute preserve.

☞ Note how Broadway and the Bowery (a.k.a. Fourth Avenue) belt up from the south and southeast. To the north, the Bowery, still disguised as Fourth, continues uptown, corseted into finishing-school straightness as Park Avenue. Untrammeled Broadway exits the ground to the northwest on its grid-defying sweep through the city.

(It was technically the *Bowery* that was the root link to the Upper West Side, not lower Broadway, a canard that most writers [including this one] sloppily repeat. The 1707 statute allowing Hudson River landowners to pay for a tract [the Bloemendael Road] to their estates from the lower city ordered the new joinder to start at *New York Lane* [the old name for the Bowery]. As Broadway and the Bowery converged here, it's just a technical win. The old street's secret romp still cheers me, however, even though I don't pursue the point as custom [let alone the street's present name, which gradually became known as Broadway for its entire stretch] is so overwhelmingly against it.)

Another factor keeping the square from being a gentry preserve, even in its residential heyday, was its role as town forum. By the 1860s the would-be enclave had replaced City Hall Park as the place for public gatherings. In part the shift resulted from the general northward expansion of the town; in part it was spurred by the relocation of the Democrats' Tammany Hall to nearby 14th Street. (People crowded in the corners of the square—today's parking spaces.)

After the Confederate Army fired on Fort Sumter, politicians rallied New Yorkers to defend the Union cause under Washington's statue (draped in Sumter's tattered flag). During the course of the emotional meeting the 100,000-strong crowd turned from an antiwar stance to support the federal government, as speakers keened and huzzahed, a group process hard to imagine today, as we don't come together for news but receive it privately in our homes from TV or newspapers.

The third factor skewing Union Square's brief moment as a sheltered green outside of New York's commercial velocity was the energy of the city's merchandising forces, which had been gathering momentum in the 1840s and 1850s.

Just before the Civil War, a new strip of stores, hotels, restaurants, and theaters opened to serve the city's wealthy residents. The retail and entertainment district started immediately below here and ran north along Broadway and parallel avenues to Madison Square. Remarkably in this town that erases its past, the greater part of the buildings are still intact. The block-size hulks startle by their sheer immensity.

Our walk will follow a route that explores the evolution of an era as well as a neighborhood.

The first point in setting out is to think about where we are. The salient geographical fact of the new commercial node was its site in the *center* of Manhattan.

Until the 1840s, stores had remained near the seaport, as shipping was still key to their operations. At that time, some stores followed patrons inland to the residential district. The wealthy, who had moved to escape waterfront commerce, first welcomed the new services; as hubbub grew, however, they fled north. Once again, trade followed.

The consumer market was worth chasing even though it was just beginning its expansion. In the three decades between 1840 and 1870, the population of Manhattan tripled, from 312,852 persons to just under a million: New York was now the national power as well as the world's third-largest city. Money flowed in from western land speculation, southern cotton, trans-Atlantic trade. Above all, it came from the manufacturing boom begun during the Civil War.

The well-to-do clamored for even more commercial facilities. Ladies' Mile grew up to supply demand, its nickname coming from the female majority who shopped there. Until the 1850s the men of the house had done the buying; now, women became the dominant consumers. The turn-around followed the specialization of neighborhoods, the separation of work and residence, the consequent segregation of sexes.

From this period, wives who could afford to stayed home when their husbands commuted to the office. As growing modern conveniences made for (somewhat) fewer household tasks, first charity work, later shopping provided a compensatory realm for old activities. They also got women out of the house, allowing them to reconfigure and enlarge an acceptable public sphere—a pattern persisting, largely unexamined, through the 1950s. Soon, many comfortably off females began defining themselves as consumers, a process hastened by the new art of advertising.

Captain R. H. Macy from Nantucket and Ulster merchant A. T. Stewart were the first to build stores in this part of town. Originally, Stewart had run a dry goods store near the seaport. Next, in 1846 he opened a "marble palace of trade" on Chambers Street. Even if the term *department store* was not used until decades later, Stewart's Chambers Street operation already fit the formula. The store sold a large volume of varying commodities under one roof and used fixed prices, aggressive advertising, and cash payments. All of these were innovations here and abroad. (Unaccountably, the credit usually goes to the founder of Bon Marché in Paris, who set up shop only in 1852.)

In 1862 Stewart moved up to 10th Street and Broadway in the wake of fashionable New Yorkers settling in Union Square. Civil War technology enabled his cavernous new cast iron store: a spending spree spurred by wartime profits assured its success. In the 1840s the whole country had produced just twenty millionaires; by battle's end, New York alone held several hundred.

Cross-ties between newspapers, the recent public life-style of rich New Yorkers, and new entertainment possibilities pushed trade to even greater volume. A dozen journals reported on the gowns society women wore to soirees at the city's grand hotels and theaters. Stewart himself owned several theaters as well as his celebrated store and he incorporated theatrics to boost sales. Organ music at his emporium simultaneously speeded and soothed shoppers. Large street-floor windows, a city first, induced ambivalent passersby inside. Stewart relied on the view people glimpsed of happy customers inside his store, but most shops used their windows to frame attractive displays. Window shopping, which the French called *lecher*, related to the English *lecher* (from the same root as *to lick*), became a new city sport.

As plate glass became commonplace in the 1870s, store windows could show off changing displays, reinforce the ephemerality of style, deepen the compulsion to buy. Novelist Emile Zola wrote in his novel *Au Bonheur Des Dames,* shopping is "le poème de l'activité moderne." Women were the poem's protagonists.

Stewart understood the erotics of consumption, the sexual and sensual appeal of wanting, possessing, and he underscored this aspect of purchasing by choosing his male clerks for their looks. Critics called the young men "counter jumpers" because of their eagerness to please the ladies.

In one year alone, 1865, the store did over $8 million in trade. In one day alone, over 60,000 people, mainly women, came to buy.

Increased materialism brought tension. In the past Protestantism had trained people to save. Now, the expanding market needed to "educate people out of their old frugal ways" and create *wants.* Some feared the new values could lead to frustration and strife. As mass production increased, clothes became democratized to the point a style magazine argued that working men should wear smocks "so people once again would know their status."

Stewart, a self-made man, had no qualms about creating discord. Any customer who could pay was welcome. In point of fact, the very poor, intimidated by the palatial spaces and elegantly dressed floor walkers, didn't shop at his store or at any of the other Ladies' Mile emporiums.

They did, however, serve in them. Like his fellow merchants, Stewart integrated production into his operation and employed several thousand seamstresses and laundry workers, who arrived (on foot) at the shops from their tenement homes near the East River between five and six in the morning. Their workday was twelve to fourteen hours long. Often, they didn't see their families by daylight.

In a store that sold $2,000 paisley shawls and $600 lace handkerchiefs, Stewart paid his seamstresses $9.00 a week. It was better than most.

With apologies for starting with a semi-ghost, we'll begin our route with an annex that is the last trace of the Ulsterman's New York empire. Walk down (south) to 770 Broadway, on the east side of Broadway to the block between 8th and 9th streets.

In 1896 Philadelphia merchant John Wanamaker bought Stewart's, reopening it under his name and management, building this **annex ❷** which he linked by a walkway to the old emporium across the street. Fire destroyed the main store in 1956.

Mass producers, such as these seamstresses at A. T. Stewart's department store, made wide-scale consumption possible in the era before and following the Civil War.

***R**etrace your steps north on Broadway to* **Grace Church,** ❸ *on the northeast corner of 10th Street.*

At this bend on Broadway, you have three institutions that were instrumental in setting the framework for New York's gilded age. A social church that arbitrated the new money society, a celebrity hotel that served the entrepreneurs arriving from all over the country, and a dry goods store that catered to women's status needs.

☞ Look across Broadway to the **St. Denis Hotel** ❹ (now stripped of ornament and painted taupe) on the southwest corner of 11th Street (1848).

By the mid-nineteenth century, so many out-of-towners came to New York, upscale hostelries published their own city guidebooks.

☞ James Renwick, Jr., designed the St. Denis a few years after he planned Grace Church across the street. Be sure to enter the 11th Street door and see the original spiral staircase, its marble treads velvety with use.

Until the palatial Astor House opened down by City Hall in 1836, New

ST. DENIS HOTEL. - - BROADWAY & 11TH STREET. - - NEW YORK CITY

York City hotel fare had been simple. Common baths, often located in the hotel barbershop, were the norm. Mattresses came
stuffed with corn husks. Dinner was served

New York saw the rise of
palatial hotels.

boarding-house style at shared tables. By the time the St. Denis opened, the
only carryover from earlier days was its dining arrangements—residents
still ate at common tables and ate standard fare at scheduled hours. The
fancy new menus, however, foretold the future: they were in French, a language nobody, including the waiters, understood.

Hotels were off-limits for unescorted respectable women, but entrepreneurs provided "acceptable" consumption zones. Taylor's Ice Cream
Parlor on the hotel's Broadway front, was one. Earlier, the restaurant had
been an old favorite down by the first Stewart emporium but had shifted
to this location when the store moved north. Women shoppers came here
to recoup from buying expeditions newspapers called "notoriously fatal to
the female nerve."

The absence of liquor was one criteria making Taylor's respectable for
ladies. In part this was a marketing strategy, but mainly it was chance—
Grace Episcopal stood close by and New York blue laws forbade selling alcohol near churches. At first, even serious dining was considered outré.
Originally, the kitchen here just served snacks, ice cream, pastry, and oysters. When women grew more brazen, the restaurant added light entrees
such as chicken.

*W*alk back over Broadway to the **Grace Church complex.**

☞ It wasn't only stores that followed their patrons around town. This incarnation of Grace Church, a lacy Gothic Revival valentine, opened here in 1846. Its first building had been located down near Trinity, when the wealthy still lived in lower Manhatten.

By the time of its move, Grace had become a key player in the city's social politics, as many elite and would-be elite Episcopalians worshiped here. Up through the 1840s a coalition of Dutch-descended families and New England Yankees had formed New York's mandarin caste. Now with the new fortunes pouring into the city, the upper class had expanded to the point that "society" was becoming a relatively meaningless concept. Money, not bloodline (i.e., old money), became the definitive social credential. A persistent old guard minority tried to save its ascendancy in the face of the new tycoons. Or at least they tried to save the *concept* of an ascendancy by setting parameters. A few givens were enshrined—aside from pure cash— as the bottom line for social acceptance and one of them was worshiping at Grace Church. Other essentials were owning a carriage, living above Bleecker Street, subscribing to the opera, having a country house, giving balls, and attending fashionable parties. (The custodian at Grace, who assigned the church's pew seating—a hierarchical affair—was hired by society hostesses to draw up their guest lists, advise them on who was worth cultivating.)

*W*alk diagonally north to **McCreery's Department Store ❺** on the northwest corner of 11th Street and Broadway.

☞ Architect John Kellum, who built Stewart's venture across the street, designed this look-alike cast iron store. The resemblance was deliberate. McCreery emulated his Ulster compatriot, rival and mentor, and had moved here to be near him.

McCreery's building was one of many to go up in 1868, a year that produced a construction boom, as everything was in place for city expansion, including the imminent arrival of rapid transit.

I suggest you walk back to your bench at Union Square to read the following.

During and after the Civil War, the commercial beachhead Stewart and a few others had established burgeoned into a full-fledged commercial zone that overwhelmed the residential neighborhood. Once again the wealthy withdrew north, this time to Madison Square, leaving their old houses to trade. One abandoned mansion here first held a restaurant and later a costume store supplying ballet tutus for P. T. Barnum's elephants.

Many of the new ventures opening were theaters, making the area the city's first rialto. The maiden enterprise here, the Academy of Music (a new incarnation of the tainted Astor Place Opera House), had offered classical music that was far more serious than its wealthy patrons, "who arrived late and departed early." As the square commercialized, however, most local theaters and concert halls forsook earlier pretensions and took on a more popular tone. As theater managers brought raunchy popular culture uptown from the Bowery and packaged it for wider consumption, a mass audience, including middle-class women, developed and grew as popularizers sanitized the old Bowery variety acts into a milder guise known as "vaudeville." The new formula left enough sexual and ethnic grit to titillate, but not enough to alarm. New Yorkers who would have never considered going down to the risqué and possibly dangerous Bowery ("where the mob is tickled and good taste disgusted") came in droves.

Theaters of all sorts took over the neighborhood. One held a flea circus featuring polka-dancing fleas who also drew miniature carriages and impersonated Don Quixote and Sancho Panza. Another housed a Gettysburg cyclorama, where audiences stood on a center patch of bloodied earth and mechanically driven canvasses furled battles around them.

☞ Look down Broadway to an early commercial building on the southeast corner of 14th Street and Broadway, the gray three-story building that's layered with posters and "going out of business" signs. The short wing is an 1868 extension of the **Union Place Hotel** built twenty years earlier. The original section remains behind the giant billboards. In 1871 the Union Square Theater opened in the hotel. If you stroll down and look at the building from Broadway, you can see the roof's steep pitch that allowed for vertically raked balconies to pack in a maximum audience.

In the 1890s B. F. Keith, of later RKO fame, took over the theater and screened kinetoscope peep-shows, hand-cranked loops of film that played for two minutes. Union Square became an early film production center; rooftops were used for locations and aging vaudeville actors and actresses as supporting players.

Walk across 14th Street to **Luchow's ❻** on the south side of the street, 110 East 14th Street, several doors east from Fourth Avenue.

☞ Watch out as you go for the confluence of traffic, still a hazard today. First omnibuses and then horsecars on rails coursed up and down Broadway *15 seconds* apart. In 1893 cable cars finally arrived. The section of 14th Street veering off to the east took the name "Deadman's curve." The swerve of the track was so sharp, sometimes hapless commuters pitched off the trolley as it lunged around the corner. A subway following this same route swung off course in 1991, at the cost of five lives.

The city's German population gave the new middle-class consumer group critical mass. By the 1870s scores of restaurants had moved to Union Square. A number were German enterprises spilled over from the East Side. Eating became so extensive, journalists complained that New York harbor was "unhealthy with decaying food from tables wasted by the capricious fashionable."

☞ This gold-trimmed, red Italianate building now stalked by pigeons is all that's left of the period's restaurants, and by the looks of it, it won't be here long. The empty building dates from the 1840s when the neighborhood was still residential. A German baron first converted it into a beer hall, and a Bavarian waiter, August Luchow, bought it in 1882. The late space is one of the city's great losses. Dining in the mirrored, paneled rooms was like entering a Renoir.

If you look closely, you'll see the building is actually several structures joined. Originally the short three-story wing was **Hubert's Wax Museum,** which displayed criminal effigies and live humans with deformities: "freaks of good character" lived in the top-floor dormitory.

Return across 14th Street. Walk north through the square to Union Square West.

☞ Notice the building on the southwest corner of 15th Street (11–15 Union Square). The 1869 **building by John Kellum ❼** now houses the Amalgamated Bank, which harks back to the square's ties to labor and unionism that grew out of its early role as public rallying ground. To many New Yorkers the link is so strong, they assume the square took its name from this aspect of its history. When the building opened, however, it served not man but mammon, being the third incarnation of Tiffany's jewelery store. Today it's faced over in something resembling bathroom tile, but the original structure is just barely discernible. Note the long second-story windows, the progressively smaller windows on each successive story, the tapering mode reflecting the architect's interest in perspective illusion.

At the time this Tiffany's opened, New York tied London for diamond consumption. Only czarist St. Petersburg surpassed the volume here. Among other uses, New York women bought diamond dust for cosmetics.

☞ The short, massively changed buildings on Union Square West, between 16th and 17th Streets, housed sheet music stores such as **Schirmers** and several piano stores. (Steinway had a hall and showrooms on nearby East 14th Street.)

So many popular music businesses followed the theaters to Union Square that many credit it with being the city's first Tin Pan Alley. As new mass printing techniques made the widespread sale of piano scores possible, most Ladies' Mile stores featured sheet-music departments. Some scores, including an 1873 top tune about A. T. Stewart's, celebrated shopping itself.

***W**alk to the north end of the square, site of the great Metropolitan Fair.*

In 1864 the city's middle- and upper-class women opened a charity bazaar at this end of the square to raise money for Union Army hospitals (an isolated example of women managing public space). During its three-week run the Sanitary Commission, which grew into the Red Cross, raised half a million dollars. (See Walk 7 for the Brooklyn fair.) This was about the only time a crossover occurred between the wild spending in the city and the war. Despite the mass casualties of New York regiments, the consumption mania of those who could afford it continued untouched by the age's larger grief.

***W**alk north along Broadway to the 1869 **Arnold Constable Store** ❽ on the southwest corner of 19th Street (now the ABC Carpet and Home Furnishings Annex).*

☞ Make sure to look down 19th Street at the gargantuan mansarded pile. Enter the ground floor of the store and marvel at the vast space, the capacity of cast iron columns to bear huge loads.

As years went on, this tradition-minded firm, opened down by the East River in 1825, stayed more conservative than most of its competitors. Even while most other luxury stores had begun to switch to female clerks in the Civil War, Arnold Constable kept an all-male sales force until well after the turn of the century. In part, most shops hired women to replace men who were off fighting; in part, they hired them to break strikes when male clerks rallied for shorter hours. Eventually, the organizers won an official ten-hour day but unofficial hours were much longer, as store workers opened and shut the businesses on their own time.

Despite its conservatism, Arnold Constable quickly recognized women's role in spending. In 1864, when inflation soared 176 percent in that one year, its managers sent letters to its female customers, not their husbands, informing them of the store's new monthly billing policy. Because of its canniness, the store prospered in the panic of 1873 and added two more stories.

☞ The present mansard roof capped the effort. The sloping style was the height of Francophile fashion and also brought the store a tax break. Assessors charged mansarded floors as attic spaces—the reason some builders crammed so many floors inside them.

Arnold Constable's line of elegant dresses became a staple from the 1880s, when ready-to-wear clothes for women had become the rule. Ten years earlier "off the rack" clothing had still been déclassé at luxury stores, as despite the citywide rise in garment production, wealthy shoppers preferred their wardrobes custom-made by in-house seamstresses.

Walk north to the old **Lord and Taylor** ❾ at 901 Broadway, the southwest corner of Broadway and 20th Street.

☞ Notice that the building, shorn of its frilly roof adornment, continues down to 19th Street.

A decade earlier public opinion had castigated store owners for tying up working capital in extravagant buildings; by the time these block-size buildings went up, most felt the new rites of consumption deserved, even demanded, opulence. Enthusiastic New Yorkers boasted this store was as luxurious as the grand salon of first-class steamboats. Others used the steamboat simile disparagingly. In fact, underneath its froth, the building was an arsenal of Civil War technology, full of up-to-the-minute devices. So many customers came just to ride the elevator (recent improvements had made the invention safe for passengers) that the management was forced to install a settee: some called the new device "a little parlor going up by machinery." The futuristic technology of Ladies' Mile stores enchanted visitors as much as their palatial ornament.

Like Arnold Constable (first, just Arnold), Lord and Taylor's had started down near the East River in the 1820s and then moved inland in lower Manhattan. This building opened with earnings made during the

Civil War. Soon after the conflict had begun, Congress had outlawed trading with the South, so the firm's stock of rationed cotton goods had zoomed in price and profit. Along with other city stores, it also had benefited from Union Army contracts. (See Walk 8 for more details about merchandising during the war.)

*R*etrace your steps back toward Union Square on Broadway passing the old **Gorham's** (1883) on the northwest corner of 19th Street and Broadway.

☞ The upper reaches of this fussy Queen Anne-hybrid building once housed a silver factory.

Craftsmen here made the accoutrements sold downstairs for gilded age dinner parties. Table settings for the era were suitably elaborate—one host recreated Central Park complete with live table-top swans paddling in a gold basin.

☞ The former **W. and J. Sloane** ❿ (now the ABC Carpet and Home Furnishing Co.) stands diagonally across the avenue on the southeast corner of Broadway and 19th Street. Be sure to enter the rosy brick building and enjoy the interior space with its elegant balconied mezzanine.

Sloane's carpet store opened here in 1882. During the next decade the store blossomed, as women cushioned their parlors to soothe urban ills, palliate "over heated nerves." Today, ABC serves the same needs.

*C*ontinue walking back along Broadway to 17th Street.

☞ The red and white Beaux Arts Building at the north end of the square (33–37 East 17th Street) belonged to the **Century Publishing Company.** ⓫ Note the limestone pomegranate, garland, and sunflower motif.

Since the 1870s, artists and writers had used the sunflower to signify physical love and the world of the senses. Despite the flower and other generative icons, the *Century* had no time for the sexuality (or politics) of some writers submitting work here. Its editors roundly rejected Stephen Crane's *Maggie: A Girl of the Streets*—the tale of a city woman turned prostitute from poverty, the "streets" in the title just one step away from the river where she ended her life.

Although the Century publishers didn't print *Maggie,* they did publish Edith Wharton, who wrote a more refined version of the same saga. Wharton, born in 1862 at the north end of Ladies' Mile, was the signal interpreter of this neighborhood and era. (She only occasionally used the Century, at first publishing mainly through Scribner's, and later D. Appleton.) Until the recent Wharton retrospective, critics tended to denigrate the gently born writer as a mere chronicler of "old New York," but her portrayals of characters adrift in social change (as was Wharton's own family) were psychologically astute. In *The House of Mirth* Lily Bart sinks from a sheltered, moneyed existence into the lower depths of working-class life and dies as miserably as Maggie.

Continue back south on Union Square West to 15th Street; turn right on the north side of the street and walk halfway down the block to the red brick and sandstone building, the back side of an early **YWCA Dormitory.** ⑫ *(Today, it's a union health center—another legacy of the square's long union ties.)*

The "Maggie Lou," as residents called this dorm, provided a home for single working women who wanted to keep their "self respect." Wealthy patrons, disturbed by the thought that independent women coming to the city to find jobs would lose their way in the urban jungle, built "Ys" as refuges and hired dorm matrons to oversee the boarders and reinforce their (Protestant) "decency." If their attitude was patronizing, the urge for moral stewardship also had its useful, caring side.

The building next door to the west of the dormitory at number 7 opened as the **Central Hall of the YWCA.** ⑬

Elite architect R. H. Robertson designed this cultural center and library for the YWCA in 1887; it was New York's first and was to remain one of the very few institutions for women in the city.

☞ The building's embattled Romanesque Revival style makes you know it's a citadel of some sort. The heavy rusticated stones, the low squat arches, the massive balustrades all say "keep out." At the same time, the architect tried to replicate the exiled women's (supposed) childhood dwellings. Note the big bay windows of the old common rooms here, the central gathering places meant to substitute for the parlors of "each long lost home."

At first, Bible studies were heavily featured here; later, practical secretarial skills were offered also.

Walk west on 15th Street to Fifth Avenue, turn left, and walk down to 14th Street, crossing the avenue to the west. You will pass a few marble-faced

*rowhouses on both sides of 14th Street be-
tween Fifth and Sixth. Try to find a safe
place to stand aside from the hectic street
vending to look around you and to read the
following.*

From the 1860s on, the affordability of
sewing machines made home garment production a nationwide undertaking. By the
1870s, so many local emporiums around
Union Square sold the device, some people
called Union Square "Sewing Machine
Square." A New York woman, Mme. Demorest (the "Madame" from snobbery and
fashion ties with Paris), profited by invent-
ing clever patterns in colored tissues. The
entrepreneuse, remarkable even by today's
standards, ran part of her multimillion dollar concern from a dozen or so old rowhouses like these that she and her realtor
husband bought in this neighborhood and
converted into shops and factories.

City drawing schools opened to train
new talent for the business, and artists
copied European styles onto Demorest's
tissues. As new low postal rates encouraged

The number of women entering
the work force during the Civil
War caused civic leaders worry.
In the 1880s philanthropists
built the city's first YWCA to
shelter them (and keep them
behaving properly). Note the
building's fortressy appearance.

selling designs through mail-order catalogues, the parlor floors of every little house across America rustled with the company's designs. Sales grew so
big that the firm used several tons of paper every day.

Fashion magazines spurred consumer interest. The Demorests also
published a monthly journal. Because of the confusing choices mass production offered, a readership rose for advice books, many of them on dress.
Over two hundred manuals came out in the decades before the turn of the
century.

***C**ontinue along the south side of 14th Street to numbers 34–40, a **remnant
of Hearn's Department Store. ⑭** To see it, look up above the street-level
storefronts.*

By the time Hearn's set up on 14th Street in 1878, the wealthy had already abandoned their homes on this once residential thoroughfare and

moved north. The same year the store opened (probably the reason for its debut here), surface cars had begun to ply along the street from the Brooklyn ferry at the East River to the piers at the Hudson. A large part of its passengers were middle-class women shopping in the city for the day. By now it was quite conventional for such women to take public transport. Two decades earlier, when they had first started riding the city's horse cars, it had been the cause for scandal and alarm. If stores provided safe areas and select company, bowdlerized miniature terrains for indoor flaneuring, public conveyances did not. Cartoonists had made much of the depredations on female modesty, the body contact women endured. Their tone was ambivalent, partly caustic about the poor transport conditions, partly censorious about women's boldness in moving about. As late as the date Hearn's opened (and the proprietor particularly noted that he built the store on 14th Street's south side so *women* could stroll and window shop in the shade), some men chose to contest women's right to public space even here in Ladies' Mile.

It didn't work. Fortified by the joys and possibilities of being out and about, middle-class women held their ground. The year Hearn's opened here, the merchant declared, "I would not give a snap of my finger for all the trade we obtain from

> Middle- and upper-class women carved out an acceptable public sphere for themselves in the Ladies' Mile shopping district, though some men tried to intimidate them.

men. . . . In olden times the lords of creation used to accompany their wives on shopping expeditions but this custom has gradually disappeared until now never or seldom men enter stores."

Men might not have shopped much anymore, but they were the reason many women did, as buying consolidated a husband's social status. These women's odalisque lives attested their husbands' credit rating—a mid-nineteenth-century invention by a Mr. Dun, whose firm became Dun and Bradstreet. During hard times it was even more urgent to keep up appearances. Wives learned to mass finery on themselves, just as they massed bibelots on their end tables at home.

A curmudgeonly contemporary wrote, "affluent women do not wear the same dress twice, but don and doff dry goods, spending their day fluttering the latest tints and modes in the glare of gas light." The year Hearn's opened, a fashionable wardrobe included two velvet dresses at $500 each; $1,000 of lace collars; walking dresses costing $50–$300; a ball dress— usually imported from Paris—for $500–$1,000; traveling dresses of black silk, velour, pongee, or pique that cost from $75 to $175; and evening robes in Swiss muslin valued at $75–$175. Walt Whitman rued the "webs of silliness, millinery and every kind of dyspeptic depletion" that kept women enthralled.

It was not just the wealthy who were driven to buy. The day's democratizing media seduced poorer women also. Doctors editorialized against the starvation diets many working girls undertook to save money for fashionable clothes. The stress of maintaining caste and keeping up with novelties (from *nouveauties,* the French word for dry goods that comes from "newness") could overwhelm. Some women became kleptomaniacs. (That is, they became kleptomaniacs if they were rich—if they were poor and shoplifted, they were simple thieves.) Anger as well as compulsion may have driven the phenomenon. A number of women went out of their way to be caught. (The problem was not confined to New York. In London the psychosis grew common enough that popular songs recorded it in scores such as "Ladies Go a Thievin'.") Special magistrates courts opened to handle genteel offenders with discretion.

Mary Todd Lincoln, the president's widow, was among other obsessive shoppers of the day. The poor lady, pilloried in her time for excess though she seems to have been acting out a larger societal dynamic, ran up huge debts at Altman's and A. T. Stewart's (the former for her wardrobe, the latter for furnishing her house).

Continue west on 14th Street. Stop at **Macy's**, ⑮ *number 56, a sliver building faced over in the 1890s with a Beaux Arts facade.*

Signs claiming slashed prices plaster the shopfronts of the stores that currently occupy the ground floor of the old Macy's building. They are a tie with the past, as the store's founder invented bargain sales.

This stone slip is a remnant of the complex that Rowland Hussey Macy began to assemble here in 1858, the first commercial enterprise to arrive on this residential street. The heart of Macy's new venture was a 60-foot deep, 20-foot frontage on the corner of Sixth Avenue (Avenue of the Americas), but it soon sprawled out piecemeal on 14th and 13th Streets.

The date of the store's debut is important: 1857 had been one of the city's great depression years, and land was cheap. Macy, the innovator of bargains, was quick to spot one and soon opened his shop here with a fifteen-person sales force. Until a few years ago a painted sign on the side wall of this building read "Macy's, the world's largest department store." Weather has worn it away.

Sadder still, until 1992 a faded red sign above the door showed a faint star and gold-lettered "Macy's." The star came from the merchant's whaling days when, like all good seamen (who picked up the custom in the South Seas), he kept a lucky tattoo on his forearm. The logo still blazons the Herald Square store today.

Surprisingly, as imports and retail still had close links at the start of the Ladies' Mile era, Macy was one of the few mariners to enter retail trade. In many ways he was a transition figure between the old wholesale merchants of South Street and the new entrepreneurs of mass retail consumption. When this store opened, Macy lived above the shop as earlier businessmen had done at the port, and like his forerunners, he exercised strict control over his employees' personal lives. Among other rules, Macy made his clerks go to Sunday school, give five dollars a year to church, take the abstinence pledge, and forswear dancing and "amusements." In some ways this supervision harked back to the old apprenticeship system, but the differences were profound. By this time workers had almost no chance of rising in the profession and usually served as disposable cogs in an ever-growing machine. Alienation went deeper than simple paternalism could assuage.

Walk north on Sixth Avenue (Avenue of the Americas) to 18th Street, staying on the west side of the avenue.

☞ Look north at the immense stores lining both sides of the street. These stores were the culmination of the commercial forces that moved up Broadway, filled Union Square to overflowing, and then rolled up this thoroughfare to 23rd Street and beyond. The strip is perhaps the closest the city ever got to an imperial boulevard, albeit crossed with a midway.

Transport had been key to the street's development. From 1851 horsecars had run along Sixth Avenue. From 1878 until 1938 the street held the shadow and shriek of the El.

☞ The cast-iron **B. Altman store** ⑯ on the northwest corner of 18th Street was one of the first arrivals here.

Altman's and other Sixth Avenue stores' full-block frontage were and are unusual in this city, where, as a rule, plots are only 20–25 feet wide. (The unit of measurement is generally said to be based on multiples of the "bay" or span big enough to accommodate a team of oxen.

Rapid transit, in the form of the elevated trains introduced in the 1870s, helped create a huge customer base.

More simply, the standard width might have been established by the average length of the trees that had provided earlier crossbeams). Most older stores had been cobbled assemblages, such as those we saw on 14th Street, but Altman bought his large tract inexpensively during the depression of 1873, building his emporium using laborers whom he paid cut-rate wages.

Small boys loitered outside the door of this cast iron palace, hoping for tips from overburdened women. Or at least a glimpse of ankle. Women departing by horsecars had problems with their 5-foot radius hoopskirts as they struggled to enter the 30-inch car doors. Inside the store navigating was easier—the architects had made the mahogany corridors vast enough to accommodate the most outlandish fashions. (Metal hoopskirts grew popular in the 1850s at the same time as cast iron buildings and used similar modular construction—an interesting crossover.)

As well as buying luxury clothes here—Altman's sealskin capes were the rage—one could buy fine arts, a big market item since the Civil War. Not all the paintings, however, were for sale. Like today's corporations that hang paintings in their lobbies to lend transcendence, early merchants, including Altman, graced their emporiums with their own collections. Altman's holdings later formed a nucleus of the Metropolitan Museum, which opened a few years before this store began. For good and bad, the museums and the stores both grew out of the impulse to acquire and display.

*T*ake a short walk to **Altman's Stables,** ⓱ *on the north and south sides of 18th Street west of Sixth Avenue.*

Even after the El arrived, Altman's and other stores kept a foot in the older order, and for the sake of prestige continued to use horse-drawn delivery wagons.

*R*eturn to Sixth Avenue and cross to the site of **Siegel-Cooper** ⓲ *on the east side of Sixth Avenue between 18th and 19th Streets. This store was one of the last of the emporiums to arrive on Ladies' Mile.*

☞ Note the owners' initials scrolled above the door. The building, which had been shut for many years, now holds the Bed, Bath and Beyond Center, and you can once again go in to see the extraordinary ground-floor interior. Unfortunately, the spectacular space has been carved into a maze of tiny units, so it's hard to see the building, which runs almost the full block to Fifth, as a whole.

The Siegel-Cooper Department Store, New York.

In its day, the establishment was famous as "the big store—a city unto itself" or simply as "the big store." Everything about it was larger than life, including its advertising. At night the gold domed central tower (only the stump is left) beamed a searchlight that threw ads on the underside of clouds for a thirty-mile radius. Some say that Batman comics copied the idea from here. When the store opened in 1896, 150,000 shoppers showed up on opening day, most of them women who'd traveled by El. The crush punched in the glass doors, and ambulances were called to cart the critically wounded to St. Vincent's Hospital.

> Gargantuan stores such as Siegel-Cooper grew up to serve the expanded middle class.

☞ Notice how different the light-toned brick and masonry building is from the cast iron emporiums, including Altman's, across the street. By the 1890s, fashion had declared the "utilitarian" iron mode passé and called for the return of antiquarian grandeur.

When customers arrived through the gargantuan doors flanked by bronze torches, they were transformed into minor royalty. Inside, the store's sweeping staircase, columned rotunda, chandelier-lit mezzanine, and opulent restaurants carried out the illusion. Single women particularly appreciated the ambience, as the city's grand hotels (which gave the same effect) still banned unescorted females. Like Niemann Marcus today, the store's seventy-two departments had everything, including a pet department featuring lions. The rooftop gardens here were celebrated for their matchless orchids. The greenhouse still stands.

Another not quite so upbeat way that Siegel-Cooper made its way into popular consciousness was in dime novels recording the hard lives of its "little shop girls." Writers from Theodore Dreiser to O. Henry also portrayed the big store and the woes of its employees—3,100 regular staff, 4,500 during holiday season.

Despite a study the store conducted on Japanese managerial efficiency (in 1904!) and a spurt of paternalism (among other efforts, it started compulsory calisthenics on the building's sprawling rooftop to prevent typewriter hunch, a new problem besetting the first stenographic work force), Siegel-Cooper shut down before World War I. In part it closed because the owner was caught speculating, peculating, with millions of dollars that customers had deposited in the store to serve as a credit bank. The deeper reason was that the store had arrived in Ladies' Mile too late. Just ten years after Siegel-Cooper opened here, Altman's led retail's exodus to midtown Fifth Avenue, where Manhattan's rump department store nucleus remains to this day.

Cross back to the west side of the avenue and walk north to the former **Simpson Crawford Store ⑲** between 19th and 20th Streets.

☞ This block-big granite and limestone building replaced the 1879 original store in 1900.

A bank of eleven "tread mill" escalators amazed customers, who found it was as easy to get to the second floor as to stand still. Purchasing was equally smoothed by the store's policy of not using price tags. The clientele here was so wealthy, cost was irrelevant.

Continue north to the former **Hugh O'Neill Department Store ⑳** on the same side of Sixth between 20th and 21st Streets. Note the name in the pediment.

When O'Neill's opened in 1876, corner towers with onion domes enlivened its roof line. To top this, it was painted in gaudy yellows set off by burnt umber. Contemporary newspapers debated pro and con about this departure from the *usual* red paint of the cast iron buildings here! So Ladies' Mile was red? We tend not to dream or see history in color.

Unlike other stores on Sixth, this north Irishman's store was relatively democratic. Many lower-income customers came to buy O'Neill's cut-rate sewing machines, which he sold as loss leaders. He also was the first in the city to offer installment buying. The store shut in 1915 with the demise of its founder and Ladies' Mile itself.

*G*o still farther north on the same side of the avenue to the former **Adams Dry Good Store ㉑** *(1900) between 21st and 22nd Streets. Make sure to enter and visit the central atrium.*

☞ Siegel-Cooper's architects designed this ornate Beaux Arts emporium, which newspapers saluted at its opening for capping a $15 million improvement to Sixth Avenue that they credited to "McKinley prosperity."

Although the store preferred its carriage trade customers (richer than those who arrived by El), it pioneered men's ready-to-wear clothing. Men's measurements had been standardized during the Civil War to allow the mass production of uniforms for the Union Army, but at battle's end civilian male ready-to-wear was slow to gain acceptance (basically, because of male conservatism). When men, at last, were ready to buy, stores began to place orders for male fashions, the sizes pegged to the dimensions drawn from the thousands of recruits who'd served the army as statistics. We still use these today.

*C*ontinue north to the former **Ehrich Brothers store, ㉒** *also on the west side of Sixth between 22nd and 23rd Streets.*

☞ The 1899 Ehrich emporium held a famous toy department featuring early Barbies who bowed and tossed their feather boas. Today, the blearing brown building suffers a sweatshop, where Asians and Hispanics work under garish neon lights.

By the 1870s many theaters and amusement arcades had moved up here from Union Square. Edwin Booth's theater occupied the southeast corner of Sixth Avenue and 23rd Street.

☞ The **Beer Garden annex of Koster and Bial,** New York's beloved vaudeville house, still stands on the southwest corner of Sixth Avenue at 24th Street. Peer up the avenue, or, if you have the energy, walk up to see the name in the building's pediment. Today, a topless bar operates on the ground floor. Vaudeville would not have sanctioned this, as it had prudently, prudishly, cleaned up its act to attract broader audiences.

Turn right and walk east along 23rd Street to the former **Stern Brothers' Department Store** ㉓ *on the street's south side between Sixth and Fifth Avenues. Note the Sterns' name in its pediment.*

Once, doormen in blue and gold greatcoats and top hats assisted customers in this elegant store, handing them down from their carriages, shouldering their packages when they departed. The liveried staff and the store's stylish design failed to endear it to its near neighbors, however. Sterns' arrival in 1878 affronted many, as despite proof to the opposite, local householders of the day liked to think the street was still a residential thoroughfare.

Keep on east to the north corner of 23rd Street and Fifth Avenue to Madison Square. ㉔

Even when the first settlers had moved here at midcentury, two decades before Sterns arrived, they'd run into entrenched commercial ventures. A circus seating 4,000 people stood on one corner of the square; the New York and Harlem Railroad depot, freight shed, and stables occupied the northeast. (In 1879, the train shed became the first Madison Square Garden.) This corner held a large hotel.

☞ Note the **Seth Thomas Clock** made by the Hecla Iron Works standing like an oversized pocket watch on the pavement at Fifth Avenue and 23rd Street. The 1888 clock is all that remains from the days of the famous Fifth Avenue Hotel that stood on the Toy Association site from 1858 to 1909. The present building looks remarkably like pictures of the old hostelry.

Edith Wharton (then still Edith Jones) and her family spent hours watching the clientele's comings and goings from the windows of their house across 23rd Street. "The hotel," Wharton wrote, "was full of Westerners and politicians, two classes of citizens my mother's intonation always seemed to deprive of their vote by ranking them with illiterates and criminals."

By the 1880s, among other culpables the Jones family would have seen from their vantage point were the high-class whores who sent business cards with photos, taken in Union Square studios, up to hotel guests. (Newspapers obligingly published lists of resident celebrities.) Prostitutes

sauntered outside the lobby doors underneath the new **bishop's crook street
lamps**—the city's first electric lighting, intended to keep the square safe for the gentry. Mocking the recent civic boast "one
lamp is as good as a policeman," "nymphes
de pave" stood vigil here throughout the night, the light flaunting their
beauty.

New technology, including
electric lighting, added to the
sense of the city as a
comestible—for some.

Aside from the area's massive prostitution (including a block-sized
brothel at Broadway and 23rd), several hundred gambling dens also flourished in the neighborhood. Despite these realities, local residents who'd
fled here from Union Square's hurly-burly tried to live as if this new re-

doubt was an oasis from commercial culture. (At least, they pretended to try. In fact, most of the male householders were patrons of the nearby gambling tables and brothels.)

Officially, even store owners were held beyond the social pale. Edith Wharton wrote about her childhood, "No retail dealer no matter how palatial his shop-front or tempting his millions was received in New York society until long after I grew up."

In fact, aside from the usual transgressions of sex (a nice phrase combining moral and spatial overtones), there was intense crossover at all levels between old guard New Yorkers and the new commercial forces serving them. Despite the Jones' scorn of the new hotels and their nouveau riche patrons, the novelist herself was briefly engaged to the son of the Fifth Avenue Hotel's manager, a detail she never wrote about.

R*etrace your footsteps back a hundred yards along the south side of 23rd Street to* **Edith Wharton's birthplace** ㉕: *14 West 23rd Street.*

☞ The denial couldn't last. By the 1880s trade was rampant. Two decades after Wharton had been born here in 1862, the old rowhouse had become a store. The present iron frontage is a later addition when yet another retail firm moved in.

The novelist would have probably been amused by the "desecration," even pleased. She despised brownstone buildings—both the material itself, which she called the most hideous stone ever quarried, and the stultified lives and mentalities that, to her, the houses personified. "Narrow houses crammed with smug and suffocating upholstery."

W*alk back toward Fifth Avenue and the former* **Western Union Telegraph Building** ㉖ *on the southwest corner of 23rd and Fifth Avenue.*

☞ The red brick Queen Anne style building (designed by Henry Hardenbergh) opened a couple of doors away from Wharton's birthplace in 1883. It's a good architectural example of the impulse at this time to look backward while actually going forward. Though the telegraph company by then had been a catalyst of national change for the past half-century, its executives ordered the firm's architect, Henry Hardenbergh, to make its head office look quaint, even archaic. The roofline's gabled dormers are intended to evoke "old world" domestic spaces. In case you missed the point, the decorative plaques depicted medieval jesters. The white bands on the facade were there to reinforce the building's horizontality, make you perceive the structure as low to the earth, a series of stacked ground floors—actually, the office is eight stories high, a relatively tall structure.

*P*osition yourself to see the **Flat Iron Building** ⓦ *by Chicago architect Daniel Burnham, which stands at the 23rd Street juncture of Fifth and Broadway; the nickname drawn from its shape.*

Edith Wharton once lamented that New York was a "crimped horizontal gridiron of a town without towers, porticoes, fountains, or perspectives." In 1902 she finally got her longed-for tower and perspective. Or at least her childhood neighborhood did. Wharton herself was long since self-exiled in multi-spired Europe. From the current residents' point of view the looming tower came all too soon, a violent intrusion in their ersatz enclave.

☞ Stand on the northwest corner of 23rd and Fifth to see the Telegraph Building and the skyscraper together. Look up at the height and power of the later building. Although it has some delicate horizontal banding like the telegraph headquarters, the twenty-story structure stalks up, proudly self-confident.

Several years after the building arrived, a newspaper exulting that the building heralded a new age wrote, "Its front lifted to the future . . . it is surrounded by staring wayfarers. Sometime a hundred or more til ordered on by the finest. . . . If it fell over eastward, it would almost reach Madison Avenue." But many shared the locals' apprehension. The same year the paper made this boast, the photographer Edward Steichen took his (now) famous nocturnal picture of the tower, deliberately capturing it in cloud to blunt its impact.

By 1907 shimmering obfuscation was not a viable refuge. Neither was the effort of some gentry square dwellers to live free of the consequences of commercial velocity. Hundreds of sweatshops and other factories that had followed the stores up Ladies' Mile moved directly into the residential neighborhood itself. The New York *Herald* wrote, the "riffraff of humanity is in the city squares . . . they are now tainted by diseased and filthy vagrants who have almost driven away those for whom the park was intended." When the local elite bailed out, they pushed north on Fifth Avenue's fluid conduit (analogous to the open-endedness of "society" itself). With one exception—Gramercy Park—New York's upper class no longer tried to hunker around squares to preserve stasis.

*W*alk south along Broadway to 20th Street and turn left to visit the **Theodore Roosevelt Birthplace** ㉓ (28 East 20th Street). The upper-middle-class rowhouse is similar, if not precisely so, to some homes of the Ladies' Mile era. Telephone (212) 260–1616, Wednesday–Sunday.

Teddy's uncle built the original house in 1848. (This is a good reconstruction, refurbished as it looked in the years 1865 to 1872.) Usually, the asthmatic child (born in 1858) suffered the "gloomy respectability" of the sunless middle parlor. Only on Sundays was he allowed to venture into the bright front room.

☞ The rooms here are full but not loaded with ornament. Like Edith Wharton's family, with whom they were acquainted, this branch of the Roosevelts were junior members of the clan, so their house was relatively modest. Moreover, and probably more important, the Roosevelt family's old-guard sensibilities checked excess. Or at least to a degree. On the second floor a double parlor reflects the competing ethos of the day that touched even conservative households. The front room is pretentious, stippled in taffeta and burnished with gilt. The center parlor is "sincere," somewhat homier, though stiff horsehair sofas make it far from inviting. Ironically, as the Roosevelts had made their money from importing the new plate glass that enabled stores to have dazzling windows, the house is dark, sequestered. The heavily draped rooms (typical of the Ladies' Mile age) turn in on themselves, keep outside tumult at bay.

Today, New York's middle and upper class have sequestered themselves still more thoroughly. This time, instead of fleeing north once again and buying still more curtains, they have fled to the suburbs. As customers have departed, many of the city's department stores have died, or at least they have died in town. (Retail employment in the city has declined to less than 350,000 from 440,000 in 1968.) In the same way stores once chased their clientele around the city, for the past three decades they have been following their customers out of New York where they operate in malls, drive-in palaces of trade. Despite the fact that the city gave rise to department stores (and for years they virtually symbolized urban life, its material focus, its abundance, its chance to construct identity through things), urbanites are now on the receiving end, and suburban malls have preempted the power and prestige that stores such as Siegel-Cooper once possessed and generated. (Home shopping, a field even Macy's is considering entering, might, in turn, replace malls.) In great part, New York's mainstream theater also survives only because it is largely written for and supported by a suburban audience.

Except for the sweatshop economy, which is also moving out to the suburbs for cheaper rents, the current city is not a production center either. What are we?

10

Harlem

Subway: IRT Broadway–Seventh Avenue line local (train 1) to 116th
Street (Columbia University stop).

*Start by the Carl Schurz statue at 116th Street and Morningside Drive,
where there are benches where you can sit to read the introduction.* ❶

☞ When the trees are leafless or just budding, Morningside Heights is a
good place to view the central Harlem Plain. Near where the Harlem and
East Rivers meet at 119th Street, the Reckgawawanc kept a fishing camp,
Schorrakin, and cleared surrounding land.

In 1637 Europeans moved up here to homestead and farm. Today, we
call the flatland near the river that held the first—and only consolidated—
settlement in Manhattan's north East Harlem, or sometimes Spanish
Harlem, as it's home to the city's Puerto Rican community. During the first
part of this chapter the eastern district will just be referred to as "Harlem,"
as it became known under the Dutch. Because of the constraints of time
and distance, this walk will not visit the neighborhood that grew up quite
differently from the western and central areas of Harlem this tour will explore.

Two years after the European arrival, a map of Manhattan shows a
"Quarter of the Blacks," West India Company slaves, at approximately 75th
Street and the East River, the southern apex of what would become the new
Harlem hamlet. We know that the company profited by renting out its municipal slaves to white settlers downtown for private purposes as well as
making them work on the "public" fort and warehouses. It's likely (if undocumented) that the colony here worked cutting wood for the new houses
going up to the north. The barracks lay alongside the bank of a creek that

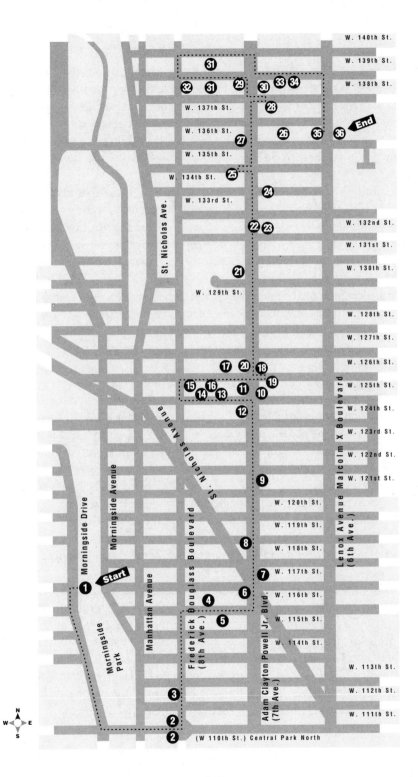

later powered a sawmill. A guess is that a mill already operated here. No other reason for settlement at the site comes to mind.

Though New Amsterdam's West India directors would have gained from the rents paid for its captive work force, and depended on the food the up-islanders shipped to Manhattan's tip, they didn't pay much attention to the northern region until the dispossessed Reckgawawanc made trouble.

Trouble came soon enough. In 1655 two thousand tribesmen slashed and burned their way down the length of Manhattan to avenge the death of a murdered Indian woman. Governor Stuyvesant told the up-island survivors to move within walls and ordered a rectangular plot surveyed near the East River. Rather than take time from farming, villagers hired West India Company slaves to build a stockade. (This is documented.) The fortified settlement took the name Nieuw Haarlem after a Dutch city famous for bleaching and weaving linen because of its large emigré population of Walloons who had brought the craft there. Interestingly, most of the European settlers in Nieuw Haarlem came from this community. (See Walk 1 for more about the Walloons.)

Private fields and common grazing land ringed the walled enclosure. In 1883 descendants of original holders banded together as shareholders in a Harlem Commons Syndicate to sue the city for residual rights to the old patent. As late as 1932 heirs were still trying. ("Oh, no," said Manhattan borough president Ruth Messinger, learning of the story, "*that's* all we need.")

Stuyvesant ordered the company work force to build a wagon way from New Amsterdam to Harlem after the debacle, but a connecting link to the old Kingsbridge Road was cut through only in 1706–1707, well after the British conquest. By then the route was not for defense, since remaining tribals had long been routed, but to speed produce down island.

Despite the road connection and a short-lived try at rechristening Harlem "Lancaster," nothing much changed under British rule. The hamlet (mapped and administrated by the new regime to include most land above 79th Street) remained agricultural. Because of its farming economy, more slaves lived here than in the downtown port. One in four Harlem residents was black, enough to warrant a separate burial ground. One historian suggests there was a black uprising here against the European farmers in the 1690s, but I've seen no substantiating evidence. Before the Revolution, still more slave labor arrived, as downtown merchants made country houses here and started ambitious plantations. (A plantation is different from a farm in that it grows just one cash crop. In Harlem wheat, corn, and tobacco were the main harvest.) By 1790 African Americans represented one-third of Harlem's population—the same ratio as in Brooklyn, another agrarian community.

In the 1830s, when big property owners here began to sell off their estates to speculators, free blacks arrived with Irish immigrants, to live and to farm. In the next decade two black churches opened in Harlem—a mission of the African Methodist Episcopal Zion near (today's) East 117th Street and a rival Methodist church, Bethel African Methodist Episcopal Zion, which stood close by.

Unlike east Harlem, where immigrants had been moving since 1837 after the railroad trundled up Park Avenue, west Harlem's population remained thin until the 1870s, when the city filled marshland here. Soon after that New York annexed the still independent suburb and extended Manhattan's grid. Asphalt drowned Harlem's natural topography. Only these cliffs and some western swamp above 140th Street remained.

A decade later the El clattered through: German Jewish speculators sold off tracts to developers who ribboned mud plots with housing for Germans from Kleindeutschland. Upper-middle-class Anglo-Saxons also arrived, many from a Greenwich Village recently "invaded" by Italians. Bringing their synagogues and churches with them, the newcomers shaped a genteel precinct, remote in mood and geography from lower Manhattan, now ruled by commerce and new immigrants.

But it wasn't that far removed. East Harlem had long been home to a working-class population, and after 1880, as other Irish, Germans, and Italians arrived from the Lower East Side, its numbers had grown. Meanwhile, second-generation east European Jews filled lower Harlem— the area north of Central Park to 125th, west of Lexington Avenue to Lenox.

The guarantee of subway construction along Lenox in 1900 brought exponential speculation. Bargain hunters (mainly second-generation Russian Jews from the Lower East Side) bought wildly. The price of land and housing catapulted. Blocks of new rowhouses changed hands every month—until the process short-circuited. In 1904 the subway arrived as predicted, but the expected middle-class tenants didn't. Desperate landlords slashed rents. The wildly inflated market crashed. By 1905, financial institutions canceled loans to speculators here, foreclosing their mortgages.

Coincidence saved the investors. Ever since 1890, southern blacks had been migrating north to escape lynchings and poverty, the failed promises of Emancipation and Reconstruction. By the turn of the century three-quarters of the black population in New York were newcomers—chiefly from the South. Despite the relatively small size of the black population—only 2 percent of the town's inhabitants—available housing was short. Racial prejudice kept African Americans from melding into the city's mainstream, and even old ghettos were under threat. Shortly after the turn of the century, construction for the new Pennsylvania Station supplanted a large black neighborhood in the west thirties. Race riots tore at other black districts—notably, the blocks near today's Lincoln Center.

African Americans needed a new safe zone. For their part, real estate men in Harlem were ready to forgo racist principles, or most were. Rather than declare bankruptcy, many landlords, particularly in the blocks above 130th Street, opened their houses to blacks. That is, they did as long as they could pay the high rents African Americans had always been forced to pay wherever they settled. Soon, two African American real estate brokers, John Royal and Philip Payton, set up businesses for themselves.

Resistant white associations bought up houses to bar black tenants, but Payton and Royal finessed their moves by buying other houses and evicting white residents. After bitter checkerboard battles, the minority firms eventually closed, and wealthy black churches took up the housing struggle.

When not fighting, the white companies tried cajoling, hinting they'd give unlimited financial help if blacks would build colonies on unimproved land outside the city. The idea was remarkably similar to a plan floated in the 1980s to remove poor African Americans from Manhattan to Yonkers.

To make sense of the promised-land aura Harlem evoked at the turn of the century (easily understood from this Morningside Heights Charlton Heston–Moses vantage), it's useful to review earlier black landholding options in New York.

In 1644 the West India Company allowed half freedom to eleven slaves (who petitioned for the "right"), providing they pay annual tithes or provide stints of unpaid labor. They also "granted" the status to their wives, whom the company had thoughtfully imported in 1626, two years after instituting slavery. Little is known about the men, less about the women.

To make the families self-supporting, the company awarded farm lots in what would become Greenwich Village, Astor Place, and the district north of City Hall. All the plots sat in swampy soil and perched on the town's rim—a buffer against Indians or other enemies. Worse, the grants were tenuous and could be seized and sold to pay the debts of each slave's former owner.

Life was to get harder still when the British arrived and canceled even these marginal entitlements. In 1712 the new rulers struck all black property rights after a slave rising the same year. From this time until 1809, African Americans couldn't own land or shelter in New York.

Property wasn't the only right snatched back. The British canceled freedom of movement as well. Under the Dutch, black New Amsterdammers had mingled rather freely in their spare time, particularly on market days and holidays. From 1683, laws banned blacks from gathering in "groups" of more than four. By 1702 it was down to three—a variation on Arlo Guthrie's contention in his "Alice's Restaurant" song that two is a conspiracy. Slaves riding horses or walking at night without lanterns could get forty lashes. (An exception to the gathering rules continued at city markets, particularly the Catherine Street market on the Lower East Side, where black youth were known for doing a low-to-the-ground "break-down" jig that sounds remarkably similar to our era's break dance.) In 1741 whites blamed the slave uprising of that year on the free mingling of blacks at a Methodist revival in the fields of present-day City Hall Park.

Even after the state outlawed the last traces of slavery in 1827, the second to last northern state to do so, African Americans remained in civil limbo for decades to come. "No Admittance" signs for blacks appeared for the first time the year slavery ended, and in the next years racism actually increased in the city, as immigrants from Ireland competed with African Americans for jobs. (And brought homegrown prejudices.) Some blacks formed multi-racial communities such as the settlement in Central Park near today's Great Lawn, but violence forced others out of old mixed neighborhoods. Greenwich Village became a sanctuary under the aegis of patrician whites who loathed the Irish. Following the Civil War draft riots, many African Americans moved to Brooklyn. At the turn of the century, blacks lived squeezed in poor pockets on the West Side between 32nd Street and the low sixties.

The move to Harlem was the first time in Manhattan's history that African Americans got decent housing in a desirable area. Turn-of-the-cen-

RIOTERS CHASING NEGRO WOMEN AND CHILDREN THROUGH THE VACANT LOTS IN LEXINGTON AVENUE.

Over the centuries New York's African Americans had to flee from one enclave to another.

tury Harlem housing was elegant, probably the largest swath of first-rate dwellings in the city. Deterioration started only when realtors doubled rates after blacks arrived—a common ghetto practice forcing tenants to share space. (Some critics then, as now, tended to blame the poor themselves for the bad housing they endured, but activist-photographer Jacob Riis, not usually very sympathetic, singled out African Americans as model residents in his reporting on the city near the time of the uptown migration.)

By the teens of this century, as southern blacks and West Indians arrived to work in the war industries, Harlem's population had grown 600 percent, and African Americans owned $5 million in real estate. Black intellectuals called their new neighborhood "the home of Negro Zionism."

"The question naturally arises," wrote historian James Weldon Johnson in the late 1920s:

"are the Negroes going to be able to hold Harlem? If they have been driven northward for the past hundred years and out of less desirable sections, can they hold this choice bit of Manhattan Island? It is hardly probable that Negroes will hold Harlem indefinitely, but when they are forced out of it it will not be for the same reasons that forced them out of former quarters in New York City. The situation is entirely different and without precedent. When colored people do leave Harlem, their homes, their churches, their investments, their businesses, it will be because the land has become so valuable they can no longer afford to live on it. But the date of another move northward is very far in the future. . . . What will Harlem be and become in the meantime? Is there danger that the Negroe may lose his economic status in New York and be unable to hold his property? Will Harlem become merely a famous ghetto,* or will it be a center of intellectual, cultural and economic forces exerting an

When black New Yorkers arrived in Harlem, it was the first time the majority had been able to occupy good housing in a desirable area.

influence throughout the world—especially upon Negroe peoples? Will it become a point of friction between the races in New York?"

The author answered his rhetorical questions with an optimistic conclusion, positing three reasons for black success in Harlem: the native-born status of African Americans (as opposed to new immigrants), the district's integral links to the greater city that wouldn't allow it to be isolated, and New York's job opportunities for all.

Johnson's poignant, prescient question about black tenure in Harlem raises questions about exactly what Harlem is, and by extension, who it belongs to.

☞ Look across the street up the block to the Beaux Arts houses owned by Columbia University.

---

*As much as blacks in the 1920s had identified with the promise of Israeli Zionism, by the 1930s they identified with the plight of European Jews: the term *ghetto* became increasingly used in the community to describe local conditions.

Because of unfairly high rents, doubling up grew common and housing stock deteriorated. The Depression took a further toll.

Until the turn of this century, Columbia, Barnard, St. John the Divine, City College, and St. Luke's Hospital all would have been considered Harlem institutions. Not surprisingly, the organizations decline the older, more inclusive designation, and (with the notable exception of some health and housing outreach) identify more with the unassailable eyrie, the precipice barriers.

Today, the eight square miles called Harlem is defined as bounded by Morningside Heights and St. Nicholas Park on the west, the river on the east, Central Park on the south, and 155th Street on the north.

Harlem-based or not, these palisade citadels exert a powerful impact on the plains below. (The cliff-top black community has long since been dispossessed, along with poor white residents, to make way for facilities belonging to these institutions, which own an estimated 70 percent of the property up here. The university alone owns 6,250 apartments in the neighborhood.) Recently, Harlem activists have been contesting a plan by St. Luke's Hospital on Morningside Drive to shift its center for birth and newborns to midtown. Morningside Park below here still has the 1968 bulldozer scars of the Columbia gym foundation, halted when students and Harlemites protested park expropriation in a much publicized campus uprising. Farther down in the valley, some, though by no means all, fault the quality of care provided by Columbia's College of Physicians to Harlem Hospital.

Definitions of Harlem have changed over time according to what interest groups wanted it to be. Today, the term *Harlem* has come to mean the designation of virtually all turf held by blacks in north Manhattan. The inverse, of course, is that land *not* held by blacks becomes something else.

Even though the manipulation often goes unrecognized, the politics of naming shapes how we perceive place. During the 1980s real estate boom, the phenomenon here was rife enough that it was hard to miss. The designation *Harlem Gateway,* coined for the blocks just north of Central Park, caused anxiety to many, suggesting as it did a *drang nach* north by downtown developers into areas the black population was not strong enough to hold. Some investing companies even sported racist names like Minority Games and Oreo Uptown Gambit.

☞ Look down at the boarded-up housing on Morningside and Manhattan Avenues. Except for their cinderblocked windows, the buildings are still architecturally handsome. So is much of Harlem's housing stock (facades at least), despite the ghastly conditions of the past thirty years.

From 1950 to 1970 Harlem's population fell from 227,000 to 159,267; the middle class leading the exodus. Today just under 100,000 people live here, even though the percentage of blacks in the overall city has grown from 19.3 in 1970 to 27 in 1990. In part, the middle class left for the positive reason that suburban discrimination eased. (Recently, as "few" as 44 percent of blacks looking to buy homes outside the city met resistance.) In greater part, they left because drugs and the economic plight had fueled a toxic culture, making Harlem painful from the 1960s on. The trickle of elite black in-migration, mostly young professionals, could not counterbalance the loss.

Side by side with the middle-class departure, white landlords refused to maintain buildings, even torched property to get insurance. Banks pulled out and red-lined the area. (The term *red-line,* which dates to early nineteenth-century Britain, was first a ledger phrase to do with striking soldiers off payrolls. It gained American currency and geographic meaning in the 1960s when first insurance companies, then banks drew no-go zones on maps.)

As a result of abandonment and default on taxes, the city is the largest landlord in Harlem, owning close to two-thirds of the housing stock. Only 7 percent of Harlemites actually own their property. More than a quarter of the houses stand empty.

In the early 1980s wary residents and community boards, fighting for more input, feared the city was deliberately letting Harlem die so that it could develop it anew for a new wave of downtown investors (the polite local name for nonblacks) attracted by the low prices and once elegant housing stock. This anxiety was aggravated by an early city policy of auctioning off its *in rem* property for one dollar, plus giving the buyer a $43,000 rehabilitation loan per apartment, to get it off its hands—a policy later rescinded after neighborhood outcry. In that period, some planning journals drew up battle plans for a "pincer" movement in Harlem's western and southern edges—the less risky margins. Property speculation before the 1987 crash grew so steamy that owners flipped one run-down apartment on 116th Street five times—its value rising from $6,000 to $600,000 despite its disrepair.

Ironically, or tragically, one safeguard holding back even more outside investment in Harlem at the time was the perception of the neighborhood as a dangerous area. A disheartening corollary to this is that interactions alleviating fear (including my walking tours) were and are often seen as undermining defenses.

Walk south down Morningside Drive to Cathedral Avenue (110th) and turn left (east) to the **Frederick Douglass Circle**. ❷ Do not go through Morningside Park, which can still be dangerous despite relandscaping.

This circle was key to early gentrification here. In 1985 a federal urban development grant gave the city $6 million to subsidize the Towers on the Park condominiums, the last hurrah of serious federal money here—the next year the Reagan government slowed housing aid to cities to a near halt. At the time of the 1985 grant, Chemical Bank gave a loan of $47 million to finance construction on the Towers—an act of unprecedented generosity for the bank and nearly its last. Since then, Chemical Bank had all but packed up in Harlem until its recent merger with Manufacturers Hanover, when neighborhood activists forced it to fulfill its CRA (Community Reinvestment Act) requirements mandated by Washington in 1977, a rule forcing banks to contribute to neighborhoods from which they profit. (There are, by the way, almost no ATMs in Harlem except the one close to [white-organized] Harlem Hospital. For that matter, there are no ATMs along Broadway in the poor black and Hispanic area all the way up from 113th Street, near white Columbia, until you reach the white Columbia-Presbyterian Medical Center at 165th Street. This is *real* landscape architecture—the most telling environmental detail I've learned in a long time.)

As one might guess, most of the apartments at this key location near the park, and the citadel institutions above, sold at upper-middle prices, with Columbia University's staff getting first pick.

Turn left and walk north on Frederick Douglass Boulevard (hereafter called Eighth Avenue for brevity). At 2079 Eighth note the **red brick apartment complex** ❸ *built in tandem by the Elks and the HUDC. (HUDC is short for the Harlem Urban Development Corporation, a subsidiary of New York State's planning arm formed under pressure from black and Puerto Rican legislators in 1973.)*

In 1986, after Congress threatened to end all federal aid to the urban homeless and the Reagan government had cut $25 billion from low-income housing across the nation, Mayor Ed Koch proposed to rebuild every abandoned building in New York and to renovate every city-owned apartment with money from the city's capital budget and state sources. Earmarking a staggering (and most say somewhat fictive) $5.1 billion fund to be spent between 1986 and 1998, the Koch administration set a citywide goal to rehabilitate hundreds of thousands of rental units for the homeless and low-, moderate-, and middle-income tenants. (Critics said that far too low a proportion of apartments was designated for the very poor and homeless.) The goal in Harlem, alone, was 10,000 renewed units.

Koch's hope was that, eventually, most of the rehabilitated property, albeit restored through public or private initiative or a combination of the two, would revert to private ownership. (One channel for this, aside from the soon aborted auction policy, was for the city to hire a contractor to fix up a building and then turn it over to a nonprofit group to run.)

It's hard to get a perspective on the plan and the many nuanced rehabilitation partnerships established, as the agencies involved are so numerous and overlapping.

Because of defaults on taxes, the city owns two-thirds of the neighborhood's buildings today. The massive rehabilitation program, started a decade ago, has ebbed with the recession.

Also, sundry revisions of the project have surfaced, died, and surfaced again. Sheer numbers make it hard to imagine. Performance estimates vary.

For a brief spell, the chink of hammers on masonry, the clouds of stone dust filling the air made walking in Harlem feel as if you were in a rising cathedral. After the 1987 crash most investors lost their taste for playing, and some Harlemites say that city-sponsored work also seems to ebb and flow with election periods. Despite this, downtown newspapers say that 6,000 units of revamped housing have been completed with help from all sectors, which, if so, would seem a relative success, though other buildings have fallen apart even as these have risen.

One big remaining problem, among others, is that despite the city government's hope to return the housing to private ownership, it still owns most of the property—a de facto housing estate for which it has no master plan.

Regardless of what even critics call a valiant effort, living conditions in many of the older buildings are imaginably horrible, as the city has been left in the position of managing the discarded buildings for hundreds of thousands of tenants, of whom at least one third are generally on relief. Private sector managers are said to be equally ill equipped, but at least their buildings get inspected for violations by the city. Or, sort of. Recently, cuts have savaged the inspection budget, and more than half the staff have been laid off. Municipally owned buildings do not get inspected (on the principle that the city could not violate its own code), and some residents live with tangles of open wiring (or none at all), sinks on the floor, and buckets for plumbing. With a few exceptions, city activists seem less hopeful than they once were about the goal of returning these apartments to private hands. (Or, at least into deserving tenants-group hands. Recently, Mayor Rudolph W. Giuliani's office has started to throw city-owned property back on a semi-open market.)

Continue north on Eighth and turn right (east) on 115th Street, passing the community garden twined with roses on the street's north side. At 203 West 115th Street, the 1908 **McKim, Mead and White Public Library** ❹ *remains from Harlem's grander days.*

☞ The building's architecture—rusticated limestone, arched windows surmounted by a carved municipal seal—was intended to recall Italy's Pitti Palace. Until former Mayor David Dinkin's library drive, in recent years it had been virtually as inaccessible as the Italian palace—open three hours a day, three days a week.

***K**eep walking east on 115th to number 215, on the south side of the street.*

☞ The copper-towered **Wadleigh Junior High School, ❺** built in 1905, is doing better. (Too well, some people think, or at least, the city's School Construction Board has done too well. The building's Flemish roof and stained-glass windows by architect C. J. Snyder has just undergone a $47 *million* restoration, and a new auditorium is under way.)

Today, Wadleigh, once a contender for the city's leading public school, runs a dropout prevention center for local children. The problems facing the city's 16 percent black students who leave high school without graduating have worsened as blue-collar work disappears. Between 1970 and 1984 half a million manual jobs evaporated or, rather, were exported to cheap labor states in America and third world countries.

In this climate, addiction is bound to flourish, particularly as few youngsters have positive male models. (And they certainly are not finding many in the corruption-plagued local 30th precinct!) Fully 82.5 percent of Harlem's mothers raise children by themselves, double the city average. Most of them live in projects, adult female ghettos within a racial ghetto. Memory walls ghosted with names of young men dead from overdose or drug turf wars commemorate the fallen—the remembrances painted by friends "to keep their spirit close."

***W**hen you reach Adam Clayton Powell Junior Boulevard (hereafter, for brevity's sake, called Seventh Avenue), turn left and walk north along the avenue's west side to 116th Street.*

☞ At this point look (don't walk) a block east to the gold-domed mosque on the south side of the street (102 West 116th Street.) It is the **Malcolm Shabazz Mosque Number Seven,** formerly the Temple of Islam and before that, in Harlem's high-life era, the Lenox Casino.

Mullahs here assume fatherly roles for Harlem's young male Muslims. Malcolm Little, later Malcolm X, ultimately El Haaj Malik El-Shabazz, who founded this center, was himself helped through conversion to Islam to establish goals and shake youthful drug dependency and petty crime. In 1954 he founded Temple Seven on the top floor of the old casino. During the 1960s and 1970s, a time when Malcolm and other Nation members (Black Muslims) were working out the ideology of black power, this mosque served as a center for the Nation of Islam.

In 1964 Malcolm X broke with the Muslims following disputes with their leader, Elijah Muhammad. Soon afterward, assassins killed him at a rally in Washington Heights. Some allege that the FBI or the CIA (or both) and the Nation of Islam backed the murder, but despite murky politics and bitter feelings, Elijah Muhammad's successor Louis Farrakhan renamed the mosque for the fallen leader out of deference to his continuing popularity.

Today, the Nation of Islam movement still dominates Muslim life in Harlem, though many Nation members converted to orthodox Sunni Islam after Elijah Muhammad's death in 1975. The latter organization, more pan-Islamic, less exclusively focused on race power than the Muslims, keeps its New York headquarters in Brooklyn. The division is one of several differences between Brooklyn and Harlem African Americans.

☞ The fanciful building on the southwest corner of 116th and Seventh by architect Thomas Lamb, opened as a theater and later became the flagship movie house of Samuel Lionel ("Roxy") Rothafel. It now houses a **Baptist church, ❻** the leading denomination in Harlem.

As much as men are paramount in mosques, women dominate Harlem churches, even though here also, with one or two exceptions, the powerful preachers remain intractably male. "Mothers of the Church" form the great majority of Harlem's congregations and serve every role, from hosting church dinners to dispensing federal aid. Like other Harlem churches, this one is bright with elegant parishioners. (As early as 1817, a European visiting the city praised the "finely dressed black women in white muslin and pink shoes—the only fashionable in New York.")

The church is known for its gospel singing, an urban evolution of camp meeting spirituals. Traditionally, congregational music provided a temporary sense of bonding, a reaffirmation of community eroded by white society.

From early on the white establishment recognized the subversive potential religion held. Colonial governments banned black churches; African Americans had to worship in segregated spaces belonging to white congregations. Several chapels with slave galleries—cramped ceiling crawl spaces—survive today in downtown Manhattan. (See site 16, Walk 3.) The only time blacks were allowed free association in an independent space of their own was after death. As most churches refused black burials in their graveyards, separate cemeteries opened for them in the seventeenth century, but white control continued even here. Laws prohibited more than twelve black mourners to gather and forbade palls on the coffins lest they conceal weapons.

Ironically, gospel has become something of a white tourist commodity in Harlem. Church members treat visitors with almost painful graciousness. A few have officially recognized the presentation aspect and arrange their services for outsiders' convenience, putting hymns up front before the sermon. It's a difficult problem to resolve, as visitors not only bring cultural affirmation but much-needed revenue as well.

If you would like to attend a service at First Corinthian Baptist or at any local church, please be sure to offer a donation and behave with reverence, not just dropping in and out. Call the Greater Harlem Chamber of Commerce, (212) 427–7200, to find sightseeing companies that include parish stops on their tours.

For years black Harlemites marched through their wide boulevards for justice. This silent parade of 1917 protested race riots in East St. Louis. Today, the boulevards are empty, as Harlem's population has left the neighborhood (and the will to organize has faded).

☞ Before leaving here, note the sign by the door advertising a gospel revival meeting. During the Depression era Harlem had its own permanent gospel tent on 137th Street, and the streets rang with hose and hydrant baptisms. Now that vacant lots (and despair) flourish as blocks of housing are pulled down, outdoor prayer meetings are back.

Cross Seventh Avenue to the east side.

☞ Harlem's spacious tree-lined avenues, the imperial boulevards never realized in other parts of Manhattan, encouraged flaneuring and parades—formal and informal.

From the 1920s on, funeral processions, patriotic marches, strikers, and housewives demonstrating for "buy black" campaigns furled through uptown Manhattan. Neighboring Lenox, now a bleak De Chirico track, was the main venue, but Seventh had its share. (Other street activity has disappeared as well, particularly the soapbox orators who used to be a big part of life here. For that matter, presumably as they commute to beg, you don't even see the homeless that now are a staple in Midtown streets. Neither do you see break-dancers, who go downtown to perform. For their part, many Harlem mothers try to keep their young indoors and view summers with dread. In some neighborhoods the local precinct has organized "safe corridors" two or three days a week for several hours to allow people to do their errands protected by an extra police presence.)

☞ Note the **Graham Court Apartments ❼** at 1923–1937 Seventh Avenue on the northeast corner of 116th Street.

In 1932 this apartment complex was home to the writer and folklorist Zora Neale Hurston.

Luxury apartment building in Harlem preceded development on Manhattan's midtown West Side. Like later West Side buildings, flats here were palatial, equipped with elevator banks, servants' quarters, butler's pantries, perambulator rooms, and baronial communal dining halls.

☞ In 1901 the architectural firm Clinton and Russell (which went on to design the look-alike Apthorp Apartments for the Astor estate on West 78th Street) designed Graham Court for the Astors. Its courtyard and stately entrance, arched and flanked by marble pillars, make it Harlem's most elegant complex. Despite a long tenants' dispute, the suites are still sumptuous, with marble fireplaces and parquetry.

Continue north on Seventh along the east side of the avenue. At 118th Street, cross the avenue and take a few steps west to number 206–210, the **Cecil Hotel** *for the elderly.*

In the 1940s the building housed **Minton's,** ❽ a beloved jazz club where Dizzy Gillespie, Charlie Parker, and Thelonius Monk improvised after work. A period mural of musicians playing with everything from whiskbrooms to base viols is being restored, and the owners here hope to reopen the cafe and jazz center if they find an investor. (If you're able to enter, it would be right to contribute something toward the restoration.)

REOPENING

Return to Seventh, recross the avenue, and keep going north past the **Paris Blues Nightclub** ❾ *at the southeast corner of 121st Street.*

During World War I, New York's Fifteenth Regiment of the National Guard,* the Hell Fighters, an African American regiment from Harlem, popularized black music throughout France. Fame for the troop's heroism and culture trickled back here and spurred interest in this country also: at least, it helped establish the rhythms; the demobilized soldiers fared less well.

The French love for jazz, blues, and Harlem still holds today. Far more French than American tourists visit here. Sadly, the Paris Blues has no music. If you're interested in hearing some, call the Chamber of Commerce.

☞ This is a good place to look up above you (to the west) and see **Grant's Tomb** grinning over Harlem Plain like an imperial joke.

Keep north to the **Refuge Temple of the Church of Our Lord Jesus Christ** ❿ *at 2081 Seventh Avenue on the northeast corner of 124th Street. The boxy white building once held the Harlem Casino—a beer and zither center for German Harlemites. The* **Theresa Hotel,** ⓫ *a 1910 hostelry that also served German Jewish society, stands diagonally across the street on the southwest corner of Seventh Avenue and 125th.*

☞ The building's size shows how confident local white developers were of their own continuance, despite black settlement to the north.

For years the opera house, vaudeville halls, theaters, and social gathering spots on this street remained off-limits to blacks. (They could come

---

*Forming the regiment was a struggle: during training, the men practiced with brooms instead of guns; once in combat, the troops fought under the French flag since the U.S. Army forbade them to serve at the front.

to stores but were treated badly.) Eventually the Theresa went on to become the nation's "Black Waldorf," but only began to admit African Americans in 1940.

The tour will now briefly explore 125th Street's epochal layers—the white era, the 1930s white-black conflict, and the present-day African American struggle to claim space. First, we'll visit the street's back side on 124th Street, as more evidence from early times remains there.

*B*efore turning west on 124th Street, you might like to look inside the **Ennis Frances Houses** ⑫ at 2070 Seventh Avenue.

☞ The HUDC subsidized this residential senior center—an example of what good housing can be. Sympathetic spaces include a small garden and an art gallery that holds changing exhibits of community artists.

*T*urn left and walk west on 124th Street on the north side of the street.

☞ Note the **L. M. Blumstein** ⑬ sign on the large white building. Blumstein's Department store opened here in 1896.

Like other white store owners on the thoroughfare, the proprietor discriminated against black shoppers and refused to hire blacks in staff positions until 1934. That year, the Reverend Adam Clayton Powell, backed by a coalition of Harlem clergymen, forced this store and others to change. By using boycotts, humor, and evidence, activists were able to get policy improved. (African Americans paid their Con Ed bills in pennies and gathered receipts for the amount of money they'd spent locally on food and clothes—$4.5 million in one year alone.) The meager gains were not enough—discriminatory hiring practices were a main cause of the 1935 Harlem riots.

☞ Next door to the west, at 243–251 124th Street, the 1913 building with the barrel-vaulted roof and saucy stonework around the arched windows sheltered **Pabst's Concert Hall and Weinstuben.** ❶

German Jewish fraternal societies came here to celebrate, and the Harlem Chamber of Commerce, an all-white association of merchants, held its meetings upstairs. (African American businessmen weren't invited into the latter organization until 1960.)

☞ By 1920, this building had become the Kress 5 and 10 Cents store. (See the faded logo, barely discernible on the upper right hand corner of the brick exterior.)

ANNUAL BANQUET *of* HARLEM BOARD OF COMMERCE
From Flashlight Photograph Taken at Pabst Harlem Tuesday Evening,
January Fourteenth, Nineteen Hundred and Thirteen

In 1935, ten thousand black Harlemites rallied here on the rumor that police had killed a dark-skinned Puerto Rican youth accused of shoplifting. Their larger protest was against the nation's racial prejudice that undermined so many aspects of black life. The Harlem Merchants Association, another all-white group, appealed to the governor to send troops. The police fired on the crowd, which began to loot.* The result was three deaths—all African American, two hundred civilians seriously wounded, and property damage of more than $2 million. Afterward, the city permanently doubled the number of police in the precinct.

This 1913 photograph of the Harlem Board of Commerce shows whites only. This is not surprising given that African Americans had just begun arriving uptown in numbers. What is remarkable is that some local organizations did not allow blacks until the 1960s.

C*ontinue walking west to Eighth Avenue and then turn right to walk north toward 125th Street. The* **House of Prayer,** ⓯ *belonging to Bishop C. Grace, or "Daddy Grace," occupies the southeast corner. Note the hanging sign.*

*Outsiders watching inner-city riots on TV are often scornful of minorities looting "their" neighborhoods. The scorn comes from ignorance that many, if not most, stores in black neighborhoods are owned by people from outside the community. Also, however negatively, the neighborhood riots (called "street jitterbugging" in the 1930s) show local rule over local domain—grafitti with firepower.

After the turn of this century, the Holiness Pentecostal movement expanded rapidly in northern cities. Evangelist churches helped rural newcomers accommodate and warded off desperation in the Depression. Daddy Grace and Father Divine, who promised utopias and, in varying degree, provided social services, were the most celebrated of the prophets pouring into the city at the time. Tens of thousands of believers attended services at their brownstone "heavens" and "peace missions." Prayer gatherings continue upstairs here today, and a homey cafeteria serves up smoky pork, fragrant greens, and sweet potatoes at Depression-era prices.

Perhaps owing to the current hard times, Pentecostal sects are once again the fastest growing of Harlem's hundreds of religious institutions.

☞ At the corner of Eighth Avenue and 125th Street, look up and down the street to get a feel of it.

The well-endowed House of Prayer owns several commercial buildings on 125th Street. It's an exception. Despite "buy black" efforts that have continued from the 1930s (see posters in many stores), outsiders dominate much of the street. HUDC has tried to restore a sense of black participation as well as revitalize the down-at-heel strip. It is an uphill undertaking.

For years banks red-lined the street, and property owners wouldn't rent to blacks. Today it looks better than a decade ago, but 125th Street's economy is still largely run by downtowners. Absentee Jewish and Italian landlords own many properties. Chains, including Baskin-Robbins, Kentucky Fried Chicken, Florsheim, and Woolworth, own the majority of stores. Jewish, Korean, Chinese, and, to a lesser extent, Hispanic merchants operate many of the small businesses that do exist.

Since the 1970s the earlier resentment of blacks against Jewish businessmen has been transferred to the Koreans, who run almost a third of the stores here. The sad fact is that the Koreans, who seem relatively prosperous, are just middlemen for absentee downtown landlords. The real problems are systemic, have to do with the larger economy. Church conciliation groups work to ease friction.

☞ Note the street sign at the northeast corner of Eighth and 125th, named the "Jackie Robinson Walk"—a bit of cosmetic geomancy. A more real view of local reality or realty is at the nearby Freedom Bank, founded by the former baseball star.

Robinson started the bank in the 1960s because he felt blacks still had little economic freedom despite gains in civil liberties.

Today, beggars sit on the doorstep of the failed institution, once the largest of the nation's (few) black banks. Even though Chase Bank gave Freedom start-up capital ($3.7 million), it prided itself on being a local institution. Unlike big bank branch offices, which had mostly pulled out of

Despite black activist efforts from the 1930s on, economic power in Harlem remained in white hands. Many, if not most, of the stores on 125th Street still belong to people from outside the community.

Harlem by then in any case, it reinvested in the community, underwriting projects the neighborhood wanted. (Today, storefront check-cashing operations, some of them run [discreetly] by mainstream banks, have replaced the banks themselves along 125th Street. Fees are high, extra services zero.) Sadly, as Freedom had no backup to offset bad loans, the bank couldn't stand on its own. When it failed in the 1980s, uninsured depositors lost $11 million, though the FDIC was bailing out (white) suburban savings banks at the same period.

If Harlem's wariness toward outside institutions has foundation, it also finds it hard to do without them. The Harlem Commonwealth Council (HCC), a subgroup of HUDC founded to run its profit-making ventures, lobbies for tax incentives to attract diverse companies here. (As this book goes to press, I'm still trying to find out if the "Commonwealth" refers back to the old commonwealth here. So far, no one can say for sure.)

Even the Apollo, a showcase for black talent by the period this picture was taken, started life as a white-only theater.

***W**alk east along 125th Street to **Mart 125** ⑯ (number 260) across from the Apollo Theater. ⑰*

One of the projects belonging to the HCC reveals some of the problems of top-down intervention in a basically fragile ecology.

☞ The mart holds a battery of booths selling souveniry African American and supposedly African African products, T-shirts, oils, and so on.

Most of the shopkeepers are cynical, saying they are only there because the city subsidized the space to get African American vendors off the streets. (They've been replaced by newly arrived Senegalese.) It's doubtful the mart could sustain itself on its own.

☞ Even the **wall mural** by school children to the west of the Apollo theater is subsidized. The work is stiff and forced, and the references to Harlem's renaissance seem remote, as if the children had little sense of what they drew. How could they? The **painted security gates** nearby are much better—a first-rate example of homegrown art. A local artist, conceding that security gates are a way of life along 125th Street, has glorified the corridor's storefronts with swaggering scenes of Harlem highlife circa 1920.

One institution aided by HUDC (a $1.4 million loan) that gets popular support is the recently renovated Apollo. The theater was white only when it opened in 1913 as the Hurtig and Seamons burlesque house. After Mayor Fiorello La Guardia banned burlesque from the city in 1934, the theater reopened as the Apollo under new white management that welcomed blacks. Soon it became the center of popular Harlem music, showcasing Bessie Smith, Billie Holiday, Duke Ellington, Count Basie, Charlie Parker, Dizzy Gillespie, and Aretha Franklin, among others. Audiences here, jaded from the wealth of talent, were notoriously critical, once even booing Ella Fitzgerald off the stage.

In the 1980s Percy Sutton, the former Manhattan borough president, opened a cable TV studio in the theater, which had gone dark in the 1970s in a decline stemming from the 1940s when black entertainers had less trouble getting spots at Midtown clubs and started commuting to work. (Not all were allowed. Arcane cabaret licensing laws, lasting from the 1930s to 1967, kept some African American entertainers from working at Midtown clubs. The police had the right to grant ID cards and could withhold them from musicians "not of good character." Some detected racial bias.)

In the 1960s the Apollo's plight worsened when most middle-class Harlem theater-goers left for the suburbs. Ironically, the theater performed global service during these years, as white devotees, including Mick Jagger, carried African American rhythms and melodies developed here into the world's commercial mainstream—a bittersweet realization of James Weldon Johnson's projection that Harlem's influence might span oceans. Today the Apollo, gone nonprofit to survive, once again hosts live reviews. All across the country alumni performers stage benefits, and even hard-nosed banks forgive its debts. The theater now holds city, state, and national landmark status.

☞ A few doors down, another HCC project (originally budgeted for $8 million) has been rerouted. A 1980s plan had called for converting **the old Loew's Theater** into the Harlem Center for Cultural Arts, a performance and exhibit space for third world artists. In 1992 the rehabilitated theater reopened more modestly as a multiplex cinema under black ownership. One

125th Street institution that thrives without help is the **off-track betting office** to the east of the old Loew's at 215 West 125th. The smoke-soiled gambling rooms occupy ground-floor space in what earlier had been a clinic belonging to nearby Sydenham Hospital.

Local black and Puerto Rican community groups and a suburban real estate company opened Sydenham in 1971. Every month its emergency room handled more than two thousand patients, and more than fifty local agencies used its prenatal and baby care center. In 1979 Mayor Koch, bent on cutting funds for municipal hospitals come what may, shut the facility. (It stands a few blocks below 125th Street, now an old people's home, after it narrowly missed being turned into condominiums.) Police bodily removed Harlem's clergymen, who staged protest sit-ins. In the past twenty years, half a dozen upper Manhattan hospitals have closed. The single new one, North General, an AIDS hospital, was funded out of the community's own pocket and only later subsidized by the state.

May has come, so to speak. Or rather, December. Health is correlated with income. Income is correlated with race. Race is correlated with neighborhood. The Harlem death rate is nearly double that for the rest of Manhattan. Today's city health maps look like nineteenth-century cholera maps, where epidemics, poverty, and swamplands were virtually synonymous.

In 1984 crack's arrival here brought havoc. During the next two years Harlem's infant mortality jumped 22 percent, to a rate worse than that of many third world countries. Since then AIDS and drug overdoses have soared. Drug-resistant TB thrives. The life expectancy for men in Harlem is less than in Bangladesh, though the high local murder rate skews this last statistic.

C*ross the* **Plaza of Afro-American Unity** *at the corner of 125th and Seventh. The optimistic name comes from Malcolm X's organization, which he proclaimed at a 1963 rally in the Theresa.*

Even before then, the hotel had already served third world solidarity. In 1960 Cuba's Fidel Castro, on tour to address the U.N. General Assembly, left the Waldorf and swept up here with live chickens and all the city's media in tow.

☞ During the civil rights struggle, the plaza became a gathering point for community stump speakers. Not so the building across the street. The razor wire and twines of graffiti ringing the **Harlem State Office Building 18** at 163 West 125th on the northeast corner of Seventh Avenue suggest it is *in* but not necessarily *of* the community.

The state built this office tower here after the 1964 Harlem riot, triggered by the death of a black youth shot by an off-duty police officer, but rooted in the larger cry for social change. The struggle cost one life, left 141 injured, and caused grievous property damage. Some local residents think the gift of this building was intended to salve Harlem's pride rather than tend to its basic needs.

For years, a mega-building has been slated for the lot next door to the office, but the ground still stands empty. The HCC has (or had) planned an "International Third World Trade Center" here. The scheduled project—a $160 million 42-story office and housing complex scheduled to include a 500-room luxury hotel as well as a 3,000-seat convention center is (was) expected to get funding from the public and foreign investors. It's still on the books, though one wonders whether the putative tenants, supposedly government agencies, international and national trade companies, and minority entrepreneurs, would have shown (will show up) in sufficient numbers even if the building had gone (does go) through.

The vision for this site is nothing compared with the project drawn up in the 1980s for the Hudson River end of 125th Street. A luxury hotel tower anchored by a 75-boat marina was supposed to open on a 40-acre complex stretching from 125th to 133rd Streets, from Hudson to Broadway. Residents could sail in and never set foot inland. If they wanted local culture, an in-house 5,000-seat theater was planned to showcase local talent. A new street was to have been built for added ambience. The brochures promised "black and Latino performances" on a brand-new "street of sound modeled after Bourbon Street in New Orleans."

Before the 1987 crash, Japanese realtors expressed interest in investing here so "they might better understand minorities," but this project is also on hold.

***C**ross back south across 125th Street to the* **Studio Museum 19** *at 144 West 125th Street (one dollar suggested admission.)*

Despite problems, Harlem's cultural institutions shine brighter than most in the city—in part, because of the collective struggle linking local intellectuals, artists, and activists. The Studio Museum, founded in 1968 for local and national black art, shows new artists as well as Harlem Renaissance greats—Romare Bearden, Robert Blackburn, and James Van Der Zee. Farther down the street at Fifth Avenue, the National Black Theater not only hosts acclaimed shows but also exemplifies good urban architecture.

***W**alk north on Seventh on the west side of the avenue, passing the former **Alhambra Vaudeville Hall** ⑳ (now a branch of the Motor Vehicles Department) on the southwest corner of 126th Street.*

☞ The 1884 church with the dramatically pitched roof on the northeast corner of 128th Street houses a congregation founded by a former slave, the Reverend Willis Brown, in 1896. Sundays will find half a dozen tour buses at **Metropolitan Baptist** and a large audience of Europeans enjoying gospel music.

***C**ontinue walking north along Seventh Avenue.*

☞ If it is open, be sure to enter **Salem United Methodist Episcopal Church** ㉑ (formerly Calvary Methodist Episcopal), built in 1887, at the northwest corner of 129th and Seventh. Countee Cullen's stepfather held this pulpit, so the poet-to-be grew up in the neighboring vicarage. Fittingly, the Harlem Literary Society sometimes meets in the church's theatrical auditorium.

***C**ontinue walking north.*

☞ The center island of Seventh Avenue at 131st Street holds the stump of the **"Tree of Hope** ㉒**."** During the Depression, actors and other unemployed gathered here to share job tips and touch the tree for luck. Harlem's unemployment at the time was dramatically higher than in the rest of the city. Recently, someone has replanted a seedling. It's needed.

☞ Don't miss the mural of the tree and its petitioners on the wall north of the Lafayette Theater: the Theater, now the **Williams Christian Methodist Church** ㉓, is located at 2225 Seventh between 131st and 132nd Streets.

Formal black drama in New York goes back to 1821, when the African Grove Theater in Greenwich Village staged new plays (including one about the Haitian liberator Toussaint L'Ouverture) and Shakespearean classics that incorporated traditional community music. Within a couple of decades, the effort was subverted, as minstrelsy—white men caricaturing blacks—swept theaters across America. From this time on, blacks themselves were suborned to play fatuous, white-created roles—black men in blackface.

In 1913 the Lafayette's white owners began the large-scale commodification of black culture in Harlem when they staged the "Darktown Follies" for white downtowners. In the 1930s African Americans seized back their own representation at the Lafayette when the Negro Unit of the WPA-backed Federal Theatre Project based itself here. Fittingly, one of the company's first performances was a newly minted presentation of "Toussaint L'Ouverture."

Today, a city landmarking controversy surrounds the old theater, or at least as much as one man with a cause can surround something. Michael Adams, a zealous Harlem preservationist, struggles to get this building (currently being defaced by its owners) designated, along with 113 others. Despite Adams' efforts, only a tiny fraction of Harlem's stunning buildings are landmarked. Ninety-five percent of Manhattan's landmarks are below 96th Street.

The loss of several black leaders in the 1960s hurt Harlem. So, too, have regional economic woes, the drug epidemic, and federal cutbacks.

Recently, the city's Landmarks-Preservation Commission has proposed twenty-five sites in upper Manhattan for designation—better than before— but nothing compared with other parts of the city and the worth of Harlem's architecture.

Some Harlem householders have a fear of landmark designation, an apprehension that it will constrain ownership and add to the cost of repair. During the protracted struggle over the proposal to demolish the uptown Audubon Ballroom for a Columbia University biomedical research facility, Adams gained increased local support. The possible loss of the Malcolm X assassination site raised general consciousness about the need to commemorate social history as well as to safeguard "good" architecture. Not just Harlemites were sensitized, but New Yorkers and planners in general. (African Americans are leaders in thinking holistically about the urban built environment. In part, this comes from a way of seeing; in part, it comes as, until recently, with a few exceptions, the establishment had considered mainly white-owned, pretty buildings worth saving. In 1994 a new group, Landmarks Harlem, has been formed, which vows to enlarge the traditional approach to preservation and to save Harlem's heritage in the doing.)

*K*eep walking north to 133rd Street on the east side of the street.

☞ The nightclub block between Seventh and Sixth (Lenox) ㉔ was a space designed to showcase "the primitive essence" of African American life, a mini Mau Mau mall. Depending what fantasy you held, this strip was "Beale Street" after the Memphis strip, or "Jungle Alley." In the 1920s popular literature promoted Harlem as an exotic playground—America's answer, along with Greenwich Village, to Paris. Breaking Prohibition laws at the white-owned speakeasies added to the thrill.

Black Harlem satisfied the needs of an urban, white middle class weary of the machine age and urbanization. By World War I, work-driven Protestants yearned for the hot-blooded and impulsive, or, as Freud had recently articulated, the id as opposed to the super ego. In theory (or wish), by listening to the "abandoned, driving rhythms of jazz," one could get back in touch with one's sexuality, wholeness. Ironically, given the African American diaspora, whites envied the perceived integrity of the black community.

*C*ross over Seventh at this point and walk one block north, then turn left (west) half a block. **St. Philip's Church ㉕** stands on the south side of 134th between Seventh and Eighth Avenues.

☞ African American architects George Foster and Vertner Tandy (New York's first licensed black practitioner) built the 1910 church. The salmon-colored brick is an odd surprise.

Venerable African American churches were the leading agents of black settlement in Harlem and remain a source of stability and hope today.

White racism prompted St. Philip's birth downtown in 1809. The church's founder, Peter Williams, Jr., began the New York African Society for Mutual Relief and was the first African American to be ordained in the city as an Episcopal priest. When his superiors at Trinity silenced him for preaching abolition, Williams and Trinity's black parishioners left to open a new church in Five Points, which they called St. Philip's after the only known apostle to have converted an African. In 1834 white toughs, allegedly acting for prominent citizens, sacked the church but failed to shut it down.

Racism didn't end there. Even though St. Philip's was cash rich when it arrived here (the Penn Station developers had bought its most recent site), no whites would sell it land. To get this property, the congregation's pale-skinned minister had to pass himself off as a white man.

Traditionally the black church had always been the most stable and wealthy community institution; now churches became Harlem's largest black property owners, helping African Americans and West Indians to settle in Harlem. "Buy property" became the text of sermons.

Property is still key—in the past decade, St. Philip's alone has channeled more than $30 million to rehabilitate and construct low-income housing to stabilize Harlem families. Part of the funds came from what remains of its endowment, the majority from money raised in and out of Harlem. The church provides more than shelter. As in the past, when religious groups offered arriving migrants almost total care, St. Philip's and others have become multi-service centers with job training, civil rights organizing, co-op food shopping, credit unions, family-planning units, day care services, and meal programs.

In recent decades, one internal problem troubling this church and, to a lesser degree, some other old guard Harlem congregations is the age of their parishioners. Most of the parishioners here are elderly (the median age at St. Philip's is over sixty), and many live in the suburbs. The shortage of new blood has an historical context. Even as St. Philip's and other old lineage churches helped poor blacks settle here, they tended to feel superior toward the "cotton field" southerners and show it. Despite its present-day good works, some Harlemites find St. Philip's uncongenial.

Return to Seventh and walk north to 135th Street, then turn right and walk partway down the block.

☞ The original housing stock ㉖ St. Philip's bought to rent out to its members stands between Sixth (Lenox) and Seventh on the north side of the street. Recently, the church has restored almost two hundred apartments in this row.

Traditionally, 135th Street served as the black institutional hub. The YMCA, the Schomburg Library, the NAACP, the Urban League are all nearby, as is the *Amsterdam News*.

Return to Seventh, cross, and continue walking north on the west side of the avenue, passing the former **Big Apple Bar** ㉗ *at the northwest corner of 135th Street, now the Big Apple food store.*

· The name and the bar go back to the jazz era when musicians popularized the term for the city. Most sources credit the Edenic phrase to Alain Locke, a Howard University professor and promoter of the arts renaissance in Harlem during the 1920s.

At 137th Street cross Seventh to the east and walk down to the **A.M.E. Zion Church,** ㉘ *the city's first African American congregation, which many call Mother Zion.*

Like St. Philip's, this church, founded in 1801, had its roots in the struggle against racism. Unlike Trinity, A.M.E. Zion's parent church, the John Street Methodist had spoken out against slavery from early on, but the congregation was far from egalitarian and refused to allow black preachers. In 1796 the church's sexton, Peter Williams, Sr. (father of the pastor at St. Philip's), left along with other African American parishioners and founded A.M.E. Zion a few years afterward.

In later years the church remained a defender of African American rights, earning the soubriquet "Freedom Church" as well as "Mother Zion" because of its links to abolitionists, including Sojourner Truth, Harriet Tubman, and Frederick Douglass.

*R*eturn west across Seventh and keep north again to 138th.

☞ During the 1930s, A.M.E.'s activist pastor often went with his younger brother, the singer Paul Robeson, to strategize with other community leaders at the **Red Rooster Bar** ㉙ on the southwest corner of Seventh at 138th Street.

Community organizers hashed out ward politics here, as well as rights issues. The two were often linked. Until 1917, blacks had *no* political representation in New York. Despite the uptown wards' 70 percent black population, gerrymandering allowed whites to rule local politics through the 1930s. In 1935 blacks (by then strongly Democratic because of New Deal programs) wrested control of their first district.

Internal rivalry between West Indian and African American politicians added to the problems of specious zoning. For several decades the West Indians took whatever posts blacks could hope for as they arrived politicized from the Caribbean.

In the 1950s black Harlemites, still circumscribed by gerrymandering, formed a separate political association. The regular Democrats reacted by throwing sops (including the borough presidency) while continuing to block potential black mayoral candidates. Mayor Dinkins was the first African American to break through the obstacles in the process.

☞ Also at 138th Street, you will see the 1925 **Renaissance Casino** ㉚ on the southeast corner of the avenue.

If whites in the 1920s held blacks politically at bay, they happily embraced black culture, as we've seen earlier at "Jungle Alley." The Renaissance opened here only a few years after whites had pulled out of this section of Harlem, but, even so, sophisticated downtowners taxied up to this combination ballroom and casino without qualm. The absence of fear (despite the brutal battle whites had recently waged against blacks to stop them moving to this neighborhood) contrasts to our own day, when dread has overcome a sense of entitlement. After the 1935 riots whites still came to Harlem for music (and more), but in fewer numbers. By the 1940s, many African American musicians went downtown to play for white audiences and white tourism declined even further.

*A*t 138th walk west to Eighth Avenue, taking time to enjoy the varied architectural detail of the 1891 **King Model Houses** ㉛ that extend from the south side of 138th Street to the north side of 139th between Seventh and Eighth Avenues.

☞ The block's developers hired three architectural firms to give tenants choice. McKim, Mead and White did the neo-Italian Renaissance houses in the center; James Brown Lord did the south tier; Bruce Price, the north.

These luxury houses saw real estate trench warfare when blacks moved to Harlem. Eventually the developers surrendered, but not to the newcomers. Instead, they sold out to the Equitable Life Assurance Company, who, along with Metropolitan Life, were large uptown real estate speculators. Even with its heft, Equitable was unable to stem the flow of African American settlement. Ever since the late 1920s, the blocks became *the* place for successful blacks to live in Harlem—"Strivers' Row." The other elite location is Hamilton Heights, technically outside Harlem's present borders, but often blurred with Harlem (by downtowners) because of its largely black population.

☞ The Historic District has an active block association that even maintains the signs on the carriage gates leading to backyard service areas. Freshly lettered notice boards remind visitors, "Please Walk Your Horses."

*C*ontinue west to Eighth Avenue and turn right, to walk north.

☞ Note the elegant new housing at Eighth Avenue and 138th, the start of a $17 million project, promised fifteen years ago but started fairly recently. The **duplex condominiums**, ㉜ laced with the same brickwork gracing the houses on neighboring "Strivers' Row," are the first of a 116-unit upper-middle-class enclave.

These "St. Charles" condominiums cost only $110–$125 thousand, thanks to the sponsoring partnership that includes several banks that are working off their local obligations under the federally mandated Community Reinvestment Act. (They call their program INVEST, or Increasing neighborhood Values with Secure Transactions, making *neighborhood* the only uncapitalized word other than the passive joining word, *with*.)

***C**ontinue north to 139th Street; turn right and walk east back to Seventh. Cross over the avenue and turn right to walk one block south; then turn left (east) on 138th Street and walk to the* **Abyssinian Baptist Church** ㉝ *at 132 West 138th.*

Four thousand to five thousand people belong to this church, founded in 1808 down in Five Points. It's one of America's largest Protestant congregations, but as in St. Philip's, many of the parishioners are elderly and live in the suburbs.

☞ Inside the parish house, a church official has mounted a one-room exhibit tracking the career of the Reverend Adam Clayton Powell, Sr., who moved the church here in the teens of this century (it had had several locations since Five Points); and that of his son, Adam Clayton Powell, Jr., who succeeded his father as minister. If you would like to see the collection, you should call before coming and make a small donation for the church's upkeep. Telephone (212) 862–7474. The display—an appealing example of taking charge of one's own institutional memory—follows Powell Senior's life and politics, virtually the same thing. Its focus, however, is on Powell Junior, New York's first black congressman, and his role in winning civil rights.

Over years, the church's activism has not gone unpunished. During Mayor Koch's administration, the city cut off the funds other churches received for their social services. In 1987 its new minister, the Reverend Calvin Butts, sued the police commissioner and Mayor Koch for organizing a "black spy desk" to discredit African American nonconformists, including himself.

Since then, pressures have eased, and Reverend Butts has mediated several racial crises. Mainstream papers are ambivalent about the minister, but nevertheless they grant him more coverage than other Harlem personalities. For his part, the Reverend Butts, while publicly more cautious than earlier, as he might run for election, continues to take on issues, personalizing some. Recently, he strode through Harlem hauling down the many cigarette ads veiling the neighborhood since educated whites quit smoking. Aside from toning down some of his public statements as he ponders a political bid, Butts has also moved back to Harlem from the middle-class suburb in New Rochelle where he lived before. Because of city conditions, a painfully large number of Harlem (and Brooklyn) clergy live outside their parishes, along with their wealthier church members.

*W*alk east along 138th, passing the site of **Liberty Hall,** ㉞ headquarters of Marcus Garvey's Universal Negro Improvement Association (UNIA), which stood to the east of the church at 120 West 138th Street.

The adopted Harlemite, who got more press than any before or since, was Marcus Garvey. After settling in New York in the 1920s, the Jamaican-born immigrant organized this century's* first black nationalist association to circle the globe.

Garvey used rallies at Liberty Hall to preach race pride and segregated social and economic institutions. Although some middle-class blacks and churches decried Garvey's separatist style and his sentimental promotion of Africa, the movement attracted many. At its peak, the UNIA claimed between two and four million followers, the largest mass movement of blacks in history.

During Garvey's reign, the streets around 135th and Sixth (Lenox) housed the organization's shops and storefront factories, which subsidized the cause. A pier at the Hudson and 135th berthed the UNIA's shabby steamships. Many whites wrote off the shipping company as comedic, but the effort was one of the few times Harlemites were somewhat successful in engendering their own economy—an uphill task for a community with a small consumer base.

It didn't last. By 1924 Garvey was in federal prison charged on a minor mail fraud count. Authorities deported him from jail to Jamaica.

☞ Eastman Kodak has donated historical plaques for some of the sites identified with Garvey in Harlem; the trail has the best interpretation of any markings in the city.

*T*urn right at Sixth (Lenox) and walk down to 136th; turn right to go to the Countee Cullen branch of the public library, 104 West 136th Street, between Lenox and Seventh.

The library stands on the site of a mansion built by A'Lelia Walker, a

---

*Black New Yorkers had had a pan-African political identification ever since 1791, when they thrilled to black Haitians' revolt against their French rulers. For decades, American whites feared the Caribbean example—a fear compounded in New York by the rush of emigré planters here after the troubles.

salon for intellectuals during the 1920s. Walker's money came from her mother, a St. Louis laundress who invented a hair-straightening process, became a multi-millionaire, and opened businesses to train and employ blacks.

Harlem's other cultural gathering spot at the time was an earlier library that stood back-to-back with Walker's house on 135th Street. Little theater, art, literary magazines, political discussion groups, even a symphony flourished there.

In 1926 Andrew Carnegie bought the material that archivist and activist Arthur Schomburg had gathered on the African diaspora and ensconced it at the 135th Street library, making Schomburg the curator.

Retrace your steps to Sixth (Lenox) and turn right (south) to the* Schomburg Center for Research in Black Culture ㉟ *between 136th and 135th Streets.

☞ In 1978 this handsome new building opened to house Schomburg's original collection and later accessions. It is one of the city's greatest resources, worth a special trip to New York, though many New Yorkers have never been here.

Visceral passion inspired the founder, a Puerto Rican of mixed German and Afro-Spanish descent, who left his native land when police hunted him down for his involvement in the island's independence movement. "History must restore what slavery took away," Schomburg wrote. One feels a (pleasant) intensity in the reading rooms even now.

☞ Old and new versions of **Harlem Hospital** ㊱ stand across the avenue from the library.

The hospital got its first black nurses in 1919, thirty years or so after opening; its first black doctors, only in 1925. Today, the facility, with 3,500 staff members, is the community's biggest employer and hosts intensive programs to train more health workers and nurses.

During the Depression this was the single health center in the neighborhood—a horror show owning only 270 beds despite its mandate to care for more than 350,000 blacks and many thousands more Puerto Ricans, Italians, and Jews on Harlem's fringe. In those days, recently operated patients slept on benches and chairs, even the floor. Twice as many people died here as at other city institutions; locals nicknamed it the morgue or butcher shop. Even so, the underserved community kept coming, in particular, African Americans who were refused admission in most other city institutions.

Despite heroic efforts by a core of dedicated doctors, conditions at the hospital remained abysmal for decades, drawing mainstream publicity recently when a friend of Mayor Dinkins died following an eighteen-hour wait in the emergency waiting room. Some blame Columbia, which has jointly managed the hospital with the city for thirty years. (The latter gives Columbia's College of Physicians and Surgeons more than $45 million annually to provide nurses and doctors.) Those who fault Columbia charge that the university does far more vigilant work at its private hospital, Columbia Presbyterian, in Washington Heights. Columbia defends its record, and many blame the city. In fact, Harlem's problems, compounded by recent slashing budget cuts, reflect those of inner-city hospitals across the country. All of them have far higher mortality rates than centers in healthy, wealthy parts of town.

Whatever the case, seventeen directors have come and gone here during the past twenty-four years, and for a time the facility was under review by a national accreditation board. A loss of accreditation (it fortunately never happened) would have jeopardized the hospital's Medicare and Medicaid payments, which provide two-thirds of its income. Among others to lose if the hospital had failed would have been the crack babies treated here under one of the institution's most successful programs.

☞ Look west to the YMCA at 180 West 135th Street, midway along on the south side of the block. If you're not exhausted, walk down to see the mysterious Aaron Douglas mural in the ground-floor barbershop there.

Redcaps at Penn Station used to point African Americans and West Indians arriving from out of town up to the Y, so it became *the* stopping place for the black diaspora in New York. Many writers, including poet Langston Hughes and writer Ralph Ellison, stayed here when they first reached the city.

Hughes, who'd traveled the world, wrote, "I can never put on paper the thrill of the underground ride to Harlem. . . . I went up the steps and out into the bright September sunlight. Harlem, I stood there, dropped my bags, took a breath and felt happy again."

By James Baldwin's day (he grew up here in the 1930s), Harlem was someplace to escape or endure. The early optimism of writers and intellectuals that African American talent would diffuse white hostility, allow the two societies a common humanity, never happened. Harlem did not become the bridge many of both races hoped. Instead, the quarter has become physically isolated in a way James Weldon Johnson, for all his prescience, could never have imagined.

Harlem's spaces are tattered. So is the dream. Still, the memory of hope is embodied here, an inconsolable promise.

11

The Upper West Side

Subway: IND B, C lines to 81st Street (American Museum
of Natural History).

*Walk into Central Park at the 81st Street entrance on Central Park West.
There are benches nearby where you can read this introduction.* ❶

In Dutch days, homesick New Amsterdammers called the land from
Chelsea to 135th Street on Manhattan's west side Bloemendael, "blooming
valley," for a Netherlands suburb. Unlike uptown Harlem, Bloomingdale
was never an organized village, only a scattering of farm hamlets.

When the British took the island in 1664, the new colonial government
doled out fiefs here to its favorites. During the next decades, wealthy families summered along the Hudson in lordly fashion. At first they traveled
here by river sloop. After 1707, when the city made a link route downtown,
they risked their carriages on the Bloomingdale Road, a farm track in the
bed of an old Indian trail that wandered into the Bowery and lower Broadway at Union Square. (The summer folk paid for the tie.) The track, later
called Broadway in this section also, ran approximately to 114th Street,
then stopped dead at the barn door of a particularly well-connected gentleman.

In 1807 estate owners who belonged to downtown Trinity organized
an Episcopal church, St. Michael's, close to the Bloomingdale Road near today's 96th Street. It shared a pastor with St. James, its gentry East Side counterpart, as several rocky cartways forming east-west links made the economy possible. A lane approximating 71st Street wove across what would
become the park to the Boston Post Road—today's Third Avenue. Two other
paths crossed at the rough equivalent of today's 86th and 96th Streets.

Ten years later, enough year-round people started living here to warrant a full-time minister at St. Michael's. The church, whose crypt holds an

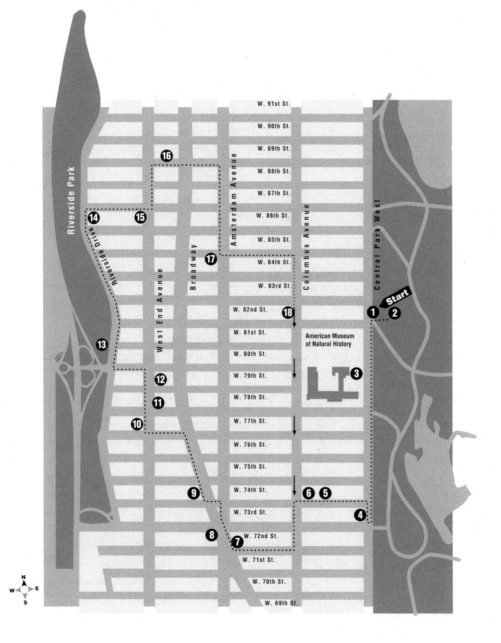

W. 91st St.
W. 90th St.
W. 89th St.
W. 88th St.
W. 87th St.
W. 86th St.
W. 85th St.
W. 84th St.
W. 83rd St.
W. 82nd St.
W. 81st St.
W. 80th St.
W. 79th St.
W. 78th St.
W. 77th St.
W. 76th St.
W. 75th St.
W. 74th St.
W. 73rd St.
W. 72nd St.
W. 71st St.
W. 70th St.
W. 69th St.

Riverside Park

Riverside Drive

West End Avenue

Broadway

Amsterdam Avenue

Columbus Avenue

Central Park West

Start

American Museum
of Natural History

N
W · E
S

early graveyard, still functions at 99th Street and Amsterdam Avenue close to its original site.

Thirty blocks downtown, also near the Bloomingdale Road, Dutch Reform families had built a church in the "Harsenville" area the year before the Anglican congregation opened. The so-called Harsenville tract (its name came from a local property owner following the Revolution) ran from 59th to 79th Street, the present-day park to the Hudson.

Compared with St. Michael's, the Dutch church was socially conservative as well as aesthetically dour. Even at mid-nineteenth century, worshipers considered organ music satanic—a preceptor led the singing with a tuning fork.

For decades the two communities remained fairly isolated, though in 1819 a stagecoach from the lower city rumbled up here, and in 1845 two horse-drawn buses made a daily round trip. Unlike the East Side, where the New York and Harlem Railroad had flung its way overland since 1834, on this part of the island the railroad only appeared in 1851 and then sloped along the Hudson shore not directly through the West Side plateau itself. While the East Side gentry had departed en bloc after the train arrived, many old families in this area hung on despite the growing blight of factories near the river and down at present-day Lincoln Center.

The gentry's roots here were secure enough and their life-style unimpeded enough, they lingered even after a number of asylums and other charities moved to the neighborhood. In fact, they sponsored several. An orphanage associated with the Dutch church survived on Broadway and 74th Street until 1899, when the Ansonia began to rise in its stead.

The institutions had a long run before development pushed them farther uptown. A few buildings remain. The south wall of St. John the Divine holds part of the 1831 Leake and Watts Orphanage. Columbia University's campus holds the old dormitory of the Bloomingdale Asylum for the Insane, now its French language center. (Columbia bought the hospital grounds in 1892. "Oh, *that's* why everyone's so crazy," students say, hearing this.)

***W**alk east into the park to the Great Lawn, formerly the outskirts of an African American village.* ❷

Unlike Yorkville, which began to have coherent working-class neighborhoods by the 1840s, most poor on the West Side had to provide for themselves. By the mid-nineteenth century, the rocky land that later became Central Park was home to several thousand shanty dwellers, some living in slanting lean-tos, some in two-story cottages with pristine gardens.

In the 1820s, or perhaps even earlier, free blacks had lived on a hill just west of today's Great Lawn. When the city dug a reservoir to hold water from the new Croton aqueduct in the late 1830s, it leveled the mount, and the hamlet's residents shifted to Seneca Village, a nearby colony also founded by African Americans. The latter hamlet ran along three short lanes on the lines of West 83rd, 84th, and 85th Streets between Eighth and Seventh Avenues, one of the first organized communities set up by African Americans after they'd won back the right, denied for a century, to own houses and land. Seneca's residents bought their plots from an Anglo-American family named Whitehead. (A senior cleric at the John Street Methodist Church also named Whitehead had been championing the African American AME Zion Church in a complex institutional and doctrinal wrangle near the time of the sale, but the common name may be just coincidence. Even so, it's intriguing, as many of Seneca's population were Methodist.) The most important point is that Seneca's residents were title holders. Often, outsiders deemed all park shanty dwellers *squatters* whether or not the occupants held deeds—a willful diminution of their legitimacy.

The tiny hamlet was well run and well churched, holding not only a branch of Mother Zion but a rival Methodist sanctuary too. In time, St. Michael's Episcopal also opened a mission here—All Angels, a Sunday school, and an "industrial" school. By the 1850s, more than 250 people lived in the village including Irish, Germans, and Native Americans.

When the townlet disbanded, St. Michael's relocated its mission well away from the park. All Angels survives today, upgraded into an elegant church for middle-class parishioners at 251 West 80th Street. Explorers claim to have seen the foundations of one of the old churches in Seneca Village, but, most likely, the stones are traces of the old reservoir's retaining wall.

☞ In 1930 the city filled its first catchment when it built the present reservoir to the north. Look closely at the Great Lawn. If you squint and blink, the grassy ellipse begins to dissolve into a calm green pond, the surface of memory.

Realtors complained about the many shanty dwellers on the West Side plateau and blamed them for blocking the onset of high-end settlement here. Once they earmarked an area for development, however, they weren't shy. Some engineers literally dynamited out recalcitrant squatters by blasting the rocks from under their houses.

*E*xit the park and cross the avenue to the American Museum of Natural History ❸ at Central Park West and 81st Street.

☞ As you leave the park, notice the high schist outcroppings inside the park wall at 83rd Street that were the real factor in delaying large-scale building on the West Side. The striations on the rock run north to south, the drift of the glaciers 13,000 years ago. All the rocks in the park conform.

In the 1870s the city agreed to locate the museum, organized a few years earlier, at this site to catalyze neighborhood development. The private institution was the first major building on the Upper West Side. The original wing faces Columbus Avenue; the second section, the rose stone Romanesque castle, runs along 77th Street. The limestone Central Park West front we see here is a 1935 Beaux Arts addition.

The museum occupies the site of one of several stillborn city squares mapped in 1811 and never developed. The old name of the fictive space, Manhattan Square, has recently been renamed Margaret Mead Green—another nonevent honoring women, a spatial version of the Susan B. Anthony dollar.

The city-owned plot was bleak and stony, raddled with mud. When the appointed museum director surveyed the site in 1871, he wrote dolefully of the desolate hills, the shanty dwellers' goats who were his only companions. Developers trying to oust resistant families complained that they fed their eviction notices to the animals.

West Side promoters tried to turn the plateau's rough topography to advantage, advertising the locality's "forest solitudes" and "crags that proudly tower." The reality was depressing, an engineer's nemesis. Cavernous furrows ran north to south between schist ledges rising as high as thirty feet. The blasting and filling needed to make the land habitable daunted even the determined. Aside from terrain, transport, too, remained abysmal. In the years after the Civil War, the only way to reach the Upper West Side was by omnibus along Broadway, then named the Boulevard.

Despite tribulations, a few developers persevered, particularly as large estates like the Harsen property (divided for sale into 500 residential lots) came on the market. Once the museum opened, a group of boosters who'd formed a West Side Association met there regularly to coordinate strategies for land use north of 59th Street and to lobby the government for local transport and infrastructure. Arguing that tens of thousands of the city's middle class were fleeing Manhattan for new suburbs opening in Brooklyn,

the association urged the city to stem the flow by helping create a luxury residential neighborhood on the island's West Side. As a start, they demanded the city cut 79th Street across Central Park to speed building materials from the East River lumber yards.

Rocky West Side terrain and bad transport kept this part of the city relatively undeveloped until the mid-1880s.

Until now developers had to freight supplies for the West Side up that river through the Harlem ship canal and then offload them at the West Side's solitary 79th Street wharf.

Even with the group's goading, city input lagged, and few developers built, though enough speculators bought acreage to jack up prices. From 1863 to 1873, land values here had risen by 200 percent, only to plummet again following the crash of 1873. As the investors were mainly Jewish, the West Side became known as the "Jewish cemetery."

*W*alk south on Central Park West to 72nd Street and the **Dakota.** ❹

☞ You might like to sit on a bench by the park wall to read the following. The vantage provides an overall view of the old apartment house, which is hard to appreciate close up because of its bulk.

Some members of the West Side Association refused to surrender after the 1873 debacle. One of them was Egbert Viele, chief engineer of Central Park and a competitor against Frederick Law Olmsted for the design commission. Viele still believed the plateau above 72nd Street was destined to become the city's fashionable quarter, as it was the last place left in Manhattan for upmarket development. Investors had long written off the blocks below 72nd Street as irredeemably blighted by industry and malaria.

Likening this part of the city to the western districts of London, Paris, Vienna and Berlin—the choice precincts of those capitals—Viele claimed that the prevailing winds here were the same, that smoke and stench would blow eastward. Not stopping with the supposed meteorological similarities, he went on to compare built spaces here with Europe, equating Central Park to Vienna's Prater and the Grand Boulevard (later Broadway) to the avenues of Second Empire Paris. Interestingly, given the large Jewish settlement to come, the engineer made a special pitch for "Hebrews" of New York to move here rather than to Harlem, where many German Jews were migrating at the time. The "Hebrews," he said, were closer than other New Yorkers to European culture and would particularly savor this new neighborhood's "continental" atmosphere.

Unlike the East Side, which had had its street patterns fairly set by the 1870s, the western plateau was less constrained if not exactly a blank sheet. There was more room here to plan in the grand French manner, to introduce Beaux Arts vistas as well as lapidary individual buildings. Knowing this connection helps one see this district in the way its developers intended. Today, without articulating why, many Europeans tourists instinctively prefer this part of Manhattan.

Edward Clark, a businessman who'd built a successful apartment house downtown, was, next to Viele, the West Side Association's driving force. As president of the Singer Sewing Machine Company, which profited from the expansion of the middle class following the Civil War, Clark recognized the need for new dwellings. The year after a new street railway ran up Eighth Avenue in 1877, Clark bought a block of land from transport king August Belmont stretching from 72nd to 73rd Street, Central Park West to Columbus Avenue.

It wasn't the Eighth Avenue transit tie that made Clark buy, however, as the single tram that turned at 125th Street to go south on the same track was a limp link at best. What prompted his interest was the announcement of an elevated train along Columbus (then Ninth Avenue), and the deci-

sion to make a 72nd Street station stop. Clark dug the Dakota's foundations the year after the El arrived in 1879.

Even *with* transport, he still had a lot to do to make his project viable, including installing his own utilities, as the neighborhood had none of its own. For years, Clark's boilers provided steam and electricity for blocks around. (At first hearing this private source for what we have come to think of as a public utility is surprising, but we may be heading back in that direction again, as the city continues to give away building rights with the proviso that prospective developers maintain local infrastucture. Witness the rather paltry demand on Donald Trump to rebuild the 72nd Street subway station in return for granting considerable city favors to his West Side "Riverside South" project.)

The American Museum of Natural History had been sited on the West Side to attract development here, but investors were slow to follow. The announcement of an elevated train along Columbus Avenue encouraged Edward S. Clark to build. This picture shows the lonely museum and Clark's apartment house, the Dakota.

*W*alk into the park at 72nd Street, taking the first path to the left to view the building across the rocky ravine—probably how the first apartment dwellers here perceived their situation.

☞ Absorb the size of the complex designed for only forty families. Clark tackled the problem of his building's isolation by making it big enough to overwhelm its wild surroundings.

While today we think of the park (three sides of it, anyhow) as a prestige location, at the time the building went up, popular opinion viewed the vastness as unnerving, even potentially dangerous. Clark and other developers felt individual townhouses could never domesticate the tract, relieve residents' anxiety. Only structures of the Dakota's size could provide true and imagined safety.

***R**etrace your steps from the park and cross back over Central Park West.*

☞ Note the dramatic iron railing forged by the Brooklyn Hecla Iron Works around the would-be moat. The moat and guard rail added a modicum of real security but also enhanced the building's chateauesque pretensions.

It wasn't just the tenants' fear of wildness that the Dakota's architect addressed. A more profound concern weighing on many new apartment dwellers was the dread of losing caste.

Clark knew that luxury apartment houses would appeal to many women who were sick of housekeeping. The Dakota had every amenity.

Clark's dealings with the female markets through his sewing machine empire had taught him that many middle-class women were ready for apartments. Common sense told him that high rises were the solution to the city's population boom and

rising land prices. Even so, he knew many people resisted the idea. Like other developers of the day, Clark felt obliged to counter alarm about collective living by adding niceties.

☞ Architect Henry Hardenbergh (who'd done Clark's downtown venture) picked showy yellowish Nova Scotia stone and fine pressed brick for the apartment. It matches the true color of the park wall under its grime. For further effect, he added the elaborate copper-trimmed roof with its peaked and gabled battlements. Many of the interior suites had baronial 40-by-20 feet deep drawing rooms.

Even though our mind's eye tends to hold a Christmas card image of prosperous Victorians in single family homes, most middle-class New Yorkers had lived in some form of multiple dwellings from the 1850s, be they boarding houses or hotels. In the 1870s "French flats" arrived—small apartment houses modeled after Parisian examples. Despite people's familiarity with the concept and fact of collective dwelling, the mode still made some uneasy. Many critics viewed apartment life as infra dig, imagining that it suggested tenement-house sharing or, worse still, the fancied promiscuity of Paris.

Oddly, as we have heard so much about Victorian women homemakers, it was mainly middle-class *men* who wanted to guard their social and psychic status as private householders. Many women leaped at the idea of apartment dwelling. Aside from the relative ease of maintaining the smaller units, in-house janitors allowed one to shut the door on them and travel— an important feature now that vacations had become a regular part of middle-class life. Apartment houses also offered communal services.

As early as 1872 feminist Sarah Gilman Young had published a book promoting Paris-type flats to ease women's burdens. Quoting John Stuart Mill, Young wrote, "there remain no legal slaves except the mistresses of every house." Women residents at the Dakota were delighted by its common laundry, central kitchen, and public banquet hall, which supplemented the individual dining rooms in each suite. As servants grew scarcer near the turn of the century, they valued the housekeeping services still more.

☞ Note the smallish windows in the Dakota's pitched roof. The Dakota's service rooms, maids' rooms, and collective nursery occupied the building's attic.

The placement grew out of the Paris model, where the middle class had lived in apartments for centuries. In pre-elevator France the wealthy had lived on the more convenient bottom floors, the poor and servants (as we know from opera) in the garrets. After elevators became widely available in the 1880s, it was possible to fill entire buildings with wealthy residents. Nonetheless, the idea that upper floors were déclassé persisted.

☞ Aside from the attic space, the rest of the Dakota is democratic. Note the uniformly long windows. Clark—who died before the apartment opened—planned to live on a high floor to overcome negative associations with upper stories. Since he wanted floor-to-ceiling windows for his own suite, the architect designed others to conform. Take a look in the courtyard, a French innovation like the apartment house itself, as far as the guard allows. (Since John Lennon's shooting here, security has been strict.) Aside from providing light and air to most rear rooms, the courtyard also offered privacy through its multiple access to surrounding apartments. Each of the yard's four corners contains an entrance and hydro-powered elevators leading to suites. There is no central foyer. After the turn of the century developers promoted lobbies as glamorous selling points, but initially tenants viewed them as embarrassments forcing unwanted intimacy on building residents.

Despite the attention Clark and Hardenbergh paid to detail, the venture remained a hard sell. In 1885 the Dakota was still half empty. Moreover, though renters here were wealthy and influential, a good number of them were just a tiny bit "artistic," not the solid merchant types moving east of the park. Ward McAllister, New York's acerbic Society arbiter after the Civil War, sniffed he couldn't be bothered to pass judgment on the West Side social set. (Even in my schooldays, many "old guard" children did not go to the West Side except to the Natural History Museum. Remarkably, I never came until I was in college. More remarkably still, some East Siders hold this view even today.)

It was Clark himself, incidentally, not detractors, who nicknamed the remote apartment complex after the distant badlands. New York tycoons were exploiting Western minerals at the time this city frontier building went up, and the designation was a boast of frontier conquest—not, as folklore has it, a sarcastic commentary on the building's remoteness.

Despite its sluggish start, the Dakota served as a magnet, and builders from the East Side began to move here to take advantage of the area's lower costs. By 1886, 778 buildings were under way on the western plateau, $20 million invested, and 20,000 men at work in construction. Nevertheless, the strip facing the park stayed vacant—now, not because of investor wariness, but because of inflated prices. For many years after the Dakota was up and functioning, its adjacent blocks remained warehoused with blacksmith shops and saloons. The lot to the south stayed empty but for shanties until 1894.

*W*alk north to 73rd Street and turn left (west).

☞ Originally, the gate at the rear of the Dakota's courtyard was a servants' entrance. Later, the management barred it shut except for the funeral corteges of building residents.

*A*s you walk along 73rd, note the **rowhouses** ❺ across the street on the north.

Before embarking on the apartment house, Clark had built a string of single-family houses on 73rd Street to cover his bets. Numbers 15A through 19 on the north, numbers 41 through 65 on the south side of the street are remnants.

☞ The houses, whose basement pipes hook up with the Dakota, resemble the structure, catering in mini-version to the same chateau needs. (The rich facades of olive sandstone contrasted with buff or reddish brick echo the larger complex.) As much as the first apartment promoters felt obliged to appease renters' vanity, by now rowhouse builders were forced to make their single dwellings super-elegant in order to compete against the efficiency of apartments. In any case, Clark wanted a harmonious ensemble. The row abounds with texture and styles, but all relate. Pairs of house fronts alternate musically with their near neighbors. Houses billowing with oriels and projecting windows stand next to houses hollowed with recessed balconies. The effort at variation continues at the roof line. Some houses are capped in peaked gables, some hipped with squat, down-turned roofs.

The harlequin rowhouses on Manhattan's West Side were a reaction away from the uniform Italianate brownstone of the earlier Civil War period. (As the tour progresses, you'll see older brownstone buildings painted white to brighten and update them.)

Despite women's ambivalence, the cost of maintenance and the growing scarcity of city land, rowhouse building continued apace through the close of the century. In a rootless society where families moved every few years, a private house offered the illusion of permanence, the grace of "home." Between 1880 and 1900, over 4,500 rowhouses went up on the

In case people resisted living under one roof, the developer also built a block of rowhouses along 73rd Street.

Upper West Side—the majority built on speculation for prosperous families making $25,000 to $100,000 a year.

By the turn of the century, rowhouse development here was virtually complete.

When the city announced the subway, land became too valuable to waste on single-family dwellings. By the time the IRT finally arrived in 1904, developers had already torn down many rowhouses, replacing them with apartments.

*W*alk west to Columbus Avenue.

Columbus Avenue took its present form between 1885 and 1895 after the El's arrival. The street's name change in 1890 from Ninth Avenue to Columbus was intended to raise its tone, but the street's utilitarian purpose remained much the same. Grimed by smoke and dinned by the noise of the elevated railroad, the avenue held a welter of tenements, breweries, lumberyards, and factories.

☞ Having said this, however, I should note that many of the tenement houses along Columbus are quite pretty, frosted with limestone decoration, patterned with fancy brick designs.

Because of the large sites available, West Side property owners often developed entire blocks as unified ensembles. Even tenements fronting directly on Columbus tend to be linked in scale, material, and architectural detail to the nearby side-street rowhouses. This is particularly true of the better-lit and -ventilated buildings on the corners of the avenue, which were more desirable than those in the middle of the blocks and rented at higher prices. Note the block of **flats at the Columbus end 6** of the side street we have been walking down. This was also a Clark enterprise, designed by Hardenbergh to meld rowhouse gentility with the roominess and relative cheapness of the tenement houses facing the commercial corridor. As you can see, the building's front door is on the more prestigious side street, away from the El's sparks and hot oil spills.

After looking at the side street section, walk around to the Columbus Avenue face of the building.

☞ Here you can understand the architect's effort, through mock cornice lines and party walls, to create the illusion that the building is actually several single-family dwellings. As a further badge of middle-class respectability, some better-class corner tenements had names over the door. This one doesn't, but it does have two charming terra-cotta roundels of a girl and a boy in bonnet and tam-o'-shanter to let passers-by know it was a decent building with solid tenants. Another badge of probity you often find on tenements are outscale pediments.

Developers popped these on multi-tenant houses in an attempt to make you experience a multi-family structure as *one* building (the reverse of Hardenbergh's trick). Architects also added pediments to storefront factories to soften their function, make them appear domestic.

☞ An example of the pediment strategy can be seen one block north at 74th Street, in the building once belonging to the **Horton Ice Cream Company,** a firm supplying three-fifths of the city's ice cream in the 1890s. (It's on the far side of the street.) Not only did the pediment drape the building in respectability, but it also served advertising purposes. The Horton name near the roofline is a reminder that the street once held an elevated train. From ground level the self-promotion would have been almost invisible unless you were looking for it; El riders would have seen it right away.

Walk south along Columbus Avenue to 71st Street, and then turn right (west) to Broadway.

A few old rowhouses near here predate the panic of 1873. Some survive at West 71st near Broadway at numbers 64–72. In 1886 Civil War General William Tecumseh Sherman, one of many new West Side residents, lived at 75 West 71st Street. Unlike our image of him astride a horse (and very gold), when he retired from the army Sherman became a straphanger who rode to his downtown brokerage consultancy job from the 72nd Street station.

☞ Look south toward Lincoln Center from the corner of 71st and Broadway.

Until century's end, malarial swamp and the clutter of factories (and the poor) below here stopped the thoroughfare from becoming a grand boulevard. The fifties and sixties blocks of Broadway stayed depressed until the 1960s. Then "urban renewal," spearheaded by Lincoln Center, "improved" the neighborhood but ruined the neighbors. Thousands of working-class Puerto Rican and African American residents left for uptown.

Back in the 1860s Boss Tweed's government had toyed with turning Broadway into a grand residential boulevard rivaling those in Paris, but Paris was safe. Except for widening the avenue and making the present-day central islands, little else occurred, and Tweed's demise and the 1873 depression ended any thought of a grand allée. This stretch of Broadway remained a muddy crater until the 1890s, when it finally got asphalt. Even then the street's future was still undetermined.

Retrace your steps a few yards to the **Dorilton Apartments ❼** at 171 West 71st Street on the corner of Broadway.

Serious change came only after people were certain the subway would arrive. The same year the city announced that private investors led by August Belmont (backed by Rothschild) would finance the rapid transit tunnel construction for the new IRT, Columbia and the Cathedral Church of St. John the Divine announced *their* plans to build on the Upper West Side. Predictably, land prices soared and rich apartments like the Dorilton opened.

☞ The architects made the 1900 Beaux Arts building ruffled and flourished to popularize their venture, maximize their returns. The strategy backfired, and the *Architectural Record* called the structure's Second Empire pretensions an "aberration, the sight of which makes strong men swear and weak women shrink affronted."

It was not only "nouveau" New Yorkers who were insecure enough to overdo
the French style. Many backwater builders
(particularly in Budapest) did the same.
Even now, numerous nationalities consider
Beaux Arts buildings the symbol of the

The announcement of a subway
along Broadway brought
speculation here at the turn of
the century.

good life, a badge of arrival. Next time you're on the East Side, notice where
the former East Bloc consulates in New York have housed their missions.
(An interesting aside that just struck me as I was writing this is that almost
all diplomatic missions seem to be on the East Side; this is from old snobbery, surely, not just because the United Nations is handier.)

☞ After being properly affrighted, walk around to see the building's voluptuous amazons on its Broadway facade. Then look north up Broadway to
the IRT station at the intersection at Broadway and 72nd Street.

☞ The subway took 12,000 men working ten hours a day (at twenty cents
an hour) four years to build. It opened in 1904.

☞ To mark its importance, the city chose fashionable architects Heins and
LaFarge to design several stations. The firm gave this one a Dutch gabled

roof for panache, as local realtors were hyping the neighborhood's "Knickerbocker" roots.

At the time the kiosk went up, nostalgia was big real estate business in the West Side (as in Brooklyn). Descendants of colonial landowners turned developers wrote several engaging local histories at this period, and, as late as 1914, some old family realtors in the area formed the Olde Settlers Association of Ye West Side, with the object of keeping "alive memories of yesterday . . . to uphold and beautify the city of tomorrow." Original membership requirements for the club, where members read items about bygone days over "Harsenville" cocktails, demanded a minimum twenty-year local residence. As numbers lagged, however, officials settled for a fifteen-yesteryear tenure "until they got on their feet."

One of the traditional values the realtors liked to claim for the neighborhood was "Family." They tirelessly portrayed the new section as a sanctuary of upper-middle-class respectable homelife, Manhattan's answer (after Harlem) to bourgeois Brooklyn.

*W*alk north on the east side of Broadway to 72nd Street. At this point, look across the avenue to the **Colonial Club** ❽ on the west of Broadway.

The association took the name "to perpetuate Revolutionary days." Members here were particularly proud of their collection of cannon balls and the club's proximity (relatively speaking) to a Washington skirmish site uptown near today's Barnard College.

☞ The limestone and yellow brick club was the West Side's first social gathering place. Because of the neighborhood's family orientation, it encouraged women guests—a Brooklyn innovation. The ladies had their own side entrance.

*C*ontinuing along on the east side of Broadway, cross 72nd Street to the north.

☞ Stop and look back at the quaint rowhouses across the street above the groundfloor shop fronts. (Some have balconies to catch the Hudson breeze.) Today, the commercial activity on this once genteel thoroughfare—a tree-lined extension of Central Park—is so dense it's hard to remember (or to see) that the buildings were once residential. Commercial conversion had already begun by 1909.

*C*ontinue north to 73rd Street; cross over Broadway to the **Ansonia** ❾ through "Verdi Square." An Italian American sculpture committee donated the statue on the triangle in 1906.

Its agenda was to distance its members through high culture from the (Anglo-American) elite image of Italians as a race of subway diggers and hod carriers—to distance them in fact, from the same laborers who had dug the subway line and built the ornamental new buildings. Ironically, for several years until 1904, when the Ansonia opened, this triangle had served as a campsite for scores of Italian stone masons who worked on the extravaganza across the street.

Newly arrived immigrants from Italy built much of the subway and elegant housing stock.

☞ Instead of becoming the luxury residential axis some had hoped, Broadway became a commercial strip, punctuated by grand apartment houses. W. E. D. Stokes' seventeen-story residential hotel was the doyenne. French architect-sculptor Paul Duboy carried out Stokes' vision of a Beaux Arts Parisian hotel blown up to American size, clamorous with peninsular towers, cupolas, and balconies.

Stokes knew what he was about. Before starting on his apartment hotel, he'd built fifty rowhouses on the West Side (like Edward Clark) and set up his own construction company. His hands-on approach was such that he not only oversaw the entire building process but even designed the thick masonry walls that made the Ansonia fireproof, a necessity now insurance prices had reeled upward. Later on, the solid, soundproof rooms attracted musicians to the hotel, boosting the West Side's early identification as Manhattan's "cultural" quarter.

Inside, the Ansonia had all the latest scientific gadgetry the Dakota offered, and then some, including central heating and air conditioning. Electric blowers in the basement circulated over coils that were steam heated in winter and cooled by freezing brine in summer.

The complex also offered the now usual communal features of other apartment houses—on a grander scale. Its dining room provided for 550 guests; its basement held an Olympic-size swimming pool as well as stables and a garage for cars, the era's new toy.

In contrast to the gigantism of its communal features (and in contrast to other new luxury buildings in this neighborhood), a number of the apartments here were small. Despite their baroque planning—ellipsoidal living rooms, circular parlors, oval reception halls, and so on, many had only three rooms. (Women blamed the new convenience apartments—"bachelor flats"—appearing in town for exacerbating the trend toward singleness: 25 percent of New York's adult men were unmarried at this time.)

In a related development, many of the suites here, even some of the larger ones, had no kitchens or provisions for servants, as the Ansonia offered full maid service and a staff that served food in private suites.

Another way the Ansonia differed from most other West Side palace buildings at the time was its grand lobby. Other apartment blocks tended to shun grand foyers to protect tenants' privacy, but the Ansonia's lobby was splendid with banks, bookstalls, doctors' chambers, and a telegraph office. Supposedly—this has not been documented—baby seals flounced in lobby fountains to provide amusement.

At this writing, it's still possible to enter the Ansonia. The building, in decline since the Depression, is less defended than most in the area, as it's only in the process of going co-op because of the mountain of legal problems and tenant-tenant, tenant-landlord conflicts that slowed the effort of some residents to re-upscale the venerable complex.

☞ Today the lobby is shabby and partitioned but boasts relics of past glory in an institutional history nook near the 73rd Street entrance. Note the picture of an annual Christmas party, the rows of sailor-suited tots solemnly frozen in magnesium glare. Children in these grand buildings formed peer groups often further cemented in the summers, as many families vacationed at the same resorts.

*C*ontinue north on Broadway to 75th Street.

☞ Across Broadway (at 201 West 75th Street between Broadway and Amsterdam), you can glimpse the **1889 livery stable of the New York Cab Company,** now a garage. The massive Romanesque Revival arches accommodated carriages.

In the 1880s Amsterdam Avenue, formerly Tenth Avenue, developed as a service strip like its neighbor Columbus. Stables lined the side streets between Tenth and Broadway. An active one, the Claremont, at 175 West 89th continues today.

*K*eep north on Broadway to 76th and turn left; walk west on 76th Street to West End Avenue. To get a general view of the **block of rowhouses ❿** on the west side of the street between 76th and 77th Streets, stay on the east side. Cross over if you want a close-up of their sensuous details.

The lower part of this thoroughfare (Eleventh Avenue at its lower end) was an extension of Hell's Kitchen, packed with asylums, breweries, grain elevators, and slaughterhouses. In 1880 the indefatigable Viele sponsored the street's name change in this stretch to invoke London's gleaming suburb.

☞ The architectural firm of Lamb and Rich designed these townhouses in 1891—deliberately varying them to seem as if they had been individually built. Some sport copper-framed dormers at the roofline; others, terra-cotta crests. The row is a vestige. Until after World War I when developers razed single family-houses for big apartments, much of West End Avenue looked like this.

The architectural firms of Hardenbergh, Lamb and Rich, C. P. Gilbert, and Clarence True built over four hundred houses on the West Side. True owned his own properties and wrote his own publicity, a charmingly falsified history of the area. All the firms worked in related Arts and Crafts styles stressing textures, contrasting colors, and a desert trolley of medieval confections. The houses resembled residences in Brooklyn's Park Slope from the same period. The similarity is not surprising, as the same firms designed houses there for the same sort of upper-middle-income families that were moving here. Though by today's lights these houses, now subdivided, represent a dizzyingly high standard of living, they were originally intended for the comfortably off. With only a few exceptions, the very rich stayed on the East Side.

***W**alk north on West End Avenue to the* **West End Collegiate Church and Collegiate School,** ⓫ *opened in 1892 at the northeast corner of 77th Street.*

The buildings dramatically announce the church and school's ancestry, which dates back to 1628. (The first schoolmaster of the Dutch Reform Church supplemented his meager salary by making his students bring in beaver skins.)

Realtor promoters of the precinct hyped it as a bourgeois, immigrant-free suburb, Manhattan's answer to Brooklyn. Architects drew on its supposed "Knickerbocker" roots.

☞ Rather disarmingly, given the aristocratic pretensions, the architect modeled these dramatically gabled buildings after a seventeenth-century public meat market in Holland.

Ten blocks up from here on West End a public school, circa 1893, flaunts similar Netherlandish decor. At the same time that old-family New Yorkers organized genealogical societies and resurrected their Dutch or Anglo-Saxon origins in architecture, they also tried to impose their identity on new arrivals through built environs and curriculum. Near the time these Dutch distillations were going up, a local historical society commemorated Henry Hudson's *Half Moon* trip up river. Unfortunately, a wayward steamboat rammed the craft and it sank.

☞ The architect of the row buildings on the northwest corner of West End and 78th Street, built in 1885–86, also used crow-stepped gables to suggest the West Side's Dutch inheritance.

*C*ontinue north to the **Apthorp Apartments,** ⑫ *which occupy the block bounded by West End Avenue to Broadway and West 78th Street to West 79th Street.*

Even if inflated as a sales pitch, the Netherlands references here did have some legitimacy. Because of the neighborhood's slow earlier development, several old houses with genuine Dutch elements had survived into the twentieth century, dissolute as taverns and boarding houses. One such was the Van Heuvel house, built as a summer home in 1792 by a Dutch governor serving in the Caribbean. It occupied this site for 115 years—the equivalent of a thousand years in New York's time frame. Possibly, the Holland brick dwelling, alleged to have had gables (I can never see these in sketches of the house), square Dutch windows, and Delft tiled fireplaces, may have inspired the houses across the street.

In 1905 William Waldorf Astor's estate managers tore down the colonial mansion, which they'd bought and warehoused three decades earlier, to make way for the present building. By the time the Astor estate built this limestone complex, the ground lot, which they'd bought for a pittance, was worth $10 million.

☞ The Apthorp Apartments take up an entire city block—11 1/2 acres of floor space—and use 25 miles of steel infrastructure. The building surrounds a central courtyard entered through a carriageway guarded by a bronze portcullis. The first floor held the requisite services, including a private bank. Upper floors had the usual luxuries and communal conveniences as well as introducing another feature—shaded promenades on the twelfth floor. Walkers who have been to Harlem will recognize the building's resemblance to the prototype Graham Court Apartments at 116th Street and 7th Avenue (see site 7 in Walk 10). Astor's estate managers had used the same architects (Clinton and Russell) for their 1901 uptown venture. As Harlem's luxury development had begun a decade earlier, many West Side developers and architects got their start there.

*T*urn left (west) on 79th Street and walk to Riverside Drive; turn right and continue north, noting the promontory, **Mount Tom,** at 84th Street.

Back in the 1840s Edgar Allen Poe had lived on a country road near here and liked to sit ruminating on the rock that later withstood efforts to blast it away.

In 1871 the city bought the land for **Riverside Park** ⑬ and passed an act to create the park and drive, but, to the rage of West Side developers,

Frederick Law Olmsted's design wasn't carried out until 1885. The West Side Association blamed the sodden, untended grounds for stalling local development in general and also inveighed against the delay in landscaping Morningside Park, another plot left unimproved for decades. It was only when the city finally covered the rail tracks along the Hudson in the late 1880s that this part of the drive received attention at last. Olmsted planned it to complement his park plan—a romantically curving route unusual in this straight-gridded city.

Before the park's creation, developers built few residences here, as despite the land's inherent beauty, the region's isolation, open train tracks, and stench of passing cattle cars discouraged speculators. After the park opened, developers were quick to invest.

☞ Speculator-architect Clarence True was one. Some of his bow-faced, gabled rowhouses are visible from here at 105–107 Riverside Drive, across the street (they're south of the big apartment house).

Despite True's massive promotion of private dwellings in general, and his holdings in particular, rowhouses were on the way out. After the new Broadway subway brought a property boom in the early 1900s, West Side developers razed many single-family homes for luxury apartment buildings. True's houses are among the few Riverside survivors. Today, of course, they are cut up into multi-family flats.

Cross the drive at 86th Street to **the Clarendon, ⑭** *137 Riverside Drive, on the southeast corner of 86th.*

The rage for named buildings on the West Side was intended to ennoble a multiple-family dwelling, make you feel you were in a *hôtel particulaire* (a Parisian palace), or a feudal manor. The omission of a number was supposed to make you forget you were on a city grid, that you weren't quite *particulaire* enough. (The 1980s saw the return of this fad. Cab drivers, unsure of manorial destinations, railed at the revival.)

Many here were secure enough to have done without a title on the door. In 1907 publisher William Randolph Hearst moved to the Clarendon just after it opened. Leasing more than thirty rooms on the upper three floors of the building, he converted the topmost into a gym. Further aggrandizement proved harder. When Hearst tried to oust tenants from the Eighth and Ninth floors to make a three-story living room, the management unaccountably balked, and the publisher was forced to buy the apartment house.

*T*urn right and walk east on 86th Street to West End Avenue, make a short loop right (south) on the southwest corner to see the **converted rowhouses,** **⑮** *531, 533, and 535 West End Avenue.*

At the start of World War I, a real estate slow-down accompanied by the looming cost of building materials caused construction to halt. By war's end the city's housing shortage was dire. Because of the population rise on the West Side (up 16 percent as Jews arrived from Harlem), the need here was still greater. Perversely, despite the lack of affordable housing, hundreds of rowhouses went unoccupied as costs grew prohibitive and servants nonexistent. (From 1914 to 1919 inflation raised living costs 79 percent.) To redress the situation, or at least address it, the New York state legislature passed a law allowing developers to remodel single-family rowhouses into multiple-family dwellings.

☞ Note the multiple buzzer systems by the front doors of these houses showing each holds at least ten families or individual tenants.

When activity started again on the Upper West Side following the war, developers dealt with inflated land values by demolishing rowhouses for apartments. Because of the residential shortage, the city granted a ten-year tax exemption for all new buildings begun between 1920 and 1922. West End Avenue, once a byway and byword of single-family dwellings, now became a rather grand apartment alley similar to Park Avenue. Razing continued wholesale until the Depression, then ended abruptly. In the next decade conversion and subdivision became the mode. Economic downturns, it seems, have always proven the strongest guarantor of New York's old buildings—at least of their outer shells.

*W*alk north on West End Avenue to 88th Street; turn right and walk to the **B'nai Jeshurun Synagogue, ⑯** *on 88th Street between West End Avenue and Broadway.*

☞ The city's oldest Ashkenazic congregation, founded in 1825 on the Lower East Side, built this Moorish-Romanesque synagogue in 1918.

At the time, it was one of two synagogues west of the park. A decade later, when Jews left Harlem after blacks arrived, there were ten. Jews now accounted for one-third of the population between 79th and 110th streets, Broadway to the Hudson. By 1934, as many Anglo-Americans relocated to the suburbs, Jews represented more than half of the West Side population from 72nd to 96th Street.

The new settlers—mainly descended from East Europeans—moved here when they left Harlem for several reasons. The subway link between the West Side and the downtown garment center where many worked attracted some. The prestigious German Jewish nucleus along Central Park West drew others. A negative reason for settlement was exclusion. A number of apartment buildings on the Upper East Side had sub-rosa covenants barring Jews from buying or renting.

(In 1994 several West Side congregations suggested putting an *erov,* a Jewish ritual thread, around the whole district from Central Park to the river, 59th Street to 110th Street, that would make the area one sacred neighborhood defined by existing masonry boundaries and translucent fishing line strung from city street lights in the gaps. The official reason is that the *erov*—already in existence in some other American cities, including Boston—would allow believers to do the thirty-nine acts forbidden on the Sabbath, which include pushing elevator buttons and wheeling prams. A more profound reason than allaying material inconvenience might be the impulse to make a spiritual and territorial claim on an area in demographic flux. Incidentally, apropos of the para-landmarking phenomenon, the Lubavitchers in Crown Heights have built a perfect replica of the late Chief Rebbe's Brooklyn house in the Israeli desert in the event he should materialize there as the Messiah. It's said to be exact, down to the surrounding razor wire and, some say, graffiti.)

Go east to Amsterdam, then turn right and walk south on that avenue to 84th Street along the west side of the street. Turn right a few steps to 202 West 84th, the **Saint Michael's Botanica, ⑰** which offers "fresh herbs, card reading, cigarettes."

Despite the gentrification of the past several decades, you'll still find a shrunken Hispanic population in the neighborhood; this store is one of the few Latino shops remaining below 86th Street. (Even this botanica is not a true Latino institution, however, as its English advertising shows, but a mixed-use operation catering to Anglo Yuppies as well as Hispanics.)

When jobs opened up in the city following World War II, thousands of unemployed Puerto Ricans, rocked by U.S.-related crises in the island garment trade, emigrated to the West Side for the same reason most of the Harlem Jews had come—rents were still low and transport ties to New York's garment center handy. The densest Puerto Rican concentration hubbed the neighborhood east of Amsterdam above 86th Street and the low sixties blocks (later "cleared" for Lincoln Center). By 1954 Puerto Rican children formed almost half of the West Side's elementary and junior high school population.

In the face of the in-migration, which old-timers called an invasion, working and lower-middle-class West Siders—mostly Irish and Italians—left for New Jersey suburbs en masse. Overall, almost a million whites quit the city in the 1940s and 1950s, as Caribbean newcomers (25 percent of them black) arrived. The two working-class streets of the West Side, Columbus and Amsterdam, changed demography but stayed the same in feeling and class, as bodegas and social clubs replaced Italian delis and Irish pubs.

Decline set in when banks red-lined the community after the majority of the white working class and middle class pulled out. An exception to the retreat were elderly Russian Jews near Broadway and upper-middle-class German Jews along Central Park West.

During the Depression many middle-class families left the Upper West Side. In the 1940s Puerto Ricans relocating from the island settled here, as subway ties were convenient to jobs in the garment district.

***W**alk west on 84th Street to Columbus, then turn right and walk south along the avenue to the Endicott, **⓳** an early West Side apartment house between 81st and 82nd Streets.*

Conditions grew so bad that in the mid-1950s the city switched its policy from malign neglect to "urban renewal," passing new housing laws to woo the middle class back from the suburbs. The catalyst of the so-called Upper West Side renaissance was the J-51 Tax Exemption and Abatement Law, a formula providing rehabilitators of income-producing residential buildings with a twelve-year exemption from real estate taxes. Proto-Yuppies arrived to renovate abandoned or overcrowded tenements and rowhouses into livable apartments. The new brownstoners, a pioneering term coined at the time, felled long-term inhabitants like timber. The Endicott, which had housed poor tenants from the late 1940s to 1960s, is an emblem of gentrification.

In the start of a chain leading to today's homeless catastrophe, rooming houses and single-room occupancies evaporated. If necessary, landlords hired thugs to ensure renters got out while developers paid off tenants protected by rent control and stabilization. New West Side public housing, underprovided with low-income apartments, couldn't begin to relieve the consequences. In the past decade alone, city spending on the shelter system for homeless families has grown from $18 million to $290 million, as the number of families sheltered has risen from fewer than 1,000 to a record 5,600.

☞ Lampposts and bus kiosks along Columbus are scabrous with moving van ads, an archaeology of loss.

By 1960 the population of the Upper West Side had fallen 13 percent as gentrification routed thousands of poor tenants. The clearances continued throughout the seventies and eighties. By then rent hikes had squeezed out many of the new middle-class brownstoners from the neighborhood as well.

From the 1960s on, displacement of the poor spiraled as tax breaks encouraged suburban youth to rehabilitate the neighborhood's rowhouses. Later, even middle-income people suffered from gentrification.

Keep walking south on Columbus to 72nd Street (from where you can walk east to take the A train at Central Park West or west to catch the IRT at Broadway).

At the same period the clearances were taking place, so many high-priced boutiques and restaurants opened here that basic service stores—shoe repair, hardware, stationery, and the like—grew scarce. Soon, however, ratcheting rents brought their own aftermath. Though most of the restaurants here look mildly Yuppie even now, most stores do not. Notice the number of low- to moderate-end national outlets and the many vacancies. As rents rose, luxury retail folded. Its local clientele, young professionals with scant disposable income after their monthly rent or co-op payments, could afford only designer ice cream. Following the 1987 crash, the street became a playground for suburban tourists Seduttoed into thinking the much-hyped stretch was trendy still.

For the duration at least, pressure is off Manhattan Valley, the area north of here.

Until the "correction," the Hispanic population there was under threat of ripple displacement, as marginalized young professionals explored the neighborhood's softer
edges. Today, rents have come down a little, and some of the new co-ops on Broadway pray for buyers.

Despite the degree of leveling, the
West Side teems with disparities, incon-
gruities. White-uniformed black maids
push white infants in Baby Gap dark
glasses, beggars and the crack-brained lie full length on Broadway's wide
pavements, elderly Jewish ladies bowed with age and Fairway groceries
shoulder past roller bladers and jewelry vendors—a dissonance softened
only by the tree-lined side streets and gracious wide-lapped row houses.
More roil is still in the offing. At this writing, it looks as though the long-
anticipated (mainly with dread) Trump development by the Hudson below
71st Street is winning approval—albeit in modified form. Scale-backs have
halved the potential numbers of new residents in the proposed 75-acre project, now called Riverside South, not Trump City. The projected population has gone down from 20,000 to 10,000. (Where will they come from?)
The 150-story tower has been modified, the TV spire dropped. No network
wanted it, in any case. Though borough president Ruth Messinger, a West
Sider herself, once tried to get the city to develop the site, the best she could
achieve was to temper the private project through prolonged negotiation.
Local community boards are stiff with fear that even the semi-gigantic plan
will be realized. From Viele till now, entrepreneurs have led the West Side
for particular constituencies. Is it too late for the city to engender, insist on
a plan that would consider and benefit *all* its citizens?

12

Fifth Avenue
Urban Chateaux

Subway: IND B, D, F to Rockefeller Center (47th–50th Streets).

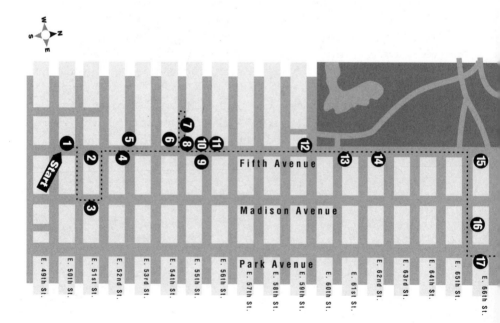

*S*tart at **Rockefeller Center ❶** in the **Channel Gardens,** the flower-filled allée leading off Fifth Avenue between 49th and 50th Streets.

From the 1830s on, lower Fifth Avenue was home to New York's old
guard and newly rich "avenoodles," as wits called them. Not so its upper
stretches; 42nd Street marked society's pale until long after the Civil War,
and the avenue wasn't paved or graded above 59th Street until the 1870s.
As late as 1875, an invalid out for a park airing complained that he had to
give up the excursion because the fissured road rocked his carriage, rattled
his bones.

How did the street get to be the premier boulevard of New York, perhaps of all America? A corollary question to the avenue's rise is, how did
the Upper East Side as a whole become a byword of social status, the last
redoubt of the city's rich?

Let's go back in time. In a pleasing continuum, this site held flowers in
1804 when it came into record as a botanical garden. Soon afterward, its
horticulturist owner sold the ground to the state, which, in turn, allotted the
plot to Columbia for its new campus. Even forty years later, when college

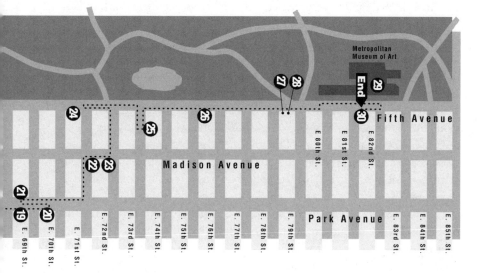

trustees traveled north "a mile beyond civilization" to assess their property, few buildings other than shanties stood in the area—all of them charities.

Columbia chose to rent the nearby Deaf and Dumb institution instead of moving here. Nevertheless, it held the ground Rockefeller Center occupies until 1985. That year, it sold out to its long-term lessees (the Rockefeller family), who held the property until 1989, when the Mitsubishi Estate Company bought 80 percent of the shares. Valuations of the ground's worth have plummeted since the sale, but by a circular reasoning that says any land here must be *inherently* valuable, stock owners swear they are sanguine about their investment.

*C*ross Fifth Avenue diagonally north to the front steps of **St. Patrick's.** ❷

☞ Today this cathedral has become Fifth Avenue's high landmark.

Officials often review parades at this spot, and marchers dip their colors. Because of the site's prestige, people sometimes say that building Saint Pat's here showed the Irish had "arrived." Perhaps the ambitious construction project using the Episcopalians' own architect, James Renwick, Jr., *did* challenge the establishment, but the location at the time did not. It was too barren even for burials, the reason a downtown Catholic church had bought it decades earlier. When Bishop John Hughes laid the foundation stone in 1858, Fifth was still a drovers' route for the Westchester cattle that blundered bawling and shitting into the city. Stockyards abounded in the low fifties above the paupers' cemetery lying below here from Park to Lexington, 48th to 50th Street.

By 1879, when the reigning archbishop dedicated the cathedral, the immediate neighborhood had become somewhat more acceptable. So had the Catholic Irish—if they happened to be rich. Money was now the overriding criteria of social preeminence in the city.

After the Civil War, New York's quota of millionaires jumped exponentially. Some were New Yorkers who'd done well in army contracts; more were newcomers, many of them mineral and transport kings. By the 1880s New York led America in banking, insurance, shipping and manufacturing. All in all, a third of the country's trusts moved their headquarters here, the firms' chairmen relocating to the city as well. Since New York's downtown had fallen to commerce decades ago, most settled in this part of Fifth, the coming residential quarter when they arrived. The pioneer mansions belonging to Commodore Vanderbilt's sons lent the neighborhood impeccable credentials.

In fact, mansions were now mainly constructed as credentials. New York's earlier wealthy might have lived in style, but their houses had been relatively modest, at least on the exterior. New dwellings tended toward the Mad King Ludwig mode. Architects became the undisputed leader of the arts. (It's hard to think of a New York painter from the time.) Most lived as palatially as their clients, wintering on "the" Avenue, summering in Newport.

We'll start at the home of railroad baron Henry Villard. Unfortunately, the house is on Madison, but we must make do. Of the nearly seventy mansions that once lined Fifth, only a handful remain.

*W*alk east to Madison Avenue on 50th Street.

☞ Stand on the raised terrace at the rear of St. Patrick's between the cathedral's twin vicarages, built in 1882. Look across the street from this vantage to the **brownstone Renaissance palazzo** ❸ built on land bought from the archdiocese. Henry Villard designed his complex in 1883 to match the cathedral's double-wing vicarages. Seen together, the ensemble forms a small square bisected by the avenue. Note the glass high rise behind the palazzo's central section. The brownstone building in front is so shallow it's a virtual facade. In the 1970s a watershed city landmarking case argued the propriety of gutting an historic building and keeping the shell. This is the compromise outcome.

The brownstone wings exist relatively intact. The southern extension serves as the public space of the (until recently) Helmsley Palace Hotel; the northern one houses the Architectural League and the Municipal Art Society, founded in 1892. The society was the city's first planning group, an outgrowth of the elite's new urge to rationalize cities through classical architecture and spatial reform. Today it continues—somewhat more democratically—to lead landmarking efforts and social design advocacy in New York.

When Villard dug his foundation, the neighborhood still held asylums and noxious industries even though it boasted the recently completed cathedral and the new Vanderbilt enclave. Immediately behind Madison on Park, Vanderbilt's railroad shuddered and smoked through open cuts and surface track on its way to Harlem. The mansion's sheltering courtyard arrangement served a practical function.

Actually, it's not a mansion at all, but six dwellings built around a court of honor—a sophisticated version of the unified rowhouses popular in the city since the 1830s. Despite its elegance, the concept never caught on, as builders with less money than Villard refused to throw money away on sheer space. Masonry was *so* much more telling.

Joseph Wells of McKim, Mead and White, a megafirm in the luxury residence trade, drew the plans for the innovative complex. Charles McKim, an early student at the Parisian École des Beaux Arts, had ties to Villard through marriage. As most of the architects who built the houses in this new millionaire precinct studied at the school, its background is important.

Louis XIV's Cardinal Mazarin founded the Beaux Arts academy to provide architects for the state buildings needed by the newly centralized country. After a training stint in Italy researching antiquities, students apprenticed in the French capital, adapting classical styles to suit Parisian needs. Architecture was only part of the program; city planning, the other.

In the 1860s Napoleon III revived the school in a bid to reclaim Paris from the poor, who'd literally *taken* the streets in recent uprisings. His chief engineer, Baron Haussmann, enforced a massive "urban renewal" program, shunting the working class to the suburbs, slashing diagonal boulevards through old neighborhoods—a restructuring providing imperial vistas and throughways for vehicles, including armaments.

The academy's revival coincided with rich Americans going to Europe (and a bid to reclaim cities from our own poor, particularly new immigrants). Richard Morris Hunt, who drew the plans for the central section of the Metropolitan Museum, was the first American to attend the institute. He became such an expatriate, for a while he had trouble speaking English, and his wife had to translate for him.

Hunt's Blois-type chateau for Commodore Vanderbilt's son William Kissam Vanderbilt was the template for successive Loire look-alikes on the Upper East Side. Commissions accelerated in the post–Civil War building boom. Hunt and his followers designed ornate tangles of Gothic Revival and Italian Renaissance styles. Newly arrived Italian immigrant stonecutters made the mode possible. For enough money, clients could live in a masonry theme park. Edith Wharton wrote of one character: "His facade is a complete architectural meal. If he had left out a style, his friends might have thought his money had given out."

Not everyone liked the sensibility, particularly Chicago architects, who had begun to veer away from Victorian fancies toward elegant modernism. Nonetheless, in 1893, the New York school won the day in a facade-off at Chicago's Columbian Exposition. (Though theoretically a culture-consumption festival to honor the fourth centennial of Columbus' arrival, the event became a stylistic battleground of participant architects.) For two more decades the backward-looking mode flourished in New York, until World War I brought its end, and, for that matter, an end to mansion building altogether, as most of the wealthy gave up townhouses and moved into apartments or country estates.

☞ If you have time (and disposable income), stop in for tea at the old music room of the Villard mansion, now the Gold Room (open from 2:00 P.M. until 6:00 P.M.) to see the Luca della Robbia stuccoes, the painted lunettes above the gilt musician's gallery, and the coffered ceiling designed by Stanford White. White, by the way, was the only eminent New York architect not to attend the Beaux Arts school, though its spirit guided his work.

Villard was more cultured than most entrepreneurs of his day. During the Civil War he worked as an abolitionist journalist and went on to publish the *Nation*. In other ways he was fairly typical of the neighborhood's new residents. Like many of the recent millionaires, he had made his money from transport, in his case, the Northern Pacific Railroad.

Just before this house was completed, Villard's business failed and he went bankrupt—this, also, was not unique. The volatile financial era caused a fair degree of mansion turnover. Villard had overextended himself in laying track and buying rolling stock. Trying to win further investment, he'd brought European bankers out west in Pullmans, sprinkled loam and greenery along the track to make the land look prosperous, and in a grand finale arranged for 1,500 Crow Indians to stage a scalp dance in honor of ceding their land to the railroad. The Indian chief's polemic in Crow against the railroad's land heist was rendered innocuous by the translator, but the investors glimpsed the bare hills through the Potemkin shrubbery and dumped their holdings anyway.

The monolithic look of this assemblage added to Villard's troubles. Ruined stockholders charged him with concealing assets. The thought that the former tycoon occupied the *whole* structure enraged the crowd who gathered daily outside the still-unfinished complex. As soon as he could sell, Villard retreated. Later, of course, he landed on his feet and died rich.

Return to Fifth Avenue on 51st Street and turn right; continue north to the **Morton Plant House ❹** at 52nd Street, on the southeast corner, now Cartier's.

☞ Villard's architects had begged him to use marble or at least the Indiana limestone recently introduced to New York. His house was one of the last mansions veneered in brownstone. A new limestone era led by the Vanderbilts had begun. Aside from a shorn Vanderbilt house at Fifth Avenue above Olympic Airways at number 649, this ponderous white beauty is the only (tenuous) survivor of the dynasty's former enclave.

By the turn of the century, midtown Fifth Avenue was growing commercial. In fact, this house was part of a last-ditch effort to stem trade. In 1904 the Vanderbilts induced a mini-tycoon, Morton Plant, to build his house on their land here to swell the neighborhood's residential mass. By 1914 the game was up. Once again the rich were being forced north by the stores that had come to serve them. In part, the rout was the consequence of a split in tycoon ranks—several of the Astors were already entrepreneuring commercial ventures in the vicinity. In the end, Plant sold the house back to the Vanderbilts, who, no longer having a vested interest in protecting the neighborhood as they'd since moved farther uptown or out of the city, resold the mansion to Cartier's, a store that had been trading across the avenue since 1907.

W*alk north along Fifth, noting the "Swing Street"* ❺ *sign at 52nd Street.*

In the late 1930s, jazz clubs employing African American musicians lined the street. Even before that, however, the transverse had had links to the black cabaret section farther west between Sixth and Eighth avenues. In the teens of this century, when fast dancing became the rage, the Vanderbilts and other wealthy residents hired club performers to come to their Fifth Avenue homes and teach them the racy new steps. Society was getting restless.

C*ontinue on to* **St. Thomas' Church** *(1914) on the northwest corner of 53rd and Fifth.* ❻

☞ This building by medievalist Richard Cram follows a first incarnation on the site opened in the 1870s. Both versions were known for society weddings. So many wealthy people married in this church, stonemasons carved a dollar sign (actually, an old Episcopalian symbol fudged to resemble a dollar sign) above the bride's door. (It's south of the main entry.) Inside, J. P. Morgan's initials are carved on the kneeling rail in front of the choir stalls.

By 1914, when this second St. Thomas went up, over five hundred American heiresses had married high European nobility. The most infamous ceremony was an ordeal at this church in 1895 when Mrs. William

Kissam Vanderbilt imprisoned her daughter until the hour of her wedding to the ninth Duke of Marlborough. A prenuptial agreement gave the groom $2.5 million. While new-money women married out, old-money women were wedding new American tycoons, adding a patina of sorts to fresh fortunes. Many recent millionaires got social sanction through marriage with "patrician" women—often from families eclipsed by the new rich.

Aside from the snob value they lent, the women's backgrounds made them instrumental as hostesses. As money became the main social criteria and the "in group" expanded, showy parties grew vital for defining, proclaiming status. Many houses along Fifth were primarily designed for balls and receptions.

*C*ontinue north to 54th Street, turn left and walk west to 13 West 54th, John D. Rockefeller, Jr.'s house. **❼**

John D. Rockefeller, Sr., came to town in 1884 when the Standard Oil trust shifted its headquarters to New York. Unlike the Vanderbilts, J.D.R. Senior didn't build but settled in a furnished brownstone that stood where the Museum of Modern Art is today. (The house's brothely furniture, oddly disparate from the founding Rockefeller's Baptist taste, is on view at the Museum of the City of New York.) The family was one of the few new dynasties in the city to shun the social rat race, if quick to "legitimate" their line through marriage. John D., Jr., moved to this building in 1901 after his wedding to an old guard New England woman. It was just one of several houses the family owned in the block. By the turn of the century the neighborhood had become a thoroughgoing Rockefeller preserve rivaling that of the Vanderbilts.

The Rockefellers withdrew to Westchester in 1914, when many other wealthy people also left town for safer precincts. The remove from 54th Street, however, was sped by daily street picketing following news that the family owned 40 percent of Colorado Coal—a company that had ordered the state militia to fire on striking miners and their children. Rockefeller Center's presence in the neighborhood indirectly owes in part to the debacle. When the Depression canceled plans to build the Metropolitan Opera on the site the center now occupies, Rockefeller's public relations man advised him to build the complex, not just to maximize his imperiled investment (he held the lease) but also to refurbish his image.

*T*urn back toward Fifth and walk to 1 West 54th Street: **The University Club. ❽**

By the late 1880s numerous clubs (copied from London prototypes) had arrived in this neighborhood to serve upper-class men. Like the dinner-party guest lists, the associations served to demarcate an "in group." The Social Register, a directory begun at this time, listed club memberships.

☞ The University Club put up this building in 1899. Its oak-paneled dining room and red-and-gold drawing room, more Borgia than bourgeois, comforted caste needs. So did the entrance hall lined with monolithic columns of green Connemara marble. The heraldic carvings on the granite exterior, however, caused anxiety, went to the heart of the elite's identity problem. Was New York's upper class established through birth or achievement? Look up over the doorway at the coats of arms representing universities belonging to the club. (Sculptor Daniel Chester French invented some for the occasion.) The shields are at once aristocratic in pretension, and democratic—stressing professional attainment in the shape of a university education.

At first, members resisted having the insignia, but consented when told it was the done thing in Medici Florence. (In general, city millionaires felt more at home with the Medici mode than its French equivalent. It was—slightly—easier to identify with the great Florentine bankers turned rulers than to relate to Francis I, source of the pinnacled chateau fantasy.)

Even if clubs theoretically had opened as a refuge from the volatile business world, inevitably they became networking centers, the reason women want to join them today. Stanford White, the architect of this building, belonged to more than a dozen associations and used them for landing commissions. A dinner party here introducing J. P. Morgan to Andrew Carnegie's lieutenant, Charles Schwab, resulted in the creation of the United States Steel Corporation in 1901. It was America's first billion-dollar company.

***W**alk on north along Fifth, to the* **St. Regis Hotel,** ❾ *the southeast corner of 55th Street.*

At the opening of the twentieth century, grand hotels served entertaining and networking needs as well as simple accommodation. In part, John Jacob Astor IV built the mansarded St. Regis in 1904 for his own dinner parties. Even mansions were becoming too small for functions as society expanded.

The plot the St. Regis occupies had fallen into Astor hands because of the misfortunes of a second New York heiress married to yet another Duke of Marlborough—the dissolute Eighth. The woman used up her $6-million dowery restoring Blenheim Palace, and then had to raise $500,000 more by selling this ground lot in 1891.

Astor bought the hotel's furnishings from other impoverished aristocrats. Just as local mansion dwellers were packing their houses with historic trophies from around the world, Astor's agent spent two years ransacking Europe to bring back the hotel's silver bathroom fixtures, Waterford chandeliers, forty-seven grand pianos, and Royal Sevres dinnerware. The Watteau panels gracing some suites came from the Chateau de Chambord by way of an earlier Astor hotel. Scribner's assembled the several-thousand-book library of "volumes suitable for gentlemen and gentlewomen."

All agreed it was the city's finest hostelry. (Perhaps now, again.) Its immediate neighbors, however, weren't reconciled. Rockefellers joined the Vanderbilts in buying up surrounding land to block more of the same.

*C*ross Fifth Avenue west to the old **Gotham Hotel,** ⑩ *now, the Peninsula.*

Despite local residents' alarm over the threat to neighborhood property values, at heart most of the bon ton were ready to embrace the grand hotel life themselves. Leading the way were upper-class women bored with their job hosting competitive functions. Their husbands had been out enjoying the town for decades. (Most recently with showgirls from chorus lines just introduced to the city.) Now their wives wanted the freedom of socializing, if not of sex.

The Gotham was the city's only luxury hostelry to fail. Blue laws killed it—you couldn't sell liquor within 200 feet of a church—in this case, the Fifth Avenue Presbyterian.

*C*ontinue walking north on the west side of the avenue.

☞ The baroque interior of the **Fifth Avenue Presbyterian Church** ⑪ between 55th and 56th Streets gives an idea of how far the Presbyterians had traveled from their ascetic origins by 1875. Note the nave's theatrically raked seating and the horseshoe balcony.

*A*s you continue north on the avenue, you will pass the **site of Duveen's Gallery,** on the northwest corner of 56th Street.

Today's gallery world along 57th Street off of Fifth is not a coincidence. It comes from the longing of Fifth Avenue tycoons for immortality through their art collections—their urge to "convert pork into porcelain . . . railroad shares and mining stocks . . . into the glorified canvas of the world's masters." Conspicuous consumption could not guarantee one a posthumous image as a cultured man. An art collection could. By the 1880s art was big business in New York. Joseph Duveen, an English dealer aware that Europe had the art but America had the money, became mentor, purveyor, and above all validator of art('s worth) to New York collectors.

*W*alk up Fifth to the **Grand Army Plaza ⑫** across 59th from the southeast corner of Central Park, passing Bergdorf Goodman. The store occupies the site previously filled by Cornelius Vanderbilt II's 137-room castle. (It stood from 1883 to 1927.) You might want to sit on the fountain steps while reading the following.

Promptings for a large city park had begun in the late 1840s. Newspapers and wealthy merchants thought it would confirm the town, and thereby their own stature, as a world center of commerce and culture. Furthermore, a park would improve the poor's health and socialization, undercut middle-class flight to the suburbs, provide the rich a place to drive their carriages.

Uptown landowners pushed the project but were divided. Some locals who stood to gain favored developing "Jones Wood," an old estate running from 66th to 75th street, Third Avenue to the East River. Many downtown realtors, who resented the new park's cost and had no stake in its creation, balked altogether.

Aside from quarreling over its location, sundry interest groups differed over *what* the park should be. After bitter debate, the state legislature appointed a Central Park Commission to decide. Its majority, Anglo-American merchants, wanted a formal, pastoral park on English lines. (Scenery, not sports and other activity.) The winners in the commission's design competition were Frederick Law Olmsted and Calvert Vaux, a Londoner, who drew up plans to suit.

To make the "naturalistic" park in the 700 swampy, stony acres the city had assembled over time, labor crews drained marshland with a ninety-five-mile web of underground pipes and reoriented waterways. Workmen smashed squatter's shanties, hauled mountains of earth, and turfed over or bared any rocks that were too big to explode.

When the park opened section by section after 1860, the affluent carriage set living downtown near Murray Hill was the first group to come. A decade later the park grew less exclusive, less pastoral. New playgrounds drew neighboring Yorkville's* working-class immigrant families.

Until the 1890s the stretch of Fifth Avenue along the park remained empty or had held shanties. Even though real estate men bought lots for speculation hoping the rich would arrive, few came. Quite apart from the drastically inflated prices of land here, buyers considered the park potentially dangerous. Building on this section of Fifth took off only after Cornelius Vanderbilt's mansion and the first Plaza Hotel brought this juncture critical mass and cachet.

☞ The Beaux Arts (and Brooklyn)-inspired Grand Army Plaza in front of the French-style hotel is probably the city's most beloved tourist spot—certainly its most emblematic. Hollywood movies use the site, along with virtually nonexistent Checker cabs, as their key identifying shot of New York. Ironically, the cause of the plaza's popularity is that it breaks the grid, the reason for its charm. As the grid is basic to Manhattan, the site is completely misleading, the opposite of what the city represents. Note the Karl Bitter **Statue of Pomona, Goddess of Abundance** (the nude surmounting the fountain.)

Ever since the Civil War, architect Richard Morris Hunt had campaigned for grandiose entrance-ways at both corners of the park's southern end. (Olmsted fought off Beaux Arts inroads on his naturalistic park all his life. The threats weren't confined to the edges but even posited an imperial boulevard down the park's center itself.) Though Hunt's vision of a terraced extravaganza here never materialized, his protégé, Karl Bitter, the sculptor who designed this statue, took up his mentor's cause.

Money for Bitter's work came from a bequest left by the publisher Joseph Pulitzer. It's worth going into the background of the statue's arrival, as it sheds light on the politics of site and representation.

Joseph Pulitzer, who'd come to New York from St. Louis in 1883 to buy the *New York World* newspaper, had already used statuary for self-promotion. His first effort, fund raising for the Statue of Liberty, had brought him and his journal fame. His second effort here at this site had drawn humiliation. In 1893, when Pulitzer and other German notables had lobbied

---

*Yorkville was still considered to include the whole area above 59th Street east of today's Central Park to the river—a German and Irish area from the 1840s, and more recently, home to a few middle-class families settling in the brownstones going up on some side streets.

At first, the raw new park kept lots along Fifth Avenue empty. Land was expensive, and the park scared people.

to erect a statue of the philosopher Heinrich Heine at this corner, the recently formed National Sculpture Society had rudely rejected the offer. Worse—one of the officers of the pro-French, anti-German association reportedly suggested the statue should be down in Tompkins Square Park "with their sauerkraut eating countrymen." Heine eventually wound up shipped to the Bronx, then home to many middle-class Germans. The defeat stung.

Pulitzer's urge to glorify and be glorified by this site was further fueled by the announcement that his journalist rival, William Hearst, would build a monument at the park's southwest corner. Hearst's monument honored American sailors killed in the Cuban War of Independence, a conflict both papers had promoted to raise circulation.

Pulitzer commissioned Bitter to make his donation ultra-classical (read "upper classical") to contrast with the ebullient statuary on the park's far side. The "tastefulness" quotient of Pulitzer's bequest also lessened the likelihood it would wind up in an outer borough.

The recently regilded **statue honoring General Sherman** after his death in 1892 also has politics behind it. Originally, the city planned to install it at Grant's tomb in Union Army togetherness. The Grant family, however, preferred solo honors.

☞ Augustus Saint-Gaudens, who cast the equestrian statue, often worked with the Beaux-Arts trained architects who built the mansions along this stretch of Fifth Avenue. The intermingling of sculpture with architecture was basic to the French school.

Eventually, a Vanderbilt chateau down at Grand Army Plaza and some nearby luxury hotels, including the first Plaza, emboldened other well-to-do to move north.

The academy's other tenet—that buildings should relate to site—came to grief in New York. The city's wealthy refused to sacrifice a cent for surrounding space even on this part of Fifth, where big plots were available. Builders jammed new mansions together like tenements. In 1900, when the city widened Fifth Avenue (planned by Olmsted to form a transitional extension of the park), the dwellings lost their 15-foot front gardens also.

☞ The 1907 French Renaissance **Plaza Hotel** is the second here, the replacement for an earlier version that proved too small—a good index of Society's growth spurt. Architect Henry Hardenbergh made this building immense but rounded the corners to soften the effect. He also shaded the mansarded roof green to echo park trees, meld the building with its location. Play Eloise, and enter to explore the Louis XVI marble lobby, the Palm Court suffused with light from a leaded glass ceiling, the Oak Room frescoed with German feudal castles.

Many of the city's rich lived here when their mansions were going up. The first to sign the register was a Vanderbilt. Before World War I, 90 percent of the residents were permanent, only 10 percent transient—the opposite of today.

Continue north and cross Fifth Avenue at 60th Street to see the **Metropolitan Club.** ⓭

J. P. Morgan and other disgruntled members of the Union Club opened this offshoot in 1892 after the old guard parent body blackballed a candidate the financier had proposed. (The name was intended to evoke the Metropolitan Opera House, founded a decade earlier as a slap in the face to old family worthies who preferred the elitist Academy of Music on 14th Street.)

☞ Stanford White designed most of the Italian Renaissance building, popularly known as "the Millionaire's Club." The club's exterior is elegantly simple.

Its interior, however, is a congeries of styles based on Italian quattrocento and cinquecento prototypes. White's thousands of photographs taken on his European travels made the copying possible. European craftsmen, especially imported for the task, made the project doable—until, that is, the American Plasterers Society struck in protest.

Detour east on 60th Street to see the club's **carriage court.** (This brief sidetrip is not shown on the map.)

Coachmen who had to turn their equipages around in the dime-sized court were wont to grumble. It was near the end for carriages anyway. In 1900 electric buses with seats for twelve replaced horsedrawn conveyances on Fifth Avenue. By 1905 the Fifth Avenue Coach Company introduced double-decker buses from France; in 1907 the city ordered all horses off the street.

Return to Fifth and walk north to The **Knickerbocker Club,** ❶ 2 East 62nd Street.

☞ This 1914 building by Delano and Aldrich (replacing an earlier mansion) is in a countervailing mode to the grand tour architecture. By this period, a revival of red brick Georgian and Federal styles had become popular in the neighborhood, and many earlier Queen Anne and Italianate style rowhouses on the side streets off Fifth had been refaced in this manner. The rediscovery of the look coincided with a defensive impulse to flaunt colonial roots against the immigrant tide sweeping the city. (According to Brendan Gill, the parlor floor windows here are in the ogle mode. Members voted to keep the sills low so they could see the ankles of women pedestrians.)

*W*alk north to 64th Street, turn right (east) a few steps to **New India House,** 3 East 64th.

☞ Warren and Wetmore, architects for Grand Central Station, designed this paradigm of Beaux Arts architecture (molded limestone with slate and copper roof, arched drawing room windows, and small oval dormers) in 1903. The top floor held servants rooms; on average, the ratio of staff to family members along Fifth Avenue was four to one. Note also the **mansion at the southeast corner** of 64th Street and Fifth built by Edward Berwind, at one point the nation's largest coal owner as well as the CEO of the new IRT subway.

The (rather depressing) brick and limestone Italian palazzo served Berwind's entertaining needs—when in town. Berwind also owned the "Elms," one of Newport's grandest mansions, as well as other pieds-á-terre. Real sojourns on Fifth were often short, as families piled up global vacation homes—100-room Newport cottages, Scottish deer parks, Burgundy chateaux, English country estates. Elite boarding schools for boys opened around this time. Girls could be packed up and moved from place to place along with the staff.

*W*alk one block north on the avenue to **Temple Emanu-El, ⑮** on the northeast corner of 65th and Fifth.

German Jews, followers of a reform movement dating back to the 1830s, built this temple after two congregations, Temple Beth El and Temple Emanu-El, merged in 1927. The synagogue occupies the site of an old Astor mansion, the big ground lot allowing for the temple's large size. In contrast to St. Patrick's, which has almost no local congregants, Emanu-El is very much a neighborhood institution despite its rather intimidating dimensions.

*W*alk east on 65th Street to Madison Avenue. Note **two rowhouses** with ground-floor storefronts on the east side of 741–743 Madison.

Madison Avenue's development preceded that on Fifth by more than a decade. From the 1880s, people from farther downtown moved into the rowhouses proliferating here. Several millionaires, including Richard Morris Hunt and Charles Tiffany, built mansions at the summit of Lenox Hill (named after the area's nineteenth-century landowner).

Until the 1920s Madison stayed essentially residential, even though the earliest storefront was recorded in 1904. Heavy automobile traffic and decrees ordering house owners to remove all stoops beyond the building line speeded the conversions. One by one, as families moved out, old rowhouses here got ground-floor shops. From this time until it became boutique heaven, the avenue functioned as a service strip for the new apartment buildings on Park and Fifth Avenues. Today, the street level holds such a cornucopia of designer everything one rarely thinks to look up at the domestic fronts above the stores.

*W*alk east to the **house** at 47–49 East 65th Street. ⓰

Franklin Delano Roosevelt's mother commissioned Charles Adams Pratt to design the twin buildings in 1907, shortly after her son married. Eleanor and Franklin lived in one, the oppressive mother-in-law in the other. Aside from the single entryway, interconnecting doors linked the two dwellings on each floor, enabling rude burstings in by Franklin's mother.

*C*ontinue east to the end of the block, to Park Avenue.

The city laid out Park Avenue as Fourth Avenue in the grid plan of 1811 but did not develop the route because of the granite ridge that ran its entire length. In 1832 the city granted the New York and Harlem Railroad a right of way along the strip, also giving it permission to run its steam engines here. Train traffic began in 1834. In the 1870s the city ordered the firm (now controlled by Commodore Vanderbilt) to funnel its trains through deep cuts. Surface track, however, remained at crossings, and guards flagged down pedestrians when engines approached.

The first stretch of the avenue to get the upscaling designation "Park Avenue" was the section below Murray Hill, which assumed the honorific in 1860. 43rd–96th Streets took the name in 1888—a big year for renaming on both sides of Manhattan. In 1896 the whole route up to Fordham received the appellation. Despite the honorifics and the fact the railroad mainly ran underground after the seventies, the route remained a septic slash spewing out grit and blight. Tenements and modest rowhouses formed the only dwellings along the avenue. When they could, developers oriented the buildings toward the side streets in an effort to shield them from sparks and oily fumes.

C*ross the avenue to the east side and note* **629 and 631 Park Avenue** ⑰ *be-tween 65th and 66th Streets.*

☞ The walkups, built in 1869, were intended to hold three families. The one with the fire escape looks particularly (endearingly) incongruous on today's streetscape. In early times it would have been at home with the other tenements, truck farms, small factories, breweries, and charitable institutions here. The blocks farther east of here were even more industrial. Third Avenue held marble works, printing ink factories, sawmills, livery stables, and cigar factories. Scuffed wall signs on the few remaining tenements still advertise five-cent brand name stogies.

The railroad, which had run along Park Avenue from the 1830s, made the street an unsightly mess. Posh apartments went up only in the teens of this century after the trains were electrified and the track cuts covered. (This picture is a rare photograph from 1865.)

*A*t *66th Street is* **the Armory,** ⓲ *which stands on land that once formed part of Hamilton Square.*

Today this neighborhood holds many public and semi-public institutions. One reason is the several charitable bequests left by James Lenox, an early nineteenth-century landowner here. Another reason for the institutions is the extent of city property. In 1806 the municipality had bought a local tract called the "Dove Lots," after the colonial-era tavern at 66th Street and present-day Third Avenue. The Sign of the Dove Restaurant at 1110 Third Avenue commemorates the old coaching inn.

In 1811 the city mapped the lots (on paper) into "Hamilton Square." The plan set one acre aside for an academy, another acre for a church. The rich merchants who then summered along the East River easily persuaded the city the new parish should be Episcopalian. Trinity obligingly paid for a wooden outpost at 69th and Lexington. For several years the new St. James Church shared a minister with St. Michael's on the West Side, which served summer residents near the Hudson. To get there, the minister rode across island on the old Harsenville road at 71st Street. Several houses that once fronted the old road still survive near Lexington Avenue.

In the 1820s St. James started year-round services for the handful of gentry now living in the area full time. Despite the presence of the elite church and the site's panoramic views, the square languished. In 1837 the city rented out most land here for pasture. Eight years later it tried to popularize the grounds by putting up a statue of Washington with much attendant hoopla.

The effort failed. In fact, the ceremony coincided with the departure of the remaining gentry, who fled in droves as growing waves of immigrants arrived from the Lower East Side. In 1865, the city converted a portion of the square into a parade ground. Two years later it trimmed the old holding still more, shutting the last remnant two years afterward. When engineers leveled the summit of Lenox Hill, they carved out the present cross streets and extended Lexington Avenue north, demolishing the Episcopalian sanctuary. Despite the pleading of St. James' minister to rebuild close by to serve Yorkville's needy, church trustees insisted that the new building relocate near the cluster of gentry houses going up along Madison Avenue. (Today, in a turnabout, St. James has forged strong ties with Yorkville's homeless, risking wrath from wealthy neighbors—and some parishioners—by starting an East Side shelter and running a soup kitchen out of the church.)

After the revamping, the city gave away the leftover land on the square, or rather the rights to it, to public (and publicly aided) institutions. Among those benefiting were the Seventh Regiment, which built its new armory here, and Hunter College. Other organizations included the Foundling Hospital, the Institute for the Deaf, and Mount Sinai Hospital on Lexington, which are all now gone.

The new public institutions here buffered incoming merchant class house-buyers along Madison Avenue and its side streets from the immigrants and tenements farther east. As the poor in Yorkville were working people, not the radical unemployed, it might seem overstating it to talk about class tensions at the time the armory went up, particularly as in our lifetime—until a decade ago when it began to house the homeless—this building was known mainly for its up-market furniture shows. Nevertheless, when the Victorian fortress opened in 1878, real estate journals touted it as a conspicuous security system standing between the two zones. Its siting near the railroad tracks didn't hurt, either. The year before the Armory's opening, violent rail strikes had swept most of the country. (An update on the safety patrol front is that, in 1994, East Side realtors have proposed creating a five-hundred-man private security force to police the neighborhood from 59th to 96th Streets, the park to the river.)

When the Seventh Regiment Armory opened on Park Avenue in the 1880s, local realtors touted the Frenchified fortress as a buffer between the rich moving to Madison Avenue and Yorkville's working-class families.

☞ Do not miss seeing the building's interior, one of New York's truly great spaces. If you have no other excuse, visit the public bar on the top floor, as this allows you to pass in front of the baronial staircase on your way to the elevator. Look up at the threadbare regimental banners, membrane of memory, that hang in the opalesque chandeliered light. Upstairs in the barroom, ancient colonels reconstruct campaigns with salt sellers on damp linen table cloths. (Honest.) If you are organized and call the curator to request an appointment, (212) 744–2968, it may be possible to see the Veterans' Room and Library. Louis Comfort Tiffany oversaw the renowned artists who decorated the rooms, and designed the windows himself in modern, almost Mondrianesque geometrics. Unfortunately, unless you attend an antique show (or something), it's hard to enter the great drill hall at the Lexington Avenue end, as the resident brigade usually trains here. If you do go in, look up above floor level. The stunning 187-by-290 foot ceiling recalls the era's great glass-roofed markets and reminds us of the train yards at the late lamented Penn Station.

Walk north on Park Avenue to **Hunter College,** ⑲ between 68th and 69th Streets.

☞ In 1873 the Board of Education opened the Normal College (an odd name) on the city-owned site to train teachers for the hundreds of thousands of new immigrants arriving in the city. The original Gothic structure burned in the 1930s. This bleak barrack went up following the fire.

Continue north along the east side of Park to the **brownstones** at 709–711 Park tucked behind the Union Club of New York between 69th and 70th Streets. ⑳

☞ Note the steepening gradient as you go. Despite the cropping of the hill in the 1860s, you can still feel the rise in the road, one of the rare inclines in Manhattan. The **Flemish gabled rowhouses** date from the 1880s.

When the houses went up, one belonged to St. James' minister, whose daughter, Nathalie Dana, wrote a memorable account of her childhood here—*Lenox Hill in the 1880's: A Girl's Memories of Saint James Parish*.

☞ This upper-middle-class row was an anomaly in the otherwise working-class houses on the thoroughfare. Notice that the dwellings are on the *summit* of Lenox Hill. (The other exceptional housing cluster stood on top of the peak later called Carnegie Hill.) The reason—and it's always a delight in Manhattan to find a natural cause—was the ground's elevation, which allowed the steam from underground trains to dissipate. Householders here could live pollution free. In other blocks, steam spuming through the street vents blanketed buildings and passers-by.

In 1903 the city legislature finally demanded that the Vanderbilts replace their steam engines with electric power after several influential people died in gruesome smash-ups caused by smoke-blinded engineers. At the time of the switch, the Vanderbilts also covered the cut along this section of Park Avenue and sank remaining surface track. The street's present **central islands** date from then.

The start of electrification in 1906 hiked local property values as high as the old hill. When institutions sold out, wealthy downtowners readied themselves to build.

Cross over the avenue and walk down the west side of Park. The three **Georgian brick buildings ㉑** *between 68th and 69th Streets were the first townhouses to arrive on the avenue. The earliest one is the southernmost residence, begun by Stanford White in 1911.*

When the mansion served as the Soviet Mission to the United Nations in the 1960s, Krushchev made his impromptu "we shall bury you" speech from the front balcony to cheering Hunter College girls across the street. (Some say he actually said, "we shall marry you.")

☞ The **white Georgian house** just below these houses on the south side of 68th Street, number 58, was, in fact, a wedding gift from the Brooklyn Standard Oil tycoon Charles Pratt to his son in 1919. It was the last great city townhouse. From the onset of World War I, apartment houses became Society's mode. Today, they shadow the street—a gloomy, if officially elegant, thoroughfare.

Return up to 71st Street, then turn left one block to Madison to the third incarnation of **St. James Church, ㉒** *which stands on the northeast corner of the intersection.*

Richard Cram built this version in 1883. The bell comes from the old Hamilton Square building.

Walk north on Madison to the **Gertrude Rhinelander Waldo House ㉓** *by Kimball and Thompson next door.*

The Rhinelanders, whose seed money came from colonial-era sugar refining, owned vast tracts of Upper East Side land.

☞ Note the statuary of kings, knights, and bishops intended to ennoble the Francis I facade. Finally, we get to see the chateau style popularized by Hunt through his work for the Vanderbilts. You can see a fair amount of the interior, which once held a billiard room, library, and ballroom, by braving the Ralph Lauren store. The imposing staircase has been revamped. Reportedly, Lauren applied for $4 million plus federal tax credits to renovate the badly eroded building; he later resold and currently rents. Before his occupancy the mansion had stood empty for three decades.

The poor woman who built it never moved in. Her new husband died before it was complete, and she lived across the street, a sad recluse, more genuinely Gothic than her building.

***W**alk west to Fifth Avenue and turn left; walk down two blocks to the* **Frick Mansion ㉔**. *(The entrance is on the northeast corner of East 70th Street.)*

When Frick (Andrew Carnegie's partner in the coke and steel business) first arrived from Pittsburgh, he rented the William K. Vanderbilt house down on Fifth and 51st Street. While enjoying the sense of dynastic connection, he abhorred being anyone's tenant. In 1906 he bought this site, which housed a library deeded by the late James Lenox and tore it down. The books went to the new 42nd Street Public.

Masonry is grander than gardens, so few houses on Fifth had any grounds. Slight as they are, Frick and Carnegie's front yards were bigger than most.

☞ Frick chose this location because it crowned Lenox Hill's vestigial summit, a tiny mount, but the best around. The house

Frick built is one of the two set-back mansions along the avenue. The other belonged to Carnegie, who also commanded a mini-hill in the 1890s which later took his name. Frick is reputed to have said he wanted to build a house that would make Carnegie's mansion look like a miner's shack.

What he built looked like a museum, which it now is. In fact, it was intended all along to become a museum, like writing a diary for publication. Frick claimed he moved from Pittsburgh to New York to enter the city's art world, to show off his paintings as well as launch himself into national politics. Another factor just might have been that his own hometown was no longer utterly congenial since he'd hired 300 Pinkerton men some years earlier to shoot down striking steel workers back in Pennsylvania. In any case, once here, Frick added to his holdings. His dealer, Joseph Duveen, not only supplied more objects and paintings but also advised the collector on the layout and decor of his "house."

☞ Go in to see the collections and experience what the mansion felt like, the Aubussons mossy under your feet. Tuesday–Saturday, telephone (212) 288–0700.

Cross Fifth Avenue at the Frick to see an 1898 **memorial that honors architect Richard Morris Hunt,** who led the Loiring of New York.

☞ A bevy of names attest the architect's connections. Among others are the Architectural League (Hunt helped to found it), the Municipal Art Society (Hunt was its first president), the Metropolitan Museum (Hunt was a trustee and latter-day architect), and the Society of Beaux Arts Architects. In the gilded 1980s Hunt became fashionable again, the subject of several retrospectives.

Retrace your steps north on the east side of Fifth. At 73rd Street walk into the block a few steps to 11 East 73rd Street, the **Joseph Pulitzer House ㉕** (1903) by McKim, Mead and White.

☞ This mansion, inspired by the Ca'Rezzonico Palace in Venice, has tactile, deeply worked textures. When Pulitzer commis-

Some mansions aped those in Medici Florence, but many were in the Mad King Ludwig mode, or as house-proud New Yorkers liked to think of it, the Loire look. Architect Richard Morris Hunt led the Loiring.

sioned the house, he was going blind and he, apocryphally, approved the model for his new house through touch, not sight. As the elderly publisher's blindness increased, so did his sensitivity to noise. Despite the use of sound-proofed, double-walled construction throughout his home, the ailing publisher still suffered from the throb of boilers in the cellar and eventually withdrew to the garden bedroom annex, whose double walls were packed with mineral wool.

***W**alk back to Fifth and turn right; continue north to the* **Harkness House,** **㉖** *1 East 75th Street.*

☞ The architectural firm of Hale and Rodgers, which did much of Yale University's faux Gothic additions, built this luminous limestone palazzo for the Standard Oil heir in 1909. Note the sills on the ground floor raised above eye level to give the ground floor privacy.

In 1910 a horrifying booklet published the names and addresses of all Fifth Avenue's prominent residents for passengers riding the new double decker buses. Its title—"Palatial Homes In the City Of New York and Dwellers There-in As Ranged for the Convenience of the Passer-by."

***C**ontinue north to the* **James Duke House** **㉗** *on the northeast corner of 78th Street, built with tobacco monopoly money. This 1912 copy of an eighteenth-century Bordeaux Hotel de Ville shares the Harkness house's simplicity and gleaming limestone facade.*

☞ Request the desk officers of the building, now gifted to New York University for its Graduate Arts program, to let you look at the ground floor of the 54-room house. Depending on their schedule, they sometimes oblige. If you are fortunate enough to enter, you can see how the avenue appeared from the householder's point of view. The proximity is alarming. You can also feel the cold atmosphere of the oak-paneled erstwhile library and the white and gold ballroom, which resembles the one in the Plaza. The institutional feeling is inherent in the structure, unrelated to NYU's tenancy here. It's hard to imagine family life above the sweeping staircase that pours into the ground-floor reception room.

***K**eep on north, noting the tension between the Duke house and its neighbor, the* **Payne Whitney House,** **㉘** *at 972 Fifth Avenue. The two houses stand in each other's shadow. Fortunately, the families had close ties; among other links, the Whitneys backed Duke's tobacco company.*

☞ Though a landmarks report says the Duke house "maintains its imposing dignity by the space around it, especially the garden between it and the Payne

Whitney house," there is not enough room for a decent-size clothesline. The embossed elegance of the Whitney house side-wall befits a courtyard; what it gets is a dark alley. It's puzzling why Whitney, known as the Grand Seigneur of Graft for his Byzantine political and financial manipulations, couldn't have done better.

> Mansions were often built as social credentials and featured glitzy reception areas for staging galas.

*C*ontinue north, passing the **Disneyesque Chateau** *on the southeast corner of 79th Street and Fifth by C. P. Gilbert (1899). The moated, gargoyled mansion once was home to the last direct descendent of Peter Stuyvesant, fittingly, a realtor.*

*W*alk north to the **Metropolitan Museum,** **㉙** *the repository of many art collections from Fifth Avenue houses.*

☞ The city's elite founded the museum in 1869. When it moved up here in 1874, its first wing faced the park, not the street. Calvert Vaux, the park landscape designer and architect who worked in a rather pastoral mode, got the commission. In 1894 more city funding paid for the present Fifth Avenue front after mansions lined the thoroughfare. Richard Morris Hunt, who loathed

Even tycoons like Payne Whitney, known as the "Grand Seigneur of Graft," lived squeezed next-door to their neighbors.

Vaux's style, drowned the earlier building in the massive new Beaux Arts structure. (It's possible to see a remnant of Vaux's boxed-in work in the Petrie European Sculpture Court.) From this time, the museum was re-oriented away from the park, its axis toward its Fifth Avenue donors. McKim, Mead and White built the latter-day North and South wings in 1911 and 1913. Notice the four large masonry blocks above the columns of the central facade. The original plan called for them to be sculpted into allegorical groups representing the four major periods in the history of art, but, somehow, the museum never found the funding. The niches intended to house allegorical figures also stand empty.

It wasn't just a question of money or even much of a question about money. It was about choice, the breakdown of older

After World War I, many wealthy left their mansions and townhouses for apartment high rises or the outer suburbs. Most residences along Fifth were torn down; those along Madison, converted to stores.

social and cultural hierarchies that once made civic art possible. Three out of the four periods of art that Hunt suggested—Egyptian, classical Greek, and western Renaissance—were easy to symbolize. The fourth, modern art, flummoxed everybody. Though people say art grew less representational at the time, it was life itself that grew less representational. Or at least more prismed. In an age of increasingly pluralistic social and cultural values, agreed-upon public art was no longer possible. Ironically, the aim of the Beaux Arts movement to impose a unifying ideal on a polyglot city came to grief in its own palace.

Perhaps New York's impulse to impose a rational schema had never been too real anyway. The exuberant robber barons in the chateaux valued rambunctious self-aggrandizement above spatial order. From now on the wealthy staked their (residential) salvation on zoning. The ideal of one shining city lay in shards.

Many wealthy moved to the suburbs or to the defensible high rises going up on Park Avenue or Fifth. Much of the museum's collection dates from this time as mansion dwellers triaged their belongings.

> A number of new apartments kept the Medici look, but their height made Fifth Avenue closer to San Gimignano than to Florence.

Walk back south to **998** **Fifth Avenue** ㉚ *(the entrance is at 1 East 81st Street).*

☞ Following 1916, apartment houses like this one replaced most residences along the avenue. Note that much of the detail from earlier houses has been kept. The Medici high rise has a rusticated base, an elaborate cornice whose coffered underside is carved with rosettes, pedimented windows, and inset balconies.

By the late 1920s, 90 percent of Manhattan's wealthy had moved to similar buildings. While the Upper East Side's premier architecture continued to be Florentine, the life-style of its defended inhabitants became ever more San Gimignano.

13

Asian Flushing

Subway: IRT train 7 Flushing line to Main Street
(travel time about 45 minutes).

I suggest you read the following introduction on the train—once you ar-rive in Flushing, it's a melee of sight and sound; few nooks offer space where you can recoup, reconnoiter.

In 1643 English colonists living under New Amsterdam's rule settled Flushing on Long Island's north shore. Dutch farmers from Brooklyn soon joined them. From early on, local English Quakers fought Peter Stuyvesant for the right to worship outside the Dutch Reformed Church. Despite fines, arrests, banishment, and torture, the "ranters" continued to gather secretly at the (extant) home of sect leader John Bowne. After seven years of suf-fering, the Dutch West India Company's headquarters in Amsterdam legit-imized the movement, and in 1694 Flushing's Quakers built a saltbox meeting house. (It still stands, and is on today's route.) Local histories now solemnize the town as "America's cradle of religious freedom." Unfortu-nately, the high-mindedness of the early Quakers did not extend to slave-holding: all of them, including Bowne, had bondsmen who formed the gen-esis of Flushing's African American population.

Despite a spurt of Irish and German immigration in the mid-nineteenth century, the sleepy hamlet was slow to grow, and land around the village and neighboring market towns remained semi-rural, thick with truck gardens until the turn of this century. Foreshadowing large-scale Asian settlement one hundred years later, several Cantonese nurserymen raised bok choy, bit-ter melon, and jade squash for restaurants in Manhattan's Chinatown.

Flushing's expansion followed the merger of Queens with New York City in 1898. Physical links concretized official ties. Eleven years after con-solidation, the borough got the Queensboro Bridge at 59th Street. The next

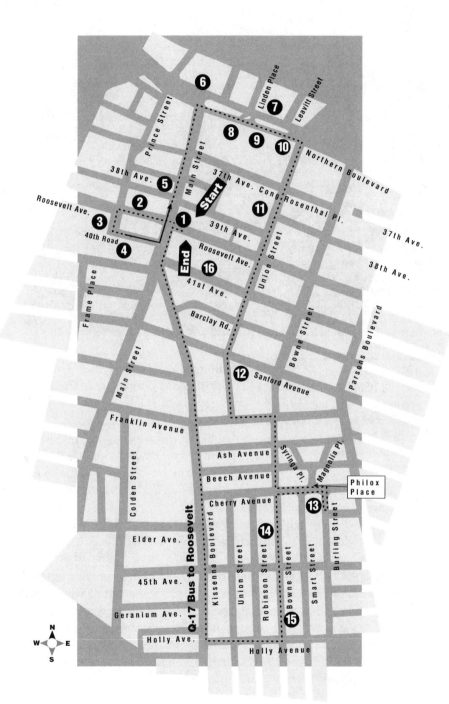

The opening of the Queensboro Bridge in 1909 helped change Queens from a self-sufficient, near bucolic preserve to a vast bedroom dormitory for Manhattan's overflow.

year brought the Pennsylvania (Long Island) Rail Road Tunnel to Manhattan. Soon, vistas of single- and two-family working-class houses replaced the vegetable fields that once shaped Queens' economy and landscape. While Queens has many residential modes, ranging from experimental courtyard complexes to apartment towers, it is the image of the single-family brick and frame housing, mostly painted white, mostly holding whites, that has become engraved in popular consciousness, a blanched dreamscape that still sticks despite dramatic change.

During the 1920s Queens' population swelled from less than 500,000 to well over a million, accelerating near the end of the decade when three events brought still more householders to the bedroom community. In 1928 the IRT and BMT subways opened, not only making an easy commute but bringing the crews who had dug the tunnels. At project's end, many of the Italian workmen and their families settled close by in new housing tracts. In 1936 the onset of construction on La Guardia Airport

Queens has many sorts of dwellings, but the borough is engraved in many minds as a dreamscape of small white houses.

(across Flushing Bay) and the World's Fair grounds (in Flushing Meadows) drew even more working-class families. Not only did Queens' growth *owe* to its transit system, but in some cases, literally depended on it—the latter two projects rest on a bloat of landfill excavated when the IND subway was extended, a midden of Indian flints, farmers' hoes, and stifled cabbage. Smoldering ash from local dumps made up the shortfall.

In 1964–1965, a second World's Fair opened on the constructed site, now bound by expressways to the city's urban sprawl. Skeletons of the sputnik-style pavilions stand today, their space-age bones visible from the lefthand side of the number 7 train like rotting futuristic ghosts. Many Korean businessmen who came to the fair struck roots.

A few years earlier they'd have had a problem. Now, by chance, their way was smoothed by a new ruling. The same year the fair ended, President Lyndon Johnson signed an immigration law raising the annual ceiling for eastern hemisphere applicants to 20,000 places per country per year. The civil rights movement influenced the unaccustomed generosity. Earlier, a niggardly quota system had discriminated against Asians and, in some periods, blocked whole categories. From 1882, the first of a series of Exclusion Acts barred entry to all Chinese but wealthy merchants. In 1917 Indians eluded an otherwise sweeping ban on Asians, as romantic western scholars pronounced them de jure Caucasians—the "ancestors of the Aryan race."

In the decades following the quota turn-around, Asian arrivals gradually made up almost half of Flushing's population. The multi-ethnic, multi-racial communities massed under the category come from Asia itself, the Caribbean, and Latin America, a comprehensive mix special to Queens. Other city enclaves tend to hold immigrants from one race or another. Manhattan's Chinatown, for example, essentially houses Chinese immigrants (mainly of Cantonese ancestry), be they descended from colonies in

Rail and subway links drew settlers in the teens of this century. Construction work on La Guardia Airport in the years before World War II brought more population.

Burma, Vietnam, Malaysia, or elsewhere. In contrast, a 1989 guesstimate of Flushing residents recorded 110,000 Koreans, 100,000 Chinese, and 94,000 Indians, followed by smaller Pakistani, Filipino, Japanese, and Afghan communities.

Another way Flushing differs from Manhattan's older Chinatown is that until recently most Asians here were relatively well off, as the 1965 admissions policy favored affluent professionals. The monied newcomers by-passed New York's traditional "first arrival" neighborhoods in Manhattan and Brooklyn for the same reasons middle-class blacks and whites were leaving town at the time. They saw no reason to live in a failing central city racked by economic crisis. Positive reasons to move to Queens included its relative newness, which saved it from the urban blight afflicting Manhattan, Brooklyn, and the Bronx; its good schools; good housing; good social services; and the absence (until recently) of the organized crime besetting Manhattan's Chinese settlement. A simple but heartfelt cause to locate here was the borough's link to Kennedy International Airport.

One of the characteristics of today's immigrants is the possibility, for many, of keeping in touch with their roots. The jet age allows the flow of homeland news and goods, the chance of frequent return to one's birth country. The link is so strong, many see their tenure here as temporary and dream of retiring, dying, on native soil. The sky bridge makes home feel closer. As you walk around town, you'll see the jeweled bellies of jumbo jets low overhead as they come in for landing at the nearby airfield. "At night, my husband sometimes stands at the window watching the planes," one Indian professional told me, "especially if things aren't going too well."

Aside from keeping native ties, a second attribute many Flushing immigrants share is their ability to keep connections with fellow nationals across state lines. A car culture has made "the tri-state area" replace the city as a governing concept. While some, such as Korean wholesalers, might commute to Midtown, most work outside of the central city, and the far majority live in the suburbs. Although from the Manhattan-centered approach of this book, Flushing is treated as a suburb, in many ways by now it, too (from its own perspective), has become a semi-urban receiving center, and many immigrants move farther afield into more exurban areas when their salaries permit.

The suburbanites' ethos contrasts with the attitude of earlier ethnics who have "moved out." The latter feel a nostalgia for old roots as well as such an articulate revulsion to the current city that it affirms the city core (albeit negatively). Many new Asian tri-staters have no memory of New York's city center and often hold dismissive aversion toward it rather than imaginative dislike. Many have come from the most privileged, villa'd, and condoed parts of Asian cities and don't share old New Yorkers' sometimes sentimental feelings for the picturesquely decrepit. Or at least this is the view presented in much of the new immigrant literature from the East Coast, which is generally middle class and often set outside Manhattan. Bharati Mukherjee is not only a poet of immigration, but a patio poet of the greenbelt area, where many of her stories occur.

Today, the median income in Flushing is somewhat lower than at the onset of Asian migration because in the 1970s the Congress broadened the 1965 statute to include workers, as American employers were then pressuring the government for "cheap" foreign labor. (Also, by the late 1970s, various home countries had just begun to grant travel documents to a wider segment of their citizens, allowing them to leave their countries. In America, we take passports for granted; not so, citizens in other states.) Though by far the majority of poorer immigrants who came after the new rulings settled in Manhattan's Chinatown, in recent years some have begun following sweatshops out to Queens. Other new poor here are the dependent relations of earlier professionals who were brought over by their kinfolk after they grew established.

Despite the recent leveling, however, many Asian Flushingites still fall under the rubric the "model minority"—the prize-winning, well-educated group touted by conservatives for succeeding without public aid and often singled out by the media for its "old fashioned" (i.e., just like white) perseverance. Little mention is made that many new arrivals came with cash in hand.

On this walk we'll see some poorer immigrants (particularly newly arrived Koreans), but the tour will concentrate on the middle-income Asians who characterized Flushing until the 1980s—at least, this will be the strategy as far as is possible, as the more professional echelons have less street presence. The three main communities the walk will focus on are the Koreans, the Chinese, and the Indians, whom we'll meet at the end of the route when the tour nears the Bowne Street Hindu Temple of North America.

Most Chinese in Flushing came from the north of China, generally by way of Taiwan, where they'd fled after the Communist takeover in 1949. Recently, smaller numbers have arrived from Hong Kong, as the date nears for that colony's return to China. By and large, Flushing's Mandarin-speaking Chinese cannot communicate with the south Chinese in Chinatown and, in any case, seek minimal contact with them. Not only do many feel socially superior* to Chinatown's new arrivals, but they also look down on Chinatown's long-term residents, who are descended from Cantonese workers who came more than a century ago.

As the suburbs now hold all the stores and services they need, Flushing Chinese don't even have to shop "in town." As you exit from the subway station, you'll see many Chinese stores, real estate offices, restaurants, and construction companies clustered around Main Street and Roosevelt Avenue.

You'll also find some Korean stores, though Union Street is that community's commercial stronghold. Christian missionaries in Korea spurred their flock's emigration from the turn of the century on. Converts left partly because their cultural ties had weakened, partly because they had access to an international Protestant network. Their early arrival explains the power of local Korean Christian churches today.

After the war ended in 1953, orphans and brides drifted here, their

---

*This social superiority doesn't stop some of Flushing's Chinese from profiting from the new emigration, however. Reputedly, several-well off Taiwanese here were involved in bringing over illegals, including the cruel cargo of souls in the *Golden Venture*.

way smoothed by immigration concessions. When the quota opened up in the 1960s, professionals followed. Some of these were North Korean refugees, including a high proportion of Christians already deracinated by schooling. Some were South Koreans uprooted by the war and the American occupation of their country. Postwar changes in South Korea were arguably good as well as bad. All, however, caused flux. For example, medical improvements in the nation boosted the population from 25 million in 1960 to 40 million in 1984. The jobless emigrated.

The first wave of immigrants in the 1960s, largely doctors and nurses trained in Korea, easily found work here, as Medicaid and Medicare had just extended hospital care. Immigrants from other professions had problems despite their urban middle-class background. Their English was too shaky, their knowledge of U.S. ways too slight. Though few had commercial training, many bought small businesses in Flushing, while others bought out Italians and Jews weary of coping with inner city implosion.* (Immigration and Naturalization Service [INS] policy at the time gave preference to newcomers who could make sizable investments in the United States.)

By now, most earlier Korean immigrants have quit retail to enter real estate, law, and other white-collar work. The stores and services you'll see on this walk belong to more recent settlers.

*T*he walk begins with the **subway station on Main Street, ❶** where you exit the train to start your Flushing tour.

In the early 1970s new suburban malls drove Flushing's downtown to near ruin. By fortunate timing, cash-rich Asian immigrants had just arrived, looking for investment. Within years they developed Flushing into the city's fourth-largest retail center. In 1984 the Flushing Chinese Business Association, seeking to symbolize the role Asian merchants had played in the town's recovery, adopted this station and paid for its restoration.

*W*alker Alert: For the next part of the tour the walker will largely be on his or her own. As the streetscape changes so rapidly here, this chapter will

---

*An odd link here is the late Jackie Kennedy Onassis, who started the rage for "falls," which became a national mania coincident with the Korean arrival. The new Korean expatriates opened hair stores in black neighborhoods, where 89 percent of the women followed the First Lady in wearing wigs of some sort. Back home in Korea, wig factories boomed, and hair pieces outstripped all other exports. By 1970 Seoul alleyways and cliff-side mountain towns rang with the calls of scalpers buying tresses.

provide (in the main) little precise locational guidance except a suggested route and a list of typical features and stores to watch for.

☞ The welter of nearby stores, restaurants (800 in the neighborhood), and banks dazzles as you exit the subway onto Roosevelt Avenue.

Thirty-five banks operate here. Some are branches of big American companies chasing immigrant money. Some, including Asia Bank, the oldest Chinese American bank, founded in 1984, are Asian American concerns. Most are branches of Pacific rim companies such as the Taiwanese China Trust, a private bank that gained a reserve of $6 million in its first two months. (What makes the sum interesting is that the money came from just a few depositors.) Many of the banks hold flight capital, wealth brought out by elite nationals fearing the political future of their homelands. This isn't the whole story though. Countries to the left, including mainland China, and the right, that once had stringent currency regulations, now want part of the overseas action.

W*alk west down Roosevelt toward Prince enjoying the gamut of bank architecture.*

Since the 1970s well-to-do immigrants from many Asian countries have been changing the borough's profile.

☞ Though there is a trace of kitschy pagoda styles, most are in various modern styles. Unlike Manhattan's Chinatown, which originally shaped itself for tourists expecting the exotic, Asian Flushing shapes itself for itself. The block also holds a gauntlet of bakeries, nail parlors (popular enterprises as they don't need licenses), real estate offices, restaurants, and driving schools. Many are so new their red-ribboned opening day plants still bloom in windows and doorways.

Note the signs in Chinese and Korean. It's easy to distinguish between the bold Korean letters and the complex, fluid Chinese script. Chinese is ideographic, pictorial. The Chinese character for mountains, for instance, actually depicts mountains. In contrast, the Korean alphabet, like English, is phonetic. To widen their appeal, many institutions use both languages, and English is a sorry third runner. Many black and white ethnics complain that they don't know what's for sale. At heart, they feel far more displaced than that.

Stores here are delightfully underpresented. Joss paper jostles Saran Wrap on shelves, redbean popsicles stand next to Breyer's. The spectrum of commodities provides an interesting view of immigrant assimilation and its opposite—the perpetuation of homeland cultures. Some of the stock is "mainstream" American stuff. Some, such as electric woks, are adaptations. Others, such as the "Hell money" paper offerings ceremonially burned at the altar to ensure a good afterlife, are purely Chinese products. (Even this latter "purely" Chinese item shows shades of assimilation, however: half the paper notes are embossed with gold, half represent approximations of greenbacks. Are Hell credit cards in the offing?)

New arrivals try to make the neighborhood look like home, adding to the sense of displacement some earlier residents already feel.

☞ The scale of some merchandise is unusual to Western eyes conditioned to nuclear families or single living. Aluminum cooking pots intended to serve many eaters seem almost institutional in size; even the ladles are gigantic, bigger than some "regular" frying pans. Meat portions, conversely, look miniscule. No haunches and roasts are displayed in the butcher sections. Mainstream American cuts are useless for Far Eastern cuisine, even repellent. Many of the Asians who have moved farther out on Long Island return here on weekends to buy not just specialty foods but meat familiarly sliced to suit traditional recipes.

To paraphrase Napoleon, many New Yorkers think Koreans are a nation of vegetable shopkeepers. In fact, Koreans (unlike Chinese and others) have little respect for retail. If you have a degree, running a small business is looked down on. The first **Korean green grocery ventures** opened in 1971, their proprietors mainly North Korean immigrants from Latin America. Though popular opinion holds that the Korean stores started the health boom here, the boom had already started, and the new arrivals merely stepped in to serve it. Twenty years later on New York held an astonishing 1,500 Korean produce stores—3,500, if you include supermarkets and delis.

Some city dwellers hold a conspiracy theory about the vegetable explosion and surmised that the Reverend Moon was behind the success. In fact, other than sheer pluck, the community's grocery "monopoly" was the result of two factors—the abundance of household labor (the 1965 ruling allowed three generations of a family to settle) and informal credit unions formed by friends. For several decades a Korean produce retail association has provided legal services and training seminars to members, but until a year or so ago there was little umbrella coordination at all as the high turnover rate of ownership (stress is so bad that bloody urine is common) made it hard to form a buying co-op. In recent years the recession has devastated many who would like to sell out to fellow Koreans but can't find takers, as immigration has slowed to almost a halt.

☞ Notice, when you visit the stores, most are Mom-and-Pop operations; if you come after school hours, you'll often find children at the till acting as interpreters. Because of their superior language skills, the children are increasingly uppity to their parents; in the past, traditional Korean social mores promoted individual sacrifice for the good of the family. Today, under Americanizing influence, that may be changing.

The five hundred **Korean fish stores** in the city are another ethnic specialty business. This is an even harder occupation than grocering—note the swollen red hands of the proprietors as they work scaling fish.

In the past twenty years two thousand **Korean dry cleaning establishments** have opened in New York, a "good" industry for newcomers, as the start-up capital for this business is relatively low. Conversely, drip-dry fabric and home machines have made Chinese laundries, begun by "bachelor" males when INS laws forbade Chinese women migrants, ever more obsolete. (From the 1880s, Chinese laundrymen worked in Queens earning "an eight-pound livelihood"—a reference to the heavy irons they hefted all day.)

Tall wedding cakes list in many **bakery shop** windows along Roosevelt and adjacent streets. The multi-tiered extravaganzas hold choruses of dancing plastic figures in tails, sugary holograms of Fred Astaire movies. Invariably, the bridal couple are Caucasian, though the stores are evenly split between Chinese and Korean proprietors.

Flushing's **candy and news stores** are plangent with Hindi film music, radiant with calendars of deities. The near Indian news monopoly came when a New Delhi businessman bought the Union News company controlling many of New York's franchises. (Actually, a Pakistani runs the main kiosk near the subway, an exception to the rule.) As well as mainstream papers, the stores stock dozens of ethnic journals that reinforce nationalism and home country culture.

*C*ontinue on Roosevelt to the **Sheraton Hotel** ❷ at 135–15 on the north side of the street.

☞ The fourteen-story copper and glass Sheraton is owned by Taiwanese, and caters to Asian tycoons landing at Kennedy and LaGuardia who want to avoid even insulated stopovers in Manhattan. The hotel's virtually impossible to enter from Roosevelt Avenue, protected by an impenetrable mall maze—*not* a community-friendly space, though the hotel belatedly has begun to offer its function rooms for local Asian gatherings. Note the 1830s swaybacked house with twisted chimneys next door.

☞ The **traditional medicine and tea shop** across the street at 135–18 Roosevelt Avenue is a trove of roots, herbs, and ginseng from China and America. Interestingly, New England ginseng was the first product New York traders *exported* to China after the American Revolution. Chinese visitors here still buy Wisconsin ginseng to take home.

The **Red Coral Lobster Restaurant** at 135–07 Roosevelt (the same side of the street as the Sheraton) recalls the Japanese presence in Flushing. Some Japanese settled here from California in the 1920s, more arrived after the West Coast incarcerations in World War II. Today, however, the majority of the community works in professional jobs and has moved out to farther suburbs in Long Island and Westchester. Only a smallish number of restaurants, food stores, and Japanese Buddhist centers remain in Flushing to mark earlier ties.

*T*urn left at Prince Street (named after William Prince, who founded a botanical garden in Flushing soon after Independence) and stop across from the **James Bland Public Housing.** ❸

Asian money and ratcheting rents have caused grief to Flushing's working-class white ethnics and blacks—the latter of whom now form 10 percent of Flushing's population. African Americans are the main occu-

Although not all Asians are rich (and more poor and working-class Asians have arrived in the past decade), the town's earlier inhabitants sometimes blame the entire Asian community for hiking rents.

pants of this subsidized housing. For the past two decades Prince Street has been an Asian–black divide, the aggravated sense of turf coming from the strained relations between races. Local churches work to bring groups together, but feelings remain raw. Blacks often decry Asians as a racist elite who ignore the well-being of the general neighborhood. For their part, Asians, who are slow to ask for public assistance, sometimes denigrate African Americans as delinquents and welfare cheats.

Although up until now Asians have had an easier time, suffering less economic discrimination than African Americans, Asian communities have also prospered because of collective self-reliance. The Korean rotating credit club, the *gye,* for example, allows members to borrow capital without turning to banks. The *gye* is run by housewives, who gather in the kitchens of members' houses. The women's network, operating out of clapboard houses just a block away from the male-dominated, glitzy banks on Roosevelt Avenue, is an example of female space and the alternate institutions women provide. It's also an example of how the sexes can inhabit different *times* as well as locations, with women often, but not always, conserving earlier patterns.

Turn left at Prince and 40th Road, noting the **Long Island Rail Road bridge** ❹ *on your right.*

☞ This short block is a palimpsest or pentimento. Traces of the neighborhood's old Italian population remain at the Roma Restaurant at 135–11 40th Road. (You can date the restaurant by its menu, which still serves spaghetti, not pasta.)

White ethnic groups have been moving out of Flushing since 1980, complaining that the town—despite its palpable rebirth—has gone *down* because of traffic gluts, dirt, burglaries, prostitution, and most recently, Chinatown gangs who have spread out of Manhattan. A particularly strongly felt complaint decries the churches, mosques, temples, and other community buildings that have taken over private homes and "destroyed" neighborhoods. Another grievance is size—that Asian-sponsored skyrises (such as the hotel and a nearby mall at 39th Avenue between Prince and College Point Boulevard) doom single frame houses and little stores.

A Coalition for a Planned Flushing formed under Democrat Julia Harrison, a City Council member, demands a moratorium on new projects. The thirty-plus civic institutions, churches, and businesses who make up the coalition deny racism and say they are just thinking small, though to date its constituents have all been white ethnics. For their part, Asian developers insist that growth is essential to keep Flushing alive and well. (Harrison has a mixed record. The Queens Chinese Women's Association endorsed the politician's council bid in 1985, the same year she organized multi-racial seminars after the tragedy in Howard Beach. Others claim her agenda tends to favor earlier settlers.)

*A*t *Main Street turn left toward Northern Boulevard, or if you have time, detour right, to walk to the Public Library at the junction of Main and Kissena, then return.*

The space around the library is a happy exception to ethnic friction here. At night various communities stroll and sit companionably in the small fronting plaza. The library hosts multi-lingual projects, holds books in scores of languages, and screens multi-cultural films.

*C*ontinue *back again on Main, going toward Northern Boulevard. You will pass the Gothic Revival* **St. George's Church** *on the southwest corner of 38th Avenue and Main.* ❺

☞ The 1854 stone building is the third incarnation on the site. The first opened in 1746 to serve a congregation organized in 1702. Many Asian Episcopalians attend today, and signs post schedules of Chinese masses.

Chinese and Korean immigrants often observe a folk religion in their homes but officially they are overwhelmingly Protestant. (None of the four hundred Korean Protestant churches in New York, incidentally, are related to the Unification Church. Though outsiders sometimes assume Moon to be omnipresent, his movement generally attracts lonely Americans and is anathema to most Koreans.)

The heavy Christian proportion among local Koreans and Chinese reverses the situation in their home countries, where Buddhists form the overwhelming majority. Ironically, given their earlier westernizing role, the denominations now reinforce national cultures. Korean churches, for example, sponsor folk-dance, tae kwon do, and Korean-language classes.

Sundays in Flushing are garden-bright, as mothers and daughters walk to church in the long silk tunics folded away the rest of the week. Single Korean women value the centers for their social role. Churches are one of the few places to meet eligible men. Unlike the old days, when bachelor societies were the rule, there now is a surplus of women. The fact that many men, though themselves Americanized, mistrust local women as too independent intensifies the situation. Some of the cheap air charters you see advertised in local travel agencies cater to men traveling to Korea to find ruly brides.

As well as strengthening traditional mores, churches also help immigrants face mainstream America by providing job, housing, legal, and health counseling.

Continue walking toward Northern Boulevard past a battery of wildly glitzy furniture stores with Playboy circular beds, jetting sconces, and groves of futuristic lamps. On Union Street you will find more traditional craft items.

Most Asian households keep one room, or the corner of a room divided by a screen, outfitted with old-style furniture. If there are elders in the household, they live there; otherwise, the traditional nook serves as kinesthetic memory center, sometimes a shrine room.

☞ Note the Deco theater on the street's west side, and AT&T's "global communication center," which urges passers-by in several Asian languages to reach out and touch someone. The block's jumble of styles ranges from mansarded Victorian to a corner high-rise office that Taiwanese entrepreneurs built at the junction of Main and Northern.

Cross to **RKO Keith's** ❻ *on Northern Boulevard.*

☞ This former 1920s movie palace arched with a starlit ceiling (by architect Thomas Lamb) stands at the heart of the struggle for and against large-scale development in Flushing. The lobby and foyer of the boarded-up building are city landmarks, but its present owner, Thomas Hong, wants to build a mall in the nonprotected area. The opposition seeks to preserve and restore the whole complex.

Community board meetings are bitter. Many Asians say that the controversy has been used to mobilize anti-Asian feelings, stigmatize all new immigrants, even though they are not behind Hong, and they, too, suffer from new capital pouring in.

Until recently, Asians without the big money of men like Hong have been politically voiceless. Despite their numbers, few vote. This is changing at a glacial pace, as Korean and Chinese American associations work to encourage naturalization and voter registration. (One big difficulty here is that, so far, the election commission has balked at printing ballots in Asian languages, a "courtesy" that the Refugee Women Council has been urging for years.)

Many of Flushing's old-time white ethnic residents and its African American community, which goes back to colonial days, resent the high rises.

☞ You are now at the hub of historic Flushing. Ever since the eighteenth century the sliver green, barely more than a patch in the road junction, has served as the town's civic center.

*Walk along Northern to Flushing's **Victorian Town Hall,** ❼ which overlooks the public island at 137–16 Northern Boulevard—the corner of Linden Place. Today, the prim porched building serves the Queens Council for the Arts.*

For the past decade, various groups have vied for the venerable hall's prestige. Among other seriatim functions, the building has served as an Indian social center and a Korean church. During the Korean occupancy, Taiwanese (who had lost out on the bid) recouped honor by starting a spatially rivalrous center across the Village Green in the old Halloran office, which once housed an Irish American firm that had built up much of Flushing at the turn of the century. The move was play-school territorial politics for the inventors of feng shui ("wind and water"), the art of auspicious and hieratic siting.

*C*ross the boulevard to the **Taiwan Center** ➑ *at 137–44 Northern Boulevard.* Inside the pink marble structure, ping-pong tables and racks of popular magazines belie the political seriousness of this Kuomintang club run by friends of Taiwan's Nationalist government.

In early years, most Chinese in Flushing were pro-Nationalist because of the United States' policy favoring wealthy immigrants. Today, there are many more varied points of view. A basic difference is between those who support Taiwan's independence (under the Nationalist Chinese government, not under the indigenous Taiwanese Formosans) and those who want unification with the mainland. Some Chinese talk in guarded generalities about the pink palace—occasionally the focus of demonstrations against the Taiwan government—and hint their fears of the Nationalists' wide reach. Others say local concerns have long eroded old battle lines.

*T*he **Friends Meeting House,** ➒ *one of the country's oldest worship sites, also stands across the green at 137–16 Northern Boulevard. Turn into the tree-lined roadway for a closer view of the brooding shingle house, begun in 1694 to serve the town's Quaker community.*

Friends still gather in the shadowy rooms for services and still work here for collective justice.

Though some Flushingites like to boast that the town's tradition for tolerance has continued unbroken from Bowne to now, the real continuum seems to lie with the Quakers' efforts. (I'm excepting the sect's early acceptance of slaveholding, a big exception.) The American Friends Service Committee, which operates out of this house, runs a conciliation center staffed by many Asians for the town's multi-cultural population. As well as mediating between different Eastern communities, the Friends also serve as a link between recent immigrants and earlier ethnics, both white and African American.

*W*alk east along Northern, passing the **Victorian armory,** ➓ *now a shelter for Flushing's homeless population (primarily displaced African American families); turn right into Union Street and walk south on the west side of the street.*

☞ Stop and explore **Oriental Foods,** the large Japanese grocery and sit-down sushi bar on the corner at 137–80 Union. The store, hung with posters for a local Nippon Club, sells huge sacks of Japanese-style rice from California, bowls, books, and magazines. (The books all open right to left, a disorienting experience for Western browsers.) A few nearby kimono stores heighten the Japanese neighborhood presence.

Flushing began life as a farm hamlet, becoming a center of Quaker dissidence early on. Friends who built this meeting house in the 1690s led the successful struggle against Peter Stuyvesant for religious freedom in New Amsterdam.

K*eep walking south, noting the posters in the shop windows and entryways.*

Some fliers advertise the autumn festival, when thousands of Koreans come from all over the East Coast to meet their friends and offer ancestor worship together.

☞ A **Korean craft outlet** at 36–14 Union sells traditional women's dresses cut from bright rayons. Telephones inlaid with mother-of-pearl pagodas and willows are just one of the east-west combo items for sale. The store looks like a misbegotten souvenir shop. The bastardized offerings, however, are not for outsiders, but for Koreans themselves, tourists of their own past. Across from the crafts shop, a **Chinese-Korean acupuncture clinic** advertises itself next to Western-style medical offices run by Asian doctors. The juxtapositions continue, with a karate school adjacent to a Korean golf store, and a Buddhist-Christian bookstore.

*C*ontinue past 36–16 Union, a **clothes store** *with cone-bosomed Western dresses that remind us of the four hundred Korean garment factories in the city, most of them now relocated from Manhattan to Queens to cut costs.*

Local rents are $4–$5 per square foot, compared with $15–$20 in Chinatown. Also, the unions hold less sway. Seven thousand Korean women in New York do "homework," as the Reagan government euphemistically designated it, some of it here in Flushing.

☞ Walk around the residential side streets in the morning, and you'll see trucks dropping off materials in front of innocent clapboard houses. At night, pastel remnants of the day's work lie bagged on the curb.

Flushing's Chinese American community has subsidized an after-hours day care center in the public school to help working mothers and keep children away from cutting rooms choked with fluff and thread.

*W*alk past the **Holistic Health Care Center** *on the corner of Union and 37th.*
The center houses many sorts of medical specialists, most of them Asian. Even at Flushing Hospital many doctors are Asians who filled in when white doctors fled to the outer suburbs two decades ago. In 1980, only fifteen years after immigration quotas opened up for Eastern applicants, Koreans, Filipinos, Pakistanis, and Indians staffed more than half the internships and residencies at New York's municipal hospitals. The high number of Asian compared with black doctors is another cause of resentment for African Americans, who lack the training opportunities middle-class Asians receive in their birth countries. There are more Korean doctors and nurses in the States now than in rural Korea—a blow to homeland welfare, though the phenomenon is tapering off as the U.S. government trims services.

☞ The **municipal parking lot ⑪** diagonally across the street at 37th Avenue and Union was a local battlefield until recently, as the city planned to build "Flushing Center" with private developer William Zeckendorf on this lot.

Local African Americans, white ethnics, and many Asians were enraged. The mooted complex, two sixteen-story towers, a seventy-store mall, and a ten-screen movie theater was a burdensome last straw for people already infuriated by displacement and gigantism. Among the leaders of the alliance to defeat the complex were congregation members of **the Macedonia AME Church,** organized in 1811, which still stands in its original sanctuary (1837) on the de-mapped vestige of 38th Street.

☞ The church, blocked from Union Street by the boxy day care center on the road front, rests on land that once was the hub of Flushing's free black community. Across Union Street between 38th and 39th Streets, **two pent-roofed frame houses,** now holding Korean nail-wrap parlors, go back to the era the church opened.

A coalition stopped a giant project due to go up on this city-owned parking lot, which would have dwarfed this historic black church.

Keep walking south along Union across the railroad bridge. By now you will have entered Flushing's more residential section, a neighborhood of 1960s brick complexes meshed with new Asian-sponsored high rises.

Many Koreans make do with apartment living instead of buying single-family homes, which Asians, like most other Americans, prefer. As a rule, Koreans rent their dwellings to keep their capital free for buying businesses, whereas Indians and Chinese buy their real estate. Realtors, delighted with most immigrants' readiness to invest even during the post-crash slump, enthuse about the "Asian long view." Banks, which once checked the source of cash-down payments and demanded to see green cards, now suspend their monitoring and crow over the flow of "mattress money." (Deposits in cash of 25–50 percent are usual in most real estate deals here, and sometimes the whole sum is paid up-front.)

Continue to P.S. 20, the **John Bowne Elementary School,** at Union and Barclay.

Traditionally, one reason people from the inner city moved out to

Queens was to get more space for growing families. The borough has always had a high percentage of children; the same holds true for the Asian
population living here now. Today, the Queens school system serves children from 120 countries. One school district alone has a student body
speaking 65 languages.

Roughly 40 percent of the children at this school are Asian. The remaining student body is 25 percent Hispanic, 14 percent African American, and 20 percent white ethnic. While the immigrant influx brings energy, finding qualified teachers for the dozens of language groups is hard.
Parent volunteers have organized to offer bilingual instruction; others mediate inter-ethnic conflict in the classroom but family involvement isn't always so positive. Many first-generation children face crushing pressure to
excel in school, as their parents have sacrificed, even left their countries, to
give a future to their offspring. Student achievements often come at a high
price. As far as they can, churches help allay mental health disorders.

☞ Note the calendar outside the cobblestone **First Baptist Church** ⑫ at the
southeast corner of Sanford and Union that announces services in a half-
dozen languages, including Yiddish, Hindi, Pushtu, and Urdu.

☞ At this juncture, Union Street begins to take on an older, more expan-
sive aspect, its leafy sidewalks lined with movie-esque small-town houses graced by comfy, turn-of-the-century porches. Yards get bigger, and we
see shingle houses dating from the last quarter of the nineteenth century
and six-story Tudor courtyard buildings. A good example of the latter
form, developed by visionary architects as an antidote to Manhattan's airless working-class tenements, stands at 42–37 Union on the west side of
the street.

*T*urn left on Franklin and walk one block east to Bowne Street. Turn right
here and walk south to Cherry; go left (east) for two blocks to 143–42
Cherry Street, the southwest corner of Cherry and Burling. The **Won Buddhist Center** ⑬ belongs to a radical Korean sect founded in 1916.

In a modern version of an age-old immigrant dynamic, many of the
successful Koreans who once lived in this neighborhood have moved up
and out. In this case, the out is to Long Island's Nassau and Suffolk coun-
ties. As earlier immigrants discovered, there are down sides to leaving the
matrix. An important drawback for some is the rapid Americanization of
their children.

☞ This Korean Buddhist center, designed in stark suburban and stripped-down temple style, is one of four hundred weekend schools for young Koreans in New York. It opened to teach second-generation children their ancestral language and culture. As one nun here endearingly puts it, "not to talk back." (The temple's hybrid architecture looks oddly familiar because of the postwar impact of Japanese architecture on Americas' suburbs by way of Frank Lloyd Wright—which raises the thought that despite the sideways Asian influence on many U.S. suburban houses, the phenomenon *and the houses* have been little examined, little discussed.) If you want to visit the center, call (718) 762–4103 to see if it can be arranged. You should offer a donation for their up-keep. If you're lucky enough to come during Sunday school hours, you may be rewarded by the sight of flower-faced infants rustling in concentration as they try to sit quietly and cultivate serenity.

Before leaving, note the central meditation object here, a simple stone circle. In contrast to the Hindu temple we'll see near the end of the tour, classical Buddhism shuns images as reductive. During his lifetime, Sakya-muni, the historical Buddha, refused to have his "likeness" enshrined, and the first statue of him came only a hundred years after his death, the shift in values probably owing to Hellenic armies then occupying parts of India.

***R**etrace your steps west to Bowne Street and turn left (south) on Bowne toward the Hindu Temple.*

☞ If you wish (though it doesn't look welcoming), you might stop first at the **Sikh Gurdwara,** opened by Punjabis from North India on the east side of the street at 43–69 Bowne between Cherry and 45th Avenues. If it is open and you are allowed in, be sure to make a small offering. The central object of respect here is the Grantha, the Sikh scripture lying open on the dais.

Sikhism, founded in the fifteenth century, was very much a religion of the book. Despite the sect's origins as a reformed version of Hinduism, repudiating caste and a multiplicity of deities, its emphasis on monotheism and righteous living make it philosophically closer to Islam and Christianity.

☞ The whitewashed walls of the bare room reflect Sikhism's inherent simplicity as well as its lack of local financial clout. The few adornments—portraits of the movement's founder, Guru Nanak, and maps of the Punjab—reflect its politics.

As Flushing's immigrant communities are recent (the Indian population, for one, has grown from 6,000 in 1970 to 94,000 twenty years later), many still define themselves through divisive homeland issues. The Sikh-Indian conflict is an example. The wall maps at the gurdwara flaunt "Khalistan," the independent nation some Sikhs in India have been fighting for since 1984 when the Indian government attacked the sacred Golden Temple in Amritsar to wipe out seccessionists. In 1988, many of the 7,000–8,000 Sikhs in New York's metropolitan area made an end run around New Delhi by mounting a parade in Manhattan—an act some organizers wistfully considered akin to virtual recognition as a sovereign state. Actually, as the parade was routed down Broadway and not Fifth Avenue, at most the city accorded only partial autonomy, not independent status!

With the spread of Punjabi terrorism and ensuing police repression—or vice versa—more Sikhs have emigrated here. You see their presence in the number of Sikh gas stations throughout the city. Gas stations are a vulnerable, robbery-prone business. The Sikhs are known as a brave, self-reliant people, the backbone of the Indian Army even after the conflict with New Delhi began.

*R*etrace your steps on Bowne ten or so yards north to the **Gujarati Hindu Temple, ⑭** Aksar Pushottam, at 43–48 Bowne on the west side of the street.

Not all separatism is hostile. Leaving aside the global Indian diaspora caused by colonialism, even innate cultural differences from one Indian state to another can be extreme—at least for first-generation middle-class arrivals. (At a poorer working-class level many immigrants have made an identity-melding alliance that often extends to people from different subcontinental countries, Pakistan, and Bangladesh as well as India.) Food can be a particularly big dividing point, the subject of intricate taboos, even the cause of riot between communities. Many Hindus won't eat meat at all, others are appalled at eating beef, devout Muslims shun pork. Mealtime communalism is the reason why few Indian restaurants have opened in Flushing as opposed to Manhattan, where establishments cater to outsiders or westernized Indians.

Language groups generally stick together. This Hindu temple, virtually a garland's throw away from the theoretically ecumenical temple farther down Bowne Street (founded in 1970 by South Indians), was established by Gujarati speakers from west India.

*R*eturn south down Bowne once more to the **Hindu Temple of North America ⑮** at 45–47 Bowne.

☞ A tiered and towered magic mountain complex arrayed with hierarchies of garudas, peacocks, and elephants, the temple looks charmingly odd among the street's modest frame houses. At first glance. As you peer longer and see the Sanskrit religious school adjacent to the temple and a classical dance school across the street, you start to see its supporting ecology.

The temple is open every day early mornings and evenings. On weekends it stays open full time, as people from all over the tri-state area come to do puja. Prosperous doctors in brass-buttoned blazers and gray flannels prostrate themselves in front of gilt gods. Occasionally, if there is an overflow of worshipers, videos show close-ups of the Brahmin priest making offerings in his niched sanctuary—an American immigrant adaptation. Overhead electric lights (never seen in homeland temples) dispel more mystery.

Over time, however, even exotic structures such as this south Indian temple are starting to become familiar.

All Hindu holy days are observed here, though they sometimes are celebrated on weekends to accommodate American work schedules. If you should come during a festival, you might find the Archie Bunker street itself incorporated into the eastern cosmos. Devotees draw chariots carrying temple images past little houses clad in checkered siding. (Many homes in Queens look as if they're perpetually wearing pajamas.) According to Madhulika Shankar Khandelwal, a historian who has written her doctorate on Indians in New York (and is the source of much information in this chapter), a first level of meaning for the godly outing is personal. Devout Hindus treat the deities rather like cherished family members. At deeper reading, the excursions can signify cycles of death and regeneration. Every September devotees drape an image of the elephant-headed deity Ganesh with flowers, fete him with feasts of coconuts and oranges, then carry a clay replica of the statue to the Flushing Meadow Lake for immersion, a return to the land of the dead. (Flushing Meadow Lake is becoming a cosmic node: several other religious groups including Orthodox Jews also do offerings or make ritual disposals here.)

☞ When the temple opened in 1972 (one of the first in America), it was a simple stucco building. Later, its South Indian founders raised more money both in Queens and in Andrha Pradesh for the embellishing statuary cast in India and reassembled in Flushing. As the community grows richer, ornament and rooms proliferate. Recently, a team of imported Madrasi workmen have added a $4.5 million wedding hall, auditorium, and banquet chamber. Reflecting the same rise in fortune, the temple now supports seven full-time priests. Originally, volunteers stood in. Visitors are made to feel welcome and then left on their own like other celebrants. If you enter, make sure to offer a small donation. To the outsider, the interior space, iridescent with Shiva spinning his cosmic dance, Laxmi the goddess of wealth, and Ganesh the god of wisdom, seems brightly cluttered, cheerfully unhieratic.

Aside from the disarming casualness of spatial ordering, *time* also feels nonchalant. Devotees, huddling familiarly with their deity of choice, appear spontaneous, without immediate agenda. Even the offerings, a mix of flowers and milk and spices, seem lighthearted, domestic, recalling the old hearth origins of many Hindu rites. According to Madhulika, temple worship is just another extension of devotions that families hold at home. (Madhulika, herself, is a practitioner of *rangoli,* the ancient Indian art of creating sacral space in the home by painting the floor with designs in turmeric, indigo, lentils, and other natural materials meant to purify and adorn.)

When you leave the temple, walk down the residential block south toward Holly Avenue.

☞ Despite the modest size of the houses here, many dwellings hold joint family households—several brothers and their wives and children. Some even shelter unrelated, long-term guests from India that the host families support until the migrants find their feet.

The obligation may rankle, but the hosts never question hospitality. Reciprocity is taken for granted, or rather, the newcomers in their turn will look after later arrivals. (Pity the poor first Indian Adam here.)

☞ Near the temple grounds before Holly, you will pass several grocery stores alight with glass vats of red lentils, green coriander, and gold turmeric. The shelves and freezers hold an increasing array of first-rate Indian processed foods manufactured in Flushing. Shamaiana products are delicious, and gourmet guides routinely vote Indian ice creams among the best on the market.

As the made-in-America Indian food shows, many individuals are rooting themselves, making a permanent infrastructure to serve local community needs, as much as others still think of return. Pick up a copy of the free magazines you'll find in the stores. Myriad articles recount the painful balancing, the conflicting self-mythologies within families. First-person stories detail the dual nationalities you'll find in a single household—one spouse holding U.S. citizenship, the other remaining Indian. Marriage-minded personals dramatize the search for mates direct from India itself. Parents rue their children's "wild" behavior, teenagers lament their old-world parents.

The sky bridge to Asia eases the wrench of emigration, alleviates the pressure to assimilate. The planes flying "home" every night, however, can deepen the sense of loss, slow accommodation, keep longing alive. Though Flushing has adopted a multi-ringed globe for its logo with the motto "a world of choices . . . (please don't litter)", the choices new immigrants wrestle with, the dislocations they survive, hurt just to hear about. Flushing is both crucible and cradle.

To reach the subway, make a right at Holly, then walk three blocks west until you come to Kissena Boulevard. Turn right and walk north on the boulevard or, better if you are tired, catch a Q17 bus back to the terminal at Roosevelt and Main. ⓰

14

Washington Heights
Dominican Imprimaturs

Subway: IRT Broadway–Seventh Avenue local
(train 1) to 157th Street and Broadway.

Caution to Walkers—*Most 911 calls here have to do with complaints about the neighborhood's pervasive music. Even so, internecine fights over drugs give the Heights one of the city's highest crime rates.*

Start at the **Church of the Intercession** ❶ *at 155th Street and Broadway. I suggest you read the following introduction in the church cloister, or if it's shut, just outside the door.*

This walk will mainly explore the neighborhood through the eyes of people from the Dominican Republic, the dominant resident group today. First, however, a bit of early history.

In precolonial times the Reckgawawanc Indians summered in Washington Heights and Inwood. Their cave dwellings at Inwood Park now shelter some of New York's homeless.

Under British rule, a few wealthy merchants, including a former army officer, Roger Morris, owned most of the land here. The colonel's residence, Mount Morris, now the Morris-Jumel mansion, was probably the first Palladian house in America. It still stands at 160th Street and Edgecombe Avenue. (Both Morris' father and his second cousin were architects who helped popularize the style in Britain. Thomas Jefferson probably used a design copy book published by the cousin when he built Monticello.)

Hills, turned into forts during the Revolution, and distance kept the area free of the commercial and real estate pressures shaping lower Man-

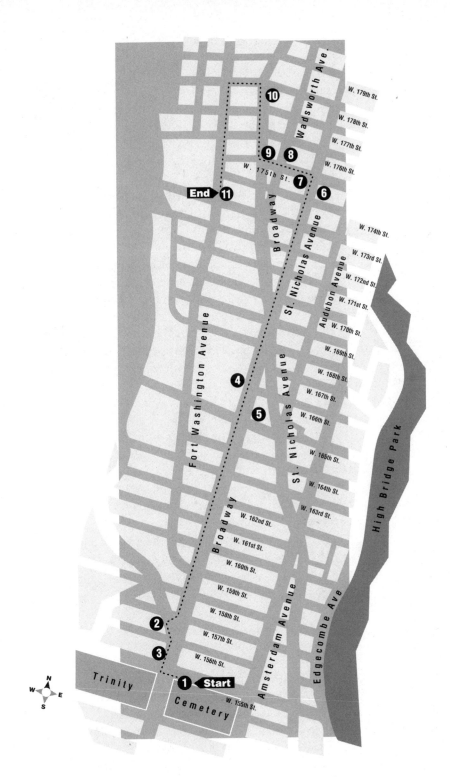

W. 179th St.

W. 178th St.

Wadsworth Ave.

⑩

W. 177th St.

⑨ ⑧

W. 176th St.

W. 175th St.

⑦

Broadway

End ⑪ ⑥

W. 174th St.

W. 173rd St.

Audubon Avenue

St. Nicholas Avenue

W. 172nd St.

W. 171st St.

W. 170th St.

W. 169th St.

W. 168th St.

④

W. 167th St.

W. 166th St.

⑤

St. Nicholas Avenue

W. 165th St.

High Bridge Park

W. 164th St.

W. 163rd St.

Fort Washington Avenue

Broadway

W. 162nd St.

W. 161st St.

W. 160th St.

W. 159th St.

Amsterdam Avenue

Edgecombe Ave.

W. 158th St.

②

W. 157th St.

③

W. 156th St.

Trinity

① Start

Cemetery

W. 155th St.

N
W E
S

hattan. Even the confident, not to say hubristic, planning map drawn by
city fathers in 1811 stopped at what later would be 155th Street. Remarkably, most of the estates here remained viable until the twentieth century,
and the 34th Precinct's map today is as green as it is gridded. Several of the
parks, including Fort Tryon (to the north of the area on our map), were
once private fiefs.

Neighborhood squires in the 1840s included James Gordon Bennett,
publisher of the New York *Herald* and ornithologist-artist John James
Audubon, owner of the estate bordering this cemetery. Audubon was already famed for his bird series and had bought the land with proceeds.
When he lived here, he wrote *Mammals of North America* and fished, winning local renown after catching a 200-pound sturgeon in the Hudson near
his home. (He was a good shot, too—the painting of him with his gun, often hung next to his sensitive representations of birds, never fails to startle
me.) Another large proprietor was Trinity Church, the parent of Intercession, whose trustees bought a plot in 1843 for burying downtown parishioners—the 23 acres running from 153rd to 155th Street, the river to Amsterdam Avenue.

A few estates near the Hudson lingered on until World War I, but most
owners sold out to developers before the Broadway IRT arrived in 1906.
One little-researched group to move to the Heights during this transitional
period were the Spanish who settled on the hill north of Intercession,
where the Audubon Terrace Museum stands today. Some of the Spanish
are said to have been consular officials, which sounds odd; others might
have worked for New York's sugar-refining industry after 1898, when
America replaced Spain as Cuba's paramount power and U.S. business won
monopoly of its trade. A large refinery had stood at the Hudson and 165th
Street from 1850 to 1870; more refineries, including the Jack Frost Company, operated across the river in Closter and Edgewater, New Jersey. The
Spanish are one of the city's least-recorded immigrant groups—more
sleuthing is needed.

After the new transport arrived, several more ethnic communities
moved to the neighborhood, bringing with them the clan divisons riving
groups in the area from then until now. Though the grid had followed the
IRT to the Heights (one hundred years after the rest of the city was carved
into neat paper squares), its geometry barely contained the steep terrain,
the wandering trunk roads. Unlike most of lower Manhattan, the mass of
natural features here was not leveled even after the grid was imposed: in
part, it was (is) the locality's ridges and gullies that allowed (allows) in-

comers to harbor a greater sense of spatial distinction, defendable turf, than in the city proper. The following account of settlement serves to situate the Dominican arrival here in the 1960s.

First to migrate in numbers after the new subway arrived were the better-off Irish workers from the Lower East Side

Washington Heights remained fairly separate from the city, full of big estates through the nineteenth century. Naturalist John James Audubon owned one.

who moved into the new tenements going up east of Broadway. Next to come were Greeks, who settled near St. Spyriton at 180th Street. In the years just before World War I, East European Jews filtered to the Heights from the Lower East Side and rented the large new elevator and walk-up apartments just opening on the ridge west of Broadway. The enclave drew further Jewish settlers in the 1930s, this time refugees from Hitler's misrule. So many Germans arrived in the neighborhood before World War II that the Heights took the name "das Vierte Reich," the Fourth Reich, and "Frankfurt on the Hudson." Incoming settlers moved into a second wave of apartments that had gone up west of Broadway after 1932 when the IND arrived along Fort Washington Avenue.

Following the war, many Irish left their now deteriorating housing on Broadway's east side, for Inwood and Rockland County across the George Washington Bridge. (The bridge had opened the year before the IND reached here.) Blacks and Puerto Ricans moved into the emptied tenements, the latter group drawn by a small colony of island garment workers who'd lived in the Heights before the war.

By the 1960s Puerto Ricans arriving from the island on the new airbuses had become the fastest growing local community, with Cubans in flight from the dictator Batista forming a big minority. Not long afterward, middle-class émigrés in flight from Castro were to follow. At first, the Puerto Ricans welcomed the newcomers, but Cuban class consciousness quickly grated, and before long the pale-skinned Cubans crossed Broadway's divide to live in the Jewish area as honorary non-Hispanics.

In the late 1960s Dominicans driven by political and economic dislocations in their homeland surged into the old Irish section east of Broadway to become the neighborhood's new majority. Dark-skinned Dominicans moved to the black and Puerto Rican stronghold in the south Heights. Cocolo Dominicans, descendants of imported West Indian sugar cane labor, joined them there. Even if Dominicans have a far more permeable definition of race and culture than white Americans, color consciousness enters into the social definitions that shape their residential patterns. The following is a summary background.

Shortly after Columbus arrived on the Island of Hispaniola in 1492, the new regime imported African labor, as the indigenous Taino tribe rebelled against enslavement and died from European disease. In the next century an African slave economy became more instrumental still after colonists there founded sugar plantations on the eastern part of the island (which came to be the Dominican Republic). Soon afterward French colonialists brought captive labor to the western side of Hispaniola, which evolved into Haiti. Today, as a rule, African blood dominates over the Taino and European component in islanders, albeit more so in Haiti, where the French colonists were that much more dependent on slavery than their neighboring imperialists. As such, the skin color of most Haitians is purer black than the essentially mulatto Dominican population, though even this statement must be modified, as the Republic's racial and cultural mix changes from area to area. In the island's northern Cibao section the country's national dance, the meringue, is based on Spanish orchestration; in the south, on African drums.

The color breakdown is important not only to Dominican functioning but to a spatial definition of the Heights as well. During the 1960s whites perceived Trinity Cemetery as a "natural barrier" to further large-scale black migration north, and the era's planning maps show the Heights' southern boundary at 155th Street. (Supposedly neutral reports of the day brim with military terms—*barriers* and *invasions*.) To most white down-towners now, the term *Washington Heights* still has shifting boundaries predicated on race. Generally, if they (we) think of the Heights at all, it means "uptown Manhattan, south of Inwood and north of the black population expanding upward from Harlem." Today, while whites often regard Columbia Presbyterian's Medical Center as the boundary and put the Heights' southern perimeter at 168th Street, many Dominicans think of the neighborhood as extending down the west side to 135th Street, where there's a substantial island presence. They also think of it as extending into the Hamilton Heights area, today home to many of New York's black elite, making some old-time residents there apprehensive (and guilty for feeling this way).

***W**alk out of the cloister to look at John Jacob Audubon's memorial, in the shape of a Celtic cross, standing east of the entry. Then return to read the following.*

The first Dominican to see New York was a black mariner by the name of Juan Rodrigues, who came from the Caribbean on a Netherlands' bark in 1609, the same year Hudson made his now eulogized entry. Arriving with a store of 80 hatchets, some knives, a musket, and a sword to trade, Rodrigues went on to become a translator for Indian trappers and Dutch fur traders.

The first Dominicans to arrive in New York en masse were white and mulatto sugar planters fleeing a slave insurrection in Hispanola at the end of the eighteenth century, their relocation smoothed by a generous grant from Congress. Among the émigrés to flee Haiti at this time was Audubon's father, a French planter and slave trader in Haiti when the revolt started, who escaped to France with his mulatto and white children. Eventually young John James Audubon reemigrated to America and can be claimed as an Hispaniolan if not an outright Dominican.

Heavy U.S. interaction with Hispaniola had begun in the 1840s when the Republic's rulers asked Washington's protection from Haiti; in 1869 the United States almost *bought* the country in a sweetheart deal with the Dominican government. Democrats in the American Senate foiled the windfall, not on grounds of anti-imperialism, but because it would have allowed brown-skinned Catholics to become citizens.

Despite the lack of formal annexation, the Dominican Republic remained a U.S. sphere of interest over time, often suffering direct intervention and American rule. From 1916 to 1924 Washington governed the Republic in concert with the United Fruit Company, who appropriated much of the communal land. When the Marines left, some of their Dominican dependents moved to Spanish neighborhoods in New York, including the Heights. Emigration ended abruptly in 1930 when Trujillo, a U.S.-backed military strongman, inveigled himself into office. It was only after the dictator's assassination in 1961 that Dominicans could travel easily once again.

Because of economic and political flux, thousands chose to, with even more emigration occurring after 1965 when the United States, fearing another "Cuba," sent the Marines to occupy the country yet one more time. (The U.S. support for yet another reactionary to replace yet another popularly elected government still offends many Dominicans in the Republic and here.)

After the U.S. invasion in 1965, Gulf and Western commandeered the country's major sugar company and became the nation's biggest landowner, holding 8 percent of all arable property. A handful of rentiers (14 percent of the population) now owned 79 percent of the remaining ground, growing mainly sugar and a small amount of tobacco, coffee, and chocolate. As prices for sugar, the most important product, have been flat since the mid-1970s, the virtually one-crop economy is in a disastrous state. Recently, American businesses have set up offshore assembly plants but made little impact to date.

According to my friend Tom Jorge, a professor of Dominican history and my informant for much of this chapter, Dominicans despise working for foreign companies. Even if sugar was flourishing, national pride and prejudice would deter people from becoming farmhands despite the Republic's 40 percent unemployment. Though cane cutting is virtually the only unskilled job available, locals see the industry as owned by outside capital, mainly North American. It is also considered slave labor fit only for Haitians. In fact, most cane field laborers are Haitians driven by an even greater unemployment and poverty rate on that end of Hispaniola. (It once provided more than half the wealth of France's colonial empire.)

Because of displacement and poverty in the Republic (heightened by increasingly stringent International Monetary Fund controls), many Dominicans continue to settle in New York. Notwithstanding the local crack trade and the dearth of manufacturing jobs (down 41 percent from 1950 to 1974), life here offers more hope than do prospects in the Caribbean. Today, the outflow from the Dominican Republic is such that only the young and old live in most villages. Those who stay behind are largely dependent on money sent from the United States.

Earliest emigration from the Republic was from Cibao, the wealthier, most educated part of the country. More recent immigration comes from the south and southeast near Santo Domingo, the capital and sugar center where poverty, dispossession, and population reel upward. On your walk today you'll see many restaurants and bodegas named after both parts of the homeland.

Wildly varying estimates suggest that from 400,000 to 800,000 Dominicans live in the New York metropolitan area, the largest nucleus in the Heights. The local precinct uses the higher number, but it's hard to be exact, considering the number of undocumented residents. Many Dominicans, sometimes risking raft runs from the Republic through shark-blooded seas, represent themselves as Puerto Ricans to settle here and get jobs.

The Church of the Intercession (1914), by Cram, Goodhue and Fergueson, was preceded on this site by a church that opened in 1849. The church has a (tenuous) tie to the long chain of sugar politics stirring Dominican emigration. Its parent association, Trinity, opened in the 1690s 30 years after James, Duke of York, took New Amsterdam from the Dutch. York's purpose was to turn the town into a depot for slave ships en route to his Caribbean plantations. The carillon here holds the bell London iron-smiths cast in 1704 to mark Trinity's opening.

Today, intercession, now quite separate from Trinity, leads legal aid programs for immigrants and undocumented Caribbean aliens. Several hundred Dominicans worship in the church, though it's Episcopalian, and attend the Spanish-language mass here.

Cross Broadway to the west side and walk north (detouring past the Audubon Museum complex) to the apartment house between 156th and 157th streets, which is surrounded by an **iron fence decorated with Stars of David.** ❷

The curving building with a tiled hacienda-style roof began life just after the turn of this century as "Hispania Hall," a rather grand Spanish apartment building that opened on this block along with three imposing neighbors, the "Cortez," the "Goya," and the "Velasques. (sic)" Several more Spanish-named buildings faced here across Broadway, the whole knoll becoming known as "Spanish Hill." When Jews moved into "Hispania Hall," they put up the present fence—a boast of occupancy.

As noted in the introduction, the Heights historically has had more than the city's usual share of ethnic politics. In the 1940s some Irish Catholics here had joined the fascist Christian Front, and anti-Semitic prejudice, sometimes violence, poisoned the neighborhood. Even children took on their elders' attitudes. When Jewish and Irish New Yorkers who grew up in the Heights and now live elsewhere meet, they often swap war stories about the circuitous paths they took home from school, the "safe" candy stores they ducked into to dodge tormentors. (New York's city treasure, dancer Jacques d'Amboise, who lived here as a child, hovered on the edge of an Irish gang that once tied [latterday] singer Tiny Tim to a tree and threw blunt knives at him.)

For their part, some current white ethnics, mostly Jewish but with a sprinkling of others, maintain a nonviolent but still combative attitude toward newcomers here, in this case, Hispanics. (The term *Hispanic* does *not* include the Spanish who lived here at century's turn, but who were gone by the time Caribbean settlers arrived. There is ethnic politics behind this etymology also. Some groups prefer *Latino,* as it begs the question of Spain.)

After the Dominicans posed their first political challenge in the early 1980s, local

From early settlement through today, working-class immigrants and second-generation New Yorkers moving to the Heights have brought their ethnic culture with them.

whites (lumped together by the Dominicans as one collective opponent, *Los Judíos,* because of the Jews' long-standing political monopoly here) staged a mid-scale war. Even though most Dominicans lacked the clout of citizenship and had poor organization, European American groups geared up to defend their suzerainty over scarce residential space, public employment, and municipal services. During the 1983 elections for the Area Policy Board, old ethnic Democrats allegedly rigged polling booths and smeared Dominican candidates as neo-Nazis—a technique reportedly used earlier at local school board elections. In a longer-term struggle to maintain ascendancy, local German Jews made a concerted effort to woo new Russian Jews settling in Brooklyn's Brighton at the time. Despite or because of the reported machinations, Dominicans won many seats—their first victory—as the community rallied and voted in strength.

Since then, campaigns have been rather less polarized, or at least the working-class group of Jews in the poorer section east of Broadway have forged some Hispanic ties. In 1991 many voters in this district backed a Dominican, Guillermo Linares, in his successful bid for a seat on the city council.

It was Puerto Rican groups who inspired second-generation Dominicans to politicize themselves, and the two groups, led by young progressives in both communities, sometimes join forces to mobilize Hispanic New Yorkers, now forming almost a quarter of the city's population. Dominicans, however, also challenge their mentors. Rivalrous areas include the school boards, where Puerto Ricans have long been the only Hispanic presence, and the public housing projects east of Broadway, south of 168th Street, a Puerto Rican preserve since the 1960s.

Some historians compare the fraternal struggle to the Irish and the Italians at the turn of this century. If that's so, it must have been a painful conflict. Puerto Ricans, generally, resent the Dominicans for staking claims not only on these Heights but to housing over east in El Barrio as well. Worse, they see the newcomers making inroads in politics, society, and the economy with an "ease" they credit to earlier Puerto Rican struggles for bilingual education, fair social and economic services, and unfettered voting rights. For their part, many Dominicans see their competitors, who control 80 percent of the city's Hispanic voting bloc, as insensitive monopolists.

*R*etrace your steps a block south on Broadway to the **Audubon Terrace, ❸** built soon after the turn of the century in expectation of continued high-end settlement here.

Archer Milton Huntington, the scholar son of a railroad tycoon, donated the Beaux Arts center for the **Hispanic Society of America,** the museum complex's anchor institute, in 1904. In part, he chose this site because of the Spanish colony here, a national identity that became stronger still when the Spanish king patronized the Church of Our Lady of Esperanza outside the complex's walls. If you're here on a Sunday and have time on your walk, be sure to see the elegant sanctuary, now a Puerto Rican center, mid-block between Broadway and Riverside Drive on 156th Street, number 624. But first, look around this would-be acropolis.

☞ **El Seedy:** As you enter the museum grounds, read the list (in English) of all the things you can't do.

In recent decades the Hispanic Society (fronted by a statue of El Cid) has shunned contact with the local community despite its founding mission "to establish a free public library and educational institute for the advancement of Spanish and Portuguese wherein those languages are spoken." Depending on how you view it, the institute's self-marooned situation in the Heights, where 65 percent of the population is Hispanic, is either ironic or infuriating. They're not crazy about visitors in general. Go in and see their remarkable Velazquezes just to annoy them.

The Hispanic Society of America, though devoted to Spanish culture, has little tie to the present-day Hispanic community.

The bilingual community college, **Boricua College,** to the left of the gate as you leave, does better at local connection, though it soon plans to leave for the Bronx. The syllabus offers Caribbean history, and its student body comes from the neighborhood. (Boricua is the aboriginal Taino name for Puerto Rico.)

As you can see by the map-related iconography on its front, the building once housed the American Geographic Society, which closed for lack of visitors. The problems of the complex's other tenant institution, the Museum of the American Indian, are legend. Despite a federal ruling (prompted by Congressman Charles Rangel) that some of the collection must stay up here to meet "a responsibility to the neighborhood," the museum is about to fold its Beaux Arts tent and move part of its collection to downtown Manhattan, the rest to Washington. As many (establishment white) New Yorkers had long written off the upper end of the island as a place to visit—just as they rarely ventured above WNCN on their radio dial to the Hispanic spectrum of the transmission band—they readily accepted the museum's plea that it had to move south to "develop audiences." In the evenings, the only time many Heights residents could come, the complex remains dark, the wrought iron gates locked.

W*alk north on Broadway to* **Columbia-Presbyterian Medical Center,** ❹ *with 1,550 beds, the largest voluntary medical center in the country—its big size possible, as it opened on the site of the old American League baseball park.*

Presbyterian is another institute which, although it's the largest employer in the Heights, has had uneasy relations with the surrounding community. Many locals depend on the hospital's affiliated clinics and emergency ward, but they generally can't use the main hospital itself, as it bars nonpaying patients. The heavy demands on the free emergency room make it a virtual war zone whose tribulations are compounded by the area's drug violence—admissions from crack problems alone are up 300 percent since 1985. The defense Presbyterian offers for its seemingly hardhearted policy is the annual loss of millions of dollars it suffers from admitting patients on Medicaid, which doesn't begin to cover costs. Recently, in return for city permission to start a new luxury branch, the hospital has opened a mixed pay or free pavilion farther uptown to treat neighborhood poor, including the undocumented who do not have access to government-sponsored care.

Another rub with the community revolves around admitting rights for doctors. Though local physicians from good medical schools in the Republic have long demanded a policy change, only a few have been invited to staff the hospital or to use hospital facilities for private patients. For its part, Columbia justifies its stance by saying that it's a teaching hospital whose standards can't be tempered, even to improve public relations. For their part, many in the community show they value the expertise here by continuing to come, despite neighborhood options.

Real estate is one more tender point between hospital and community—local rents have soared as Presbyterian has bought up surrounding property. Critics say at least some of the homeless in Mitchell Park across from the hospital (and in the infamous armory nearby) have been casualties in the chain of neighborhood displacement.

Some things the hospital might do to smooth ties seem easy—for one, they might add Spanish translations to the hospital's recorded telephone message, currently in English only, a language almost half the Dominicans have difficulty understanding. In other areas, particularly that of public health, the hospital has already made imaginative links, hosting conferences not only with the local Dominican community but in the Republic itself.

Because of the migratory nature of settlers here, the hospital's widening sphere makes a terrible sense. In May 1992, Mayor David Dinkins flew to the Dominican Republic to plead for free local AIDS treatment for Dominican New Yorkers who choose to die at home on the island. Shared epidemics, viral villages, may become a new way to define community.

☞ Look over Broadway to the east at the block-length skeleton of the **Audubon Ballroom and theater complex,** ❺ designed by Thomas Lamb and built by William (later 20th Century) Fox in 1912 when the new subway made upper Broadway a northern rialto. Note the brown foxes between each window at the second-floor level, which honor the Hungarian nickelodeon operator turned movie mogul.

The ballroom's demise is one more thing Presbyterian often gets blamed for. In this case, unfairly. The hospital will benefit, but it was Columbia University, not the hospital, that bought the Audubon grounds from the city in 1965 in order to build a biomedical research facility. The university's plan to destroy the old complex raised stormy opposition, stalling the project until recently. In part, the architectural value of the ceramic-fronted megalith prompted the outcry, but passion over the building's historical significance caused the greater torment—in 1965 gunmen assassinated Malcolm X as he spoke in an Audubon conference room.

Critics of the university say the site was essential to black conscious-

ness and accuse Columbia of racial insensitivity. Its supporters contend that New York must get into the biotech business to survive, that the community will gain jobs through the new center, that the local economy will prosper, and that a Malcolm X memorial can be incorporated into the new structure. Are sites needed for memory? Can plaques, busts, video adequately convey visceral as well as intellectual meaning? Would a white shrine have been more respected? Black activists and (mainly) white preservationists led the protests. Columbia's promise of several hundred (low- to medium-skill) jobs and training for neighborhood youth appealed to many Hispanics, and the local community board gave its assent to the demolition.

Unemployment in the post-industrial city makes life hard. So far, Columbia Presbyterian Medical Center offers most of the neighborhood's (low-level) jobs. (Note the shell of the Audubon Ballroom in the foreground.)

The "compromise" solution—saving part of the building's facade while adding a tower block—pleases some. Others are devastated.

Continue walking north on Broadway to the vee juncture where Broadway meets St. Nicholas. (A McDonald's holds the strategic site.) Look one block east to Audubon Avenue, which parallels St. Nicholas from this point north. (Stay where you are, don't detour.)

Even Dominicans who have become U.S. citizens remain minutely involved with the Republic's politics and vote in homeland elections. Most neighborhood residents support the PRD (Partido Revolucionario Dominico), the social democratic party whose overthrow in 1963 led to emigration here. Others supported a breakaway PRD faction. One battle between the two groups was over who should run the Dominican Day parade that first plumed out along Audubon Avenue.

The initial reticence of Dominicans to assert numbers, claim neighborhood space, was tied to the feeling the Republic was still home, that one day they would return "forever." Many felt shame, *vergüenza,* about becoming naturalized here. In 1980 more than three-fourths of South Americans and Central Americans in New York did not take out papers, but remained citizens of their old countries. (This shift from earlier immigration patterns extends to other groups also. In fact, only Russian Jews have become citizens en bloc in recent decades, a change that could affect how we work to shape a cohesive city and nation state.)

Until recently, Dominicans were even more prone than most other nationalities to think of themselves as migrants rather than true immigrants. (Only 18 percent of Dominicans are naturalized.) This has been changing only lately as the Republic's plight, compounded by fearsome International Monetary Fund strictures, grows sadder, illusions dimmer.

The first signal announcing Dominican intentions to become a city presence came with the inaugural Dominican parade down Audubon Avenue in 1982. That day 100,000 people showed up for the ceremony (inspired by the Puerto Rican Day celebration). As Dominicans have grown more assertive, the parade has moved out of this neighborhood to midtown Manhattan. A rite has become a declaration of *right,* even if the impact is diminished as the parade is not on Fifth since the city has put a ceiling on marches there—a policy effectively allowing that honor only to earlier nationality groups.

At this point, veer east (to the right) and continue walking north on St. Nicholas.

☞ The community is still not rich enough to influence its built environs, i.e., put up its own structures; nevertheless, a Dominican presence suffuses surrounding streetscapes in this part of the Heights, the high spine of land

adding to the feeling of being in a place apart. Even in winter, music slants from windows. The mechanical rocking horses on the sidewalk, often a sign of nearby sweatshops where mothers tote small children, grind out a Latin beat. In warm weather the streets become public spaces for vending and socializing. Impromptu salesmen press the hoods of parked cars into service. Beepers, cellular phones, baseball caps, plastic toys line the bonnets of old Buicks. Music eddies you along.

Like earlier immigrants, today's neighborhood majority, the Dominicans, shape their surroundings in their image. Note the street vending, normally found in a warm-weather country.

For the next part of the tour, which proceeds north along the old avenue (once an Indian trail), this guide will, by and large, suggest local institutions to look out for, rather than offer precise examples.

☞ The small, all-purpose grocery stores called **bodegas** are the Heights' paramount institution, in part, because mainstream supermarket chains have been reluctant to locate in poor neighborhoods. Dominicans buy foods here from their island home to put on the dinner table, reabsorb their past. Every day, fruits and vegetables arrive in Kennedy on the inexpensive three-hour flight from the Caribbean. Stalls line Broadway, parrot-bright island produce lies mounded under cold skies.

Easy air ties to the islands heightens the Dominican profile here. Familiar food is flown in daily.

Once bodegas were a Puerto Rican preserve. Today, Dominicans own the majority—another cause of complaint by some Puerto Ricans, even if the shift seems to reflect a bettering of circumstances for both communities. By the 1970s, when many Puerto Ricans had tired of the work involved in running the stores, and their children (some, anyway) were becoming white-collar professionals, a number of Dominicans had saved enough capital to buy them out. Many of the new storeowners bought their shops with the help of the informal Dominican mutual aid associations, *san,* that provide members (usually kin) low-interest loans on a rotating basis.

If some immigrant groups, including Koreans and Indians, who tend to come from professional backgrounds, look down on store work, Dominicans dream of owning a grocery, long work days and increasing robberies notwithstanding. Proprietorship in this community confers local influence as well as employment and autonomy. The power extends back to the island also, as a hefty percentage of earnings gets sent to dependents in the Republic. Since one dollar fetches four pesos despite the official exchange of one dollar per peso, New York bodegeros can buy several retirement houses and have cash left over to care for any family still living on the island as well. Sometimes, aside from subsidizing relations, storeowners also underwrite island political candidates who travel here to solicit help.

In 1982 when the Republic's PRD presidential candidate came to the Heights to raise funds, it was mainly bodegeros who supported his campaign, and the indebted politician returned to thank them. (He won.)

☞ Step inside a store to look around. Adding to the fungible indoor-outdoor way of experiencing space, the same merengue playing on the street spills from the owner's transistor. As Hispanics are often self-employed and can listen to the radio at work, programming is round-the-clock. Glass counters, looking like some backcountry display case, hold pale loaves of bread and egg-white candies called *suspira*, or a "a breath, a sigh." Near the cash register you'll find religious essentials, votive candles, incense, as well as stacks of the ten Dominican papers flown in every day from the island.

Some of the products in the store, particularly fresh produce, can't be found in mainstream groceries, though that is changing as Hispanic purchasing power grows. The Hispanic community spends far more money on food than do other ethnic groups in the United States. The Puerto Rican Goya products are now almost everywhere, winning general converts as well as Hispanic customers.

☞ On the other hand, it's hard to find any packaged food exported from the Republic. The island's U.S.-dependent economy and small consumer base keeps it from making many processed goods. (Or, at least, goods made under a Dominican label.) Check the shelves to see if you can find a single Dominican brand of sugar.

According to my friend Professor Tom Jorge, Dominicans, like most immigrant groups, are traditional about food and want the familiar. You might live someplace different, wear different clothes, even speak other languages, but you want the comfort of the same rice and beans that your mother and father gave you. Even relatively assimilated Dominicans will not go without their yucca and platanos. Tom says Dominican households put more emotional value on communal eating than most "mainstream" Americans do. Though most Dominican women have jobs, they still spend hours making traditional dinners for their husbands. (Watch for more and more frozen Goya dinners, as urban stress catches up and values change.)

Continue to walk north along St. Nicholas.

After the bodega, the Heights' most visible institution is the **tributario, or multi-purpose travel agency.** You will see several on every block as you walk up this avenue.

☞ The personnel in the agencies, which can be clubby with circles of folding chairs, or intimidating with bullet-proof screens, act as culture brokers.

In one spot you can send money back home, buy your travel tickets to the island ($489 round trip), arrange your taxes, divorce, immigration documents, notary public needs, check cashing, and translation of legal forms—in short, do all necessary interfacing with New York life. The *tributario's* main business for clients is securing the precious *tarjeta,* or green card, allowing permanent residency here.

Another well advertised function of these agencies is obtaining divorces—$150 plus costs. This, too, is frequently tied to immigration, as some Dominican marriages to U.S. citizens are made to gain legal status.

The *tributario* provides one more service that, at first, seems unimportant to downtowners—recruiting drivers for "gypsy" cars, the unlicensed taxis that operate in the city's poor neighborhoods. Medallioned yellow cabs go only in "safe" districts, and middle-class Manhattanites who take taxis for granted are known to panic when they visit localities (even my neighborhood in Brooklyn) where they don't see the reassuring canary. For their part, the "Tigeros," who drive the gypsies up here and other parts of the city, lead a perilous life. Over a hundred have been murdered in the last

Neighborhood "tributarios" are agencies that serve as conduits between Dominican "Yorkers" and the Republic, two domains fast becoming one.

few years. An accurate map of the city's social economics could be drawn by charting yellow cab and gypsy cab zones—a demarcation as sharp as in wall-era Berlin.

☞ The Heights' third dominant institution is also linked to immigration but harder to find because of efforts at concealment. Puffs of steam from exhaust pipes, fluorescent lighting, and bags of harlequin scraps on the sidewalk, however, offer clues. The (mostly illegal) **garment shops** are usually owned by second- or third-generation Dominicans, often from the same hometown as the workers they exploit. Look for hiring ads pasted on local buildings.

As official manufacturing left the city, garment sweatshops mushroomed. By 1980, 44 percent of industry workers were foreign born, many finding an opening in specialty work.

For a while, Dominicans inherited the pleating business, as the work is labor intensive. Skirts are folded by hand and then steam pressed. In the 1980s pleats went out of fashion: contractors lost their shirts (or skirts), and machine operators their jobs.

The link between illegal garment shops and immigration comes because sweatshops depend on squeeze practices—low wages, poor safety, long hours, no benefits. If you are undocumented, you can't complain—you might lose your niche in this country as well as your paycheck. An extension of the logic is that most workers are women, even more vulnerable to exploitation than immigrant men. In 1981 only a third of Dominican women worked before emigrating. After coming to New York, over 90 percent of them took jobs for some time, the great majority in the garment trade.

Despite conditions (and reformist urging), surveys show the women *like* the work. The main enthusiasts are the 20 percent of those lucky enough to be in unionized shops with health care; the nonunionized majority, however, also agreed. For the first time, wives controlled their own money, felt equal to their husbands. Today, when asked who is head of household, they respond "los dos"—"the two of us."

In a revealing insight into how men and women sometimes inhabit space in entirely different ways, Dominican women feel much more connected to New York than their men and would like to prolong their stay here. The voluptuous sofa stores along upper Broadway cater to wives who want to root their apartments, furnish their lives. The men, who chafe at their social isolation here as well as the city's cold weather and harsh conditions, hate belongings, see them as traps. They want only rudimentary mattresses, TVs, and card tables. Buying wastes money, delays the return home.

Yet another streetscape institution on the Heights are **restaurants;** these are dense repositories of island memory. Many use historical and political dates for their names.

☞ Notice the side entrances off the main doors marked "Los Familios" that lead to separate dining rooms welcoming women and children. The arrangement illuminates the Dominican gender divide, which continues, albeit diluted, in New York. Though the majority of Dominicans are politically liberal, the men (and perforce the women) are ultra-conservative in their domestic affairs.

At this point the walker may rather eat than read about fine dining. If you have time for a lunch stop, Dominican soups are cheap, delicious, and filling—to the point that anesthesiologists at the Columbian Presbyterian Hospital have recategorized them under solid food. (The reclassification might save lives, as operation schedules are based on the presumed state of the patient's digestive system.) If you prefer, you might try one of the Heights' Chinese Hispanic restaurants, the hybrid outcome of nineteenth-century imperialism, when contractors brought over Far Eastern laborers to the Caribbean and South America. After Castro took over, many trilingual Chinese left Cuba and set up these ventures. The food is mainly island with a dash of Cantonese.

I suggest you read the following section while sitting down in one of the many eating places along St. Nicholas. If you only want something to drink, the local cafe con leche is delicious.

While largely invisible, drug dealing is a key local business.

America is supposed to be the land of the rich. Ordinary jobs in the Heights—driving gypsy cabs, sewing garments, cleaning Presbyterian Hospital—do not provide much money. A Dominican New York merengue says, "Here life is not worth a rotten guavesa. If a hoodlum doesn't kill you, the factory will. . . ."

Many young men don't have the patience, the credit, or the capital to invest in a bodega. There's pressure to get rich the easy way. While the drug identification (and corollary violence) dismays most Dominicans, crack dealing has become a Dominican specialty, since earlier ethnic groups already controlled prostitution and gambling. Some suppliers have become famous or infamous in this trade and its attendant murders, mayhem, and arrests. Operations are split between locals who get into drugs to pay back their passage to New York and professional dealers who work the city for a few years and then retire to build a home in the island. (A particular base for retired "Dominican Yorkers" is San Francisco de Macoris.)

Recently, the recession has slowed the drug boom just a little, and renewed police vigilance has made a modest inroad. As well as trying to shut down dealers, the police have also been tightening screws on buyers, mainly family men from suburban New Jersey who arrive over the George Washington Bridge. For some time the local precinct has been impounding the cars belonging to these clients, a humorous as well as a just and semi-effective effort to punish those who demand as well as supply. (In Bridgeport, Connecticut, the city is toying with putting up concrete mazes to disorient drive-in buyers who come to drug neighborhoods. The hope in this grotesquely surreal take on city planning is that the blind wandering through dangerous neighborhoods—as opposed to the present speedy ins and outs off of highways—would scare consumers enough to curb their habits.)

☞ Not all drug users in the Heights, however, come from outside. Note the many **drug-counseling clinics** as you walk around. Drugs were not a big problem in the island (it's rising slightly now), but local youngsters are growing addicted.

☞ One of the shelters against pain and big-city loneliness (at least for men) are the dozens of Heights associations that affirm ethnic identity, solidarity. Even though many clubs went underground following the Bronx Happy Land fire in 1990, when the city re-inforced laws against unlicensed gathering places, windows full of baseball trophies, faded postcards of azure seas, and strings of Christmas lights give the show away.

Organizations generally cater to Dominicans from the same home town or province and serve a variety of functions. Some feature sports, others serve as mutual aid societies. Most have a political bias. Overwhelmingly, they are left wing, as the more conservative (and upper-middle-class) Dominicans who managed to come here under Trujillo live outside the city in affluent suburbs.

*R*esume your walk north on St. Nicholas until you come to the Roman Catholic **Church of the Incarnation** ❻ on the east side of the intersection at 175th Street.

A place that did not feel like home to many Dominicans until relatively recent times was the Roman Catholic church.

☞ Notice that the sidewalk in front of the church is virtually the only street space in the Heights free of vendors. The strong-willed priest here frightens them away.

An Irish congregation built Incarnation in 1925, and the priest is still Irish despite the church's Dominican parishioners.

☞ You can see traces of the earlier Irish presence across the street in the **McGonnell Funeral Home, ❼** which opened a few years after the church. It still functions, but with difficulty.

☞ If Incarnation is open, enter to see its severe, Gothic beauty. Saints adorn the stained-glass windows, but there are only a few statues. Some Dominicans think the building looks Protestant and miss the baroque environment of homeland churches.

The Irish intended the building to look Protestant. They had been the first Catholic ethnic group in America to be attacked and learned to defend themselves through protective coloring and the curbing of customs that might appear pagan, excessively ritualistic, or simply "foreign." In later decades the Irish Catholic clergy worried that the new immigrants, first the Italians and later the Hispanics, might threaten their (semi-)assimilated status. Moving to trim Italian religious processions and Latin emotionality within the church, the Irish became the guardians of Americanization as well as defenders of the faith.

Although the New York Roman Catholic church provides *for* Hispanic immigrants, offering refugee resettlement, legal guidance, mental health counseling, English training, and job referral services, it is not always *of* the community. In 1939 New York's Archbishop (later Cardinal), Francis Joseph Spellman, ended the old system of national parishes earlier immigrants had devised and called for "integration." It's no coincidence the call for integration came when wide-scale European immigration had ended and Puerto Rican immigration had just begun. In the 1950s educator Ivan Illich, who was then assigned to Incarnation as a parish priest, started an institute in Puerto Rico to sensitize New York's Catholic hierarchy to Hispanic communities and cultures, but Cardinal Terrence Cooke unaccountably shut the center in 1972.

There are few Dominican (or Caribbean) priests available to contest the white ethnic hierarchy, despite the fact that Hispanics now form almost 50 percent of the Roman Catholic church in New York: only two or three Hispanic seminarians attend the training school for priests in Yonkers; the single bishop with a Latin background in the city comes from Spain; New York's vicar for Hispanics, though nominated by Hispanics, is an Anglo-American. The dearth is not new. Even in Latin America there have always been few native-born clergy, as locals considered the church a largely alien (Spanish) institution.

Today, many Dominicans and Puerto Ricans are leaving the Catholic fold to join the Protestant Evangelical movement. Like Southern Baptist churches, these services are expressive, laden with music; also, they're led by ministers from the islands. To stave off further conversion to Evangelical Protestantism—a huge recent phenomenon in U.S. cities as well as Central America—Roman Catholic ministries have begun, at last, to be more flexible. Many, including Incarnation, now offer "charismatic" programs that provide born-again fervor inside a Catholic framework. Not surprisingly, the movement has become the fastest-growing sector inside the church. (The second is *pilgrimage,* showing people's need to link themselves to site as well as sanctity.)

The ambivalence some Dominicans hold toward some Catholic attitudes and issues does not extend to education. Many parents prefer parochial to public schools in order to mediate their children's exposure to "American" (non)values. Fully 1,800 local kids attend Incarnation's kindergarten-to-8th grade elementary school. Neighborhood people also applaud the church's involvement in a nearby clinic, run by Presbyterian's Baby's Hospital, for children with AIDS.

*B*acktrack one door south on St. Nicholas. Virtually next door to Incarnation, a **botanica** (a vernacular religious store) displays what looks like all the take-outs from the church.

☞ The images in the window are as racially varied and culturally complex as Caribbean people themselves. Black African and Taino protectors rub shoulders with Spanish Madonnas. These tutelary saints are part of Santería, a mix of the Hispanic version of vodou and Catholicism that many Dominicans prefer to formal church worship.

The botanica also sells party goods, which provide more insights into Dominican life. There are the crepe-wrapped thrones where young girls entering puberty preside at their *quince años fêtes*—a more explicit version of mainstream "sweet sixteen" parties. Gift baskets called piñatas hang from the ceiling—their variety showing a radius of cultural identification. Some come in traditional island form, parrots and burros; others reflect the childrens' Americanization. Two common piñatas sold represent Micky Mouse standing in front of the Disney World Castle and Sesame Street's Big Bird. Another example of cultural adaptation is the line of aerosol spray cans made in New Milford, Connecticut. These cans are technological updates of traditional lucky candles and fragrances designed to win you money, love, health, or a mix of the above. "Shake well, make the sign of the cross, think of your love object and keep well away from eyes." (Do not trifle with these. I did, and suffered broken love affairs for years to come.)

*R*etrace your steps north to 175th Street. Turn left and walk west.

☞ As you go, note the sealed synagogue on the south side of the street between Wadsworth and St. Nicholas (610–614 West 175th Street). Also see the freestanding **frame house at 45 Wadsworth** ❽ on the northeast corner of 175th Street. The little cottage sits perched on a stony ledge scarred with dynamite grooves. When blasting couldn't budge the rock, the street grew around it.

*K*eep walking west, to the **United Church** ❾ on the east side of Broadway at 175th Street.

☞ Designed by Thomas Lamb, this building was opened in 1930 as a Loew's theater.

That same year, community organizers held ethnic conciliation gatherings here aimed at diluting friction between local Irish and Jewish youth. Ten years later they were still meeting. Today, the building houses an African American church colloquially called the "Reverend Ike's Temple," after the minister who preaches material and spiritual reward in return for following Christ. Despite the sign in Spanish bidding welcome, few neighborhood Hispanics attend.

☞ After absorbing the church's exuberant Moorish exterior, take time to enter the lobby, if it's open, to see its stunning Art Nouveau detail.

*W*alk north up Broadway toward the bridge.

☞ These blocks are thick with music stores selling CDs from all over South and Central America.

Music is the common denominator of Latin groups, though each nationality has a preference or, more accurately, a passion. Cubans and Puerto Ricans enjoy the salsa, Dominicans are slaves of the merengue—"formal from the waist up—tropical from the waist down." Dominican singers are so popular, Tom Jorge says, some get elected to the National Congress just for their talent.

Aside from musicians, baseball players are the other stars in the Republic and the Heights. Thanks to long-term U.S. influence in the island, the sport has become a national pastime. Note the mini-versions of Big League outfits for sale in every childrens' clothing store. (The neighborhood has a long ball history. New York's Yankees were once the Heights' "Highlanders"—a local team.)

☞ A sign you can't miss as you walk these blocks is "Envios Diarios." Almost every store has such an ad in its window announcing that it makes daily shipments to the Republic. Curiously, even the local florist shops fly daily consignments back to the verdant island.

The greenest item people send back, however, is money, an estimated $300–$600 million a year. Most is channeled through the *tributarios,* but some goes through banks.

As you proceed north notice the **Deco bank ➉** on the east side of Broadway between 177th and 178th Streets.

Until legal problems arose a few years ago, this building housed "the Banco Dominico" and flew the red, white, and blue homeland flag. It was the only Dominican bank in the United States and grew out of public demand. The community wanted its own institution, even though a nearby Banco Popular (essentially Puerto Rican) catered to the locality and hired many Dominicans.

In truth, this bank was not a Dominican bank or a even a branch of some Dominican bank, but rather a public-relations-inspired subdivision of Banco Popular. As long as the subterfuge lasted, many Dominicans went along with the hypocrisy and felt at home in the supposed Dominican firm, enjoying the illusion they'd get an easier line of credit here or at least a sympathetic hearing.

Turn left and walk west on 178th Street to the subway at Fort Washington Avenue, where you get a good view of the **George Washington Bridge.**

The bridge is a link to Dominican garment factory and domestic cleaning jobs in north Jersey. Every morning, caravans of gypsy cabs and bright blue school buses cluster at the site to ferry workers across the river. Conversely, some suburban Dominicans cross over to the Heights to tend sweatshops here.

If you like, you might want to walk down to **Public School 173** ⓫ *at Fort Washington and 173rd Street before getting on the subway.*

Among other troubles schools face here are low teacher expectations, segregation, a scarcity of qualified bilingual teachers, and rules that push students out of bilingual classes before they are ready. Hispanic youngsters have a 21 percent high school dropout rate—the steepest in the city. (Aside from school problems, many children quit to help support their families.)

Six or seven years ago the Board of Education shut down the board of this school because of the school's low scores. Some Dominicans felt the closure owed to ethnic politics as much as to objective criticism; the school board here was mainly Dominican.

Most senior officials of Hispanic origin on the Board of Education remain Puerto Rican, but Dominicans are gradually winning representation at a local level. In 1991 the community won its first school district, a widely sung victory. Because of Dominican pressure, the Board of Education is replacing the old public school (attended by Henry Kissinger), ten blocks up from here on Wadsworth Avenue, with a $30-million model school that will be one of the city's finest.

☞ Look down into the leafy park across from P.S. 173, where young Dominicans, Puerto Ricans, and elderly Jews sit in all weathers playing chess. The friendly interaction belies the gripping antagonisms, the fierce local struggle for authority and patronage. Since the seventeenth century, ethnic politics have driven this town—in the end, however, our connections have always proved stronger than differences.

Despite conflict, racism, and too many woes to summarize, the city is still a dream, even *the* dream for immigrants round the world. In the Dominican Republic, *ir allá*, "to go there," is a (rather tragically) common phrase. Everyone talks of it, everyone does it. Though sometimes the "there" means America in general, more usually it means New York.

Illustration Credits

Reproduction of the photographs and maps in this book was made possible with the generous support of The Kaplan Fund.

Cover
Frank Leslie's Illustrated News, June 20, 1885, p. 288—New York—the torch of the Statue of Liberty. Courtesy of the Prints and Photographs Division, Library of Congress.

Walk 1: Manhattan and the Harbor
p. 5: Adriaen Block, Map of Nieu Nederlandt. 1614. From the Collection of the New-York Historical Society. **p. 7**: New Amsterdam in 1660. Redraft of the Costello Plan, engraving by John Wolcott Adams. From the Collection of the New-York Historical Society. **p. 8**. Nieu Amsterdam at New York. 1673, engr. by A. Meijer. From the Collection of the New-York Historical Society. **p. 10**: Egbert L. Viele, *Topographical Atlas of the City of New York Including the Annexed Territory,* 1874 view of lower Manhattan. From the Map Division, The New York Public Library, Astor, Lenox and Tilden Foundations. **p. 16**: The Stadt Huys of New York in 1679, Corner of Pearl St. Litho by F. G. Hayward. From the Collection of the New-York Historical Society. **p. 22**: Broad Street, 1659. *Hollyer's Old New York Views.* From the Collection of the New-York Historical Society. **p. 28**: Coffee-House Slip and New York Coffee House. Litho by F. G. Hayward, 1856. From the Collection of the New-York Historical Society. **p. 29**: Negro wench— advertised for sale. March 30, 1789, from *N.Y. Daily Gazette.* From the Collection of the New-York Historical Society. **p. 32**: Custom House, New York, Town and Davis Architects. Litho by A. J. Davis. 1834. From the Collection of the New-York Historical Society. **p. 33**: Wall Street, looking west from William Street toward Trinity Church. Wood engraving. From the Collection of the New-York Historical Society.

Walk 2: South Street Seaport and Sailor's Snug Harbor
p. 37: Port of New York. From the Battery looking South. Currier and Ives. 1872. From the Collection of the New-York Historical Society. **p. 39**: East River—view of New York Harbor, ca. 188?. From the Collection of the New-York Historical Society. **p. 41**: Sailor on Shore Leave. Lithograph by George G. Gratacap. From the Print Collection, Miriam and Ira D. Wallach Division of Art, Prints and Photographs, The New York Public Library, Astor, Lenox and Tilden Foundations. **p. 43**: W. Wade, The Seaman's Home,

Corner of Fulton and Water Streets, ca. 1845. Engraving (Eno 198). Eno Collection, Miriam and Ira D. Wallach Division of Art, Prints and Photographs, The New York Public Library, Astor, Lenox and Tilden Foundations. **p. 47:** Friday morning in the 4th ward—the women's fish market in Oak Street. Engr. by Horace Baker. From the Collection of the New-York Historical Society. **p. 48:** A dog fight at Kit Burn's. Edward Winslow Martin. *The Secrets of the Great City.* 1868. From the Collection of the New-York Historical Society. **p. 52:** William James Bennett. View of the New York Quarantine Station, Staten Island. 1833 Colored aquatint (Eno 465). From the Eno Collection, Miriam and Ira D. Wallach Division of Art, Prints and Photographs, The New York Public Library, Astor, Lenox and Tilden Foundations. **p. 55:** Sailors' Snug Harbor, After Dinner Smoke, ca. 1900. Courtesy of the Museum of the City of New York, The Byron Collection.

Walk 3: The Lower East Side
p. 65: Plan of New York in 1766 and 1767 by Bernard Ratzer. From the Collection of the New-York Historical Society. **p. 69:** Present-day St. Teresa's Church, Rutgers Street, East Broadway. Michael Wallace. **p. 71:** *Harper's Weekly.* Cheap clothing—the slaves of the sweaters. Courtesy of the Prints and Photographs Division, Library of Congress. **p. 73:** Rivington Street at Orchard Street. 1930's Photo Irving Browning. From the Collection of the New-York Historical Society. **p. 74:** Double entrance at funeral parlor, Ludlow and Canal. Michael Wallace. **p. 76:** Eldridge Street Synagogue. Michael Wallace. **p. 78:** Girl jumping rope atop Public School #126 Brooklyn. United States, Local History and Genealogy Division, The New York Public Library, Astor, Lenox and Tilden Foundations. **p. 83:** Back porch, Lillian Wald house. Michael Wallace. **p. 86:** Vladeck Federal Housing Project, Madison and Jackson Street. Courtesy of the Museum of the City of New York, The Ted Stone Collection. **p. 91:** Modern sweatshops. Michael Wallace.

Walk 4: Greenwich Village
p. 98: How can it be? Photo by H. Cotterell, Jr. Sept. 28, 1947. From the Collection of the New-York Historical Society. **p. 105:** Hyde House and workshop. Michael Wallace. **p. 106:** Woman at work, wood engraving by Alexander Anderson (MEYI #167). Print Collection, Miriam and Ira D. Wallach Division of Art, Prints and Photographs, The New York Public Library, Astor, Lenox and Tilden Foundations. **p. 107:** Grove Street Federal houses. Michael Wallace. **p. 109:** Northern Dispensary. Michael Wallace. **p. 114:** Seventh Regiment, National Guard Parading on Washington Square 1851. From the Collection of the New-York Historical Society. **p. 115:** North Row House, Washington Square, Michael Wallace. **p. 117:** Nicolino Calyo, The Richard K. Haight Family, ca. 1848. Gouache, 20″ × 15″. Courtesy of the Museum of the City of New York #74.97.2, Bequest of Elizabeth Cushing Iselin. **p. 120:** Washington Arch. Temporary arch erected 1889 for Centennial. From the Collection of the New-York Historical Society.

Walk 5: The East Village
pp. 130: Colonnade Row or La Grange Terrace. Photo H. N. Tiemann. From the Collection of the New-York Historical Society. **p. 132:** Riot at Astor Opera House. Litho by N. Currier. From the Collection of the New-York Historical Society. **p. 134:** *Frank*

Leslie's Illustrated News, May 4th 1861, Women's Central Assoc. of Relief meeting at Cooper Institute. From the Collection of the New-York Historical Society. **p. 137:** McSorley's 1854 bar. Michael Wallace. **p. 140:** Sunday Social Freedom in the Bowery. Cartoon by V. Ratzler. From the Collection of the New-York Historical Society. **p. 144:** *Frank Leslie's Illustrated News,* January 31, 1874, p. 344—The Red flag in New York—riotous Communist workingmen driven from Tompkins Square by the mounted police. Courtesy of the Prints and Photographs Division, Library of Congress. **p. 148:** Children's Aid Society lodging house, Tompkins Square. Michael Wallace. **p. 150:** Poster recalling 1988 riot in Tompkins Square. Michael Wallace. **p. 152:** curfew sign. Michael Wallace.

Walk 6: Irish History in Lower Manhattan
p. 161: John McComb, Jr., Architect of New York City Hall. From the Collection of the New-York Historical Society. **p. 165:** *Harpers Weekly,* July 29, 1871, cover, "Bravo Bravo." General Research Division, The New York Public Library, Astor, Lenox and Tilden Foundations. **p. 169:** *Harper's Weekly,* July 12, 1873, p. 604—Health officers cleaning out a "dive." Courtesy of the Prints and Photographs Division, Library of Congress. **p. 170:** *Frank Leslie's Illustrated News,* Dec. 5th, 1885, p. 245—Doing the slums,—a scene in Five Points. General Research Division, The New York Public Library, Astor, Lenox and Tilden Foundations. **p. 172:** Engr. by H. L. S. in *Frank Leslie's Illustrated News,* Aug. 13, 1859. The Police, under the direction of Inspector Downing, clearing the piggeries of Bernard Riley. From the Collection of the New-York Historical Society. **p. 173:** Illus. from *Harper's Weekly,* Aug. 9, 1879, by Sol Eytinge, Jr. Among the tenement houses during the heated term—just before daybreak. From the Collection of the New-York Historical Society. **p. 179:** The wall around Old St. Patrick's Cathedral. Michael Wallace. **p. 180:** Sarony, Major and Knapp. Departure of the 69th Regiment, April 23rd, 1861. From the Collection of the New-York Historical Society.

Walk 7: Brooklyn Heights
p. 187: After Francis Guy, *Brooklyn in 1816.* Wood engraving (Eno 452). Eno Collection, Miriam and Ira D. Wallach Division of Art, Prints and Photographs, The New York Public Library, Astor, Lenox and Tilden Foundations. **p. 188:** Map A215/1816 Brooklyn Heights. Ross, Peter, Village of Brooklyn (compiled from the first village map of that date by Jer. Lott and from Poppleton and Lott's map of the Pierrepont estate of 1819). Courtesy of the Brooklyn Historical Society. **p. 189:** Lithograph of Brooklyn City Hall. Courtesy of the Brooklyn Historical Society. **p. 191:** View of New York from Brooklyn Heights, 1849. Litho by N. Currier. From the Collection of the New-York Historical Society. **p. 193:** Brooklyn Sanitary Fair, 1864, New England Kitchen. Courtesy of the Brooklyn Historical Society. **pp. 199:** New American Sewing Machine. Litho by Miller Wagner Umbdenstock. From the Collection of the New-York Historical Society. **p. 202:** Plymouth Church proscenium. 12.5 24 Brooklyn photos and prints 31-3 Churches Congregational. Plymouth Church. Courtesy of the Brooklyn Historical Society. **p. 204:** Longshoremen, Furman Street. 1924, Furman St/ Bklyn Heights waterfront/ marine terminals warehouses and stores. Courtesy of the Brooklyn Historical Society. **p. 206:** Sunday school Parade. Parks/Prospect photos and prints. Courtesy of the Brooklyn Historical Society.

Walk 8: Whitman's New York

p. 213: Walt Whitman. From the Collection of the New-York Historical Society. **p. 215:** Reproduction of a pen drawing of Reinagle's view of Broadway at St. Paul's (Eno 138). Eno Collection, Miriam and Ira D. Wallach Division of Art, Prints and Photographs, The New York Public Library, Astor, Lenox and Tilden Foundations. **p. 217:** Old Federal houses on Canal Street. Michael Wallace. **p. 220:** Greene Street cast iron buildings. Michael Wallace. **p. 221:** The Riots at New York, July 1863. Sacking Brooks's Clothing Store. *Harper's Weekly,* Vol. VII Aug. 1, 1863. From the Collection of the New-York Historical Society. **p. 226:** Endicott and Co.—Printing House Square. 1866. Color lithograph (Eno 383). Eno Collection, Miriam and Ira D. Wallach Division of Art, Prints and Photographs, The New York Public Library, Astor, Lenox and Tilden Foundations. **p. 230:** Abraham Lincoln's funeral passing Broadway and Chambers Sts. From the Collection of the New-York Historical Society. **p. 234:** Wood house on Poplar Street attributed to Walt Whitman and his father. Michael Wallace.

Walk 9: Ladies' Mile

p. 242: Sewing room at A. T. Stewart between 9 and 10th Streets, Broadway and Fourth. From the Collection of the New-York Historical Society. **p. 243:** St. Denis Hotel—Broadway and 11th Street. From the Collection of the New-York Historical Society. **p. 251:** YWCA on 15th Street, west of Union Square. Michael Wallace. **p. 252:** *Frank Leslie's Illustrated News,* May 16, 1874, p. 152—Running the gauntlet, a scene in front of a popular hotel in NYC at 5 o'clock. General Research Division, The New York Public Library, Astor, Lenox and Tilden Foundations. **p. 255:** The El—New York Transit systems. Courtesy of the Prints and Photographs Division, Library of Congress. **p. 257:** The Siegel-Cooper Department Store. From the Collection of the New-York Historical Society. **p. 261:** Adapting the Brush electric light to the illumination of the streets—a scene near the Fifth Avenue Hotel from *Frank Leslie's Illustrated News.* From the Collection of the New-York Historical Society.

Walk 10: Harlem

p. 272: The riots in New York, July 1863, Rioters chasing Negro women and children through the vacant lots in Lexington Avenue. From the Collection of the New-York Historical Society. **p. 273:** Photograph: Interior view of stairway with banister. Photographs and Prints Division, Schomburg Center for Research in Black Culture, The New York Public Library, Astor, Lenox and Tilden Foundations. **p. 274:** Man standing in a doorway, wearing an overcoat and hat—Not Shatterproof—photo by Dummett. Photographs and Prints Division, Schomburg Center for Research in Black Culture, The New York Public Library, Astor, Lenox, and Tilden Foundations. **p. 277:** Current housing rehabilitation. Michael Wallace. **p. 281:** Photograph: Marchers in parade (Thou Shalt Not Kill). A March in Silent Protest. Photographs and Prints Division, Schomburg Center for Research in Black Culture, The New York Public Library, Astor, Lenox and Tilden Foundations. **p. 285:** Annual Banquet of Harlem Board of Commerce 1/14/1913. From the Collection of the New-York Historical Society. **p. 287:** Photograph: Picket line ("VIM are on strike"). Photographs and Prints Division, Schomburg Center for Research in Black Culture, The New York Public Library, Astor, Lenox and Tilden Foundations. **p. 288:** Photograph: Overhead view of the Apollo Theater marquee. Photographs and Prints Division, Schomburg Center for Research in Black Culture, The New York Public Library, Astor, Lenox and Tilden Foundations. **p. 293:** Malcolm X posters. Michael Wallace. **p. 295:** St. Philip's cornerstone. Michael Wallace.

Walk 11: The Upper West Side

p. 309: Brennan farm house, south side of 84th Street. From the Collection of the New-York Historical Society. **p. 311:** American Museum of Natural History under construction 1889. From the Collection of the New-York Historical Society. **p. 312:** Dakota Apartments, Central Park west at 72nd, n.d. From the Collection of the New-York Historical Society. **p. 316:** Dakota houses, north side of 73rd Street. From the Collection of the New-York Historical Society. **p. 319:** Public Service Commission, 72nd Street, north on Broadway. From the Collection of the New-York Historical Society. **p. 321:** *Harper's Weekly*, Oct. 18, 1890, p. 819. In the Italian Quarter. Courtesy of the Prints and Photographs Division, Library of Congress. **p. 324:** The Collegiate School and Church. Michael Wallace. **p. 329:** Habana-San Juan Dry Cleaners. Michael Wallace. **p. 330:** Moving ads on lamp post. Michael Wallace. **p. 331:** Yuppie scene on Columbus. Michael Wallace.

Walk 12: Fifth Avenue

p. 344: Probably J. C. Geissler, after Pierre Martel. Martel's New York Central Park 1864. Lithograph, printed by Henry C. Eno (Eno). Eno Collection, Miriam and Ira D. Wallach Division of Art, Prints and Photographs, The New York Public Library, Astor, Lenox and Tilden Foundations. **p. 345:** View south from 59th and Fifth Avenue. Photo by William Roege. From the Collection of the New-York Historical Society. **p. 349:** Looking south on Fourth Avenue down in Yorkville ca. 1865. From the Collection of the New-York Historical Society. **p. 351:** Seventh Regiment Armory, 1885, Park Ave between 66th and 67th Sts. From the Collection of the New-York Historical Society. **p. 354:** Frick Mansion with grounds. Michael Wallace. **p. 355:** Richard Morris Hunt statue at Fifth Avenue and 71st Street. Michael Wallace. **p. 357:** Payne Whitney Residence, New York City 1906. McKim, Mead and White, pl. 292. 1906. From the Collection of the New-York Historical Society. **p. 358:** Duke and Whitney houses, showing narrow garden. Michael Wallace. **p. 358:** 870 Madison Avenue at East 70th Street, ca. 1940. From the Collection of the New-York Historical Society. **p. 359:** Apartment house on Fifth Avenue and 81st Street. Michael Wallace.

Walk 13: Asian Flushing

p. 362: Photograph: Queensborough Bridge, *Changing New York* (1937) (1311 E 5) (Berenice Abbot, photographer) (Neg. no. 240). Photograph Collection, Miriam and Ira D. Wallach Division of Art, Prints and Photographs, The New York Public Library, Astor, Lenox and Tilden Foundations. **p. 363:** Dwellings built as single-family houses. Michael Wallace. **p. 364:** La Guardia Airport and Vicinity, aerial view. Courtesy of the Museum of the City of New York. **p. 368:** Asian bank. Michael Wallace. **p. 369:** Asian signage. Michael Wallace. **p. 372:** Real estate signs. Michael Wallace. **p. 375:** High rise on Main; Keith's movie theater in background. Michael Wallace. **p. 377:** Friends Meeting House. Michael Wallace. **p. 379:** Macedonia AME Church. Michael Wallace. **p.383:** Hindu Temple of North America. Michael Wallace.

Walk 14: Washington Heights

p. 389: John James Audubon, 1785–1851. From the Collection of the New-York Historical Society. **p. 394:** Star of David fence. Michael Wallace. **p. 396:** Hispanic Society of America at Audubon Terrace. Michael Wallace. **p. 399:** Audubon Ballroom shell with Columbia Presbyterian Medical Center in background. Michael Wallace. **p. 401:** Outdoor vending. Michael Wallace. **p. 402:** Fruit stand outside bodega. Michael Wallace. **p. 404:** Envio de valores signs. Michael Wallace.

End Piece

Harper's . . . Courtesy of the Prints and Photographs Division, Library of Congress.

All Maps

Shanley T. Jue.

Index

Note: Streets are in Manhattan, unless otherwise noted.

About the Author

Hope Cooke is a writer and urban historian. She lectures widely on New York history, conducts independent walking tours of New York City, and teaches history at the Birch Wathen Lenox School in Manhattan. She has directed the walking tours program at the Museum of the City of New York and written a weekly column for the *New York Daily News*. Her essays, short stories, and reviews have appeared in such popular periodicals as *Redbook, Travel and Leisure, The New York Times,* and *The Chicago Sun Times*. Among her previously published books is *Time Change,* her acclaimed autobiography which chronicles the ten years Cooke lived in a remote region of the Himalayas as the Queen of Sikkim.